# Jews in Nazi Berlin

## Studies in German-Jewish Cultural History and Literature
Franz Rosenzweig Minerva Research Center, Hebrew University of Jerusalem

*Established in 1990 at the Hebrew University of Jerusalem, the Franz Rosenzweig Minerva Research Center is funded by the Minerva Foundation, Munich, and the Ministry of Research and Technology of the Federal Republic of Germany.*

*Named after the German-Jewish philosopher Franz Rosenzweig (1886–1929), whose life and work are deemed emblematic of the German-Jewish cultural legacy, the Center seeks to honor the cultural achievements of German-speaking Jewry from the Middle Ages until the Shoah, and its subsequent reconstruction. Through its ramified research projects, the Center also endeavors to examine the "culture of modernity" through the prism of German-Jewish cultural and literary history.*

# Jews in Nazi Berlin
## From Kristallnacht to Liberation

EDITED BY BEATE MEYER, HERMANN SIMON,
AND CHANA SCHÜTZ

THE UNIVERSITY OF CHICAGO PRESS *Chicago and London*

BEATE MEYER is a research associate at the Institute for the History of German Jews in Hamburg.
HERMANN SIMON is director of the New Jewish Synogogue in Berlin.
CHANA SCHÜTZ is vice-director of the New Jewish Synogogue in Berlin.

Originally published in German as *Juden in Berlin 1938–1945* copyright © Philo Verlagsgesellschaft mbH. Berlin, 2000.

Editor of the German edition: Diana Schulle
Translated from the German by Caroline Gay and Miranda Robbins with editing by Miranda Robbins

PHOTO ON PAGE 1
After the Pogrom of November 1938. A definitive identification of this Berlin "Modellhaus" has not been possible. The graffiti *Think of Prague* refers to the Sudeten crisis, which had reached its peak that summer. Centrum Judaicum Archive.

PHOTO ON PAGE 121
Pupils of the Youth Aliyah School with their teacher Jizchak Schwersenz, around 1940. After two years of hiding in Berlin, Schwersenz escaped to Switzerland in 1944. He was able to bring with him his photographs from the years 1940–43. These are now in the Centrum Judaicum Archive.

PHOTO ON PAGE 309
The Levetzowstrasse Synagogue around 1900. Landesbildstelle Berlin.

The University of Chicago Press, Chicago 60637
The University of Chicago Press, Ltd., London
© 2009 by The University of Chicago
All rights reserved. Published 2009
Printed in China

18 17 16 15 14 13 12 11 10 09     1 2 3 4 5

ISBN-13: 978-0-226-52157-2 (cloth)
ISBN-10: 0-226-52157-5 (cloth)

Library of Congress Cataloging-in-Publication Data

Jews in Nazi Berlin : from Kristallnacht to liberation / Beate Meyer, Hermann Simon, and Chana Schütz.
     p. cm.
     Accompanies exhibition held at the Stiftung "Neue Synagoge Berlin-Centrum Judaicum" in 2000.
     Includes index.
     ISBN-13: 978-0-226-52157-2 (cloth : alk. paper)
     ISBN-10: 0-226-52157-5 (cloth : alk. paper)
     1. Jews—Germany—History—1933–1945.
     2. Jews—Germany—Berlin—History—20th century.
     3. Holocaust, Jewish (1939–1945)—Germany—Berlin.   4. Berlin (Germany)—Ethnic relations.
     I. Meyer, Beate, 1952–   II. Simon, Hermann, 1949–
     III. Schütz, Chana C.   IV. Stiftung "Neue Synagoge Berlin-Centrum Judaicum."
     DS134.3.J49   2009
     940.53'180943155—dc22

                                        2009022517

# Contents

# Foreword

Since the Centrum Judaicum opened on the eve of May 8, 1995, over a million people have visited the restored New Synagogue—that authentic old-new site of Jewish life in Berlin. They come to a place where history's scars are enduringly visible, because of the confrontation of the past with the present.

Five years after the opening, a remarkable exhibition took place within the historical rooms of that venerable synagogue, accompanied by an equally remarkable publication, the English version of which now lies before you.

It was devoted to certainly the most oppressive phase in the history of German Jews, in the history of European Jews. For the first time such an exhibition was framed entirely from the perspective of Jews themselves. Indeed, it was held on the very site where so much had happened, a place that saw flourishing, decline, and even hesitant new beginnings.

In organizing this exhibition, it gave me great personal satisfaction to be able to draw on a family connection to Berlin that dates to 1671, the year the Great Elector of Brandenburg granted Jews permission to settle in Berlin. My children are the thirteenth generation to reside in this city. Their grandparents, my parents, belonged to the small group of Berlin Jews that survived the Shoah.

This book remembers those men and women. Above all, it is dedicated to the memory of the Jewish victims of Nazi persecution.

The words of the Biblical prophet Joel are and have ever been before me: "Tell your children of it, and let your children tell their children and their children another Generation" (Joel 1:3).

*Hermann Simon*
*Director of the New Synagogue Berlin–Centrum Judaicum Foundation*

# Preface

"The life of our people would be wretched without three things that keep it going: the unshakeable courage with which the leaders of the Jewish authorities continue with Jewish work, the lively interest that American Jews show in the fate of their brethren in Germany, and the indestructible hope in a better future."[1] This is how Berlin Rabbi Max Nussbaum described the situation in Berlin late in the summer of 1940, just after his own emigration to the United States Nussbaum had witnessed the pogrom of November 10, 1938. He had himself been spied on by the Gestapo, forced to emigrate, and stripped of his financial assets. And his optimism was sadly inaccurate. By 1941—a year after Nussbaum's own escape—any hope of a better future for the Jews of Berlin had transformed itself into mortal fear. The life of Berlin's Jews became wretched indeed. The work of the leaders of the Jewish Community and the Reich Association of Jews in Germany—the Reichsvereinigung—was increasingly difficult, dangerous, and compromised. And Jews abroad showed remarkably little interest in helping their Jewish brethren in Germany. (Nussbaum's faith in American Jewry may have been understandable from his point of view, but it was not shared by many of those who shared his fate.)

IN THE YEAR 2000, the New Synagogue Berlin/Centrum Judaicum Foundation devoted a special exhibition to documenting the most oppressive phase of Nazi persecution in the capital city of the Third Reich: the years 1938–45. It examined various events that took place between 1938, the "year of fate," and Red Army liberation in May 1945. It examined the perspectives of both individuals and organizations. The exhibition drew on rich archival sources: interviews with eyewitnesses, information about those who perished, the testimony of survivors in postwar trials, case files, and the few remaining Jewish Community documents from the Nazi era. It also incorporated photographs, objects, and documents generously loaned from private collections. A multifaceted picture of Jewish life in Berlin emerged.

Anyone dealing with these years in the history of Nazi persecution soon confronts the fact that there has been no systematic historical appraisal of Jewish persecution in Berlin, the city from which so much of the Nazi policy of persecution was formulated. There is, however, a broad range of literature specific to particular Berlin districts as well as rich biographical material and sources associated with all aspects of the subject. The historian Wolf Gruner, in particular, has conducted important specific research in this area, but as yet there is no work that integrates three major aspects: Nazi policy, the social reactions to it, and the shifting but distinct perspectives of those persecuted. We sought to bring together these strands and to fill some of the gaps in research. Time constraints meant that we could realize our ambition only in part. A broader study would also have to take account of elements and personalities specific to Berlin: Gauleiter Joseph Goebbels's obsession with making the city "judenfrei"; the bullying behavior of the corrupt chief of police, Count Helldorf—a man not averse to saving a few lives if it meant he could line his own pockets in the process; and Albert Speer's ambition to turn Berlin into the overblown city of "Germania" and to clear out all Jewish tenants in the process.[2] Last but not least, all the Reich ministries involved in the anti-Jewish policy were located in Berlin.

These Nazi institutions were aware that foreign embassies and newspapers would react to any openly violent activities directed against the Jews in the capital. This became far less important after the beginning of the war, however. Berlin's was the largest of Germany's Jewish Communities. Of the 522,000 German Jews living in Germany in 1933 (566,000 according to Nazi racial definitions), more than 160,000 lived in the capital. By May 1939 roughly half had fled the country. In the summer of 1941—that is, on the eve of the first deportations—the Berlin Jewish Community still counted about 65,000 members. To this 9,000 more were added, people who did not consider themselves Jewish but whom the Nazis nonetheless persecuted as such. The greater the pressure on Jews and stateless Jews in smaller German cities, the greater the number of people fleeing to the capital in search of better living conditions—and anonymity. Berlin's Jewish Community sought to provide for its old members and the newcomers until this was made impossible by a barrage of new regulations and, finally, the deportations, which began in October 1941 and followed in rapid succession through March 1945. In the course of 65 transports "to the east" and 122 transports to Theresienstadt, over 55,000 of those deported were Jews from Berlin.

Most of them were murdered, not only in Lódz, Minsk, Riga, Piaski, Warsaw, Majdanek, Auschwitz, and Theresienstadt but also in the nearby concentration camp of Sachsenhausen. The original exhibition and the accompanying volume seek to provide a glimpse of the lives of those who remained in Berlin. At the war's end, only 1,900 of those deported returned from the camps to Berlin. Between 1,400 and 1,500 "U-Boote" ("submarines") survived underground in the city. And 4,700 people were protected through their marriages to non-Jews.[3]

Recent exhibitions in Berlin have provided a detailed examination of particular themes, ranging from the history of the Jewish Cultural Union (Kulturbund) to Jewish life in wartime Shanghai, to the history of the Lódz ghetto. Personal histories have been presented as well, such as the love story between two Berliners, Aimée and Jaguar, drawing on the work of journalist Erica Fischer (whose book was recently made into a internationally successful film).[4] Without claiming to present a complete history, the "Juden in Berlin, 1938–1945" exhibition built on this work and offered new information in a number of other areas.

Our project has differed from previous exhibitions in three ways. For one thing, we focused on the period 1938 to 1945, a period that saw a shift in state policy from "forced emigration" to genocide. Second, at the heart of the project are the people and institutions that remained in Berlin after the major waves of expulsion and deportation: the last Berlin Jews to be called up for deportation, those employed by the Jewish associations, those who hid underground or even melted into the crowd and "passed" as Gentiles. Finally, the material on view—the exhibits, documents, and accompanying texts—sought to provide insight into the working and living conditions of Berlin's persecuted Jews. In doing so, we showed their (frequently unsuccessful) attempts to assert themselves, as well as their expressions of human dignity, hope, and survival. The displays told stories in the true sense of the word, stories both typical and extraordinary. Some experiences were shared by many. Others were unique.

The exhibition included as many historical recordings and film extracts as possible, a dimension that we can only hint at in this accompanying volume. For example, the testimony given by Theresienstadt survivor Hildegard Henschel at Adolf Eichmann's 1961 trial in Jerusalem before the Israeli Supreme Court was available in full. Henschel was an employee of the Reichsvereinigung during the Nazi period and her husband, Moritz Henschel, was the last chairman of the wartime Berlin Jewish Community. Her insight into events was considerable. The show also included over fifty years of radio and television extracts. We presented the recollections of well-known eyewitnesses, among them the popular television host Hans Rosenthal and Heinz Galinski, who chaired the Berlin Jewish Community for many years after the war. Less prominent figures were

**Figure 1**

A display in the exhibition showing various objects that Jews were required by law to hand over to the authorities.

important here as well, and we were able to draw on the Centrum Judaicum's wealth of video and audio interviews with survivors who had emigrated to Israel, the United States, Great Britain, and Sweden—as well as those who returned to Berlin and other states of the Federal Republic after the war.

The exhibition and book would not have been possible without the many interviews granted to us. These individual accounts are an extremely important part of reconstructing events. Indeed, they are among the most important historical sources that we have. This is particularly the case when the task is one of reconstructing a psychological portrait of the persecuted, of presenting the experiences of persecution. Because we did not want to lose these comments in publication, this volume presents in the margins selected excerpts from the transcripts, which serve as a binding element for the individual chapters. The passages may be read independently, so long as the reader keeps in mind that they are by nature fragmentary—snapshots or close-ups of a larger, far more complex picture. We intended them to give an overview of the time and the circumstances as well as to facilitate the orientation in the publication.

A particular strength of the exhibition was that it was presented on the historical site of Berlin's New Synagogue on Oranienburger Strasse. The distin-

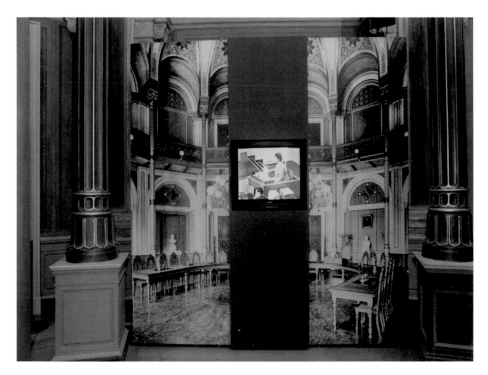

**Figure 2** A display set up in the New Synagogue's hall of representatives included footage of Hildegard Henschel's testimony during the Eichmann trial in Jerusalem, May 11, 1961.

guished synagogue and its adjacent buildings headquartered the Jewish Community of Berlin until the Nazis closed it down on January 29, 1943. Throughout the harsh years of National Socialist rule, the employees of the Community tried to maintain educational and cultural activities for the Jewish Community, to organize religious services, to arrange accommodation when Jews found themselves homeless, and to provide them with clothing, food, and other basic welfare services. It was, moreover, from Oranienburger Strasse that beginning in the fall of 1941 the Community was forced by the regime to send its "marshals" (*Ordner*) to collect those whose names had been placed on the deportation lists. And it was here that the Gestapo held the staff hostage during the *Gemeinde-Aktion* of October 1942.

THE BOOK'S NINETEEN CHAPTERS are spread out over ten thematic sections, each representing a different but related aspect of Jewish life in Berlin: the events of 1938, emigration, "Aryanization," the yellow star, Zionism, forced labor, deportation, betrayal, survival, and the Jewish Community. Some of the chapters provide overviews. Others are case studies drawn from archival material, firsthand accounts, and biographical records.

**Figure 3**
Synagogues in Berlin destroyed during the pogrom of November 1938.

It is appropriate that the book's first section begins with the consequential events of the year 1938: the *Juni-Aktion*, in the course of which Jews with "criminal" records were arrested alongside other "asocials" and Jewish shops were smeared with anti-Semitic slogans; the *Polen-Aktion*, a campaign that sent Jews with Polish passports to a grim no-man's-land over the border; and finally, the venomous November Pogrom—known to many Americans as Kristallnacht— during which synagogues were burned, shops were plundered, and some 12,000 Berlin Jews were taken to the concentration camps at Sachsenhausen and Buchenwald. Hermann Simon furnishes a vivid picture of these events as well as an analysis of the origins of the term "Kristallnacht." The November Pogrom coincided with the compulsory sale of Jewish-owned businesses and the financial plundering of Berlin's Jews as a whole. Michael Schäbitz's general overview of the emigration process (chap. 3) and Beate Meyer's case study of the Garbáty cigarette factory (chap. 4) both attest to this.

Chapters and sections overlap considerably. The frightening shadow of deportation, in particular, hovers over much of the book, the largest section of which deals explicitly with the theme via a number of case studies. Many of Berlin's Jews were not able to emigrate because they made up their minds too late or were too old, too poor, or simply unable to get out in time. A breach of just one of the many Nazi regulations (chap. 5)—particularly a failure to wear the "Jew-

**Figure 4** A display case containing veronal alongside the Jewish hospital register, open to entries for the year 1942. Again and again, the cause of death is listed as "Schlafmittelvergiftung"—an overdose of sleeping medicine.

ish star" (*Judenstern*)—could lead to "protective custody" and, ultimately, deportation and near-certain death. Young Zionists, as Chana Schütz shows, were deported from local kibbutzim, as these were transformed gradually into forced labor camps (chap. 7); other forced laborers (chap. 8) were arrested for deportation during the *Fabrik-Aktion* of February 1943 (chap. 10). The threat of capture and deportation loomed large in the lives of those in hiding (chaps. 16 and 17) and was what pushed such Jewish "snatchers" (*Greifer*) as Stella Goldschlag Kübler into the unfathomable act of hunting other Jews who lived underground in the Reich capital (described by Christian Dirks in chap. 15).

Beate Meyer's extensive chapter near the end of this volume (chap. 18) addresses the complex role played by the Reichsvereinigung and the Jewish Community during this torturous period. In several sections, Meyer's history examines the Community's involvement first in "emigration," later in deportation. It recounts the events surrounding the deportation of Community employees in October 1942. And it describes what happened after the Reichsvereinigung was officially dissolved by the authorities in June 1943 and its employees and representatives were deported to Theresienstadt. Meyer's focus then shifts to the Jewish hospital in the district of Wedding, where the hospital's director, Walter Lustig, served as a Gestapo pawn. The hospital became not so much a place for caring for the sick as a detention camp.

**Figure 5** A glass column displaying personal documents entrusted by deportees to the Jewish Community. The following comes from a leaflet distributed to deportees: "Those participating in the transports may submit such important personal documents as birth and marriage certificates and notices of death to the Jewish Religious Association (archive). These documents should be delivered personally or via post in an unsealed envelope either to one of the local departments or directly to the archive. The envelope should be marked with the sender's transport number, first and last name, and former address, as well as a precise list of the documents [enclosed.] Upon completion, a receipt for the deposited documents will be made out at the assembly area. IDENTITY CARDS (or, in the case of noncitizens, FOREIGN PASSPORTS) should not be included but should be brought along."

The next chapter provides brief portraits and biographical details of the Reichsvereinigung and Jewish Community board members or senior employees, who met a variety of wartime and postwar fates (chap. 19). Many paid for their commitment with their lives, but some survived the concentration camps. During the exhibition, this material was projected in the New Synagogue's hall of representatives, the very room in which, on October 20, 1942, over five hundred Community employees were marked out for deportation.

Lastly, Diana Schulle provides a chapter on the buildings on Oranienburger Strasse and the activities they contained, and the ways in which those functions were twisted to serve Nazi interests. For example, the upper floor of the building at number 28 Oranienburger Strasse contained the General Archive of Jews in Germany (Gesamtarchiv der Juden in Deutschland), established in 1905. The National Socialists saw the archive as a welcome collection of documents pertaining to "racial" origin and eagerly confiscated it for its own uses. The Gestapo continued to systematically expand these files in subsequent years.

MANY OF THE ARTIFACTS of deportation on display in the exhibition could not be included in the book for reasons of space. An estimated seven thousand Berlin Jews committed suicide when faced with the hopeless prospect of being "abgewandert"—"evacuated," to use a prevalent Nazi euphemism for deportation. One of the display cases contained the most common means used at the time—the sleeping pill veronal—as well as precise records kept by the Jewish hospital regarding cause of death. When a suicide attempt failed, doctors were forced to do everything in their power to stabilize the patient—so that he or she could be included on the next transport list.

Other artifacts included a luggage tag marked with the deportee's transport number; the paper seal used by the police to close off the freshly vacated homes of Jewish deportees; a selection of letters that Walter Oppenheimer and his partner Rose Scharnberg smuggled in and out of the police prison on Lehrter Strasse. A glass pillar in the center of the main exhibition hall presented various documents deportees had entrusted to the Jewish Community: insurance documents, family birth certificates, proof of cancelled debts, and so forth. These people clearly hoped that, despite their uncertain fate, they would some day be able to retrieve their documents—that they would one day return to Berlin.

Even as the years 1938–45 were a time of acute threat, many Jewish Berliners also showed self-assertion, solidarity, courage, and dignity. There are photographs, for example, of two young Jewish boys who saved Torah scrolls from a burning synagogue in November 1938. Interviews describe the tactics used to avoid wearing the yellow star. Self-help and self-assertion groups were organized and later maintained illegally among Zionists, for example. Jewish Community employees tried as best they could to stand by those who were summoned for deportation, often taking great risks to help their friends and relatives. Finally, the lives of the "U-Boote" bear witness to the will to survive, the courage, and the wits needed to live underground. In cellars, attics, garden plots, bombed-out apartments—wherever they went—they lived in almost constant risk of police checks, denunciation, and discovery. They carried forged identity cards and, often enough, fell into the hands of ruthless profiteers, private exploiters, and "snatchers." But they also received help from friends, former colleagues, non-Jewish family members, Christians and atheists, prostitutes and madams, and even complete strangers.

The exhibition relied heavily on audio and visual elements to tell its stories, and while the English edition of the catalog cannot of course reproduce the audio-visual effects, it can certainly build on them. The book will be as accessible to readers who did not attend the show as to those who did. To a certain extent, the book has the character of a historical account, even though for the reasons already stated it does not and cannot replace such an account.

IN 1941, A YOUNG Berliner named Walter Philipp had just managed to emigrate with his parents when the first deportation trains were heading east. Philipp, who now lives in the United States, very kindly lent his parents' passports to the exhibition along with the prayer book that he received one year before for his bar mitzvah at the New Synagogue. He also loaned a family menorah that he brought with him from Berlin and carefully looked after for more than sixty years. It cannot have been easy for Philipp to allow these items out of his sight, let alone to send them back to Berlin. His generosity is representative of all those who allowed us to display their personal possessions. It turned out that many had kept such objects very carefully but had, until now, never opened the boxes in which they were stored. We are extremely grateful to everyone who loaned materials to the exhibition.

In preparing the exhibition and accompanying volumes, it gave us great pleasure to work with many different authors. Alongside the seasoned academics who contributed chapters were a number of talented students and interns who have gone on to pursue interesting careers of their own. Working together were Jewish and non-Jewish participants alike, members of the second as well as the third generations following the Shoah. Many thanks to them all.

We would like to thank all of those who worked on the exhibition and the accompanying publications, especially Diana Schulle, who edited the German edition, and Philo Verlagsgesellschaft, Berlin, which published it. Caroline Gay produced the initial translation, which Miranda Robbins edited. The staff at the University of Chicago Press skillfully steered the project through to completion. Last but not least, we would like to thank series editor Paul Mendes-Flohr for helping to bring this work to an English-speaking audience as part of the Studies in German-Jewish Cultural History and Literature series.

*Beate Meyer*
*Hermann Simon*
*Chana Schütz*
*Berlin, August 2003*

**1**  Report by Max Nussbaum, Yad Vashem Archive, 01/232, p. 15.

**2**  For more on Speer, see Susanne Willems, *Der entsiedelte Jude. Albert Speers Wohnungsmarktpolitik für den Berliner Hauptstadtbau* (Berlin, 2000).

**3**  For numbers, see Wolf Gruner, *Judenverfolgung in Berlin. Eine Chronologie der Behördenmaßnahmen in der Reichs-* hauptstadt (Berlin, 1996), pp. 15, 93; and Kurt Schilde, *Bürokratie des Todes* (Berlin, 2002), pp. 75–76.

**4**  See Erica Fischer, *Aimée und Jaguar. Eine Liebesgeschichte—Berlin, 1943* (Berlin, 1994).

**1**

1938

# Chapter One
## 1938: The Year of Fate

HERMANN SIMON

Kurt Jakob Ball-Kaduri, who in 1944–47 had already started to collect reports from the persecuted German Jews in Palestine and who deposited his own memoirs at the Yad Vashem Archive in Jerusalem, wrote the following about the year 1938: "From the start of 1938, one had the feeling that disaster was on the horizon, that we no longer had time for lengthy planning and preparation for emigration."[1]

If, before 1938, many Berlin Jews thought they could work around the uncomfortable circumstances, that feeling vanished at the start of 1938. Finally, it became clear to all that they would have to leave the place they called home. Yet in many cases, those affected saw little chance of emigrating. Emigration required entrance visas to another country, and these were by no means easy to obtain. The visas required financial guarantees from relatives or friends living in the countries concerned, and not every Jew in Germany had such connections. Nazi laws, moreover, made it extremely difficult to transfer money and other assets abroad. Many Jews simply did not have the necessary amount of property and were unable to raise the travel expenses—even in the rare cases in which one could pay in German currency.

Early March 1938 saw the enactment of the Nazi "Law on the Legal Status of Jewish Religious Associations," which stripped Germany's Jewish Communities of their status as religious organizations. Berlin's Community now became an association and was registered as such. "This law," Ball-Kaduri noted, "shook up most Jews terribly. Actually it was not surprising that the law was implemented. . . . Remarkable, rather, was the fact that the Communities had been allowed status [as an official religious community] for so many years under the Nazi regime. . . . Nonetheless, the loss of this status made a terrible impression. Everyone now knew that the last hour of German Jewry had sounded, that this was the beginning of the end, and that one could no longer expect a slow development but instead a rapid sequence of events." Berlin's Jews, too, were desperate, and "a deep wave of pessimism spread among them."[2]

## Harassment

Ball-Kaduri reported on raids in areas of the city where Jews often assembled, including a trap set up on the busy shopping street, the Kurfürstendamm: "If a passer-by breached certain pedestrian codes—for example by cutting diagonally across the street instead of crossing at right angles, or starting to cross at a yellow light instead of waiting for it to turn green—he would be stopped. Aryans got off with a warning, while Jews were taken to the police station and kept there overnight, verbally abused and sometimes mistreated."[3]

This kind of bullying became more and more frequent over the course of the year, and not only on the Kurfürstendamm. There were several pedestrian "traps" in Berlin. One of them was at the junction of Berliner Allee and Lothringenstrasse in the Weissensee district—the intersection at the approach to the Jewish cemetery. The Jewish Community put up a large enamel sign warning its visitors not to jaywalk "for their own good." The sign, which has been preserved, was mounted on a stand at the cemetery's exit. When precisely it was placed there is not known, but it must have been after August 1939—when the Community was forced to append the initials "e.V." (*eingetragener Verein*, "registered association") to its name. As early as September 1938, the Jewish Community's board was urgently reminding people to "observe road traffic regulations." "Members of the Community have been punished with severe fines for breaching road traffic regulations," it announced in the *Berliner Gemeindeblatt* that month. "If the person concerned is unable to pay, there is prison instead of a fine—a punishment that can, in any case, be imposed in all cases deemed serious. We are thus publishing the road traffic regulations for pedestrians and drawing the special attention of our Community members to the fact that they should follow the regulations to the letter. In particular, it should not be overlooked that the road may only be crossed on the green light, and that it is forbidden to cross when the light is still yellow."[4] There followed an extract from the road traffic regulations concerning the "pedestrian code."

Hans Reichmann, the syndic of the Central Association of German Citizens of Jewish Faith (Centralverein deutscher Staatsbürger jüdischen Glaubens) described similar traps set up during the months of June and July 1938:

> The smear campaign stopped.[5] The word was now that "the Jewish question is being solved by law." How many times have we heard that already! The Berlin

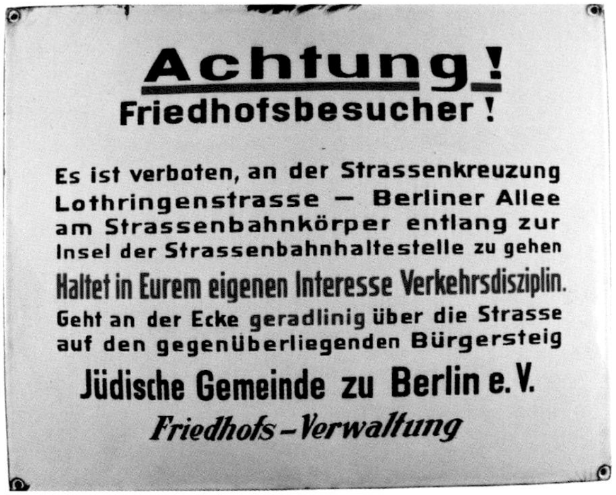

**Figure 1.1** Sign posted at the entrance to the Jewish Cemetery in Weissensee

police ordered that special Jewish license plates be put on cars to discourage Jews from driving. Detectives stopped those violating traffic regulations at main traffic points. Traps were set up in front of the Jewish hospital on Iranische Strasse and at the crossing in front of the Jewish cemetery in Weissensee to catch Jewish pedestrians jaywalking. They were fined by the police—indeed, given the highest 150 Reichsmark penalty, while Aryan offenders had to pay one Reichsmark. We searched until 8 P.M. for an employee of the Philo publishing house who had left his apartment [for work] at 3 P.M. but had not arrived by 3.15 P.M. We sought in vain for him at hospitals, at the missing persons center, at the police stations. The notorious police station on Grolmanstrasse lied to us, saying that he wasn't there. He turned up that evening. He had been caught failing to observe a traffic light, and for this Grolmanstrasse made him sit there for five hours. . . . Then came prosecution. This, too, was a contribution to the legal resolution of the Jewish question.[6]

As Ball-Kaduri relates, all aspects of Jewish life in the city were particularly tense in 1938. "Cultural life in the Jewish Cultural Union [Kulturbund], in orchestral organizations, and so forth, continued. But in a forced way. One constantly had to reckon with arrests."[7] Reichmann recalls:

Throughout the whole summer there were raids on Jewish cafes and restaurants. . . . The notorious police chief Schneider would suddenly appear and seal off these establishments with a contingent of police cars, police constables, and criminal police officers. He would then make harmless visitors show their identity papers, knock the cigarettes out of the mouths of elderly people, put handcuffs on anyone who protested, and then race off to [the police station at] Alexanderplatz with his booty of thirty, fifty, or sixty people. There the captured were held for days, even weeks—because the Jewish question is of course now being solved "legally." No Jewish establishment, not even an isolated restaurant, was safe from these lightening raids.[8]

A range of Nazi laws and regulations passed in the course of the year made the lives of the Jews ever more difficult and contributed to considerable uncertainty about what would come next. Two striking examples were the law requiring the registration of Jewish assets (passed April 26) and the requirement that all Jewish-owned firms to be marked as Jewish (passed June 14).

Certainly, many saw the second supplementary decree on the Implementation of the Law on the Amendment of Family and First Names enacted on August 17, 1938, as particularly humiliating. The law stipulated that as of January 1, 1939, the names Sara (for women) and Israel (for men) be affixed by default to any Jew whose first name was not included on an official list of allegedly "Jewish" first names. This appended list had been issued by the Ministry of the Interior on August 18, 1938, and comprised 185 male and 91 female names.[9] The fact that Jews had to register the name change in person with the authorities was yet another form of harassment.

Interestingly, the list contained very few Biblical names. In a May 1986 lecture given at the Jewish Museum in Eisenstadt, Austria, Marie Simon pointed out that in this compilation of names "one can see the discriminatory intention . . . to brand the Jews with names that were displeasing, even repulsive." Yet "this intention was not thoroughly realized." The list reveals "a chaotic variety of forms, which not only suggests that heterogeneous sources were probably used but also that various people contributed to the lists of names, from which the index was then compiled—a selection of the strangest names."[10] Marie Simon recalled her reaction to the regulation as a pupil at the Jewish school on Wilsnacker Strasse: "When the supplementary names . . . were imposed on all Jews in 1938, this measure, although despicable, provoked laughter among us. The Jewish women had been elevated to nobility—Sara means 'princess.' The men were honored as 'fighters for God.'"[11]

## Dress Rehearsals

In the next chapter of this volume, Christian Dirks examines in detail the so-called *Juni-Aktion*, the Nazi roundup of "asocials" that took place in the spring and summer of 1938 and included the arrest of about 1,500 Berlin Jews. In the course of the campaign Jewish shops were vandalized and smeared with slogans.

Suffice to say here that all Jews with previous offenses—and this included those who had been punished by the police for breaching road traffic regulations—were considered "asocial."

Reproduced in Dirks's article is a series of photographs acquired by the Centrum Judaicum in the 1980s depicting some of the vandalism that took place during the *Juni-Aktion*.[12] My maternal grandfather, Hermann Jalowicz, a lawyer whose practice was at Prenzlauer Strasse 19a, noted the following in his unpublished diary entries for June 22 and 27, 1938: "Outside children are smearing slogans on the doors and windows of Jewish shops. Later, other Jewish signs were also painted—the nameplates of the Jacobis, Egers, and Michelsohns, for example—and mine as well. After a few days, the policeman from our station came and demanded that we clean the signs. A long discussion with the Berlin authorities. The result: the Jews cleaned up what others had defaced."[13]

This comment by Reichmann was surely on the mark: "Since June, the Jews have had no peace. Over the summer they have lost their sense of feeling for nature. We no longer notice that the sun is shining; it no longer warms us. We have no sense of summery ease; the harmony of nature disturbs us. We are wounded, but our wounds are invisible. We are bleeding internally."[14]

To a certain extent, the so-called *Polen-Aktion* orchestrated by the Nazis on October 27 and 28 served as another dress rehearsal for the pogrom that would take place on November 9, 1938, and for the later deportations as well. Some 17,000 Jews of Polish nationality all across Germany were affected. Many had been living there for decades. Others were born in Germany and had no links with Poland whatsoever. In the words of Trude Mauer, all "were put on remand pending deportation, to be transferred literally at the last minute to the country where they were still nationals but which was no home for them, and which indeed had sought to exclude them forever."[15] It is difficult to say how many Berlin Jews were affected by this deportation. The number was probably around six thousand. The first expellees were allowed to enter Poland; the rest were detained in the border areas, above all in Zbaszyn (Bentschen), under unbearable conditions.

"Disaster was in the air," Ball-Kaduri recalls of the situation as it unfolded in the days that followed. "In early November came the news that the Jew Grünspan [Herschel Grynszpan] had shot the German diplomatic official von Rath [Ernst vom Rath] in Paris. A few days later came the news of his death . . . and the corresponding commentary in the German press. We now knew that terrible things would happen in the days ahead, but no one knew what. No one could conceive of what was to take place."[16]

**Figure 1.2** The Kurcer family, forced from Berlin during the *Polen-Aktion*, shown here in January 1941 in the Wolbrom Ghetto, Poland. *Left to right*: Jacob Kurcer, his wife Rosa Zuckermann Kurcer, and Adolf Kurcer

**Figure 1.3** Jews forced from Berlin during the *Polen-Aktion* of October 1938 at a station on the Polish border

## The Terminology of Kristallnacht

Since 1987, I have again and again asked eyewitnesses what term they use to refer to the events that unfolded on the night of November 9–10, 1938. When did certain names take hold? No one can really remember. Some call it the "pogrom," others "the night of the burning synagogues," others *Kristallnacht* or "the night of broken glass." Increasingly frequent in Germany today is the linguistic hybrid *Reichskristallnacht*.

We still do not know when the terms *Kristallnacht* or *Reichskristallnacht* first came into use. At Berlin's Centrum Judaicum, Christian Dirks recently raised the question in an Internet discussion forum for historians, eliciting a range of responses. It was suggested, for example, that the term *Reichskristallnacht* was a joke invented by the famous comedian Werner Finck similar to an epithet then circulating in reference to a popular starlet—*Reichswasserleiche* (Water-Corpse of the Reich)—who had twice "drowned" on the Nazi screen.[17] But this theory has little credibility. Nor was the term *Kristallnacht* first used, as Michael Cullen suggests, by the Nazi economics minister Walther Funk in a notorious meeting held on November 12 at the Reich Ministry of Aviation.[18]

As Erika Ising wrote in 1989, "the reconstruction of the origin and occurrence of *Kristallnacht* [and] *Reichskristallnacht* is, as before, difficult. The written sources prove *Kristallnacht* to be the original term." The author continues that this evidence has, "however, only been available since around 1950."[19]

In fact, as early as November 1945 the newspaper *Berliner Zeitung* used the term "Kristallnacht" in scare quotes.[20] On November 8, 1945, another Berlin paper, the *Tagesspiegel*, reminded its readers that the days of the pogrom and "the subsequent days were commonly known as "Kristallwoche."[21] That *Kristallnacht* was already used in November 1945 suggests at least that the term was in use during the Nazi period. Up to now, there has been no firm evidence that the term was created by the Berlin vernacular of the time, and it is uncertain whether such evidence will ever come to light.

In a 1978 letter to the editors of the *Frankfurter Allgemeine Zeitung*, a Berlin reader who had worked near the New Synagogue in Mitte referred to the events of November 9–10 as "Kristallnacht, which we in Berlin called the *Tag der Deutschen Scherbe*"—the Day of the German Shard. This unique designation is especially interesting for its apparent irony.[22]

## The November Pogrom

What is certain is that the night from November 9 to 10 utterly changed the lives of Berlin's Jews. At first it was only the synagogues, shops, and property that fell prey to an orgy of burning, looting, and destruction! Soon it would be people themselves. It must have been dreadful for the Jews to see their synagogues burn. Josef Goebbels personally gave the order to destroy the Fasanenstrasse synagogue in the western part of Berlin, as he notes in his diary.[23] Many eyewitnesses can still picture this burning synagogue, which smoldered for days. Over sixty years later, Ernst Günter Fontheim, a schoolboy at the time, recalled:

> The place of worship was one of the most beautiful synagogues that I had ever seen, both from the outside and the inside. . . . On the morning of November 10, I went to school as usual. My neighborhood, Westend, had no Jewish shops. Nor did I pass any synagogues on my way to school. So I had no idea that a pogrom was underway. It was only when I arrived at school that I heard terrible accounts from my classmates, most of whom lived in Jewish neighborhoods—horror stories of smashed shop windows, plundered Jewish shops, burning synagogues and prayer rooms, and so forth. When the bell rang at 8 A.M., not a single teacher appeared, neither in our class nor in the classroom across the hall. That was unheard of. We just sat, dejected, in our classroom waiting.
>
> Later . . . the door to the teachers' room opened, and they all came into the classrooms with worried faces. Our teacher, Dr. Wollheim, entered our classroom, closed the door behind him, and said that the safety of the school could no longer be guaranteed and that the school would therefore be closed, effective immediately. We were all to go home. He gave us the following instructions: not to loiter

anywhere; to go straight home so that our parents would know that we were safe; also not to go in large groups, which could attract the attention of Nazi gangs, but instead in groups of two or, at most, three. . . .

The Adass-Schule was near Tiergarten station, and my route to school thus took me via S-Bahn from the Tiergarten station to the Heerstrasse station. I lived five minutes from the Heerstrasse station. After what I had heard, I naturally looked out the window, and between the Zoo and Savignyplatz stations, I could see the synagogue on Fasanenstrasse, right next to the S-Bahn overpass. This was the synagogue where I had had my bar mitzvah three years earlier.

As the train passed the synagogue, I could see a cloud of smoke rising like a column from the central dome—the synagogue had three domes. It gave me such a shock that I forgot everything Dr. Wollheim had told us. At the next stop I leapt from the train and ran back as fast as I could to see what was happening. On a pavement opposite the synagogue there was a crowd of people being held back by the police. There was a lot of anti-Semitic . . . shouting. I stood there in the middle, oblivious to the danger, completely hypnotized by the sight of the burning synagogue—that was all I could think about.

. . . The Adass School, like most of the other Jewish schools, never re-opened. My parents thought it wise, in view of emigration, that I learn English as quickly as possible.[24]

As elsewhere in the city, firemen stood at the ready on Fasanenstrasse—but only to protect neighboring properties. The next morning when the fire had gone out they withdrew. A photo of the burning synagogue went out around the world and was printed on November 13–14 in the *Pariser Tageblatt,* a German-language newspaper founded by Germans in exile.

The great New Synagogue on Oranienburger Strasse, was on fire, too. Alexander Szanto, who worked for the Berlin Jewish Community between 1923 and 1939, reported in detail on the pogrom in his largely unpublished memoirs:

On the morning of November 10 . . . the telephone rang in my apartment. I recognized the voice of the agitated man at the other end as that of the porter [Julius Wainschel] at our Community quarters. "Don't come. Fire at 30," he shouted and hung up. It was not hard to decipher the meaning of this abbreviated message. The Community's main office was at 29 Oranienburger Strasse and its Economic Aid Office was at number 31. Between them stood number 30, the proud and beautiful building of our venerable synagogue. Clearly, fire was raging there. But why was he warning me to stay away? Could nothing be saved? It was clear that the caller with the fearful voice, who had not dared to give his name, was not only himself at risk but also knew that anyone else who rushed to scene would also be in danger. He did not call to ask for help but to give a warning.[25]

**Figure 1.4** The Fasanenstrasse synagogue in flames, November 10, 1938

**Figure 1.5** A photograph of the burning Fasanenstrasse synagogue printed in the *Pariser Tageblatt*, November 13–14, 1938

Szanto further recalled that, after receiving more and more bad news, he arranged "a meeting at midday at a neutral place near the Community office" with Dr. Bruno Mendelsohn, head of the Economic Aid Office.

From there we learned more about the situation and contacted Heinrich Stahl, the chairman of the Community. We only got confirmation of news that had already come in. All of the Berlin synagogues had been set on fire; all had more or less been burned. Fire had ravaged only the interior of the main synagogue at 30 Oranienburger Strasse, from which the alarm had first been raised. The rapid intervention of the porter [Wainschel] and some other brave people had kept the flames from spreading. A fireman was in the building at the time. Next door, the premises of the Economic Aid Office appeared to be intact but were occupied by SS officers. In the meantime the SS were said to have left the main office on the

**Figure 1.6** Kracher Ladies' Wear, Potsdamer Strasse 104 in Schöneberg

**Figure 1.7** Destroyed business on Leipziger Strasse, November 19, 1938

other side of the synagogue, but we weren't sure because the gate was locked. The ground-floor windows had been smashed, the inside of the rooms demolished. Approaching via side streets, we then tried to get into the rear courtyard of the complex though a back entrance, and we managed to make contact with Wainschel, who told us that the SS officers were lounging . . . in the front offices and freely rewarding themselves with beer and wine after their "heroic actions" of the previous night. His wife [Berta, née Landbrand] and his children [Isidor, b. 1927, and Leo, b. 1930] were forced to wait on the "heroes," get them drinks, clean their boots. We could get little more information out of this completely broken man.[26]

**Figure 1.8** The café and confectionery of Isodor Dobrin on Spandauer Brücke 7

**Figure 1.9** After the pogrom

A frequently printed photograph of the New Synagogue in flames bears in its caption the date of November 9–10, 1938, dates that, in fact, are incorrect. The photograph is a postwar fabrication. We know this because the synagogue's small east dome, including the entire tower that supports it, is missing from the image. Seeing this photo for the first time in the late 1970s, I originally assumed that the picture had been taken during the [American] bombing raids that took place in 1943, on the night of November 22–23, 1943. However, in his 1990 book *Der beherzte Reviervorsteher* (The Courageous Policeman), Heinz Knobloch clearly demonstrates that smoke and flames were retouched to a postwar photograph taken in April 1948 by a photographer named Heinscher from the Haupttelegraphenamt (Central Telegraph Office), which stood opposite the synagogue.[27.] Elsewhere, I have written about how this came about.[28]

Jewish shops, and not just synagogues, were devastated in the course of the pogrom. The city was a terrible sight, above all in the commercial districts, for example around the Kurfürstendamm in the western part of the city on Alexanderplatz in Mitte.[29]

The Colombian ambassador Jaime Jaramillo Arango described the night's events in a report to the Colombian president, Eduardo Santos: "To get a view of it by day . . . we set off about 10 A.M. to look at the scene of the events. We were of course curious to catch a glimpse of the horror on display in Berlin as well as in all other German towns: destruction, plunder, burnt-out synagogues, a certain vigilantism—images that Dante himself could not have conceived, since the torments bear the refined mark of this century."[30]

The Secretary of the Colombian Embassy, Rafael Rocha-Schloss, described the situation to his Foreign Minister, Luis López de Mesa:

As we neared our apartment on the Kurfürstendamm [on the night of November 9–10], we were suddenly astonished to see a group of people armed with iron bars systematically smashing up all of the large shops on the street. The destruction was targeted at Jewish property, and, since I was driving slowly and discreetly, I could see how these barbaric acts were being carried out along the street. Some of the vandals smashed in the windows, as others forced their way in, destroying furnishings and throwing the goods into the street, where they were . . . looted. Here and there on the street corners, under cover of darkness, stood a few cars from which people wearing the black uniforms of the SS . . . gave orders and led the vile devastation. This spectacle at the heart of Berlin was truly horrific; shards of glass windows littered the pavement, goods were shredded, and the shops were filled with rubble. And so it was that, the next morning, Berlin's population had to be present at the largest demonstration of vandalism of modern times.[31]

Rocha-Schloss's Brazilian colleague, Themistokles de Graca Aranha, also reported on the devastation in the western part of the city:

I myself saw how shops were devastated in broad daylight on the Kurfürstendamm, one of Berlin's main shopping streets, which contains most of the city's luxury shops. Police stood by doing nothing, watching the frightful spectacle with approval. They seemed to regret that they couldn't take part in the looting themselves. On the nonaction of the police, Dr. Goebbels has said that they did not feel they were in a position to intervene against this justified and spontaneous declaration of will on the part of the German people. After all, Hitler's Minister continued, there was a justified revolt against the Jews; they were enemies of the German race.

It would be wrong and indeed ridiculous to comment on this assertion by the Reich Propaganda Minister, which shows the shamelessness expressed in such general declarations.[32]

It was virtually impossible to resist the riots of the night from November 9 to 10, 1938. Nonetheless, there was some resistance, both on the part of foreign diplomats working in Germany and Berlin Jews themselves. The Colombian diplomats, for example, came into conflict with the authorities as they photographed damaged shops in the area around the Zoo station. When ordered to hand over their camera, they bravely resisted—an incident that put severe strain on German-Colombian relations.[33]

Recently, the resistance of two Jewish boys during the pogrom has been discovered. The teenagers rescued the Torah scrolls from their synagogue on Berlin's Markgraf-Albrecht-Strasse, the Friedenstempel (Temple of Peace). David Zwingermann (now David Hamilton) provided me with a detailed written account of these events. On the morning of November 10, Zwingermann, then aged fourteen, and his younger friend Horst Löwenstein discovered twelve undamaged Torah scrolls in the burned-out synagogue. They were still intact within the Holy Ark, which had very thick oak doors. The two boys carried the scrolls through the entrance into the street without anyone noticing. "Nazis in uniform, supporters and onlookers, were on the steps, the sidewalk, and in the street. . . . I tried to hail a taxi and managed to get one. Luckily the driver, a White Russian by birth, was willing to take the Torah scrolls." Zwingermann's mother subsequently arranged for the scrolls to be stored with a Jewish tea importer from England, and some time later they were returned to the congregation. The head of the congregation, Elieser Ehrenreich (1883–1941, d. Ravensbrück) learned of the action both from Rabbi Ladislaus Eliezer Berkovits (1908–92) and from a personal report by Zwingermann. He sought to make arrangements for the two boys to emigrate. He was only successful in the case of Zwingermann, who left Germany for England on December 2, 1938, with the first *Kindertransport* to England. Löwenstein was murdered in Riga on November 30, 1941.[34]

Incidentally, these two boys were not the only ones who saved Torah scrolls from the Friedenstempel that day. The Berlin rabbi Max Nussbaum, who was able to emigrate in 1940 and later held office in Hollywood, California, stated in 1958 that he, too, had saved a Torah scroll from the ruined synagogue. Nussbaum had learned of the riots after a phone call in the wee hours of the morning from the American journalist Louis Paul Lochner. Lochner told him that the synagogues were burning.

We met immediately in the street when it was still dark and went to the synagogue known as the Friedenstempel in west Berlin. The synagogue was on fire. The fire service was there but only protecting the neighboring buildings. Our *Chasan* [prayer leader] stood next to the burning synagogue and led me inside secretly though a back door. The Aron-Kodesh [Holy Ark] was already open; Torah rolls had been pulled out and ripped up using great strength. Half of the pews had been chopped up. I went behind the Torah Ark without being seen and was able to grab a small Torah scroll that was still in there, pull it out, and hide it under my

*We looked out of the window [and saw] men and women with axes and long iron bars which they used to break open large wooden chests. This hacking was the only sound that could be heard in the street.*
WALTER TICK, 1994

*We have already written to you in support of the emigration of the two boys Horst Löwenstein and David Zwingermann, who committed an act of self-sacrifice in helping to save 12 Torah scrolls from the Friedenstempel. In the meantime, David Zwingermann has been helped to emigrate, while Horst Löwenstein is still waiting for his final exit permit. We would be most grateful if this boy could also soon enjoy the benefits of being sent away.*
ELIESER EHRENREICH TO DORA SILBERMANN (AT THE DEPARTMENT FOR YOUTH AND WELFARE), LETTER DATED JANUARY 10, 1939

**Figure 1.10** The boys Horst Löwenstein, center, and David Zwingerman, right, next to the Torah scrolls they rescued from the synagogue on Markgraf-Albrecht-Strasse during the pogrom. At left is the tea importer who hid the scrolls until they could be safely returned to the congregation. Photograph courtesy of David Hamilton, London

*They hacked everything to pieces with the axes. The shattering glass also made a lot of noise. Most of the women there had prams, but there were no babies in them. They brought the prams in order to put as many goods in them as possible. That way they could drag off more than they could carry.*

WALTER TICK, 1994

raincoat. We went back out and, although the SS men looked threateningly at us, we were able to go our own way, undisturbed. I was able to take the little Torah scroll home with me.[35]

In 1958, Nussbaum continues: "Today this Torah scroll is located in the Aron-Kodesh of our temple in Hollywood. It is very well known there, and during processions, especially Simchat Torah [the Celebration of the Torah], I always carry it through the synagogue."[36]

That the accounts of Zwingermann and Nussbaum differ slightly is not surprising in view of the fact that both statements were made years after the event. Nonetheless, the complete destruction of the synagogues on the night of November 9–10, 1938, remains a fact.

In the face of relentless Nazi censorship, Jewish intellectual opposition to the regime, though muted, was often ingenious. Of the Jewish press after 1933, two quotes in particular could have served as mottos: "The truth must be spread in cunning ways" (Bertolt Brecht) and "A satire that the censor understands is a poor satire" (Karl Kraus). Thus, the *Jüdisches Nachrichtenblatt* couched its comments on the events of November 9 in a review of the film *Chicago*, which had recently been screened by the Jewish Kulturbund: "A city goes up in flames and firefighters stand by without taking any action. All the hoses are poised, the ladders have been prepared. . . . But no hand moves to use them. The men wait for the command, but no command is heard. Only when the city . . . has burned down and is lying in cinders and ashes, an order arrives; but the firefighters are already driving away. A malicious invention? An ugly tale? No. The truth. And it was revealed in Hollywood."[37]

There are also known instances of protest on the part of non-Jewish Berliners—though this was admittedly but a drop in the ocean. An anecdote has been passed down regarding Lieselotte Henrich, then a young civil servant, who would later become the well-known ancient historian Elisabeth Charlotte Welskopf. Coming from work in the late afternoon of November 10, she saw shards of glass and noted the looting. Her colleagues had also related something of what was going on, so she was therefore informed. As innocently as possible, and in a deliberately naïve tone of voice, the young woman declared to the onlookers that "surely, the Communists were responsible. Nazis would never have done such a thing; only Communists were vandals. . . . And look at how valuables have been destroyed here—only the Communists would do such a thing." The police advised her to move on. She did, but after traveling a few stops by train, she again announced, "We must explain and inform. The Communists did this." To the degree that it made people stop and think about what the Nazis had allowed to happen, even this small act of resistance was meaningful.[38]

The pogrom resulted in the arrest of around 12,000 of Berlin's Jewish men, most of whom were delivered over to the concentration camps at Sachsenhausen and Buchenwald. The conditions were appalling, as detailed descriptions testify.[39] Nonetheless, for some, arrest actually meant salvation—only, of course, for those who were later released from the concentration camps. This is because anyone who had been in a concentration camp was deemed particularly "at risk," and Jewish foreign organizations then made special efforts to help them emigrate. This was the case for Herbert Eger, a lawyer from the district of Pankow, whom the B'nai B'rith Lodge helped to emigrate to England with his family after his release from Sachsenhausen. His son recalls:

In November 1938, my father was summoned by the Gestapo. This was nothing unusual, since he was the secretary of the [Pankow] congregation and it had happened frequently.[40] Each time, he would take a toothbrush, soap, and a towel with him just in case he was kept there—except this time! On this occasion, he didn't come home. Of course, the Gestapo didn't answer any requests for information. Then we heard rumors that a truck full of men had been seen driving toward Oranienburg. My mother thought that they had perhaps taken my father to the Sachsenhausen concentration camp. A few days later she and I drove there to try to drop off a package for my father . . . but it was impossible. On the way there, we saw groups of prisoners on the road who were being marched to the camp.

Herbert Eger was released after a few weeks. His son continues: "He never told us much about his experiences in the concentration camp. But after his death [in 1953] my mother told me that he used to wake up almost every night screaming, and that this was linked to what he had gone through in the camp."[41]

In a few cases some of those arrested on November 9 were set free due to the fact that there were still some upright and respectable policemen in the city. My grandfather Hermann Jalowicz, whom I mentioned earlier, was one of them. He was arrested immediately after the pogrom and brought to the police station on Alexanderplatz, where a policeman recognized him: "Good Lord, how did you end up here, then, Dr. Jalowicz?" Jalowicz briefly filled him in, and the policeman expressed astonishment: "That's ridiculous; they haven't even looked at your papers. Be so good as to leave this hospitable place right away. Please don't take this the wrong way—but I think it best if you follow me. I'll accompany you to the staff exit and you can leave by the back." There the pair shook hands warmly and bade one another farewell.[42]

The situation changed radically after the pogrom of November 9, 1938. There was nothing left for the Jews in the Reich to hold on to. Only downfall remained.

**1** Kurt Jakob Ball-Kaduri, Sachsenhausen concentration camp (1938), Yad Vashem Archive, Jerusalem (YV), 01/46, p. 2.

**2** Kurt Jakob Ball-Kaduri, *Vor der Katastrophe. Juden in Deutschland, 1934–1939* (Tel Aviv, 1967), pp. 126–28.

**3** Ibid., 128.

**4** *Jüdisches Gemeindeblatt*, 18 September, 1938, p. 5.

**5** The "smear campaign" refers to the *Juni-Aktion*.

**6** Hans Reichmann, *Deutscher Bürger und verfolgter Jude. Novemberpogrom und KZ Sachsenhausen*, ed. Michael Wildt (Munich, 1998), p. 81.

**7** Ball-Kaduri, *Vor der Katastrophe*, p. 131.

**8** Reichmann, *Deutscher Bürger und verfolgter Jude*, p. 81.

**9** Winfried Seibert, *Das Mädchen, das nicht Esther heißen durfte. Eine exemplarische Geschichte* (Leipzig, 1996), pp. 266 ff.

**10** Marie Simon, "Zunz als Begründer der Onomastik im Rahmen der Wissenschaft des Judentums," in *Kairos: Zeitschrift für Judaistik und Religionswissenschaft* 30/31, Salzburg (1988–89), pp. 130–32. A sample of the names— Abel, Abieser, Abimelech, Abner, Absalom, Ahab, Ahasja, Ahaser—is provided by Saul Friedländer, *Nazi Germany and the Jews*, vol. 1, *The Years of Persecution, 1933–1939* (New York, 1997), pp. 254–55.

**11** Ibid., p. 129.

**12** Hermann Simon, " 'Bilder, an die Dante nicht im Traum gedacht hätte': Neue Quellen zum Novemberpogrom in Berlin" (paper presented at a meeting of the Porta Pacis Association), in *1938: Vom Pogrom zum Völkermord*, ed. Martina Weyrauch and Peter Borowsky (Berlin, 1988), pp. 21 ff.

**13** Diary of Dr. Hermann Jalowicz (1877–1941), in the possession of the author. Mention is made of the lawyers Herbert Eger and most probably Moritz Jacoby and Dr. Felix Michelsohn.

**14** Reichmann, *Deutscher Bürger*, p. 84.

**15** Trude Maurer, "Abschiebung und Attentat. Die Ausweisung der polnischen Juden und der Vorwand für die 'Kristallnacht,' " in *Der Judenpogrom 1938*, ed. Walter H. Pehle (Frankfurt am Main, 1988), p. 53.

**16** See note 1.

**17** The Swedish actress Kristina Söderbaum, later married to the director Veit Harlan, played the lead role in his 1938 hit film *Jugend*. Söderbaum embodied the Nazi ideal of the Germanic child-woman whose threatened purity had to be saved. If her honor could not be saved in the film, she had to drown. In fact, Söderbaum's characters drowned in just two of her films, but this sufficed to earn her the nickname *"Reichswasserleiche"* (Water-Corpse of the Reich).

**18** Michael S. Cullen writes that Funk "has the dubious distinction of having coined the term 'Kristallnacht.' " See "Der genius loci hat viele Facetten," *Der Tagesspiegel*, 6 November 1998, in a special supplement for the American Academy in Berlin, p. 4.

**19** Erika Ising, "Kristallnacht—Pogromnacht: Schluß-punkt oder neue Fragezeichen," in *Der Sprachdienst* 6 (1989): 169.

**20** Ursula Lampe, "Hintergründe der 'Kristallnacht,' " *Berliner Zeitung*, 13 November 1945, p. 3.

**21** *Der Tagesspiegel*, 11 August 1945, p. 4.

**22** Albert Tilmann, letter to the editors, *Frankfurter Allgemeine Zeitung*, 27 November 1978.

**23** Friedländer, *Nazi Germany and the Jews*, p. 272.

**24** Transcript of audio interview with Ernest Guenter Fontheim conducted by Beate Meyer on May 26, 1999, p. 31.

**25** Alexander Szanto, *Im Dienste der Gemeinde, 1923–1939* (London, 1968), collection of memoirs, M.E. 838, p. 211, Leo Beck Institute, New York (LBINY).

**26** Ibid., pp. 212–13.

**27** Heinz Knobloch, *Der beherzte Reviervorsteher. Ungewöhnliche Zivilcourage am Hackeschen Markt* (Berlin, 1990), p. 156.

**28** Hermann Simon, "Abschließende (?) Bemerkungen zu einem historischen Foto," in *Museums Journal* (October 1998): 44–45.

**29** For an interesting account of events in the area around Alexanderplatz, see Horst Helas et al., *Juden in Berlin-Mitte* (Berlin, 2000), pp. 79 ff.

**30** Jaime Jaramillo Arango to the Colombian president Eduardo Santos, letter dated November 12, 1938. See Simon, "Bilder, an die Dante," p. 27.

**31** Colombian diplomatic envoy, Rafael Rocha-Schloss, to the Colombian Foreign Minister, Luis López de Mesa, November 16, 1938, ibid., p. 24.

**32** Embassy advisor Themistokles da Graca Aranha to the Brazilian Foreign Minister, November 21, 1938. This document is located in the archive of the Brazilian Foreign Office and was shown to me in 1998 by the Brazilian consul general in Berlin.

**33** For a more detailed account, see Simon, "Bilder, an die Dante," pp. 24 ff.

**34** See Hermann Simon, "Aber ein stiller Widerstand glühte weiter. Einige Gedanken zum Novemberpogrom—Wie zwei Jungen zwölf Thorarollen aus dem 'Friedenstempel' gerettet haben," in *Die Welt,* 9 November 1998, p. 35.

**35** Continuation of the eyewitness report of July 11, 1958, YV 01/222, p. 2.

**36** Ibid., p. 3.

**37** Jüdisches Nachrichtenblatt, 30 December 1938, p. 3. English translation in Friedländer, *Nazi Germany*, p. 284.

**38** Note from Marie Simon to the author, September 1998.

**39** On Sachsenhausen, see for example, Siegmund Weltlinger, "Hast Du es schon vergessen?" (lecture at the Berliner Gesellschaft für christlich-jüdische Zusammenarbeit on January 28, 1954), pp. 9 ff.; Reichmann, *Deutscher Bürger*. On Buchenwald, see Ball-Kaduri, YV 01/46, pp. 5 ff.

**40** The reference here is to the synagogue association in Pankow.

**41** "Herbert Eger und die Jüdische Gemeinde in Pankow," in *Jüdisches Leben in Pankow,* ed. Inge Lammel (Berlin, 1993), pp. 140–41.

**42** See note 38.

# Chapter Two

## The *Juni-Aktion* (June Operation) in Berlin

CHRISTIAN DIRKS

The anti-Semitic, pogrom-like disturbances that took place in mid-June 1938 in Berlin and other cities throughout the German Reich should be seen within the overall context of the Nazi policy toward Jews. Following the enactment of extensive special provisions, regulations, and laws, the National Socialist powers in 1938 took further measures aimed to push Jews out of the German economy and (insofar as this had not happened already) seize Jewish-owned assets. This development reached its provisional peak after the pogrom of November 9, 1938, and subsequent "atonement payments" (*Sühneleistungen*). Nazi leadership came ever closer to its goal of stripping Jews of their economic base so as to force them to emigrate en masse. Jewish businesses were thus "Aryanized"—sold to non-Jews at prices far below market value in virtually all cases. The resulting waves of refugees affected all European countries—France and England in particular—as well as the United States. The countries were not adequately prepared to take them in.

During the first half of 1938, anti-Jewish riots had already taken place within the German Altreich. These were by no means "spontaneous outbreaks" of the "bottled-up anger of the *Volk*," as Nazi leaders maintained. Rather, they were operations organized across the Reich by the SD (Sicherheitsdienst, Security Service of the SS), SA (Sturmabteilungen, Storm Troopers), and NSDAP (National Socialist Workers' Party). Their goal was twofold: to exert pressure on the international community and to force German Jews into emigration. The problem of Jewish emigrants from Germany and Austria would be an acute one for the international community as a whole. Indeed, the international conference convened at Evian in July 1938 to address this matter had no positive outcome.

## The *Juni-Aktion* (June Operation)

During the spring and summer of 1938, the Nazis arrested some ten thousand "asocials" in two major waves and sent them to the concentration camps at Buchenwald and Sachsenhausen.[1] The order had been given by Reinhard Heydrich, head of the SD and chief of the security police, in conjunction with the campaign called *Arbeitsscheu Reich* (Work-shy Reich) and the "preventative campaign against crime." About 1,500 Jews with previous convictions were affected.[2] Two groups were differentiated during the arrests. The first consisted of "asocial" males without fixed work—"vagrants, beggars, gypsies, pimps," as well as those with numerous criminal convictions. The second comprised "all male Jews . . . who have served at least one prison sentence of more than one month."[3] Heydrich ordered that, in the week from June 13 to 18, 1938, each Gestapo district headquarters take into protective detention at least two hundred able-bodied males.[4]

The SS forced the Jewish prisoners to build new barracks at the concentration camps at Buchenwald and Sachsenhausen. Such extensions made possible the subsequent detention of tens of thousands of Jews after the November pogrom.[5]

The impetus for this wave of arrests was simple; the German economy was suffering a severe labor shortage. The deployment and forced recruitment of "asocials" was one attempt to relieve the situation. The policy blended the Nazis' stated goal of "social-biological prevention" with economic pragmatism and anti-Semitism. The *Juni-Aktion* thus fell within the rubric of the Four Year Plan, directed by SS Reichsführer Heinrich Himmler. It was the first campaign implemented by the SS itself in which a large number of German Jews were delivered over to concentration camps.[6] Members of the SA, Kripo (criminal police), and Hitler Youth were also involved.

## Events in Berlin

Early May 1938 saw an increase in the number of anti-Semitic attacks in various Berlin districts. These included vandalism of Jewish shops and damage to a synagogue.[7] In late May there was an extended campaign to arrest jaywalkers on the Kurfürstendamm. According to press reports, several hundred Jews were taken into custody in the process.[8] Eyewitness reports state that there were particularly bad riots in the districts of Tegel and Lichtenberg. An SD report from the city's "eastern sector" states that on May 27 not only were the windows of a

**Figure 2.1** Shop smeared with anti-Semitic symbols at Grosse Frankfurter Strasse 121 in Friedrichshain

Jewish-owned shop smashed but a crowd of about a thousand people assumed an "ever more threatening stance." As a result, the police took the Jewish shopkeeper into "protective custody" (*Schutzhaft*).[9]

Another SD report dates the start of the *Juni-Aktion* to June 10 and mentions that all party organizations took part with the express permission of Berlin's Gauleiter Joseph Goebbels.[10] Goebbels had launched the campaign with a speech to police officers given at his own Reich propaganda ministry, whipping up their emotions with his rhetoric and calling on them to "cultivate constant attacks" on the Jews. "Spoke in front of three hundred police officers in Berlin," he noted that day in his diary. "Really got them going. Against all sentimentality. Legality is not the motto, but harassment. The Jews must get out of Berlin. The police will help."[11]

On June 13 came a boycott of Jewish shops on the Kurfürstendamm and on Bayrischer Platz in the Wilmersdorf district, during which sidewalks and shop windows were painted with slogans such as "DEUTSCHE, KAUFT NICHT BEI JUDEN" (Germans, do not shop at Jewish establishments). On June 14 there were several raids on Berlin cafes.[12] Finally, after these small-scale campaigns came the major wave of arrests on June 16, during which several thousand Berlin Jews were brought in on trumped-up charges of organized drug dealing to the police headquarters on Alexanderplatz.[13] The crass, rabble-rousing propaganda published in the Nazi newspaper *Stürmer* included on June 16, 1938, the headline "Göring's Words Will Come True in Berlin as Well—The Jews Have to Go!" That day Jewish shops were smeared with anti-Semitic slogans on Bayrischer

Platz, at the Börse station (now Hackescher Markt) in Mitte, and on Frankfurter Allee in Friedrichshain.

Most of the Jewish prisoners arrested were subsequently taken to concentration camps, and their property was sold to Germans.[14] Survivors have reported that the people arrested during the *Juni-Aktion* were treated even more brutally than those Jews arrested in the wake of the November pogrom. According to an informant from the exiled German Social Democratic Party (Sopade), "the Jews arrested during the recent raids and taken to one of the concentration camps at Weimar or Sachsenhausen meet a terrible fate. The Jews detained there undergo the most dreadful forms of torture."[15]

Detailed and gloomy reports on the events were published in the foreign press. A report of June 17 in the *London Daily Telegraph* stated that "in the east of the city, SA troops went from shop to shop, drove shoppers from Jewish establishments, and abused the Jewish proprietors."

As embassy records attest, several foreign correspondents were actually caught up in the arrest operations, though they were later released.[16] Goebbels later noted in his diaries that the English press "took photos of the June campaigns in Berlin, which are incidentally completely over. I will have all of these confiscated."[17] A correspondent for the exile German newspaper the *Pariser Tageblatt* reported on the riots on the afternoon of June 16, 1938. A raging mass gathered on the so-called Horst Wessel Platz and voiced their approval for the arrests with chants like "Death to Juda!" and "Kill the Jewish pigs!" Apparently there were also many signs and banners referred to the Sudeten crisis, including the slogan "REVENGE FOR CZECHOSLOVAKIA."

According to a report in the English *Daily Herald,* most Berliners seemed to show little interest in the anti-Jewish measures taking place in their midst.[18] On the other hand, an informant from the exiled Social Democrats reported that in his district "the smallest incitement to Jewish persecution gets a strong reaction from the majority. For months the *Stürmer* has been producing extensive lists indicating the race of businessmen throughout the city."[19]

The Jewish journalist Bella Fromm described in her diary an instance of vandalism during the *Juni-Aktion*:

We were about to enter a tiny jewelry shop when a gang of ten youngsters in Hitler Youth uniforms smashed the shop window and stormed into the shop, brandishing butcher knives and yelling, "To hell with the Jewish rabble! Room for the Sudeten Germans!" The smallest boy of the mob climbed inside the window and started his work of destruction by flinging everything he could grab right into the streets. Inside, the other boys broke glass shelves and counters, hurling

**Figure 2.2**
The Georg Hirsch
café and bakery at
Schönhauser Allee
21, Prenzlauer Berg

alarm clocks, cheap silverware, and trifles to their accomplices outside. A tiny shrimp of a boy crouched in a corner of the window, putting dozens of rings on his fingers and stuffing his pockets with wrist-watches and bracelets. His uniform bulging with loot, he turned around, spat squarely into the shopkeeper's face, and dashed off.[20]

Fromm's diary continues: "These scenes are everywhere. They just differ in the degree of violence and nastiness. The entire Kurfürstendamm was full of painted slogans and posters. The word *Jude* had been smeared all over the doors, windows, and walls in waterproof paint. In the quarter [behind Alexanderplatz], where most of the small Jewish shops were located, the SA had wreaked dreadful havoc. There were sickening, bloodthirsty pictures of decapitated, hanged, and mutilated Jews with vile inscriptions everywhere. Shop windows were smashed, and the 'loot' from the wretched, small shops was spread over the pavements and the gutters."[21]

Sopade's reports on Germany related the systematic course of the arrests. "In June, police raids took place every night, leading to the arrest of Jews. At the same time, fairly extensive columns went house to house through the streets. Using an apparently carefully prepared list, they marked the Jewish shops with large painted slogans. . . . Police activity runs parallel to these mob-driven operations. Not a pub in Berlin has been spared from a raid, whether the owner is Aryan or Jewish, whether his clients are aristocratic or proletarian."[22]

On June 22, Hugh R. Wilson, the American ambassador in Berlin, summarized events for Washington:

> Starting late Saturday afternoon, civilian groups, consisting usually of two or three men, were to be observed painting on the windows of Jewish shops the word "JUDE" in large red letters, the Star of David, and caricatures of Jews. On the Kurfürstendamm and the Tauentzienstrasse, the fashionable shopping districts in the west, the task of painters was made easy by the fact that Jewish shop-owners had been ordered the day before to display their names in white letters. . . . The painters in each case were followed by large groups of spectators who seemed to enjoy the proceedings thoroughly. . . . It is understood that in the district around the Alexanderplatz boys of the Hitler Youth participated in the painting, making up for their lack of skill by a certain imagination and thoroughness of mutilation. Reports are received that several incidents took place in this region leading to the looting of shops and the beating up of their owners; a dozen or so broken or empty showcases and windows have been seen which lend credence to these reports.[23]

According to the Nazis' official police report on the *Juni-Aktion* (cited in the exile paper *Pariser Tageblatt*), there were raids on two cafes on the Kurfürstendamm on May 30, 1938, during which 339 arrests (mainly of Jews) were made. These two raids "gave rise" to further arrests, and on June 16 many further "suspects" were brought in, among them 143 Jews.[24] There were similar operations in Frankfurt am Main, Cologne, Munich, Leipzig, Vienna, Essen, Breslau, Königsberg, and other cities in the Reich, many of which were reported in the press.[25]

Despite outraged reports in the foreign press, the Nazi press made no mention of the events until June 21 with an article in the *Völkischer Beobachter* entitled "The Background to the 'Jewish Persecution.'" Naturally it did not mention the real reasons for the operation but instead justified the violent acts as an expression of legitimate German anger at the Jews. "The fact that the 'Aryan' population took matters into its own hands, marked the Jewish shops, and gave the Jews a spontaneous, clear and deserved response," wrote the paper, "does not represent a riot but is only an act of self-help."[26]

Here as elsewhere Nazi propaganda drew on old stereotypes of Jews as profiteers and hagglers who earned a dishonest living through cheating. The propaganda minister was an expert at fanning the anti-Semitic flames. In his June 21 speech at Berlin's Olympic Stadium, part of the midsummer celebrations, Goebbels declared, "Germans have not fought for seven years against international Jewry in Berlin for it to be more widespread than ever before in National Socialist Berlin. We really must protest the provocative stance of international

**Figure 2.3**
The Adolf Brünn
department store at
Berliner Allee 29–31
in Weissensee

Jewry in Berlin. Does it not scandalize, does it not make one blush with shame, to think that no fewer than three thousand Jews have immigrated to Berlin in the past months?"[27]

Even as he encouraged the anti-Semitism of Berliners, however, Goebbels wanted to avoid too drastic an outbreak of mob violence. And so he called on the population to maintain discipline, not to take matters into their own hands, and to leave matters to the state. Goebbels went on to emphasize the legality of the campaign, stating "that the disputes with international Jewry in Berlin were legal and implemented strictly in accordance with the law of the party and the state and not the law of the street. Moreover, legal measures had already ensured that the Jewish influence in the economy, too, would be broken in the foreseeable future."[28] The threat to the Jews of Berlin was barely veiled. "Above all Dr. Goebbels urgently advised Jews who had recently moved to Berlin to leave the city as soon as possible," wrote the *Völkischer Beobachter* on June 23.[29] Goebbels countered international censure of the riots with thinly disguised allusions to the crisis surrounding the Sudeten Germans in Czechoslovakia. If they were "talking about repression," Goebbels was reported to have said, he "could only recommend that they deal with the terrorization and brutal suppression of three and a half million Germans in another country."[30]

The riots were accurately interpreted in the international press. The *Daily Herald* wrote that "the National Socialist crusade to exclude the Jews from economic life has started up again and seems to have entered a decisive phase."[31]

**Figure 2.4**
Möbel-Cohn (a furniture store) at Grosse Frankfurter Strasse 59

The *Neue Zürcher Zeitung* reported on June 26, 1938, that "although the 'wild' operations in Berlin stopped after a few days of confusion, it should nonetheless be expected that in the course of this summer, the plan to force the Jews out of economic life will be implemented, since it is closely linked with the urgent need to finance the autarky."

It is well known that Goebbels was obsessed with finding a "solution to the Jewish Question" in the Reich capital. Already in April 1938 he had assigned to Berlin chief of police Count Wolf Helldorf the task of producing a detailed plan for future anti-Semitic measures to be taken in the city. On June 13, 1938, the "*Judendezernat*"—a department at the police headquarters for the standardized processing of the "Jewish Question"—was established.[32] As the campaign was getting underway on June 21, Goebbels noted in his diary that "the anti-Jewish operation has caused a major reaction abroad. Our party comrades are also going about it in a pretty harsh way. I am hemming this in a bit. Yet, I also let the people have free rein. The Jews of the world are grumbling in any case. But they still have not cleared out of Berlin."[33]

The Berlin riots did not take place quite as Goebbels or Hitler envisioned them. As the "healthy" expression of "anti-Semitism on the streets" threatened to veer toward mob violence, with accompanying looting and abuse, the authorities reined in the forces they had unleashed. At the height of the Sudeten crisis, the Nazis could not afford such risks. Hitler personally intervened from his retreat at Berchtesgaden, ordering an immediate halt to the riots. Goebbels

**Figure 2.5** Berlin chief of police Wolf Heinrich von Helldorf (*middle*) with Joseph Goebbels (*right*) at a presentation of decorations

passed on instructions to party authorities that all illegal actions had to stop.[34] For the time being, similar campaigns was to be avoided.

On June 24 Goebbels noted with satisfaction: "The *Judenaktion* is now over. A police major and a district leader bear the blame. And [there are] innumerable rumors. I will take the strictest measures against a repetition of events." Two days later he wrote: "Report on the Jewish Question in Berlin. Everything has blown over already. The operation is over. Proof of party discipline."[35]

The general foreign policy climate had, however, already improved for the Nazi power holders. An unexpected but highly opportune event would soon provide a pretext for anti-Semitic violence on a scale heretofore unknown. In this sense, the *Juni-Aktion* was, to use the words of historian David Friedländer, but a "a small scale rehearsal," a run-up to the devastating pogrom that would take place on November 9 of that year.[36]

**1** Wolfgang Scheffler, *Judenverfolgung im Dritten Reich* (Berlin, 1964), pp. 28–29; Ulrich Herbert, *Best. Biographische Studien über Radikalismus, Weltanschauung und Vernunft, 1903–1989* (Berlin, 1996), pp. 212–13; Michael Wildt, *Die Judenpolitik des SD 1933 bis 1938. Eine Dokumentation* (Munich, 1995), p. 55. The *Juni-Aktion* in Berlin is discussed in Saul Friedländer, *Nazi Germany and the Jews*, vol. 1, *The Years of Persecution, 1933–1939* (New York, 1997), pp. 261–63; Hermann Simon, "'Bilder, die Dante nicht im Traum gedacht hätte'—Neue Quellen zum Novemberpogrom in Berlin" (paper presented at a meeting of the Porta Pacis Association on November 7, 1988) in *November 1938. Vom Pogrom zum Völkermord*, ed. Martina Weyrauch and Peter Borowsky (Berlin, 1998). See also Hans-Jürgen Döscher, *"Reichskristallnacht"* (Berlin, 1990).

**2** Patrick Wagner, *Volksgemeinschaft ohne Verbrecher. Konzeption und Praxis der Kriminalpolizei in der Zeit der Weimarer Republik und des Nationalsozialismus* (Hamburg, 1996), pp. 279 ff. See Wolfgang Ayaß, *"Asoziale" im Nationalsozialismus*, (Stuttgart, 1995), idem, "'Ein Gebot der nationalen Arbeitsdisziplin.' Die Aktion 'Arbeitsscheu Reich' 1938," in *Feinderklärung und Prävention. Kriminalbiologie, Zigeunerforschung und Asozialenpolitik*, ed. Wolfgang Ayaß et al. (Berlin, 1988), pp. 43 ff.

**3** Reinhard Heydrich's decree of June 1, 1938, quoted in Herbert, *Best. Biographische Studien*, pp. 212–13.

**4** Reinhard Heydrich, letter dated June 1, 1938, quoted in Wagner, *Volksgemeinschaft*, p. 279.

**5** Avraham Barkai, "'Schicksalsjahr 1938.' Kontinuität und Verschärfung der wirtschaftlichen Ausplünderung der deutschen Juden," in *Der Judenpogrom 1938. Von der "Reichskristallnacht" zum Völkermord*, ed. Walter H. Pehle (Frankfurt am Main, 1988), p. 114; Scheffler, *Judenverfolgung*, p. 29.

**6** Wagner, *Volksgemeinschaft*, p. 279; Herbert, *Best. Biographische Studien*, p. 213.

**7** Michael Wildt, "Gewalt gegen Juden in Deutschland, 1933–1945," in *Werkstatt Geschichte* 18 (1997): 68. This does not name the synagogue or sources.

**8** *Völkischer Beobachter*, 21 June, 1938.

**9** Report of June 24, 1938, from the *SD Oberabschnitt Ost* (SD main sector east), to the *SD Hauptamt* (SD main office), quoted in Wildt, *Die Judenpolitik*, p. 55. On the uses of "protective custody" in the Nazi state, see Ulrich Herbert, "Von der Gegnerbekämpfung zur 'rassischen Generalprävention.' 'Schutzhaft' und Konzentrationslager in der Konzeption der Gestapo-Führung, 1933–1939," in *Die nationalsozialistischen Konzentrationslager: Entwicklung und Struktur*, vol.1, ed. Herbert et al. (Göttingen, 1998), pp. 60–61.

**10** See the *Beiträge zum Reichsleiterdienst* (Contributions to Reich Leadership) of July 1, 1938, compiled by the SD, Institut für Zeitgeschichte, Munich, MA 557. See also Friedländer, *Nazi Germany*, p. 262.

**11** Goebbels, diary, entry dated June 11, 1938, in *Die Tagebücher von Joseph Goebbels: Sämtliche Fragmente*, ed. Elke Fröhlich, part 1, 1924–1941, vol. 3 (Munich, 1987), p. 452, English translation in Friedländer, *Nazi Germany*, p. 261.

**12** *Pariser Tageblatt*, 14 June 1938. See also Wolf Gruner, *Judenverfolgung in Berlin 1933–1945. Eine Chronologie der Behördenmaßnahmen in der Reichshauptstadt* (Berlin, 1996), pp. 51–52.

**13** *Pariser Tageblatt*, 17 June 1938.

**14** A total of 824 Berlin Jews were taken to Sachsenhausen. Gruner, *Judenverfolgung*, p. 51.

**15** See *Die Deutschlandberichte der Sopade*, fifth year, 1938, vol. 7 (Frankfurt am Main, 1980), p. 761; and Scheffler, *Judenverfolgung*, p. 29.

**16** See the report from American Ambassador Hugh R. Wilson to Foreign Minister Hull ("Subject: Demonstrations Against Jewish Shops") dated June 22, 1938 in *The Holocaust. Selected Documents in Eighteen Volumes*, vol. 1, ed. John Mendelsohn (New York and London, 1982), p. 141.

**17** Goebbels, diary, entry dated June 23, 1938.

**18** *Daily Herald*, 16 June 1938.

**19** *Deutschlandberichte*, pp. 756–57.

**20** Bella Fromm, *Als Hitler mir die Hand küßte*, English translation in Friedländer, *Nazi Germany*, p. 262.

**21** Fromm, *Als Hitler mir die Hand küßte*, revised edition (Berlin, 1993), p. 295; Goebbels, diary, entry dated June 28, 1938.

**22** *Deutschlandberichte*, pp. 756–57.

**23** Report from Wilson to Hull (see note 16 above) quoted in Friedländer, *Nazi Germany*, p. 262, also in *The Holocaust: Selected Documents*, p. 141.

**24** *Pariser Tageblatt*, 18 June 1938; and report from Wilson to Hull.

**25** The synagogue on Herzog-Max-Strasse in Munich had already been torn down on June 9, 1938, on Hitler's initiative. It was the first synagogue in Germany to be destroyed by the Nazis. See the exhibition catalog *Beth ha-Knesseth—Ort der Zusammenkunft. Zur Geschichte der*

*Münchner Synagogen, ihrer Rabbiner und Kantoren* (Munich, 1999).

**26** *Völkischer Beobachter*, 21 June 1938.

**27** Goebbels's speech was paraphrased in the June 21, 1938, entry of the history almanac *Schultheß Europäischer Geschichtskalender*, vol. 79, ed. Ulrich Thürauf (Munich, 1939).

**28** Ibid.

**29** *Völkischer Beobachter*, 23 June 1938.

**30** See note 27 above. The reference was to the situation of the Sudeten Germans in Czechoslovakia.

**31** *Daily Herald*, 16 June 1938. Also see the reports in the *Times*, the *Daily Express*, the *Manchester Guardian*, and Reuters from mid- to late June 1938.

**32** See Gruner, "Die Reichshauptstadt und die Verfolgung der Berliner Juden, 1933–1945," in *Jüdische Geschichte in Berlin*, ed. Reinhard Rürup (Berlin, 1995), pp. 236–37; and Gruner, "'Lesen brauchen sie nicht zu können.' Die 'Denkschrift über die Behandlung der Juden in der Reichshauptstadt auf allen Gebieten des öffentlichen Lebens's vom Mai 1938," in *Jahrbuch für Antisemitismusforschung* 4 (1995): 305 ff.

**33** Goebbels, diary, entry dated June 21, 1938.

**34** A note from the SD main office of June 22, 1938, states that further riots were forbidden as of 5:00 P.M. on June 21, following a decision of the Gauleiter and the Berlin chief of police, preceded by a "personal intervention of the Führer from Berchtesgaden." Quoted in Wildt, "Gewalt," p. 68, note 42.

**35** Goebbels, diary, entries dated June 24 and 26, 1938.

**36** Friedländer, *Nazi Germany*, p. 263.

# 2

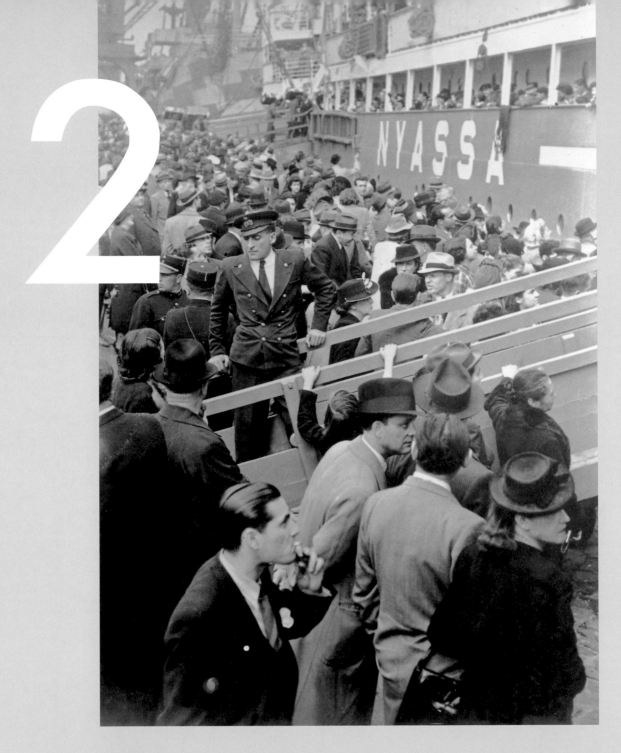

# Emigration

# Chapter Three

## The Flight and Expulsion of German Jews

MICHAEL SCHÄBITZ

After largely succeeding in driving Jewish Germans from public life during the first years of its rule, the Nazi regime identified another goal: to force Jews to emigrate from Germany. As early as May 24, 1934, a memo from the SD (Sicherheitsdienst, Security Service of the SS) Department IV/2 to Reinhard Heydrich stated that "the aim of Jewish policy has to be the emigration of all Jews. . . . The possibilities for Jewish life—not just in the economic sense—should be restricted. Germany must be a country with no future for them, a country in which the older generation may die off . . . but in which the young cannot live. So that the appeal of emigration remains constant."[1]

Despite being deprived of their rights and forced from professional and economic life, only a quarter of the Jews living in Germany had left the country by the end of 1937. (Some 129,000 of an estimated 525,000 left; in Berlin, the ratio was slightly higher—48,000 of 160,000.) Many Jews hesitated to leave for a number of reasons: bonds to home, family, relatives and friends; the fear of the unknown; a lack of emigration opportunities; the financial losses associated with emigration; or a combination of several of these factors.

The Nazi regime, dissatisfied with the results of previous efforts and fortified by its foreign policy successes (such as the reintegration of the Saarland region into the German Reich on March 1, 1935, the annexation of Austria on March 13, 1938, and the annexation of the Sudetenland), stepped up its anti-Jewish measures considerably in 1938. The National Socialists would now apply the concept of "forced emigration" (*forcierte Vertreibung*) developed by the SD in the years prior to this.[2] At the same time, the policy of "Aryanizing" Jewish property made it impossible for many people to emigrate. This policy was now carried out systematically to an ever greater extent,[3] and in most cases, it was impossible to enter another country without sufficient capital. Stripped of their resources in Germany, it was now considerably harder—and often impracticable—for Jews to build up a new existence in the country of immigration.

The perfidious nature of the regime is particularly apparent in this policy. The Jews were indeed expelled—after being robbed of all that they owned. The regime's intention, moreover, was to encourage worldwide anti-Semitism, reasoning that the unwelcome presence of impoverished Jews throughout the world would win approval Germany's own discriminatory toward the Jews.[4]

After the outbreak of World War II it became even more difficult to emigrate. There was hardly a single country still prepared to accept Jewish refugees from Germany. There was, moreover, a severe lack of transportation opportunities. The regime was simultaneously developing its concept of a "Final Solution to the Jewish Question"—that is, the murder of all European Jews. Emigration was banned at the end of October 1941 so that no Jew would be able to escape the "Final Solution."

## The First Wave of Emigration

Jewish Germans began to emigrate from Germany immediately after Hitler assumed power on January 30, 1933. This first wave of emigrants went, above all, to neighboring countries, especially France, Belgium, Holland, Czechoslovakia, and Switzerland.[5] Most of those who fled hoped for a rapid end to the Nazi regime and that they would soon return home. Some in fact did return to Germany after things had supposedly calmed down—or if the situation in their host country worsened. At this time, long-term emigration, particularly to Palestine but also to South Africa, also became more widespread.

### Jewish Aid Organizations

Several important Jewish aid organizations had offices in Berlin during this period. There were advice centers in all of the larger German towns and cities. Those people planning to emigrate to Palestine received advice and support from the Palestine Office (Palästina-Amt), a department of the Jewish Agency for Palestine, a Zionist organization. The Aid Association for German Jews (Hilfsverein der deutschen Juden e.V.) provided help in emigration to countries other than Palestine. The Central Office for Jewish Emigration Welfare was an independent department of the Central Welfare Office for German Jews. It dealt with Jews living in Germany who had foreign passports and wished to return to their country of origin. In many cases these were people whose forbears had lived for many generations in Germany but who, due to Germany's restrictive naturalization policy, still had a foreign—often Polish—passport.[6]

The Working Group for Child and Youth Aliyah arranged for the immigration to Palestine—*Aliyah*, in Hebrew—of children and adolescents without their parents. The British mandate in Palestine set aside special immigration certificates for this purpose on the condition that accommodation and education would be provided for a minimum of two years (see chap. 7).[7]

Zionist organizations vigorously promoted emigration to Palestine as soon as Hitler came to power. Most of the other major Jewish organizations, however, had called for Jews to remain in the country and stand up for their rights there. This attitude changed only after the Nazis formulated the Nuremberg Laws of 1935. Subsequently, the Reichsvertretung der Juden in Deutschland (Reich Representation of Jews in Germany) made "the preparation and process of emigration" the "central focus of aid and reconstruction work."[8] The Reichsvertretung, established in 1933, served as an umbrella for the major Jewish organizations in Germany (see chap. 18).[9] It included the Central Association of German Citizens of Jewish Faith (Central Verein deutscher Staatsbürger jüdischen Glaubens), the Reich Association of Jewish Frontline Soldiers, and the Zionist Association for Germany.

Such aid organizations had taken it upon themselves to manage the emigration of Jews from Germany, hoping that Jews would not simply flee in an unplanned and unprepared fashion. Along with general advice on emigration provisions and information about potential immigration countries, they offered retraining and language courses. They sought to organize the transfer of finances and goods. And they faced the difficult challenge of, on the one hand, easing the new start for the immigrants and, on the other hand, cultivating the goodwill—and open doors—of host countries. This required managing the emigration process as carefully as possible. Even before the Nazis launched the policy of forced emigration, it was difficult to strike such a delicate balance. Afterward, it became impossible.[10]

In 1935 the aid organizations merged into a central Emigration Committee (*Wanderungsausschuss*) in order to streamline and coordinate their work.[11]

## The Second Wave of Emigration

The second wave of emigration began after the Nuremberg Laws were declared in September 1935. Almost all European countries had introduced stricter immigration or labor conditions in the wake of the first major wave of emigration, and in 1936 entrance restrictions to South Africa and Palestine were tightened as well. Increasingly, emigrants were heading to Latin America. Then, in 1937, the United States relaxed its immigration restrictions, and the country became an overwhelmingly popular destination for Jews leaving Hitler's Germany.[12]

## U.S. Immigration Provisions

The immigration provisions for the United States furnish an interesting example of the hoops through which potential immigrants had to jump in order to gain entrance. The American immigration department stipulated an exact number of immigrants—a quota—from each country. In the 1930s, the maximum annual number of immigrants the United States allowed in from Germany was 25,957. Following the annexation of Austria in March 1938, the figure was raised to 27,370. The quotas were dramatically lower for the countries of southern and Eastern Europe—for example, Poland (6,524), Lithuania (386), Romania (377), and Hungary (869).[13] The decisive factor for an applicant's inclusion within a quota was not current nationality but country of birth. (Many Jews had moved from Eastern Europe into Germany, particularly to Berlin, in the years before and after World War I.) If the fixed number of immigrants had been reached in a year– as was the case for Germany from 1939 onward—people wishing to emigrate were put on a waiting list for the next year, and often the year after.[14]

In fact, up to 1939, the U.S. immigration quota for Germans had not been met. On instructions from Washington, the consulates prevented this through a restrictive application of the existing regulations.[15]

Certain groups of people were not subject to the quota regulations. These included close family members (minors, spouses) of American nationals. Within the framework of immigration limited by quotas, priority was given to parents of American citizens and to the close relatives (children, spouses) of people who had already immigrated legally.[16]

One of the most important prerequisites for obtaining a visa for the U.S. was proof that the immigrant would not be a burden on public welfare. If a would-be immigrant did not have resources enough to look after himself, an "Affidavit of Support" was required, in which relatives or close friends guaranteed financial assistance in case of need. The information provided in the affidavits was checked for accuracy. The affidavits were only valid for a certain period and then had to be renewed. The compulsory medical examination was another matter on which acceptance hinged. The emigrants' details were checked by the responsible consulate in Germany.[17]

The relaxation of U.S. immigration policy in early 1937 brought an influx of Jewish emigrants from Germany. The flow came to a halt, however, in December

1941 when the U.S. entered the war and closed its borders to all emigration from Germany and Austria.[18]

## The Third Wave

The third and final wave of legal emigration from Germany began with the heightening of anti-Jewish measures in 1938 that culminated in the pogrom of November 9, 1938. After this few Jewish Germans failed to notice the irretrievable hostility at home. Now, however, even the Latin American countries had begun to tighten their entrance provisions, and the search for a safehaven beyond Germany became ever more difficult. A fitting description of the situation was published in the South American supplement to the newspaper *Jüdische Auswanderung* (Jewish Emigration)[19] in January 1939:

> There can be no doubt that there is barely a single South American country that is now open to immigration from Germany to the extent that it was two years ago. . . . This disastrous reduction in the possibilities for immigration to South America—at a time when the entire Jewish population of Germany is under the greatest pressure to emigrate, and at a time when, beyond the boundaries of the extended Reich, Jews from other European countries are also attempting in large numbers to find salvation in emigration—is certainly due in part to circumstances beyond the control of Jewish people and institutions. This is particularly the case for the extreme difficulty in transfers [of funds], which makes it impossible for even Jewish emigrants with means to take any capital worth mentioning with them.[20]

Emigration was also hindered by the process of "Aryanization" and the continuing impoverishment of German Jews by the authorities (see chap. 4). Soon after the Nazis came to power Jewish shopkeepers and businessmen were forced to sell or give up their businesses as a result of boycotting measures and other reprisals. Forced "Aryanization" at the end of 1937 aimed "to eliminate remaining economic activity and to expropriate Jewish assets, most of which are already liquid." This process was halted in early 1939.[21]

In spite of these factors, more Jews managed to emigrate at the start of 1938 than in previous years.[22] This was due in large part to the pressure exerted after 1938 by the Nazi policy of forced emigration. That September an aid association reported on the increased numbers. "While in May of this year 11,156 people requested information from our advice center in Berlin, this figure rose by

**Figure 3.1** Suitcase label: "*Kindertransport* no. 16, Registered Aid Association for German Jews"

almost one thousand in June and reached 14,841 in July. The number of first-time inquiries also increased. In January of this year the figure for the [entire] Reich was 3,197, and in May 1938 it rose to 10,952 people; in other words it multiplied three times in four months."[23]

The increase in emigrants was facilitated in part by the relaxation of immigration provisions in certain countries after the November pogrom, including Great Britain. In addition, the emigrants now began to consider places and countries that had previously seen little German-Jewish immigration. Until 1941, Shanghai—a port with no entrance requirements—served as one of the main host areas for immigrants.[24]

## The Kindertransport

In Great Britain and other countries, the pogrom of November 9, 1938, unleashed a wave of indignation at Nazi brutality as well as a wave of sympathy for those persecuted. The British government, bowing to public pressure, announced in late November 1939 that it would take in 10,000 Jewish children from Germany. British aid organizations arranged the rescue operations in cooperation with the Reichsvereinigung der Juden in Deutschland (Reich Association for Jews in

Germany). The first *Kindertransport* reached Great Britain on December 2, 1939. Jewish organizations arranged for the accommodation, board, and education of the children and teenagers aged up to seventeen.

Most of the approximately 11,000 children and teenagers who arrived in Great Britain between December 1938 and November 1939 during this campaign never saw their parents again. The *Kindertransport* was the last farewell. Only a few of the desperate parents who had entrusted their children to strangers in a foreign country survived the Nazi killing machine.[25]

Ruth Wing, née Spanier, was the daughter of the actor Ben Spanier and his wife Bella. Her parents had asked her if she would like to go to England for a vacation to learn English and told her that they would join her soon. At the end of August 1939, at the age of eleven, she left for England on the final *Kindertransport* from Berlin. Ruth and her parents maintained contact through Red Cross letters—brief messages limited to twenty-five words in length. One note she received (shown here), dated January 24, 1942, simply stated: "Herzele! Happy with September letter. We are healthy, together again soon. Greetings Uncle Jacob and Grandma. We're constantly thinking of you. Million kisses, Daddy and Mummy." Contact ceased in May 1943 when her parents were deported to Theresienstadt. Ben and Bella Spanier were subsequently deported to Auschwitz and murdered there. Along with the numerous documents and photos that Ruth Spanier has gathered over the years, she still has two silver spoons that she had been allowed to take with her as mementos.[26]

Ruth was taken in by the family of a London rabbi, although he did not bother much with her once she was evacuated with her school from London to Windsor. As a German and with no means of her own, she had to drop out of school at age fourteen and was sent to an institution similar to a kibbutz in Scotland. This institution prepared young German and Austrian Jews for emigration to Palestine. Ruth Spanier had no wish to go to Palestine. After the war she returned to London, where she has lived ever since.[27]

Though they never matched the extent of the British aid operations, Belgium and Holland followed the English example. In the United States, too, some members of Congress tried to set up a similar initiative but encountered resistance from the majority in the subcommittee.[28]

**Figure 3.2**
Ruth Spanier shortly before her departure for Great Britain

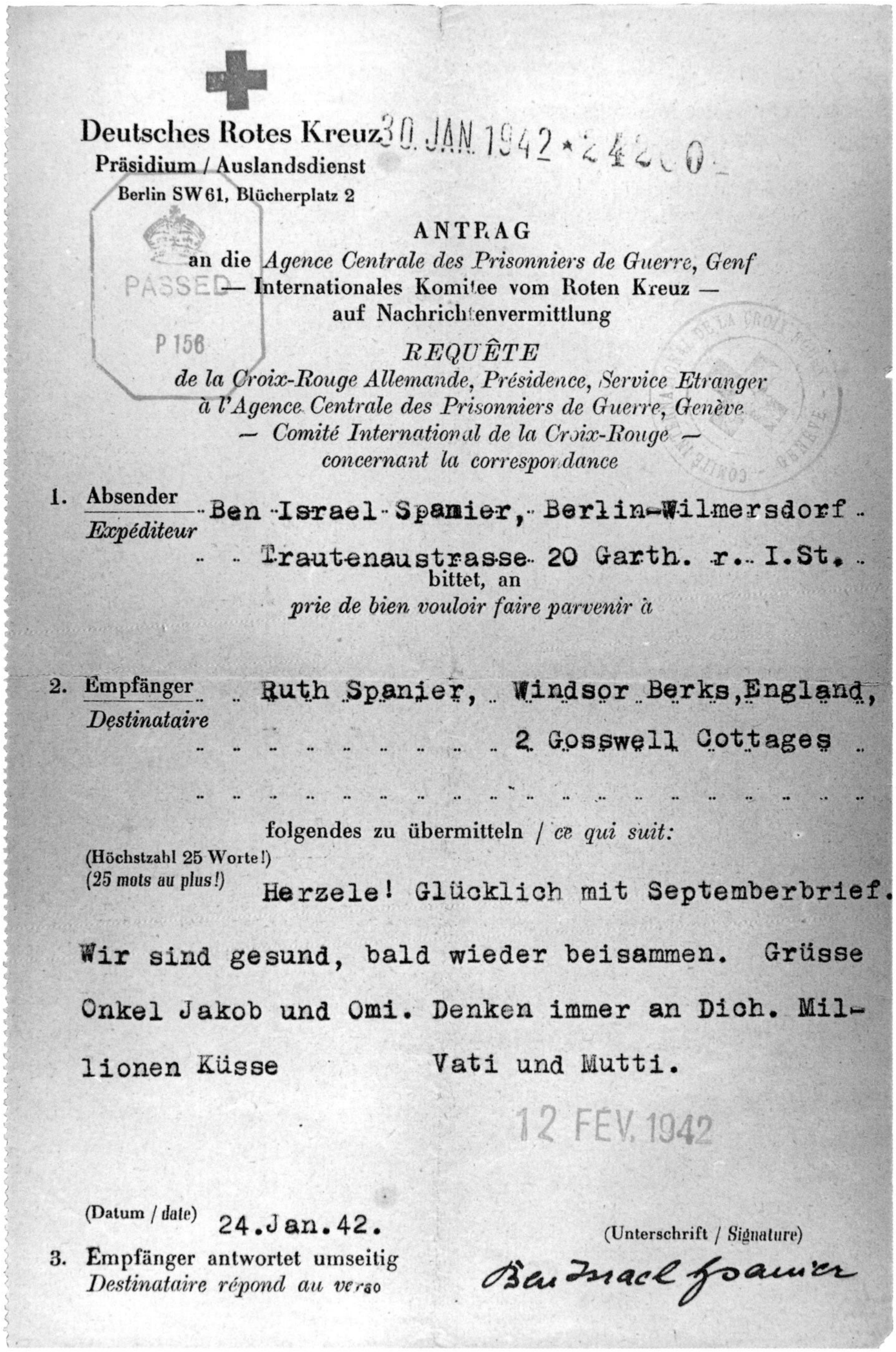

**Deutsches Rotes Kreuz** 30. JAN 1942 * 24200

Präsidium / Auslandsdienst

Berlin SW 61, Blücherplatz 2

PASSED

P 156

ANTRAG

an die *Agence Centrale des Prisonniers de Guerre, Genf*
— Internationales Komitee vom Roten Kreuz —
auf Nachrichtenvermittlung

*REQUÊTE*
*de la Croix-Rouge Allemande, Présidence, Service Etranger*
*à l'Agence Centrale des Prisonniers de Guerre, Genève*
*— Comité International de la Croix-Rouge —*
*concernant la correspondance*

1. Absender — Ben·Israel·Spanier, Berlin-Wilmersdorf
   *Expéditeur*
   — Trautenaustrasse· 20 Garth. r. I.St.
   bittet, an
   *prie de bien vouloir faire parvenir à*

2. Empfänger — Ruth Spanier, Windsor Berks, England,
   *Destinataire*
   2 Gosswell Cottages

   folgendes zu übermitteln / *ce qui suit:*

(Höchstzahl 25 Worte!)
(*25 mots au plus!*)

Herzele! Glücklich mit Septemberbrief.

Wir sind gesund, bald wieder beisammen. Grüsse

Onkel Jakob und Omi. Denken immer an Dich. Mil-

lionen Küsse          Vati und Mutti.

12 FEV. 1942

(Datum / date)  24.Jan.42.

3. Empfänger antwortet umseitig
   *Destinataire répond au verso*

(Unterschrift / Signature)

*Ben Israel Spanier*

**Figure 3.3** Red Cross letter from Ben and Bella Spanier to their daughter in England.
Such messages were restricted to twenty-five words.

**Figure 3.4**
The first *Kindertransport* to Great Britain. Exhausted children upon arrival in Harwich, England, December 2, 1938.

**Figure 3.5** Quayside farewell, 1938

## Emigration Provisions and the Transfer of Assets

One guide to emigration for German Jews was the *Auswanderungsvorschriften für Juden in Deutschland* published in Berlin in 1938. In the volume's preface, Dr. Arthur Prinz summed up a dismal economic situation:

> While *immigration* into other countries was bound up with many difficulties and problems for the Jews in Germany in the first few years after 1933, the emigration process itself was at first relatively simple. This has, however, changed fundamentally over the past few years. Along with all the problems of immigration

and adaptation to other, particularly overseas, countries, the laws, regulations, and administrative decisions in Germany regulating Jewish emigration have now become increasingly significant for emigrants. Whether these be foreign exchange regulations or the procurement of documents for moving, the emigrant faces a whole range of practical difficulties that have to be overcome before leaving Reich territory.[29]

The book provided a detailed overview of contemporary emigration and transfer provisions. The lists themselves testify to the growing difficulties faced by emigrating Jews—above all, to the virtual impossibility of their bringing any financial resources with them to their new homelands.

Any emigrant intending to transfer assets abroad was required to submit a valuation assessment from an emigration advice center. This report had to be submitted to the foreign exchange office together with the transfer application. As Dr. Prinz continued in his preface, "taking account of the few opportunities to transfer assets, which should however at the same time benefit as many emigrants as possible, only so many assets may be transferred as are definitely needed to establish a modest existence abroad."[30]

Only the following items could be taken from Germany *without* the permission of the foreign exchange office:

A) Travel expenses of RM 10 per person. Depending on the destination and duration of the journey it was possible to apply to the police for an increase in travel expenses to RM 50 per person.
B) Boarding and embarkation money of up to RM 30 per day.

The following items could be taken along, but only *with* the permission of the foreign exchange office:

A) "Removal goods" (furniture, clothes, tools, and work clothes) and jewelry: According to the Reich Economics Ministry's circular no. 8/38 of May 13, 1938, emigrants had to register the "removal goods" with the foreign exchange office at least fourteen days prior to emigration, submitting a list in triplicate of items they wished to take with them. An exact register of assets (*Vermögensverzeichnis*) for the emigrant—as well as for his parents and in-laws—had to be submitted as well. Among the items that did not count as "removal goods" were industrial machines, cars, medical instruments, jewelry, and stamp collections. Such items could not be taken from the country without explicit permission.
B) Emigrants who did not transfer any assets apart from removal goods could take an amount of up to RM 1,000 with them as "small capital transfers." Cash, however, was not permitted.[31]

The transfer of assets required permission from the foreign exchange office. Until 1934, a limited amount of free currencies (such as dollars, pounds, and Swiss francs) could be acquired. Thereafter, however, it was no longer possible.

Up to October 1937 people with limited assets were permitted to transfer amounts of up to RM 8,000 to any country they wished, including Palestine—albeit at a loss of 50 percent. In November 1937 this policy was briefly extended to amounts up to RM 50,000 but was closed to new applicants in the summer of 1938.

Special agreements were in place for the transfer of assets to Palestine (the so-called "Haavara transfer"). Immigration to the territory was controlled by the British Mandate authorities, who allowed entrance to various categories of immigrants, including "capitalists," schoolchildren, students, workers, and people who were supported by close relatives. With the exception of the "capitalist" category, the number of certificates was severely limited, and specific criteria were required for each category (see chap. 7).

The "capitalist" category was thus an important one for emigrants from Germany. If it was not restricted in terms of the available number of certificates, it was, however, restricted in terms of wealth. "Capitalists" were required to prove that they had assets of 1,000 Palestinian pounds (between RM 12,000 and RM 15,000). Because Germany exercised foreign exchange control—that is, the export of assets could only take place with Reichsbank permission—the Haavara transfer agreement was critical for emigrants. This agreement had been concluded at the end of August 1933 between the Zionist Association for Germany, the Anglo-Palestine Bank, and the Reich Economics Ministry and was still in force at the start of the war. It enabled thousands of Jewish immigrants from Germany not only to emigrate but also to start new lives in Palestine.[32]

The transfer abroad of stocks and shares, life insurance, and benefits (pensions and so forth) was generally only allowed to a very limited extent, and in progressively lower amounts. Again, Palestine was an exception; the Haavara agreement made it possible for pensions and other benefits to be transferred.

In some circumstances emigrants could take stocks and machinery with them for personal use, but here, too, the possibilities kept narrowing and the fees and penalties were ever greater.[33]

During the Weimar years, in order to help rein in the drain on capital abroad a Reich emigration tax (*Reichsfluchtsteuer*) of 25 percent of the assets to be transferred abroad had been instituted in 1931. The tax affected people with assets worth more than RM 50,000 or a yearly income of more than RM 20,000. After the Nazis took power in 1933, the calculation principles for the tax were changed to become even more unfavorable for emigrants.[34]

**Table 3.1** Reich Emigration Tax for All Emigrants, 1932–33 to 1938–39

| Year | Amount in Reichsmarks |
|------|----------------------|
| 1932–33 | 1 million |
| 1933–34 | 45 million |
| 1934–35 | 70 million |
| 1937–38 | 81 million |
| 1938–39 | 342 million |

Source: Herbert A. Strauss, "Jewish Emigration from Germany—Nazi Policies and Jewish Responses" (part 1), *LBI Yearbook* 25 (1980): 343.

The credit balances left behind in Germany by the emigrants were deemed the "Frozen Assets of Emigrants" (*Auswanderer-Sperrguthaben*).[35] Until the summer of 1938, such credit could be sold from abroad, but at an enormous loss. Thereafter, it was discontinued. Access to a frozen account required the approval of the Reich foreign exchange office. The same applied for land left behind.[36]

The processes described above ensured that from 1938 onward most emigrants arrived in their new home countries with practically no remaining resources. The majority depended on support from national and international aid organizations.

## Forced Emigration

The Nazi policy of forced immigration is associated above all with the name of Adolf Eichmann. After the annexation of Austria in March 1938 he was put in charge of organizing the expulsion of the Jewish Austrians. Following annexation, thousands of "Aryanizations" took place within a short space of time. Many Jews were arrested, tortured, and imprisoned in concentration camps. The Jews taken to concentration camps were only released when it was certain that they would soon be emigrating. At that time, Eichmann also promoted illegal transport to Palestine, along with the illegal procurement of visas.

To perfect the expulsion measures, in August 1938 Eichmann was put in charge of a new office in Vienna, the Central Office for Jewish Emigration (Zentralstelle für jüdische Auswanderung). The office speeded up the formalities associated with emigration.[37] Franz Eliezer Meyer, a witness at the 1960

Eichmann trial in Jerusalem, compared the office to "an automatic factory, like a flour mill connected with some bakery. At one end you put in a Jew who still has some property, a factory, or a shop, or a bank account, and he goes through the building from counter to counter, from office to office, and comes out at the other end without any money, without any rights, with only a passport on which it says: 'You must leave the country within a fortnight. Otherwise you will go to a concentration camp.'"[38]

After the pogrom of November 9, 1938, the same methods were applied to the Altreich. This meant that responsibility for Jewish policy was ultimately transferred to the SD.[39]

In the course of the November pogrom, 20,000 to 30,000 male Jews were taken to concentration camps throughout the country. They would be released only on condition that they would leave the country immediately, with all the required emigration documents in perfect order. The Jewish aid organizations now urgently sought opportunities for these imprisoned Jews to emigrate. As historian Dan Diner writes, "[W]ith this, the usual procedure of maintaining the long-term willingness of emigration countries to take on people could be considered a failure. The new policy of unconditional expulsion greatly endangered the sensitive process of emigration, which relied on keeping the host countries willing to take in immigrants."[40] In Berlin, around 12,000 Jewish men were taken to Sachsenhausen. Only those who could provide written assurance that they would emigrate immediately were released.[41]

In fact, many were able to do so. One enabling factor was the response of the British government, which in January 1939 introduced visas for temporary residence and gave priority for these to the men detained in concentration camps. The openings applied to three categories: people over eighteen who wished to wait in England before continuing their emigration overseas; people between eighteen and thirty-five who wished to come to England for a change of career or training; and people over sixty who did not wish to work in England. Permission was only granted, however, if the German Jewish Aid Committee in London could guarantee that the candidate concerned had means enough to live on. The committee usually "only took on such a commitment when friends or relatives can give the committee a sufficient guarantee for the support of the interim emigrants."[42]

A transit camp was set up in Great Britain to house men aged between eighteen and forty-five (at the oldest). The prerequisite for their stay was that they would definitely continue their emigration in six to nine months. Here, too, people from concentration camps were given preference.[43]

*The Jews had to get out, regardless of the constantly dwindling possibilities for immigration.*

At the end of January 1939, Hermann Göring, in his role as plenipotentiary for the Four-Year Plan, ordered the establishment of a Reich Central Office for Jewish Emigration (Reichszentrale für die jüdische Auswanderung). Headed by Heydrich, this organization had the task of promoting emigration "by any means necessary" and of speeding up emigration in individual cases through the centralized processing of applications. *Zentralstellen* (headquarters) were to be set up in cities such as Berlin, Breslau, Frankfurt am Main, and Hamburg on the model of Eichmann's office in Vienna. The Jewish Emigration headquarters in Berlin opened in the spring of 1939, headed first by Kurt Lischka, and from December 1939 on, by Eichmann himself.[44]

The policy of forced emigration was also linked to the establishment of the Reichsvereinigung in July 1939. All Jews had to belong to this Nazi-supervised body, which merged all Jewish institutions, associations, foundations, and organizations. The Reichsvereinigung's official purpose was to encourage the Jews to emigrate from Germany.[45]

## The Evian Conference

The mass expulsion of Jews from Austria had heightened the international refugee problem considerably. President Franklin D. Roosevelt responded by convening an international conference on the matter. On July 6–14, 1938, delegates convened at the French resort town of Evian-les-Bains. Myron C. Taylor, head of the U.S. delegation and chairman of the conference, summed up the problem: "Some millions of people, as this meeting convenes, are, actually or potentially, without a country. The number is increasing daily. This increase is taking place, moreover, at a time when there is serious unemployment in many countries, when there is shrinkage of subsistence bases and when the population of the world is at a peak."[46] Taylor asserted that the United States would nonetheless ensure that the German quota of 27,360 immigrants per year would be filled. Finally, Taylor pointed to the cross-border dimension of the refugee problem— that it could no longer simply be managed by private organizations but needed international solidarity and concerted government action.

Unlike the United States, most of the other thirty-two countries present were not prepared to relax their now very restrictive immigration provisions to benefit Jewish refugees from Germany and Austria. They cited the tense economic and social situations in their respective countries, as well as problems integrating the refugees who had already been accepted. It also became clear in the course of the conference, however, that there was fear that the German example could become the norm—that other countries might begin to expel unpopular groups from their own populations. This was a fairly significant factor in the decision against a relaxation of immigration provisions.[47]

Evian's only result was the establishment of a London-based Intergovernmental Committee on Refugees (ICR). In cooperation with existing institutions, this body was to seek possibilities for immigration and negotiate transfer agreements with the German government, and it had very little effect indeed. The German side let the negotiations drag on. Finally, with the outbreak of World War II, all attempts by the ICR to help Jewish refugees from Germany were negated. None of the hopes invested in Evian by Jewish aid organizations, Jewish refugees, and the Jews still in Germany were realized.[48]

## Trade in Visas

The increasing difficulty of legally obtaining visas brought about a booming black market for visas, both real and forged. Unscrupulous profiteers preyed on the desperation of people who wanted to emigrate. The American Consulate General in Berlin warned of swindlers.[49] In a circular dated September 9, 1938, a Jewish aid association warned readers of a particular con man. "The Berlin customs inquiry service today informed us that there is an alleged American marine officer in Cologne who, under the name of Henry *Bercau*, approaches Jews wishing to emigrate, saying that he can get them an American visa. The charge for men is apparently the equivalent of $2,000 and for women the equivalent of $1,000. We have been requested to issue suitable warning."[50]

Swindlers were active in Berlin as well. The Berlin State Archive, for example, contains documents on three men who preyed on desperate Jews between 1938 and 1939.[51] It seems that the trio—an economic advisor, a former South American consul, and a businessman—initially did try to obtain valid visas for their clients, even while pretending to be an economic consultancy. The former consul tried to obtain the visas through his connections with embassy staff. The businessman wanted a stake in a London firm that was to develop emigration possibilities for Jews from Germany by establishing branches throughout the world. After its initial (legal) attempts to get visas failed, the office continued its activities, obviously with fraud in mind. They demanded fees of up to RM 22,000—RM 15,000 on average—for securing "entrance permits." Charges were to be paid into a frozen account and would allegedly only be cashed in successful cases, otherwise returned. Records of a Gestapo interrogation of the office's "clients" suggests that, in some cases, this was indeed the procedure applied. It is clear, however, that the three used unrealistic promises to lure their clients in and then lead them on.[52]

*Attention! Apart from the $10 charge for the immigration visa, which is only levied by the Consulate General, absolutely no other charges shall be made for information, forms, etc. Beware of anyone offering to arrange emigration matters, quota numbers and so on and note that no one is authorized to do this.*

In some cases the trio's clients had paid the office before receiving the visa. None of them ever received a valid visa.[53] Two "clients," Kurt Glaser and Georg Schwerin, were in fact provided with invalid entrance permits for Ecuador. The shipping companies, which were obliged to check the papers of their passengers, could not recognize them. This was, quite obviously, fraud; the Ecuadorian consul in Berlin had for some time no longer been authorized to issue visas. Exceptionally, both received permits from the Consul General in Hamburg so that is was in fact possible for the Glaser and Schwerin families to emigrate to Ecuador. Following the investigation, two of the three con men were arrested and presumably also sentenced; the other managed to move to London.[54]

A statement by the investigating official in this case suggests that such confidence schemes were prevalent: "Much as the emigration of Jews from Germany is to be desired and encouraged by the responsible departments, in the inter-

**Figure 3.6** A letter from Selma Lehmann to a friend in the United States, November 7, 1941. The text hints at her imminent deportation.

ests of legal emigration one must, nonetheless, put a stop to the opportunists who are springing up all over the place, especially since such underhand wheeling and dealing has recently led almost all immigration countries to impose a freeze on immigration. The result is that Jews wishing to emigrate are at present unable to enter a foreign country."[55] Graver than these isolated instances of private swindling was, however, the massive, legal swindle taking place in public. Indeed, it is because the German authorities were methodically stripping potential emigrants of their resources that it was increasingly difficult to find countries willing to take in Jewish emigrants from Germany.

**Figure 3.7** Selma Lehmann, ca. 1940

## The War and the End of Emigration

The outbreak of war on September 1, 1939, made it next to impossible for Germany's remaining Jews to emigrate. Existing immigration opportunities often came to naught, as transportation links broke down and foreign currency grew scarce. Letters from those still inside Germany to relatives abroad asking for help with emigration grew more and more desperate.

A few months before the start of the war, Selma Lehmann wrote to her sons, Ernst and Herbert, in Palestine: "I've come back very disappointed from the P[alestine] office. . . . The result is always the same. I've still got no urgent reason [to emigrate], I'm not suffering like others, I have to see that. After many requests and much begging and tears they promised that they will mark my papers urgent. So I have to wait for months or even longer. They take no account of my mental state, my lonely life. And who knows what could happen in the meantime, and I'm all alone."[56]

In February 1940 she pleaded with her sons not to "let up in your efforts, perhaps you could get yourselves a L[awyer], but please, God, do anything and everything so that I can come to you. What is to become of me? I'm getting older and older, after all, and everything weakens me. I know that you're doing all you can but please don't let up in your efforts. My life is so pointless and then I am always so worked up and scared."[57]

Lehmann tried through a relative to get a visa and a boat ticket to Cuba, but it was no longer possible. In a postcard (shown here) to a friend in America, she hints at her impending deportation: "Dear Heinz! I'll most probably be leaving here soon, I still don't know where I'll be going. I'll write if I can. Send my greetings to Ernst & Herbert; they were unfortunately never really in the picture. I've

*And then I remember the Germans coming. And soon the fate of the Jews [in Holland] was just like it had been in Germany. With the Jewish laws, some of which had already started in '41, but definitely in '42.*

MIRIAM BLUMENTHAL- MERZBACHER

cabled Hazel; she wants to send Cuba visa and ticket. Probably not needed now. My dearest wishes and thanks for everything. Don't forget me and keep me in your heart. Your old friend Selma."

Selma Lehmann, née Peiser, born on September 21, 1877, in Posen, who lived at Sächsische Strasse 9, later Babelsberger Strasse 48, in the Wilmersdorf district of Berlin, was deported to Kovno on the Sixth Transport of November 17, 1941. All the people on this transport were murdered there on November 25, 1941.

As the Wehrmacht made its way westward, tens of thousands of emigrants who had found refuge in France, Holland, and Belgium were once again caught up in the Nazi machinery. Many did not manage to escape a second time. It is estimated that around 30,000 of them were deported to extermination camps and murdered.[58]

German troops caught up in Holland with members of a Berlin family, the Blumenthals. Miriam Blumenthal had emigrated to England at the age of ten in April 1937 with her parents, Ilse and Herbert Blumenthal. Her brother Peter

*And I can still see my father and mother lying together just before he had to go away. It must have been during the day. This was goodbye. . . . And we also took a walk together.*

MIRIAM
BLUMENTHAL-
MERZBACHER

**Figure 3.8** Passenger ship *Nyassa* in Lisbon harbor, summer 1941. Many refugees traveled to the United States on this ship.

**Figure 3.9** Frieda Philipp's passport

*When I think about what we took in our small suitcases with us for our emigration, it stands out today that there were no valuables but, rather, in many cases reminders of better, happier times. Apart from the Machsor (Prayers for the Holidays) and my little Menorah from Berlin, I took many childhood photos and a small vase belonging to my parents. And you have to remember that we were only allowed one suitcase each!*

WALTER PHILIPP

was already attending school there. Her father, however, could not practice as a dentist in England without taking new examinations, and so the family moved to Amsterdam in July of the same year. There Dr. Blumenthal was able to practice and the children went to school. Following the entry of the Wehrmacht in May 1940, the family tried to emigrate to the United States. Their visas had already been distributed, but the war prevented them from leaving. Peter was arrested during a raid in 1941 and murdered soon afterward. Miriam and her parents managed to avoid deportation temporarily with fake baptism papers. In May 1943, however, they were discovered and deported, first to the camp at Westerbork, and in September 1944, to Theresienstadt. Shortly thereafter, Herbert Blumenthal was deported to Auschwitz, where he was murdered. Miriam and Ilse Blumenthal survived Theresienstadt. Miriam Merzbacher, née Blumenthal, now lives in the United States.[59]

The first deportations from Berlin and other major cities were en route to (already occupied) Poland, when on October 19 a train carrying Jewish emigrants traveled from Berlin via Frankfurt and Paris, bound for Spain. From there the refugees, including Mr. and Mrs. Philipp and their son Walter, went to Cuba. The Philipp family had two strokes of luck. They had found an official who was willing to help by extending their passports. As Walter Philipp recalls, "when my parents went to the office in Berlin on September 29, 1941, to extend their pass-

**Figure 3.10**
Walter Philipp's menorah: "a souvenir of better times"

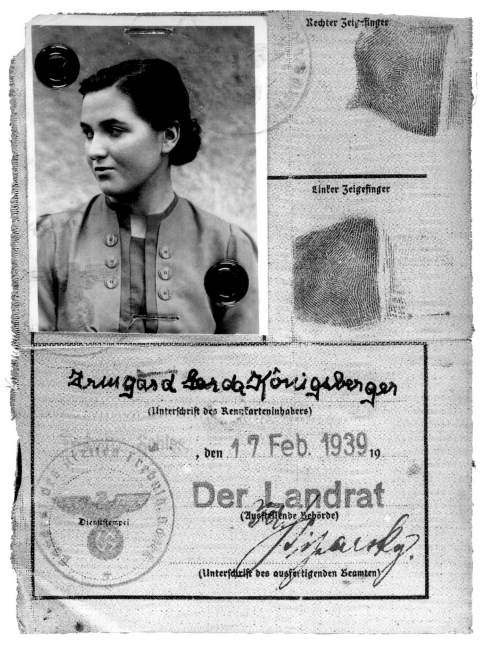

**Figure 3.11** Irmgard Königsberger's forged identity card. She had ripped out the front part marked with a "J" and changed the name "Sara" to "Gerda." This meant that she could no longer be identified as Jewish and was able to travel freely to the Swiss border.

**Figure 3.12**
Irmgard and Edith
Königsberger
in Switzerland

*We asked what kind
of excursions we
could take there. We
[said we] wanted
to go walking up
into the forest, into
the mountains. And
then the man said
to us: "Yes, you can
go here and there,
but be careful, the
border is up there."*
IRMGARD
KÖNIGSBERGER
JOURDAIN

ports, the official yelled at them and said, 'What are you doing here? You'll never get out!' After that, another whispered in my father's ear, 'Come back tomorrow, he won't be there, I'll extend them for you.' And thus we got the signature on September 30, 1941."[60]

Members of the Philipp family were among the last Jews to leave Berlin legally. "On October 19, 1941, my parents and I had the incredible luck of emigrating with around forty or fifty fellow Jews in a separate passenger carriage from the Anhalter station in Berlin. I can still remember sitting at the station on my little suitcase. Each person was only allowed one suitcase. But all were full of hope since we were traveling to freedom."[61] Just a few days later, on October 23, 1941, emigration was banned, although the ban was never officially announced. Quite simply, the policy of expulsion was gradually replaced with one of extermination.[62]

After this, only very few people managed to get out. Success required equal parts courage and luck. Two young women who managed to escape were the sisters Edith and Irmgard Königsberger. Edith, born in 1921, was a neonatal nurse and worked in a Jewish children's home in Berlin. When the deportations began in October 1941, she had to look after the children who were to be deported on the premises of the Levetzowstrasse synagogue, which had been converted into an assembly camp. Irmgard, born in 1923, had started to train as a neonatal nurse and worked in the Jewish Hospital in Berlin.

After receiving news of the deportation of their relatives to Theresienstadt, the Königsberger sisters decided to execute a plan to flee to Switzerland, which they had been weighing for a long time. In order even to reach the Swiss border they needed papers that disguised the fact that they were Jewish. Irmgard altered her identity papers by tearing off the part marked with "J" and changing the compulsory "Jewish" middle name of Sara to Gerda.[63] Edith used identity papers from her childhood, which had not been marked. With a good deal of luck, they managed to reach Swiss soil near Schaffhausen on September 2, 1942.[64] They were, moreover, lucky not to be sent back. The two had to spend the next four years in various Swiss labor centers. Both later married in Switzerland, and Irmgard Jourdain lived in France until her husband's death. At the time of this writing (2000), both sisters were living in Karlsruhe.

*When about forty or fifty of us left Anhalter station on October 19, a member of the board of the Berlin Jewish Community was at the station to tell us how lucky we were to be going away and that when we arrived the next morning in Frankfurt we should not talk too much—since on this day a transport would leave for the east.*

WALTER PHILIPP TO
HERMANN SIMON,
LETTER DATED FEB.
14, 1997

**Table 3.2** Emigration of Jews from Berlin and Germany, 1933–41

| Year | Berlin | German Reich |
|------|--------|--------------|
| 1933 | 13,000 | 37,000 |
| 1934 | 9,000 | 23,000 |
| 1935 | 6,000 | 21,000 |
| 1936 | 10,000 | 25,000 |
| 1937 | 10,000 | 23,000 |
| 1938 | 16,000 | 40,000 |
| 1939 | 16,000 | 78,000 |
| 1940 | ? | 15,000 |
| 1941 | ? | 8,000 |
| 1942–44 | ? | 8,500 |
| **Total** | 80,000 | 278,500 |

Source: Wolf Gruner, *Judenverfolgung in Berlin. Eine Chronologie der Behördenmaßnahmen in der Reichshauptstadt* (Berlin, 1996), p. 95.

**Table 3.3** Jewish Population of Berlin, 1933–41

| | |
|------|------|
| June 1933 | 160,000 |
| August 1935 | 153,000 |
| May 1939 | 79,000 (according to the Nazi racial definition, 82,500) |
| June 1941 | 65,000 (according to the racial definition, 74,000) |

Source: Gruner, *Judenverfolgung in Berlin. Eine Chronologie der Behördenmaßnahmen in der Reichshauptstadt* (Berlin, 1996), p. 94.

Note: The differences between this and table 3.1 result from the extensive internal migration from small towns and villages to Berlin.

**Table 3.4** The Main Immigration Countries and the Number of Jewish Emigrants Taken in from Germany

| | |
|------|------|
| United States | 132,000 |
| Palestine | 55,000 |
| Great Britain | 40,000 |
| Argentina | 10,000 |
| Brazil | 10,000 |
| China (Shanghai) | 8,000 |

Sources: on Palestine, the United States, and Shanghai, China, Herbert A. Strauss, "Jewish Emigration from Germany—Nazi Policies and Jewish Responses" (part 2), *LBI Yearbook* 25 (1980): 346, 362, 384; and on Great Britain, Argentina, and Brazil, Monika Richarz, *Jüdisches Leben in Deutschland. Selbstzeugnisse zur Sozialgeschichte, 1918–1945* (Stuttgart, 1982), pp. 40–73.

**1** Michael Wildt, editor, *Die Judenpolitik des SD, 1935–1938. Eine Dokumentation* (Munich, 1995), document 1, pp. 66–66.

**2** On the development of the concept of forced emigration by the SD, see Wildt, *Die Judenpolitik*, pp. 15, 32–35, 52–61, and documents 1, 9, 17, 32.

**3** See Avraham Barkai, "Der wirtschaftliche Existenzkampf der Juden im Dritten Reich, 1933–1938," in *Die Juden im Nationalsozialistischen Deutschland/The Jews in Nazi Germany, 1933–43*, ed. Arnold Paucker, Sylvia Gilchrist, and Barbara Suchy (Tübingen, 1986), pp. 153–66.

**4** Juliane Wetzel, "Auswanderung aus Deutschland," in *Die Juden in Deutschland, 1933–1945. Leben unter nationalsozialistischer Herrschaft*, ed. Wolfgang Benz (Munich, 1988), pp. 413–98; and Herbert A. Strauss, "Jewish Emigration from Germany—Nazi Policies and Jewish Responses" (part 1), in *LBI Yearbook* 25 (1980): 347.

**5** On the distinction between the different phases, see Wetzel, *Auswanderung*, pp. 417–19.

**6** Scholem Adler-Rudel, *Jüdische Selbsthilfe unter dem Naziregime, 1933–1939. Im Spiegel der Berichte der Reichsvertretung der Juden in Deutschland* (Tübingen, 1974), p. 76.

**7** Ibid., pp. 97–99.

**8** See the 1935 working report of the Reichsvertretung der Juden in Deutschland, p. 7; Adler-Rudel, *Jüdische Selbsthilfe*, p. 77.

**9** The organization was founded as the Reichsvertretung der deutschen Juden (Reich Representation of German Jews) but had to change its name to Reichsvertretung der Juden in Deutschland in 1935. In July 1939 the name was changed once again to the Reichsvereinigung der Juden in Deutschland (Reich Association of Jews in Germany).

**10** Dan Diner, "Die Katastrophe vor der Katastrophe. Auswanderung ohne Einwanderung," in *Zerbrochene Geschichte. Leben und Selbstverständnis der Juden in Deutschland,* ed. Dirk Blasius and Dan Diner (Frankfurt am Main, 1983), p. 143; and Adler-Rudel, *Jüdische Selbsthilfe*, p. 110.

**11** Adler-Rudel, *Jüdische Selbsthilfe*, pp. 76–77.

**12** Wetzel, *Auswanderung*, pp. 417, 422.

**13** Julius L. Seligsohn, *Die Einwanderung nach U.S.* (Berlin, 1940), p. 39.

**14** Wetzel, *Auswanderung*, pp. 486–87.

**15** Herbert A. Strauss, "Jewish Emigration from Germany. Nazi Policies and Jewish Responses" (part 2), in *LBI Yearbook* 26 (1981): 343–409.

**16** Seligsohn, *Die Einwanderung*, pp. 32–51.

**17** Ibid., pp. 15–30.

**18** Strauss, "Jewish Emigration" (part 2), pp. 361–62.

**19** The newspaper *Jüdische Auswanderung. Korrespondenzblatt des Hilfsvereins der Juden in Deutschland* was published by the Registered Aid Association for German Jews, with its first edition in September 1936. "The newspaper . . . which has by now produced sections on North America, Cuba, the Philippines, South America, Australia and New Zealand, with a South American supplement, has become indispensable for anyone planning to emigrate." Heinz Cohn and Erich Gottfeld, *Auswanderungsvorschriften für Juden in Deutschland* (Berlin, 1938), p. 80.

**20** *Jüdische Auswanderung*, January 1939, p. 1.

**21** Barkai, *Der wirtschaftliche Existenzkampf*, p. 164.

**22** Of the total of almost 280,000 German Jews who emigrated from Germany, some 129,000 of them had left by late 1937.

**23** Aid Association for Jews in Germany, Circular W.-A., no. 29, September 1, 1938, p. 5, Centrum Judaicum Archive (CJA), Berlin, 2 A 2, no. 17.

**24** Petra Löber, *Leben im Wartesaal. Exil in Shanghai, 1938–1947*, ed. Jewish Museum Berlin (Berlin, 1997), pp. 10–41.

**25** Ronald Stent, "Jewish Refugee Organisations," in *Second Chance. Two Centuries of German-speaking Jews in the United Kingdom*, ed. Werner E. Mosse and Julius Carlebach (Tübingen, 1991), pp. 579–598.

**26** Interview with Ruth Spanier Wing, conducted by Beate Meyer in 1999, video, CJA.

**27** Ibid.

**28** Strauss, "Jewish Emigration" (part 1), p. 328; (part 2), p. 362.

**29** Cohn and Gottfeld, *Auswanderungsvorschriften für Juden in Deutschland*, p. 7.

**30** Ibid., p. 24.

**31** Ibid., pp. 30–36.

**32** Werner Feilchenfeld, Dolf Michaelis, and Ludwig Pinner, *Haavara-Transfer nach Palästina und Einwanderung Deutscher Juden, 1933–1939* (Tübingen, 1972), pp. 23–64, 77.

**33** Cohn and Gottfeld, *Auswanderungsvorschriften*, pp. 46–55.

**34** Ibid., pp. 61–68.

**35** Ibid., p. 104.

**36** Ibid., pp. 37–59.

**37** Gabriele Anderl, "Die 'Zentralstellen für jüdische Auswanderung' in Wien, Berlin und Prag. Ein Vergleich," in *Tel Aviver Jahrbuch für deutsche Geschichte 23* (1994): 275–299.

**38** Hannah Arendt, *Eichmann in Jerusalem: A Report on the Banality of Evil*, excerpted in *The Portable Hannah Arendt*, ed. Peter Baehr (New York, 2000), p. 321. The witness, Franz Eliezer Meyer, was the former chairman of the Zionist Association for Germany. See Leni Yahil, *Die Shoa. Überlebenskampf und Vernichtung der europäischen Juden* (Munich, 1998), p. 162, fn. 68.

**39** Wildt, *Die Judenpolitik*, pp. 61–64.

**40** Diner, *Die Katastrophe*, pp. 143–44.

**41** Wolf Gruner, "Die Reichshauptstadt und die Verfolgung der Berliner Juden," in *Jüdische Geschichte in Berlin. Essays und Studien*, ed. Reinhard Rürup (Berlin, 1995), pp. 238–39.

**42** CJA 2 A 2, no. 17, Aid Association for Jews in Germany, Circular B no. 358, January 16, 1939, p. 1.

**43** Ibid., pp. 3–4.

**44** Anderl, "Die 'Zentralstellen,'" pp. 283–86.

**45** Ibid., p. 296. See also Uwe Dietrich Adam, *Judenpolitik im Dritten Reich* (Düsseldorf, 1972), pp. 228–31.

**46** Adler-Rudel, "The Evian Conference on the Refugee Question," in *LBI Yearbook* 13 (1968): 235–73.

**47** Ibid., pp. 241–51.

**48** Ibid., pp. 258–60. Also see Kurt R. Grossmann, *Emigration. Geschichte der Hitler-Flüchtlinge 1933–1945* (Frankfurt am Main, 1969), pp. 61–66.

**49** Chaje Durst Papers, CJA, no signature, unpaginated.

**50** CJA, 2 A 2, no. 17, Circular A no. 122, September 9, 1938.

**51** B Rep. 057–01, 1 Ks 1/69, R 34/26, Landesarchiv (LAB), Berlin.

**52** Ibid. On the swindlers, see sheets 4–6, 10–12, 14–15, 18–21, 60–62; on payment to funds see sheet 10b f.; on the few honest cases, see sheet 32.

**53** Ibid. The clients were Hans Wolff (sheet 36b), Abram Falkowicz (sheet 37), Paul Marx (sheet 37), Dr. Siegfried Falkowicz (sheet 37), Frieda Faerber (sheets 111–12), Georg Schwerin (sheet 120–25) and Kurt Glaser (sheets 113–15, 119). On the failure of visa provision, also see sheet 38, sheet 56b.

**54** Ibid. On the Ecuadorian counsel, see sheets 113–15. On the permits from Hamburg, see sheets 119, 125. On the arrests, see sheets 110, 135–36, 154–55.

**55** Ibid., sheet 95.

**56** Selma Lehmann Papers, letter to her sons dated June 8, 1939, CJA.

**57** Selma Lehmann Papers, letter dated February 20, 1940, CJA.

**58** Strauss, "Jewish Emigration" (part 1), p. 358.

**59** Interviews with Miriam Blumenthal-Merzbacher conducted by Beate Meyer, CJA.

**60** Report by Walter Philipp of February 11, 1997, p. 2, CJA.

**61** Ibid.

**62** Wetzel, *Auswanderung*, pp. 420–21.

**63** Private collection of Irmgard Jourdain.

**64** Edith Dietz, *Den Nazis entronnen* (Frankfurt am Main, 1996), pp. 105–137. A description of the escape can be found in the interview with Edith Dietz conducted by Beate Meyer.

# 3

Aryanization

# Chapter Four

## "Aryanized" and Financially Ruined: The Case of the Garbáty Family

BEATE MEYER

The "Aryanization" of Jewish property under the National Socialist regime represents one of the most extensive changes of ownership to have taken place in recent German history. The process of driving out Jewish enterprises gradually crept in after 1933, assumed an increasingly systematic form between 1936 and 1937, and came to a head in 1938–39 with a veritable moneymaking free-for-all among "Aryan" purchasers.[1]

Contrary to popular opinion, "Aryanization" was not the sole product of the regime's anti-Jewish policy—that is, it did not simply ensue from NSDAP initiatives and legal and administrative measures on the part of the state. In fact, for quite some time the state steered clear of such takeovers. Only in 1938 did the Nazi government enact legal regulations for the "Aryanization" of Jewish enterprises and property, and these were not formally enforced and ordered until after the pogrom of November 9, 1938.

Up to this point, the state had not made the transfer of Jewish property into non-Jewish hands a priority. Rather, its interest was primarily focused on plundering the financial resources of the vast numbers of Jewish proprietors it had bullied into emigrating. The Third Reich met its urgent need for money and foreign currency in part through a network of taxes and compulsory contributions designed to transfer Jewish assets to the Reich Treasury. Two measures that helped the Third Reich to siphon off Jewish assets were the Weimar-era Reich Emigration Tax, above all, which the Nazi's had transformed into an anti-Jewish compulsory tax, and the so-called *Dego-Abgabe* (*Deutsche Golddiskont-Abgabe*, the gold discount rate). This was levied in the case of capital transfers abroad, and in October 1936, it already comprised over 80 percent of the sums transferred.[2]

Although state measures and NSDAP initiatives framed the political climate and legal conditions of "Aryanization," the phenomenon would never have been possible without the direct or indirect participation of millions of German citizens. They assumed all kinds of roles in the process of forcing out Jewish businessmen and expropriating their businesses—as competitors, purchasers, financiers, profiteers of all sorts, brokers, trustees, experts, and finally, as representatives of specialist groups, economic associations, and chambers of industry and commerce. As the phenomenon of "Aryanization" makes all too clear, the Nazi regime was more than a dictatorship operating from the top down. It was a coherent social practice that involved German society in manifold ways.

THE CASE OF THE GARBÁTY cigarette factory and the fate of its Jewish proprietors serves to illustrate how "Aryanization" was virtually based on this effective division of labor between regime and society.[3] From humble nineteenth-century beginnings, the Garbáty company had grown into one of Berlin's most significant Jewish-owned industrial enterprises.[4] The company's founder, Josef Garbáty-Rosenthal, had started out selling "tobacco products" in the 1870s with a vendor's tray. By 1907 he employed over eight hundred workers in his factories on Hadlichstrasse and Berliner Strasse in the district of Pankow. That the company was one of the first in Germany to produce "brand-name cigarettes" contributed considerably to its success. Alongside Garbáty's Kurmark brand, the Königin von Saba (Queen of Sheba) brand was particularly popular and was famous for its pronounced "Oriental" taste. The product was patented in 1898 and distributed well beyond Berlin and surrounding Brandenburg.

Prior to World War I, the German cigarette industry was generally made up of small or medium-sized enterprises and had successfully resisted efforts to concentrate production in the hands of a few.[5] After 1918–19, however, the situation changed completely. In 1930, a conglomerate made up of the firms of Reemtsma and Haus Neuerburg controlled 82.4 percent of the national cigarette market.[6] Garbáty was unable to resist the trend. In 1929, when Josef Garbáty-Rosenthal transferred the company to his sons Eugen and Moritz, Philipp F. Reemtsma bought Eugen Garbáty's share: a 50 percent stake in the factory. (The transaction was hushed up, however, in order to preserve the factory's image as a small firm—"big business cigarettes" had a poor reputation with certain customers.)

Initially, the Nazi rise to power in 1933 did not drastically affect Garbáty's sales, but gradually, there were hints of an insidious threat to the company. On several occasions, the Nazi newspaper *Stürmer* denounced Kurmark cigarettes as a "Jewish product" and informed its readers "on account of many questions" that "the 'Garbaty' cigarette factory is a purely Jewish firm."[7] Moritz Garbáty was overwhelmed with threatening letters. Then, on the basis of an accusation alleging that he had smuggled foreign currency into Denmark, he was subjected to a Gestapo investigation.[8]

**Figure 4.1**
The Garbáty villa

The initiation of the firm's "Aryanization" came in the fall of 1937, when Reich Economics Minister Hjalmar Schacht was dismissed from his post. His successor, Hermann Göring—who was also in charge of the Four-Year Plan for the German economy—immediately stepped up the ministry's anti-Semitic measures. An edict of November 27, 1937, instructed the monitoring authorities to grant non-Jewish importers "priority" and to cut the import quotas for Jewish firms. In January 1938 the monitoring authority for tobacco thus lowered the import quota for the Garbáty company by 10 percent.

The Reich Economics Ministry action would not in itself have posed a major threat to the company's existence had Garbáty's rivals not seized the chance to join the fray and thereby increase their market share. They managed to exclude Garbáty from the so-called *Frischdienst* (delivery of newly produced cigarettes) of the cigarette producers' syndicate, which made it difficult for the Pankow factory to ensure a regular supply to its customers.[9] The process was sanctioned by the Fachgruppe Tabak (Tobacco Specialist Group), which showed itself to be very interested indeed in the "de-Judification" (*Entjudung*) of the cigarette industry.[10]

The "concerted action" had a direct and negative impact on Garbáty's turnover, which went from RM 15.84 million in the second quarter of 1937 to RM

**Figure 4.2**
Moritz Garbáty

9.26 million in the first quarter of 1938.[11] In the face of this poor performance, Moritz Garbáty saw no realistic alternative to selling the company. He thus gave his lawyer, Dr. Fritz Koppe, a tax specialist, the task of commencing appropriate sales negotiations with interested "Aryan" parties.

One of the main applicants was Dr. Jakob Koerfer, a cinema owner from Cologne, who happened to be an acquaintance of Garbáty's wife Ella. With the help of influential sponsors, he had established a financially robust buying consortium. Another member of this consortium was Emil Georg von Stauss, director of the Deutsche Bank and vice president of the Reichstag, who had become an eminence grise of the German economy in the 1930s and had excellent political connections—above all, to Göring himself.[12]

Complicating matters was the fact that Philipp F. Reemtsma still owned a 50 percent stake in the company. Neither the Reich Economics Ministry nor the economic advisors in the Nazi party's Berlin district were in favor of Reemtsma completely taking over the firm. In keeping with its policy of helping the *Mittelstand* (the middle class, that is, in this case, small and medium-sized owners), the National Socialists opposed further concentration in the cigarette industry.[13] Although Reemtsma had already secured a leading market position in the "Third Reich" in political terms—thanks in large part to regular donations of millions of Reichsmarks to Göring—he obviously did not want to stretch things too far and provoke an attack from *Mittelstand* ideologists within the Nazi party. Reemtsma eventually sold his share in the firm to Koerfer for six million Reichsmarks and withdrew completely.

THE GARBÁTY FAMILY, though it had launched the "Aryanization" negotiations on its own initiative, quickly lost control of the proceedings and was gradually maneuvered into a situation of powerlessness. The process of silent but highly effective blackmail involved a broad range of institutions. Hence, the "Aryanization official" of the Berlin Nazi party's economic advisor ultimately hired Garbáty's lawyer in March 1938 to make sure "that the Messrs. Garbáty in no way think that they can close their eyes to the necessities of the times."[14] The Judenreferent (official in charge of Jewish affairs) at the Reich Economics Ministry also pushed for the firm's rapid "Aryanization," as did the *Fachgruppe Tabak*, which urged that "the process be speeded up as much as possible."[15]

Koerfer, the company's prospective "Aryanizer," was in an excellent position. His alliance with von Stauss ensured him the political blessing of the Reich Economics Ministry, which had indeed turned down other applicants (further narrowing the Garbáty family's scope of action). At a time when the heightened climate of anti-Semitism had sent the market value of Jewish companies into free fall, Koerfer simply had to wait until the Garbáty cigarette factory fell into his lap.

While Koerfer was not the least scrupulous profiteer among the "Aryanizers," he was not a well-meaning purchaser either. His behavior marks him as one of the regime's many "silent partners," a man who pursued his personal advantage in an inconspicuous but thorough—and profitable—way.[16]

The contract dated October 24, 1938, reveals just how advantageous the take-over of the cigarette company was for Koerfer. Moritz Garbáty withdrew from the firm as a shareholder with individual liability; Koerfer entered the firm as a shareholder with liability, together with the Saarland Association for Industry and Administration, Emil Georg von Stauss, and Baron Alfred von Adelsheim as limited partners.[17] As compensation, Moritz Garbáty was to receive six million Reichsmarks and his brother Eugen would receive one million. The "Aryanizers" paid a further RM 1.74 million for the factory premises in Pankow. The calculation of an economic trustee—which stated the firm's total value on December 31, 1937, to be RM 31.6 million—shows how little these compensation payments corresponded to the actual value of the company.[18] How did such a crass under-valuation come about?

It is normal to calculate a firm's value according to a set of factors collectively known as "goodwill." These include market position, range of products, regular customers, business contacts, trade channels, and the company's good name. It goes without saying that the National Socialists assumed all Jews to lack "good-will," and the Garbáty case was no exception. The October 1938 contract thus made no provision for these factors. Nor, on similar grounds, did the Garbátys receive compensation for company trademarks and other immaterial rights.[19] Only factory buildings, inventories, and stocks were deemed eligible for compensation, and corners were cut even here, when only the so-called *Fakturenwert* (invoice value) was used to calculate the estimated value of the stock—at somewhere between 15 and 20 percent below the actual value.[20]

Moritz Garbáty suffered further losses as a result of the Reich Economics Ministry's concluding authorization decision, passed down on November 2, 1938. The Judenreferent at the ministry was SA Führer Alf Krüger, known among Jewish companies as "Judenkrüger" for his notorious reputation as an

*He was no crook; he was a sly fox, and he knew the mother. And so it was.*

THOMAS GARBÁTY, 1999, ON JAKOB KOERFER, THE "ARYANIZER"

anti-Semite.[21] Krüger peremptorily lowered the compensation payment from the six million Reichsmarks stipulated in the contract to RM 4.11 million.

Even then, Moritz Garbáty did not have direct access to the money, since Koerfer, the buyer, had on November 8 transferred funds into the bank account of a middleman—Garbáty's general representative, Fritz Koppe.[22] This loophole measure had been taken in order to get around the German foreign exchange office's "blocking order," which would have stripped Moritz Garbáty of the right of access to his account had the payment been made directly to him.[23]

IT SO HAPPENED THAT the contract was concluded and the transfers and further formalities were carried out during the grim days around the November pogrom. Under these circumstances, there was no way Moritz Garbáty could have operated as a normal businessman. To avoid the wave of arrests that followed the pogrom, he was obliged to hide temporarily in the garden cottage of a trusted employee. Meanwhile, it was too risky for the family to stay at home, and his wife and their eight-year-old son, Thomas, were stranded in a taxi, moving aimlessly through Berlin. Thomas Garbáty described the experience in an interview:

> [A] taxi was really the safest place, provided one had enough money to travel all over Berlin. People were not stopped on the street, but, above all, apartments were broken into and windows smashed. And I asked my mother, "Mummy, why are so many people standing around and smashing shop windows?" I did not understand much, and my mother did not say much either. It was somehow not real. . . . My father's best friend, Erich Zabel, was a Gentile. We eventually went to his home. Anyway, I remember . . . that the Zabels were incredibly nervous. They were really afraid, since the Gestapo of course knew who our friends were. My mother rang home from there to see what the situation was like. Our housekeeper Elise answered the phone. "Elise, how are things at home?" asked my mother. The answer was "I'm sorry, but Mrs. Garbáty is not here." Then we knew that the Gestapo were in the apartment. They were looking for us. It was Kristallnacht.[24]

*During Kristall-nacht . . . my mother and I were in a taxi, not at home. . . . When I think about it now, I have to say that inside a taxi really was the safest place.*
THOMAS GARBÁTY,
1999

Moritz Garbáty's provisional hiding place in the garden cottage had not gone unnoticed. A few days after the pogrom, Ella Garbáty received a call from the Berlin chief of police Count Wolf Heinrich Helldorf, whose home she had once decorated as an interior designer: "You know," he was reported to have said, "you can't keep Garbáty in that house for much longer. . . . My people and I—have known for a long time where he is. I have to send someone there to arrest him."[25] At Helldorf's suggestion, Moritz Garbáty had himself admitted to hospital with an alleged stomach ulcer.

The police chief's friendly gesture was in no way the result of philo-Semitism but was due entirely to selfish motives. Helldorf had found in the wealthier Jews of Berlin a flourishing source of income and imposed a block on passports for all Jews with assets over RM 300,000. They could only obtain an exit permit by making a compulsory "donation"—soon known as the *Helldorf-Spende* (Helldorf donation) by those concerned—often amounting to several hundred thousand Reichsmarks.[26] From Moritz and Eugen Garbáty alone, the chief of police extorted a total of 1.15 million.[27]

The *Helldorf-Spende* was supposedly to be transferred to a Jewish Community fund for "Emigration Support for Needy Jews." The money never arrived in this account.[28] Even contemporaries suspected that Count Helldorf, a rake who had had creditors knocking on his door for years, privately siphoned off some of these compulsory donations for himself, thereby solving all of his financial worries.[29] Helldorf was subsequently involved in the July 20, 1944, plot to assassinate Hitler—for which he was arrested and hanged later that summer.

**Figure 4.3** Berlin chief of police Wolf Heinrich von Helldorf

IN NOVEMBER 1938, the Berlin NSDAP, too, saw a favorable opportunity to make money from the assets of wealthy Jews. After the pogrom, the Berlin district propaganda leader, Wächter, extorted a "voluntary donation" of five million Reichsmarks from the city's Jewish Community as "Compensation for Damage to Glass in Berlin."[30] This so-called *Scherbenfonds* (Broken Glass Fund) was used, for example, to finance the "State Funeral of Party Comrade vom Rath" with RM 300,000. The Berlin Party organization received RM 200,000, and the SA and SS received RM 70,000 as compensation "for many days of service, even at night." Moritz Garbáty's compulsory donation to this fund alone amounted to RM 20,000.[31]

Once Helldorf and Wächter had extorted a total of one million Reichsmarks from the cigarette producer, Moritz Garbáty went on to suffer almost total financial ruin on behalf of the German Reich. First came the notorious Reich-wide reparation payments on the Jews—the *Sühnemaßnahme* (atonement measures)—to pay for the pogrom damage. Garbáty's *Judenvermögensabgabe* (Jewish Property Levy) amounted to RM 1.12 million. Then, upon emigration, the Finance Office of the Tiergarten district, where he lived, levied a Reich Emigration Tax of about RM 1.43 million. A further RM 830,000 RM was lost in foreign

*Each day, Helldorf knew exactly how far the [sales] negotiations had gone. When they were at an end, my mother received a call: "If you want your passports, come to the police headquarters tomorrow morning." . . . There we paid loads of money for the passports, . . . got them, and then we were off.*

THOMAS GARBÁTY, 1999

**Figure 4.4** From Bordeaux, Moritz Garbáty asked Count Helldorf to reduce the "contribution."

exchange rates since he could only exchange 6.5 percent of the sum transferred into foreign currency and had to pay 93.5 percent as advance payment to the Deutsche Golddiskontbank.[32] When all these extortions had been made, all that remained in Moritz Garbáty's account was a sum of 861 Reichsmarks. And this was confiscated in late 1943 on behalf of the German Reich.

MORITZ GARBÁTY, his wife, and son managed to received exit permits at the end of November 1938 and traveled by plane to Amsterdam. At the customs office of Berlin's Tempelhof Airport the Garbátys underwent a strict body search. "Something else almost went wrong at Tempelhof customs," Thomas Garbáty recounts in his memoirs:

> Father's secretary had given my mother a small package when they said farewell. 'Don't open it until you are outside,' she told mother. Mother put the package in her handbag and forgot it all in the agitation. We were then all searched, as we were not allowed to take anything with us—no money, no jewelry. My mother had to undress in front of a particularly thorough, strict female customs officer. Of course the package was found, and only then did mother remember it again. She begged the customs officer not to take offence, it was a present that only had been given at the last minute and had not even been opened. What if it were a diamond, which Mrs. Sch. in her goodness wanted to give my parents on the way so that they could turn it into money? The whole emigration would have fallen

through, and who knows what would have happened to us. The customs officer opened the package. Both saw that Mrs. Sch. had packed a small golden cross for my mother. And tears welled up in the eyes of this woman, this bitter customs officer. "Now you are safe," she said to my mother, "this is the last station of the cross for you."[33]

From Amsterdam, the Garbátys went on to Bordeaux, where they had to wait half a year before receiving their entrance visas to the United States. On June 9, 1939, shortly before the outbreak of World War II, their boat arrived in New York.

Josef Garbáty-Rosenthal, paterfamilias and founder of the firm, remained behind in the family villa, which now belonged to others. He was eighty-seven years old and had not wanted to take on the burden of emigration. His right to stay there had been stipulated in a contract—even if the Implementation Office for the New Design of the Reich Capital did not like it. It made this request of the new owners of the factory: "Further to a telephone conversation, I would like to ask you to present the authorization that the Jew Josef Garbáty-Rosenthal may continue to live there in room 21 until his death."[34]

**Figure 4.5** Josef Garbáty-Rosenthal

Joseph Garbáty-Rosenthal died three weeks later in Berlin and was thus spared further witness to the "Aryanization" process beyond the company he had founded but also of the cigarette packaging itself. His portrait had once graced the packages of the Königin von Saba cigarettes; it was now replaced with an Orientalized rendering of a "Turk's head."[35]

The Königin von Saba and Kurmark brands continued to be produced in the Pankow cigarette factory up to the end of 1942. They were then replaced by cheaper "war brand cigarettes," since there was barely any tobacco of "peace-time quality" available.[36] The factory was badly damaged by fire during the liberation of Berlin in April 1945, but it was still possible to continue production to a limited extent. Jakob Koerfer, the firm's owner since 1938, had already reached safety in Switzerland in December 1944.

After the fall of Berlin, the city administration appointed a temporary manager as a trustee. In September 1945 the manager reported in a letter to Eugen Garbáty that the factory was producing 1.5 million cigarettes a day, of which 500,000 were for Red Army consumption.[37] As the trustee assured the former Jewish owners right at the beginning of the report, "I don't need to mention that

**Figure 4.6 and 4.7** The Königin von Saba cigarette label before . . . and after "Aryanization."

we have gone through a difficult period in the meantime." Perhaps it did not occur to him that the Jewish owners might have gone through a lot as well. As such, the letter is a telling document of the German state of mind at the war's end, a period in which self-pity often replaced empathy for the victims of the Nazi regime. Similarly, the Soviet occupying forces and the government of the German Democratic Republic (GDR) disregarded the regime's original victims. In the GDR, Jewish properties were appropriated a second time, this time by communists who proved as unwilling to compensate the original owners as the "Aryanizers" had been.

In the western part of Berlin, however, Allied and Federal German compensation legislation led to a restitution process for the Garbátys. On December 20, 1952, a settlement was reached between Jakob Koerfer and Maurice (Moritz) Garbáty by which Koerfer paid a total sum of 4.25 million Deutschmarks in compensation. However, this compensation only related to the smaller branch factory located in Brombach an der Tauber. The main factory in Pankow had been appropriated by the GDR and was no longer in Koerfer's possession.[38]

From the 1950s onward, the East German firm was renamed VEB Garbáty (Nationally Owned Garbáty Firm) and merged in 1960 with the "nationally owned" firm VEB Josetti to form the Berliner Zigarettenfabrik. It began producing its legendary Club brand in the 1950s.

The fall of the Berlin Wall in 1989–90 brought the Garbáty cigarette factory's hundred-plus-year history to an abrupt end. In order to avoid standing in the

**Figure 4.8** Ella, Thomas, and Moritz Garbáty on the passage to New York, July 1939

**Figure 4.9** Moritz and Thomas Garbáty on the Empire State Building, September 13, 1942

way of a sale to a successful U.S. company, the R. J. Reynolds Tobacco Company, the family had refrained from filing compensation claims against the factory's East German trustees. The latter had signed a purchase agreement with the trustees, not for the whole company but for its jewel, the "Club" brand.[39] On October 2, 1990, one day before German unification, the trustees sold off the legendary cigarette brand. Had the transaction taken place a day later it would have been forbidden under economic law in the Federal Republic of Germany.

The amount paid was ridiculously low: ten million marks. Reynolds's net profit from this transaction must have been hundreds of times the amount of the purchase sum. In September 1991 the last cigarettes rolled off the Pankow production line. The machines as well as the fittings were sold. One hundred and ten years after Josef Garbáty-Rosenthal founded the firm, production had finally ceased.

**1** On the "Aryanization" of Jewish property, see for example, Helmut Genschel, *Die Verdrängung der Juden aus der Wirtschaft im Dritten Reich* (Göttingen, 1966); Avraham Barkai, *Vom Boykott zur "Entjudung." Der wirtschaftliche Existenzkampf der Juden im Dritten Reich, 1933–1943* (Frankfurt am Main, 1987); and Frank Bajohr, *"Aryanization" in Hamburg: The Economic Exclusion of Jews and the Confiscations of Their Property in Nazi Germany* (New York and Oxford, 2002).

**2** See Dorothee Mußgnug, *Die Reichsfluchtsteuer, 1931–1953* (Berlin, 1993); Martin Tarrab-Maslaton, *Rechtliche Strukturen der Diskriminierung der Juden im Dritten Reich* (Berlin, 1993); and Bajohr, *Aryanization*, pp. 153 ff.

**3** We extend our heartfelt thanks to Thomas Garbáty, who generously gave the complete documentation on the cigarette company's "Aryanization" to the Centrum Judaicum archives.

**4** On the following, see Petra Woidt, *Pankow und die Königin von Saba*, edited by the Pankow district authority, Department for Youth and Education, Cultural Office, Panke-Museum (Berlin, 1997); memorandum on the development of the Garbáty Firm (n.p., n.d.), Garbáty Collection, Centrum Judaicum Archive, Berlin.

**5** See Kurt Bormann, *Die deutsche Zigarettenindustrie* (Tübingen, 1910); Fritz Blaich, *Der Trustkampf. Ein Beitrag zum Verhalten der Ministerialbürokratie gegenüber Verbandsinteressen im Wilhelminischen Deutschland* (Berlin, 1975).

**6** Aribert Heilmann, "Entwicklungstendenzen im deutschen Tabakwarenmarkt in den Jahren 1930 bis 1955," doctoral dissertation (Heidelberg, 1956), p. 112.

**7** See, for example, *Der Stürmer* 8 (February 1938).

**8** Woidt, *Pankow,* pp. 45 ff.; Thomas Garbáty, interview conducted by Beate Meyer, May 10, 1999, transcript, p. 12, CJA.

**9** Memorandum on the development of the Garbáty Firm, p. 17.

**10** Ibid., Dr. Koppe, file note of May 21, 1938, Garbáty Collection, CJA.

**11** On the turnover figures, see the appendix to the so-called *Pool-Vertrag* (pool contract), Garbáty Collection, CJA.

**12** On Stauss, see Lothar Gall et al., editors, *Die deutsche Bank, 1870–1995* (Munich, 1995), pp. 352–64.

**13** Memorandum on the development of the Garbáty Firm, p. 15; Fritz Koppe to Eugen Garbáty, letter dated March 18, 1938, Garbáty Collection, CJA.

**14** Koppe to Garbáty, letter dated March 18, 1938.

**15** Fritz Koppe, file note dated May 21, 1938, Garbáty Collection, CJA.

**16** On the typology of "Aryan" purchasers, see Bajohr, *"Aryanization,"* pp. 256–59.

**17** Contract dated October 24, 1938, Garbáty Collection, CJA.

**18** Alfred Roehlicke, Formulation of the Economic Trustee, dated May 31, 1938, p. 9, Garbáty Collection, CJA.

**19** Memorandum on the development of the Garbáty Firm, p. 17.

**20** Georg Telschow to Fritz Koppe, letter dated June 15, 1938, Garbáty Collection, CJA.

**21** Alf Krüger, *Die Lösung der Judenfrage in der deutschen Wirtschaft. Kommentar zur Judengesetzgebung* (Berlin, 1940).

**22** Jakob Koerfer to Fritz Koppe, letter dated November 8, 1938, Garbáty Collection, CJA.

**23** Fritz Koppe to the customs investigation department in Berlin, letter dated December 1, 1938, Garbáty Collection, CJA.

**24** Quoted in an interview conducted by Beate Meyer with Thomas Garbáty (in Ann Arbor, MI) on November 6, 1999, transcript, pp. 3–4.

**25** Thomas Garbáty, interview conducted by Beate Meyer, May 15, 1999, transcript, p. 11.

**26** Hans Reichmann, *Deutscher Bürger und verfolgter Jude. Novemberpogrom und KZ Sachsenhausen 1937 bis 1939,* revised by Michael Wildt, Biographische Quellen zur Zeitgeschichte, 21(Munich, 1998), pp. 103–4.

**27** Declaration by the notary Dr. Georg Staege, dated October 30, 1948, Garbáty Collection, CJA. Moritz Garbáty had to pay RM 500,000 to Police Chief Helldorf on November 19, 1938, and RM 300,000 on February 9, 1939. Eugen Garbáty, his brother, had to pay RM 350,000 to Helldorf on November 19, 1938.

**28** Board of the Berlin Jewish Community to Fritz Koppe, letter dated May 14, 1940, Garbáty Collection, CJA.

**29** On this, see also Rex Harrison, "'Alter Kämpfer' im Widerstand. Graf Helldorf, die NS-Bewegung und die Opposition gegen Hitler," in *Vierteljahrshefte für Zeitgeschichte* 45 (1997): 385–22; and Bella Fromm, *Als Hitler mir die Hand küßte: Tagebücher, 1930–38* (Reinbek, 1997), p. 299.

**30** See Hans-Erich Fabian, "Der Berliner Scherbenfonds," in *Der Weg. Zeitschrift für Fragen des Judentums* 37 (November 8, 1946).

**31** Confirmation by E. Köhnen, October 10, 1948, Garbáty Collection, CJA.

**32** Confirmation by Max Heyn, March 9, 1947; Max Heyn to Maurice Garbáty, letter dated July 1, 1948, Garbáty Collection, CJA.

**33** Thomas Garbáty's memoirs, quoted in Woidt, *Pankow*, pp. 51–52.

**34** Rep. 250–04–09, no. 131, Landesarchiv Berlin.

**35** Future manager of the Garbáty firm to Eugene L. Garbáty, letter dated September 7, 1945, Garbáty Collection, CJA.

**36** Ibid.

**37** Ibid.

**38** Compensation settlement of December 20, 1950, Garbáty Collection, CJA.

**39** Woidt, *Pankow*, pp. 28 ff., and "Der Fall Garbáty," *Frankfurter Allgemeine Zeitung*, 4 February 2000.

# 4

# The Yellow Star

# Chapter Five

## Berlin Jews: Deprived of Rights, Impoverished, and Branded

ALBERT MEIRER

## The Heightening of "Jewish Policy" in 1938

For some time, foreign policy considerations prevented German Jews from being fully banished from society and the economy. These ceased to apply when the National Socialist regime started to pursue an expansionist policy. The country was to be ready for war by the end of 1938. In the view of the Nazi party, the large-scale economic exclusion of the Jews would no longer have a detrimental impact on the economy. The system of state-organized plunder was far along enough to secure gains for the state and the party from the sale of Jewish businesses. In addition, the regime's more aggressive foreign policy and increasingly repressive domestic policy heightened the need for an internal enemy.

The anti-Jewish policy of 1938 culminated in the pogrom of November 9–10, which marked the transition to outright state-organized terror. Yet this was only part of the story. This major wave of anti-Jewish activity—the third following those in 1933 and 1935—functioned, as Peter Longerich has put it, according to the "familiar dialectic between 'operations' and administrative or legislative measures."[1] The Nazi goal was to keep their "old promise from the time of struggle" (*Kampfzeit*), that is, to force the Jews from the economy and society.[2]

Berlin's Jews were, in the words of historian Wolf Gruner, living at the "intersection between two developments in terms of persecution: the anti-Jewish policy of the Reich government, on the one hand, and the anti-Jewish measures of the Berlin municipal government on the other."[3] The city authorities played an active and imaginative role in depriving Berlin's Jews of their rights and excluding them from society. In the process, they influenced and motivated the planning of central discrimination measures introduced by the regime's leaders. A raft of special provisions reduced the Jewish minority to a compulsory community, a community that was increasingly subject to the whim of the regime's representatives. The threat of extermination, which was increasingly articulated by leading Nazis, combined with official legitimization of the street terror during the November 1938 pogrom, soon made it clear that this would be a tyranny over life and death.

In the years to come, the ultimate deprivation of the rights of the Jewish minority went hand in hand with the NSDAP's complete penetration of German society and the capitulation of the general German public in the face of National Socialism's total claim to power. Anti-Semitism was used not least as a means of intimidating the population. It became clear that the system would stop at nothing. In other words, the pogroms were partially intended, in political terms, for those who witnessed them. In this way the National Socialist racial mania could become a historic phenomenon despite its obvious absurdity; it commanded respect on the basis of violence.

## Injustice

In the Nazi state, anti-Semitic ideology was to have extremely severe and inhumane consequences for the certainty of law of individuals. National Socialism had emerged in opposition to liberalism. Its claim was to push back positivism and formalism in favor of "national renewal" and to thereby eliminate the "rigid distinction between law and morals." Yet the fulfillment of this promise achieved entirely the opposite effect. The fascist form of post-liberal law destroyed the generality of law as a principle of form and abolished the independence of justice from the state.

The ideological vehicles of this process of dissolution were the principles of "national justice," the *Volksgemeinschaft* (community of the German *Volk*), and the "protection of the Aryan race." Under the camouflage of these terms, the law was transformed from a body of security and protection into a tool of terrorist elitist rule. The Nazi legal order replaced the equality of individuals with the "homogeneity of race" (*Gleichartigkeit der Rasse*), thereby abandoning the notion of people of different with the same abilities, rights, and duties."[4] Against the background of the openly emerging contradictions in the crisis of industrial society, it was easy for National Socialist ideologists to make a mockery of this notion. Two important principles were sacrificed to the supposed interests of the so-called *Volksgemeinschaft*: the protection of individuals and the equality of state citizens before the law. Hitler declared it a task of justice to protect "people of the same race" (*Artgleichen*) from "foreign races" (*Artfremden*). Special legislation was thus to be drawn up for all those classed as being outside the *Volksgemeinschaft*. This already tended to apply to political opponents and "asocials" but was developed and came to light in the course of anti-Jewish legislation and the laws for "foreign peoples" (*Fremdvölkische*).

Legislation and jurisdiction were subject to a rapid process of politicization and "de-formalization." In this way, the leadership and executive could free themselves of unwanted commitments and possibilities for appeal and instead apply "rapid-fire legislation" and absolute arbitrariness in "criminal prosecution." Laws were de facto no longer adopted by the Reichstag; in their place came decrees from the Führer (*Führererlasse*) and regulations with legal effect. As the majority of Germans wrongly imagined themselves to be unaffected by this perversion of the law, they stood by in silence while the rule of law was eroded.

## Background History

The German Jews had been systematically repressed since 1933. State departments, party authorities, and economic institutions worked in ever closer cooperation to exclude and drive Jews from their midst. The administrative thoroughness of the bureaucracy, the "idealism"[5] of the Party apparatus, and the profit motive of the economic associations all promoted the gradual deprivation of rights and expropriation.

Organized *Volkszorn* ("national rage"), boycotts, bullying, and laws and regulations were the tools used by the Nazi state apparatus, which appealed to broad sections of the population through clever anti-Semitic incitement. According to a 1937 report from the exiled German Social Democratic Party (Sopade), "[A]nti-Semitism encountered fierce opposition from the middle classes as well as the core of the organized workforce; however, the constant barrage of anti-Semitism did not fail to have an impact on the mass of indifferent workers. Even those who, before, did not even know what a Jew was now attributed all misfortune to them."[6]

Nazi economic bureaucracy always demanded clarity and legal order in its procedures. Anti-Jewish measures, too, had to take place systematically, following careful and complete plans and a legal framework. It was, for example, soon established that pogroms and street violence were costly and unpredictable and, moreover, damaged the German economy. "Such practices," notes historian Raul Hilberg, "aroused the most base instincts and also damaged Germany's image abroad."[7]

At the beginning of the regime, many Jews were convinced that they would face hard times but could not imagine that their situation would become intolerable. "They can condemn us to go hungry but not to starve," was a widespread view.[8] Along with senior Nazi bureaucrats, Jews, too, awaited the publication of regulations that would end the uncertainty and define their status. "One can live under any law" was often to be heard.

**Figure 5.1** Hitler Youth members build a snowman with a "Jewish star," 1938

The campaign for the systematic exclusion was launched in 1933 with the Law for the Restoration of the Professional Civil Service (*Gesetz zur Wiederherstellung des Berufsbeamtentums*), stipulating the dismissal of all Jews from public service. A range of subsequent regulations gradually excluded the Jews from all areas of public life—trade, healthcare, cultural life, jurisprudence, and education.

The infamous Nuremberg Laws of 1935 further defined, downgraded, and isolated German Jews; a new wave of dismissals ensued, accompanied by "Aryanization" of Jewish-owned businesses under threats and blackmail. According to Gruner, Nuremberg's "new 'racial' definition of the term 'Jew' had marked out the circle of victims more precisely than before and created the apparently legal basis for further persecution. . . . Trials of Jewish men and women from Berlin for having sexual relations with non-Jewish Germans were a daily occurrence in Berlin courts."[9]

Through the fall of 1937, cooperation between the Berlin municipal authorities and party departments often developed spontaneously. Hitler's highly anti-Semitic speech during the party conference in 1937 was to trigger yet a new wave of anti-Semitic activity, accompanied by increased standardization of anti-Jewish policy. From this point, Joseph Goebbels, Berlin's Gauleiter, pushed in particular for a rapid expulsion of the city's Jews. In spring 1938 the Berlin Gestapo presented him with a comprehensive concept for persecution commissioned by chief of police Count Wolf Heinrich Helldorf, "the essence of which becomes clear in the formulation that 'in the long term, a kind of ghetto' would be created."[10] Measures followed, blow after blow. The year 1938 marked the beginning of the end.

## The Tide of Regulations in 1938

The Law on the Legal Status of Jewish Religious Organizations (Gesetz über die Rechtsverhältnisse der jüdischen Kultusvereinigungen) came into effect on March 28. It stripped Germany's Jewish Communities (*Gemeinde*) of their protected status as "public bodies." From then on, they were treated merely as registered associations. There followed a whole range of tax burdens and discriminations, which resulted in a more rapid disintegration of the small Jewish Communities.

A severe blow was delivered with the Law on the Registration of Jewish Assets (Verordnung über die Anmeldung jüdischen Vermögens) of April 26, which placed the property of German Jews throughout the Reich under state control. Jews were forced to put their entire domestic and foreign assets under state control if the value exceeded RM 5,000. This registration of assets (*Vermögens registrierung*), combined with the third supplementary decree to the Reich Citizenship Law (Reichsbürgergesetz) of June 14—according to which Jewish commercial enterprises had to be registered and as such were to be marked out in public—laid the foundations for further measures.[11] They foreshadowed later expropriations which, together with enforcement orders, created the legal basis for the "Aryanization" of Jewish property. With respect to the events of that November, they represented what historian Wolfgang Scheffler has called a "pogrom guide."[12]

Jews were also ultimately excluded from being awarded public contracts. They were forbidden to participate in auctions. Subsequent changes in commercial law cut them off from many of the economic sectors that had, until then, remained available: peddling, credit enquiry agencies, marriage bureaus, and real estate.

The fourth supplementary decree to the Reich Citizenship Law stripped Jewish doctors of their license to practice, and there quickly followed a fifth barring Jewish lawyers from practice. Thus two more professional groups in which the Jews had been strongly represented were barred. Only a fraction of those originally licensed could now continue working—exclusively for Jews—but only under the title like "carer for the sick" (*Krankenbehandler*) and "advisor" (*Konsulent*).

Another decisive step toward defaming, isolating, and branding German Jews was the second supplementary decree on the Implementation of the Law on the Amendment of Family and First Names (Zweite Verordnung zur Durchführung des Gesetzes über die Änderung von Familien- und Vornamen), enacted on August 17. This law stipulated that Jewish women and men must assume the compulsory names of "Sara" and "Israel," respectively, if they did not bear first names that were included on an appended list of "recognized Jewish" first names (see chap. 1). It was henceforth a punishable offence to omit the name in any signature and in any dealings with the authorities or business.

By the end of the year 1938, all German Jews were obliged to apply for and carry an identity card. This card then had to be presented and the number stated in all applications and dealings with the authorities.

The Anschluss with Austria in March 1938 brought an additional 200,000 Jews under Nazi rule. In Austria, the lightening-fast process of catching up with anti-Semitic discrimination provoked, in Longerich's words, "a degree of hate and aggression that put the anti-Semitic waves of 1933 and 1935 in Germany in the shade."[13] Vienna's anti-Jewish campaigns—the Jew-baiting (*Judenhatz*), public humiliations such as the "cleaning operations" in which Jews were forced to clean the sidewalks, direct and violent attacks on Jewish property, and the first mass deportations—would radically influence "Jewish policy" throughout the German Reich.

The pressure on the Jews of Austria and Germany to emigrate intensified. This was above all the case after the mass arrests and deportations in the framework of the *Juni-Aktion*, a precursor to the more extensive expulsions during the November pogrom (see chap. 2).

## Legislation after the November Pogrom

As early as October 1938, senior representatives of the regime held meetings to discuss the exclusion of the German Jews from economic life. The pogrom of November 9–10 made it possible to thoroughly realize their intentions. On

November 12 Hermann Göring instructed, "the Jews must be taken out of the economy and into the register of debts, . . . things have to get going."[14] That day the head of Four-Year Plan announced the Regulation on the Exclusion of Jews from the German Economy (Verordnung zur Ausschaltung der Juden aus dem deutschen Wirtschaftslebens). Compulsory "Aryanization" and the closure of businesses, the final professional bans, and the looting of remaining assets rapidly led to financial and economic ruin. Furthermore, Jews were radically impoverished under the guise of new tax demands; from the beginning of 1939, all Jews were assigned to the highest tax bracket, irrespective of income and family status.

The Regulation on Street Restoration (Verordnung zur Wiederherstellung des Straßenbildes) stipulated that the Jews themselves must pay for the damages incurred during the November pogrom. A total of RM 1.127 billion was to be collected within the framework of the payments levied.

The introduction of "taxes on Jewish assets," an "emigration tax," and the Special Tax on Wealthy Jews (Sonderabgabe von reichen Juden) followed shortly. Senior Nazi representatives agreed that the public staging of the racial mania had not fallen short of its goal with regard to the increased pressure to emigrate, yet there was now a decisive call to stop what the Minister of the Interior Wilhelm Frick had called "foolishness, indeed madness (*Unsinn, ja Wahnsinn*)"—and to put the terror directly into the hands of the bureaucrats.

Regulations were now implemented to isolate the remaining Jews from the rest of the population in all areas of existence. This isolation meant that communication was cut off, that news was suppressed, that freedom of movement was restricted, and that supplies were scarce. As measures threatening their existence grew ever more repressive in following years, the intention to exterminate the Jews became increasingly apparent.

On November 15, 1938 regulations were introduced to thoroughly segregate the educational system, although "racial segregation" had been underway for a long time. Following the November pogrom, Jewish pupils were only able to attend private schools maintained by the Reichsvereinigung der Juden in Deutschland (the Reich Association of Jews in Germany).

Restrictions on where the Jews were allowed to go and at what times increasingly restricted their freedom of movement. They were forbidden to attend public cultural events of any kind. They were barred from theatres, museums, cinemas, and concert halls as well as libraries, swimming pools, sporting facilities, parks, and zoological gardens. Signs reading "FÜR JUDEN VERBOTEN" (No Jews Allowed) were increasingly common in hotels, restaurants, cafés, and on park benches; many of these were put up hastily, on individual initiative. Areas were, moreover, established where Jews simply could no longer go. In central Berlin, the *Judenbannbizirken* (area banned to Jews) stretched from Wilhelmstrasse to Vosstrasse and Unter den Linden.

From December 1938, Jews were forbidden to drive. Driver's licenses and vehicle registration documents had to be handed in. A pamphlet of the period gives an insight into the language of racism. The writer drew on the familiarity of the term *Volksgemeinschaft* to coin a new term, *Verkehrsgemeinschaft* (transportation community).

> With this defense against Jewish presumptuousness, moreover, the National Socialist state has expressed the German *Volk*'s healthy sense of justice. The German has for a long time seen it as a provocation and a danger to public life if Jews are seen at the wheel on German roads or even as beneficiaries of the streets that Adolf Hitler has built with the hands of German workers. . . . Jews no longer have any business behind the wheel of a vehicle in Germany! Instead of this, the industrious German will have more opportunity than before to discover the beauty of his homeland and to gain new strength for this with the motor car, the product of German intellect and German hands. The National Socialist state continues to strive for a community of all German people [*eine Gemeinschaft aller deutschen Menschen*] in road traffic, a community which willingly obeys the necessities and laws of traffic. Jews do not belong to this National Socialist transport community [*Verkehrsgemeinschaft*]![15]

Prior to stripping Jewish Berliners of their drivers' licenses in late 1938, the *Judenreferat* (office for Jewish affairs) at the police headquarters had, in the summer of that year, ordered an allocation of special registration plates for cars belonging to Jews, the better to mark out Jewish drivers in public: "Urgent, for immediate implementation! The *Judenreferat* of the Berlin police headquarters has drawn up an order according to which all Jewish vehicles shall be registered with new numbers. Numbers over 355,000 will be allocated. Up to now, the other numbers in Berlin went up to 310,000."[16]

As Edith Nomis recalls, she and her husband "had bought an Opel, which we could not drive for our pleasure for very long as it was assigned a car registration number over 355,000. We had to sell the car at well below its value because we were getting tickets almost every day."[17]

There followed provisions excluding Jews from the welfare and healthcare systems and deploying them in segregated labor columns. Jews were compelled to liquidate deposit stocks and shares and to sell gems, jewelry, and art items.

The regime's bureaucrats enforced total segregation down to the last detail. Jewish academics were forbidden to use libraries. As Hermann Simon points out in this volume, Jews were even prohibited from keeping carrier pigeons—by the First Decree on the Implementation of and Addition to the Law on Carrier Pigeons.

By the eve of World War II, German Jews were leading a truly miserable existence. Living in complete social isolation, they could only withdraw less than what was absolutely necessary from the frozen accounts into which they had been forced to deposit all their assets—and only then with the permission of the Gestapo. They were thus largely reliant on Jewish welfare institutions and the negligible income from Jewish labor deployment. With the exclusion of the Jewish minority from German society at the beginning of the war, the Nazis' "Jewish policy" came to a temporary halt. "After six years of Jewish policy," writes Longerich, "it was hardly opportune in terms of propaganda to continue to treat the remaining Jews as dangerous opponents."[18]

## Total War—Total Repression

The Nazi movement came into its own with the war. Wartime conditions made it possible to achieve the complete terrorist penetration of society according to racist paradigms. With the alleged material constraints of the war, they could justify the exclusion of Jews from essential resources and the comprehensive obligation for forced labor.

Each week saw a progressive tightening of the noose that the regime had put around the necks of Berlin's Jews. Private telephones were disconnected, and Jews were barred from using public telephones. The already dangerously inadequate supply of provisions for Berlin's Jewish population got worse when daily shopping hours were restricted to between 4 and 5 P.M.

There was a compulsive search for further pretexts to strip the Jewish Germans of their rights. The Nazi propaganda machine redoubled its efforts to brand Jews as spies and helpers for other countries. A nighttime curfew was imposed in 1939. In some areas it was even forbidden for Jews living on different floors of the same house to visit each other after this hour. They were forbidden to speak to members of the Wehrmacht and forbidden to enter railway stations without a permit.

In September 1939 the Reich Security Main Office (Reichssicherheitshauptamt [RSHA])—an organization formed through the merger of the Gestapo and the SD—issued a decree on the confiscation of Jewish-owned radios.

After the ban of Jewish newspapers and magazines, this made access to news even more difficult. Here, as on previous occasions, the Nazis also made efforts to link the expropriation with a particular humiliation and abuse of Jewish religious law; the day radios had to be handed over on Yom Kippur, the holiest day of the Jewish year.

Since it was forbidden for the radios to be submitted via a representative, each owner had to appear to the authorities in person, thus violating the sacred Jewish day of atonement. As eyewitness Leopold Marx recalls, "I had to take the equipment belonging to my family with my uncle on a hand-cart from Cannstatt through the park to Schlossplatz. Everyone was in a similar situation. It was eerie, but the very malice of this order strengthened inner opposition. This was just one cog in the large wheel that began with humiliation and for so many ended in the gas chambers. Anyone who experienced that day will never forget it."[19] To make sure that Jews would not buy new radios, retailers were instructed to register the names and addresses of all purchasers of radios.

Jews were forced to sell their valuables at laughable prices. They had to give up all jewelry, precious stones, pearls, and Jewish religious objects in their private possession. They could not own objects of stainless steel. Carpets and works of art such as paintings had to be handed in.

A further example of the interlinking of material interests and ideological principles in Nazi Germany was the campaign for the "De-Judification of Living Space" (*Entjudung des Wohnraums*). With the Laws on Jewish Tenancy initiated in April and March 1939, Jews had already been deprived of tenants' protection (*Mieterschutzrecht*). Using as justification the wartime housing shortage in Berlin, termination of Jewish tenancy was rapidly implemented. Jews were forced out of their homes and allocated inferior replacement apartments. Unlike the cities in the occupied territories in Eastern Europe, the allocation of housing in Berlin was not intended to form Jewish ghettos outright. Instead, the desired concentration of Jews was to be achieved "subtly," by "centralizing" the Jews in certain districts or streets. The scheme to establish "Jewish houses" was underway.

Jewish freedom of movement was further restricted by the requirement of state authorization for each time a family moved to a new address. The process of forcing the Jews out of their homes was "the first stage in the process which led from 'ghettoization' and deportation to extermination."[20] The lists that the authorities compiled in the course of such procedures later made it easier for them to deport the "centralized" Jews. These heightened controls, moreover, made it far more difficult for beleaguered Jews to go underground. Of the 160,564 Jews (defined according to the racist Nuremberg definition) who were

*My mother had lived in that house for twenty-eight years. Everyone knew her, but from the moment we had to wear the Jewish star they all cut us off. No one talked to us any more. We were simply invisible.*
ZWI COHN, 1999

*And grandfather—he was eventy-two at the time—had been sent to Sachsenhausen for six weeks in 1938. When he came back I could barely recognize him. . . . He had been such an imposing man. He had been awarded the Iron Cross first class in World War I. He was a first sergeant—and suddenly he came home like a wreck and the whole time he just said, "Horst, they have broken my legs."*
ZWI COHN, 1999

living in Berlin in June 1933, only 73,842 were left in June 1941. This group now became the target of extermination policy, and October 18, 1941, saw the first deportation of Berlin's Jewish men and women from Grunewald station to the Lódz ghetto.

## The Fate of Berlin Jews after 1941

In 1999 Zwi Cohn recalled his experience as a youngster during the period:

> From that time on, that is October/November 1941, to the day we were taken to the camp, I sat the whole time—two full years—completely alone in our apartment at Zehdenicker Strasse no. 28, on the fourth floor. . . . If there was a siren—and at the time there were many air-raid alerts in Berlin—we were not allowed, because we were Jews, to go down into the cellar [for shelter], neither during the day nor night. Mummy had to do forced labor from 1942, as did Papa from late 1942, when the home was closed. Mummy had to clean trams, and Papa had to work for the Gestapo, carrying the luggage of Jews who had been assembled to be taken to Oranienburger Strasse or [the assembly camp on] Grosse Hamburger Strasse. He simply had to take these people's luggage to the assembly point. As a result I was by myself at home the whole time. We had had to hand in all that we owned. We were not allowed to have a radio; we were not allowed to have a telephone; we were not allowed to buy newspapers. In other words, we were cut off from everything. Luckily, because all our neighbors turned up the volume on their radios, I could hear the news—"the commander in chief of the Wehrmacht announces . . ."—that is to say that, up until February 1943 and the fall of Stalingrad, the German Wehrmacht had been victorious the whole time. As a ten- to twelve-year-old child, all I ever heard was that the German Wehrmacht was marching and marching and conquering and conquering. I learned . . . that there had been raids in the streets of Berlin and that people had been taken away to the assembly camps. I was always deeply afraid that Mama and Papa would be captured somehow and that they would not come home again.

Zwi Cohn was even lonelier after the deportation of his grandparents, who had lived in the same building. "We did not know where they had been taken. From then on I was completely alone. And we knew that one fine day they would come and take us away [too]. Our fear was that we would not be sent away together. It was often the case that people were simply evacuated without the rest of the family even knowing what had happened to them and what was going on. Papa always said: 'Horst, we have to do everything possible so that we go together.' "[21]

*A key experience was also when I was standing in the subway—as Jews we were not allowed to sit—on the way home, then I suddenly felt a hand on my coat, in my coat pocket. And my instinctive reaction was to grab the hand, but then someone soothingly tapped my fingers. I no longer recall whether it was a man or a woman but the person got out at the next stop. And I soon got out too and then looked in my pocket and saw meat coupons. [That person] wanted to do a good turn, wanted to help. This happened, too.*

GISELA JAKOBIUS, 1999

With systematic cruelty, the remaining Jews were stripped of their livelihoods. Wartime rations for Jews were utterly inadequate. They were excluded from obtaining meat, milk, and tobacco. Soon they had to do without fish, white loaves, and rolls, butter, eggs, fruit, chocolate, tea, coffee, alcohol, cocoa powder, and jam as well. Infants only received half a liter of skim milk, and no special rations were granted for pregnant and breastfeeding women or the sick.

Jewish ration cards were marked with a "J" to ensure that these were only used in "Jewish shops." Those who went shopping—at the permitted times in the permitted shops—found that the minimal allocations were usually already sold out. These circumstances forced them to turn to the black market, thereby risking arrest and deportation. Jews were prohibited from purchasing soap, firewood and coal, shoes, and material for soles. In addition, Jews were not granted clothing rations, and they could not obtain any sewing materials. The Jewish Communities were obliged to set up clothing and shoe collection points. The "clothing stores" provided as best they could for Jews forced into poverty.

A state of total segregation now reigned in Nazi Germany. Jews were forbidden to enter parks, restaurants, forests, stations, and other prohibited areas. A decree from the Reich transport minister dated September 18, 1941, banned them from sleepers and restaurant cars on trains, pleasure boats, busses, waiting rooms, and pubs. They were prohibited from using public transport and ticket machines. Jews were not allowed to keep pets.

Regarding pets, the following announcement was carried in the May 15, 1942, edition of the *Jüdisches Nachrichtenblatt*:

> The Reich Association of Jews in Germany hereby announces the following instruction from its supervising authority:
>
> Keeping of pets
>
> Jews who are obliged to wear the distinguishing symbol [the yellow star] or people living with them are forbidden to keep pets, effective immediately.
>
> Jews with pets at the time of publication of this regulation are required to inform the Jewish Religious Organization [Jüdisches Kultusvereinigung] or district or administrative office of the Reich Association of Jews in Germany in writing by May 20, 1942 of the pets in their possession, under the subject heading "pets."
>
> People keeping pets will be given instructions on the handing in or collection of pets. . . .
>
> Violation of this regulation will result in police measures.

Jews were obliged to hand in any electrical appliances in their possession as well as bicycles, typewriters, and optical equipment. In this category, they had to hand in the following:

*We had already grown used to a lot of things. Jews were not allowed to own bicycles or to use electrical appliances. Jews were not allowed to use public telephones. But the regulation on woolen goods seemed so downright despicable and bloody-minded that we first wanted to see it in black and white. And it really was there in black and white. Everyone in the agricultural center went to their cupboards and picked out the woolens in best condition and gave all the other things away.*

1. Electrical goods
   Electrical appliances such as heaters, electric fires, sunray lamps, electric hot pads, cooking pots, vacuum cleaners, toasters, electric blankets, irons, hairdryers, electric watches, ventilators, kettles, ovens, etc.
   Record players and records
2. Typewriters, bicycles, and optical equipment,
   Typewriters, calculators, and copying equipment
   Bicycles and accessories
   Cameras, film, enlargers and projection equipment, light meters
   Telescopes

At the beginning of 1942, Jews had to submit all fur and wool clothing as well as skis, ski boots, and mountain boots. They received nothing in return. The employees of the Jewish Community were obliged to collect all "unnecessary" warm clothes and hand them over to the authorities. As Joel König recalls:

> The new regulation was no trifling matter. It meant that we had to wear our best and only warm clothes even when undertaking the dirtiest work. Yet the most annoying thing was that even as far more serious matters preoccupied us, we had to discuss how the regulation was to be interpreted. More and more members of our *chawerim* [Zionist comrades] were being deported. Who would be the next to be "resettled" with his parents? Are insoles made of rabbit skin to be regarded as fur clothing according to the regulation? Is it true that we can no longer send food ration cards to the deportees? And is one only allowed to keep one pair of woolen tights?
>
> Upon our return from work two days after handing in our wool and fur clothing, the girls found their room in a state of complete disarray. Two Gestapo officials from Rathenow had suddenly turned up in a car, allegedly to check that we had handed in the wool and fur items according to the regulation. They were rummaging through all the cupboards and had confiscated thirty girl's sweaters without much counting or calculating.[22]

The regulations were purposefully complicated and difficult to grasp, and many Jewish men and women were arrested and deported for infringing on them. "According to bureaucratic rules, the administrative death of the deportees was registered in files and record cards by an authority familiar with the process."[23] Deportees—who had to pay for their own deportation—were ultimately stripped of their German nationality. "In the camps the SS and industrial firms set about the final impoverishment and exploitation of the laborers. The series of robberies were completed after the death of the deportees with official theft from the bodies—gold teeth, hair, final possessions."[24]

*The regulation made my world fall apart. Up to then I had, to a certain extent, been able to live freely in Berlin. That meant that I could also sometimes go into a pub marked "Jews not welcome" or "No Jews". . . . That day was terrible. . . . It took real willpower to go out into the street at all wearing that thing. And it was bright yellow material, and 'Jew' was on it in large, Hebrew-like letters.*
EDITH DIETZ, 1999

*Many Jews tried to lessen the dangers associated with the markings by throwing them in the dirt to dull the vivid yellow color, or by removing the star in a building entrance outside their neighborhood. Some created a device that made the star removable.*
LISELOTTE CLEMENS, 1999

## The Yellow Star

*And then maybe one or two kilometers away, where we were no longer known, we went into a house and when no one was passing removed the hook, put the star in our pockets, went into the street as newly created Aryans, and went to the movies.*

ERNEST GUENTHER
FONTHEIM, 1999

*There are said to be cases when a Gestapo man went up to a Jew wearing a star and tried to reach under the star with his finger to see if it was properly sewn on.*

ERNEST GUENTHER
FONTHEIM, 1999

*Another result of this was that a white Jewish star had to be put up on our door, too, bearing the name of the Jewish members of this family. So 'Lucie Sara Gessner, Horst Israel Gessner' went up on the door so that everyone knew that two Jews were living there.*

HORST GESSNER,
1999

Leading Nazis had long pushed for the introduction of a distinguishing mark for Jews. This return to a medieval practice was born of a paranoid anti-Semitic logic, according to which the population had to be divided into *Volk* and *Volksfeinde* (enemies of the German people)—into *Artgleiche* and *Artfremde*. In the framework of modern, racial anti-Semitism the marking out of the "pest to the people" (*Volksschädling*) who sought to creep "unrecognized" into the "body of the people" (*Volkskörper*) now became the precursor and preparation for the physical extermination of the Jews.

Throughout the 1930s Hitler had often been presented with proposals and concrete drafts for introducing a Jewish symbol but had delayed approving such a measure. Marking out the Jews had lower priority than implementing other anti-Jewish policy measures. These included emigration, "Aryanization," ghettoization, and exploitation through forced labor. Furthermore, various modes of marking out Jews—the identity cards and ration cards marked with a "J," for example—were already part of particular bureaucratic processes. And there were orders, such as the one issued by the head of the Party Chancellery regarding the provision of soap and shaving soap, that were intended not only to degrade but "to make male Jews recognizable on account of their beards"[25] Another absurd instance was a decree from the Reich Minister of the Economy regarding scholarly citations. "Jews may only be cited in doctoral dissertations if this is unavoidable for academic reasons; they must then be particularly marked out as Jews. German and Jewish authors should be separated in the bibliography."[26]

The introduction of the "Jewish star" (*Judenstern*) coincided with the start of administrative preparations for deportation and extermination. The Reich Ministry for the Interior and the Reich Security Main Office agreed on the text for the regulation. It was published in the *Jüdisches Nachrichtenblatt* on September 12, 1941:

Police Regulation on Marking of Jews

§ 1

Jews who have reached the age of six are forbidden to go out in public without wearing the Jewish Star.

The Jewish Star is a six-pointed star, drawn in black lines, made of yellow fabric the size of the palm of one's hand and with the word "*Jude*" superimposed on it in black. It must be visibly displayed on the left side of the chest, firmly sewn to the piece of clothing.

§ 2

*Jews are forbidden:*

**Figure 5.2**
Car with a "Jewish"
license plate

To leave the vicinity of their community of residence without carrying written permission from the local police,
To wear medals, decorations or other insignias.

The restrictions to the freedom of movement that went hand in hand with marking the Jews out in public thereby symbolized a qualitative change in anti-Jewish policy: the transition to the process of extermination. A supplementary decree from the Reich Security Main Office followed in the spring of 1942: "From April 14, 1942, the apartments of Jews must be specially marked with a Jewish Star in black print on white paper, which corresponds in style and size to the one to be worn on clothing and is to be put up on the front door next to the nameplate."[27]

The regulation on wearing the yellow star went into effect on September 19, 1941. Within the space of a few days, thousands of stars had been produced by the firm of Geitel & Co.—"Berlin's largest flag printer," as it was listed in the directory—at Wallstrasse 16 in Berlin's Mitte district. This firm had become a large enterprise, meeting the huge demand for Nazi flags, pennants, insignias, and window hangings. In 1989, Rolf Geitel, the son of the factory's former manager, and his wife Marianne recalled the firm's past and reflected on their family's involvement in the Nazi extermination policy. Marianne Geitel:

I have since read fascinating books about the exclusion of the Jews—which began back in 1933–34—for example, about everyday life under National Socialism, which assumed grotesque proportions. It began with racial laws and ended with

*It is completely
absurd and laugh-
able that a regime
has to prove itself
by prohibiting Jews
from having irons!
And the population
looked on for eight
or ten years as the
Jews were unable
to shop in certain
shops or to be seen
on the streets during
the day—and as
they were taken
away.*

MARIANNE GEITEL,
1989

**Figure 5.3** Publication of the order for Jews to wear a distinguishing symbol in the *Jüdsiches Nachrichtenblatt*, January 23, 1942

Jews not being allowed to own irons. . . . I don't know what grandfather Geitel thought about it when he printed the Jewish stars. Perhaps one gets used to injustice to such an extent that, in 1941, one said, "Okay, that's an organizational, bureaucratic terror measure which has been preceded by many other, worse ones." It was just one more humiliation in a series of innumerable abuses, which at the time was not considered to be any worse than the other measures that had robbed the Jews of their rights, but which stands out today. We judge things differently today and so the horror was also greater when we learned about the Jewish star.

To this Rolf Geitel added: "But perhaps it was also an order! The swastika flags and the Jewish star have to be seen according to totally different criteria. The star was not a business deal but a secret commando matter to be carried out in the space of three weeks. And it seems quite natural to me that within three

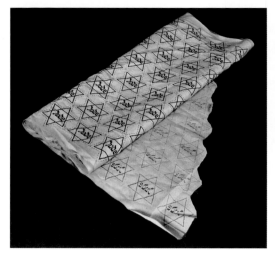
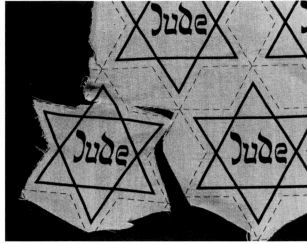

Figure 5.4
Cloth printed with
"Jewish stars"

weeks, between an order from the Führer and delivery in Vienna—which has been documented!—there was no bid to see who was the cheapest or the most expensive. Someone came and said, 'Start today, you have three weeks—and not a word! You'll get ten thousand. . . . We have calculated how much material is needed, now get printing!' And with this the matter was settled."[28]

A 1988 report by the historian Konrad Kwiet in the weekly magazine *Spiegel* described things somewhat differently. "The Berlin flag factory Geitel & Co. had its bid accepted to produce the Jewish stars. . . . Almost a million stars were delivered, printed on long rolls of cloth and packed into heavy bales. The firm made RM 30,000 from the contract, which followed the usual terms of business and offered a 2 percent discount in the event of 'payment within five days.' . . . The symbols were sold to the (Jewish) organizations at the cost price of three pfennigs [each]. The organizations had to charge ten pfennigs for the stars to cover the administrative costs associated with distribution."[29]

One final example of the Gestapo's "diabolical methods" can be seen in an instance of blackmailing the Reichsvereinigung. The Jewish representatives were forced to distribute the yellow stars punctually. Any opposition on the part of employees to these regulations or attempts to bypass them was punished with immediate deportation.

Ultimately, the introduction of the symbols wrenched the Jews from any anonymity they had previously enjoyed in the big city, to which many had fled. The typeface printed on the star parodied Hebrew script—another humiliating "subtlety" with which the National Socialist bureaucrats peppered their regulations. Violations against the regulation were frequently punished with arrest and

*We had to pick up the star somewhere. . . . They had to be cut out nicely, but were made from really cheap fabric that began to fray. We were not allowed to stitch them up. But like good citizens we stitched and lined and even put press-studs on them.*

LISELOTTE
CLEMENS, 1999

deportation. There were even cases of spontaneous murder. It was impossible to predict whether one was in more danger wearing the star or taking it off and thereby breaking the law. Wearing the star in public always brought the risk of being stopped and having one's name and address taken down by the police for alleged minor violations. This often led to being put on the deportation list.

This permanent humiliation and danger spread fear and desperation among Berlin's Jewish men and women. Many no longer left their homes. Indeed, many chose to commit suicide in spite of Jewish law. The openly violent anti-Semitism also indirectly struck back at the observers. "Looking at how the wearers of the star were treated, the population could see what happened to someone who was not agreeable to the regime."[30]

The introduction of the yellow star did not, however, entirely produce the effect the Nazis had desired. Although there were no open acts of protest in Germany, there are reports of individual expressions of solidarity with the victims (in addition to attacks and abuse from passers-by). People wearing yellow stars were sometimes greeted very warmly by strangers on the street. Sometimes people expressed regret or sympathy as they went past: "Your badge is our shame" (*Euer Fleck is unsere Schande*). Sometimes a German made a show of getting up on public transportation to offer his seat to someone marked out as *Volksfeind*. "Again and again fellow passengers—particularly the workers on the early trains—were outraged that we were not allowed to sit. They always wanted to tempt us: 'Come on, little shooting star (*Sternschnuppeken*), have a seat!'" Elisabeth Freund passed on the following anecdote. A mother saw that her little girl was sitting next to a Jew. "Lieschen," she said, "go and sit somewhere else, you don't have to sit next to a Jew." Then a worker stood up and said, "And I don't have to sit next to Lieschen." Ursula von Kardorf recalls another typical exchange, conducted in thick *Berlinisch* dialect: "*Setz dir hin olle Sternschnuppe* (Have a seat, my old shooting star)," said a Berlin worker. When a party comrade complained, he retorted, "*Üba meene Arsch verfüje ick aleene* (Where I put my ass is my business)."[31]

It was particularly hard on Jewish children, who had to wear a star from the age of six. They were persecuted and beaten in the streets by non-Jewish children.

Open solidarity and aggression were the two extremes of the reactions shown by Berlin's non-Jewish residents. Most accepted the fall into barbarism without a word.

*We were less like children from day to day. And then in 1941 we had to wear the star. . . . We were then also no longer allowed to travel by train. . . . Anyone with a journey up to one hour had to go on foot.*
EVA FRANK-KUNSTMANN, 1999

*During the time that we were still allowed to travel by train, . . . we were thrown out of the train . . . and then had to wait for the next one, because they did not want to have Jewish children in the train. Those were such cases . . . no matter where it was, at school or on the street—we were fair game, that's for sure.*
EVA FRANK-KUNSTMANN, 1999

1 Peter Longerich, *Politik der Vernichtung. Eine Gesamtdarstellung der nationalsozialistischen Judenverfolgung* (Munich, 1998), p. 156.

2 Konrad Kwiet, "Nach dem Pogrom. Stufen der Ausgrenzung," in *Die Juden in Deutschland, 1933–1945*, ed. Wolfgang Benz (Munich, 1988), p. 546.

3 Wolf Gruner, *Judenverfolgung in Berlin, 1933–1945. Eine Chronologie der Behördenmaßnahmen in der Reichshauptstadt* (Berlin, 1996), p. 8.

4 Otto Kirchheimer, "Die Rechtsordnung im Nationalsozialismus," in *Wirtschaft, Recht und Staat im Nationalsozialismus. Analysen des Instituts für Sozialforschung, 1939–1942*, ed. Helmut Dubiel and Alfons Söllner (Frankfurt am Main, 1981), p. 315.

5 Raul Hilberg, *Die Vernichtung der europäischen Juden*, 3 vols. (Berlin, 1982), vol. 1, p. 60.

6 Sopade report, November 1937. Cited in Longerich, *Politik der Vernichtung*, p. 158.

7 Hilberg, *Die Vernichtung*, vol. 1, p. 52.

8 Ibid., p. 54.

9 Gruner, *Judenverfolgung*, p. 9.

10 Ibid., p. 10.

11 Wolfgang Scheffler, *Judenverfolgung im Dritten Reich* (Berlin, 1964), p. 28.

12 Ibid.

13 Longerich, *Politik der Vernichtung*, p. 162.

14 Ibid., p. 208.

15 Kwiet, *Nach dem Pogrom*, p. 597.

16 Telex from the senior section of the East Berlin Security Service dated August 23, 1938, Yad Vashem Archive, Jerusalem, 051/OSOBl, no. 88, sheet 47. I would like to thank Wolf Gruner for his kindness in providing this document.

17 Edith Nomis in the files of the memorial book project *Berliner Opfer des Nationalsozialismus* [Berlin Victims of National Socialism], Centrum Judaicum Archive (CJA), Berlin, 5C2/no. 29, p. 2.

18 Longerich, *Politik der Vernichtung*, p. 226.

19 Leopold Marx. Quoted in Kwiet, "Nach dem Pogrom," p. 567.

20 Kwiet, "Nach dem Pogrom," p. 632.

21 Audio interview with Zwi Cohn conducted by Alexandra von Pfuhlstein in Israel, CJA.

22 Joel König quoted in Kwiet, "Nach dem Pogrom," p. 568.

23 Kwiet, "Nach dem Pogrom," p. 569.

24 Ibid.

25 Cited in Joseph Walk, editor, *Das Sonderrecht für die Juden im NS—Staat. Eine Sammlung der gesetzlichen Maßnahmen und Richtlinien. Inhalt und Bedeutung* (Heidelberg, 1996), p. 343.

26 Cited in Bruno Blau, *Das Ausnahmerecht für die Juden in Deutschland, 1933–1945* (Dusseldorf, 1954), p. 80.

27 Cited in Walk, *Das Sonderrecht*, p. 369.

28 Henry Ries, *Abschied meiner Generation* (Berlin, 1992), pp. 189–90.

29 Konrad Kwiet, "'Schrei was du kannst.' Der Weg in den Holocaust. Die Brandmarkung durch den Judenstern," in *Der Spiegel* 34 (1988): 150.

30 Kwiet, "Nach dem Pogrom," p. 621.

31 Ibid.

# Chapter Six

## The *Jüdisches Nachrichtenblatt,* 1938–43

CLEMENS MAIER

The pogrom of November 1938 marked the end of over one hundred years of the German Jewish press. Between November 8 and 12, 1938, all Jewish newspapers and magazines were banned, including those published by the Jewish Communities and the Reichsvertretung der Juden in Deutschland (Reich Representation of Jews in Germany). This ban was supposed to be temporary, but it was never lifted.

Just a few days after the pogrom some of the most respected editors of the two main Jewish newspapers—the *C. V. Zeitung* produced by the Central Association of German Citizens of Jewish Faith and the *Jüdische Rundschau*—were summoned to the Propaganda Ministry.[1] They were informed by the authorities that they had a few days to set up a new paper—the *Jüdisches Nachrichtenblatt* (Jewish Newspaper)—and that they had at their disposal the premises and finances of the now defunct newspapers. The new publication was permitted only for "circulation in the Jewish-populated areas of the Reich territory"[2] and was to serve as an official source of information for the Jewish minority—a minority being progressively deprived of its rights.

The new source of information was subject to the strictest Nazi censorship. Erich Liepmann, a former employee of the *Jüdische Rundschau*,[3] writes in his memoirs that, after the pogrom of November 9, 1938, and the ban of all Jewish newspapers, Joseph Goebbels personally summoned him to the Propaganda Ministry and gave him the "task" of setting up the *Jüdisches Nachrichtenblatt*. "An informational paper must be published within two days," Goebbels apparently yelled. "Each issue will be submitted to me. Woe to you if even one article is published without my having seen it. That's it!"[4] Although it is not clear whether Goebbels really was the person "commissioning" the task, the threat was taken seriously, and the command obeyed; all articles were duly presented in advance.

**Figure 6.1** Leo Kreindler, editor-in-chief of the *Jüdsiches Nachrichtenblatt*

The paper's initial debut was a failure. The first edition, planned for November 22, 1938, did not pass Nazi censors and only appeared a day later in amended form. From then on, Leonhard (Leo) Kreindler served as editor-in-chief and determined the paper's form and content until his death in November 1942. As editor and author of lead articles, Kreindler's voice was clearly heard in subsequent years.

For the most part, however, the Jewish staff had little control over content. Each edition was rigorously censored by the Propaganda Ministry before going to press, and the editors had to go there several times a week—often at short notice—to receive instructions. Sometimes, too, the paper's publisher—the Kulturbund (Jewish Cultural Organization)—or the Reichsvereinigung der Juden in Deutschland (Reich Association of Jews in Germany) received instructions by telephone. Orders had to be carried out as quickly as possible and passed on to Leo Kreindler just as quickly. Indeed, some of the editions were only approved by the ministry one day before publication.[5]

The censor's control of the paper stretched not only to editorial content, which was obliged to inform readers of the anti-Jewish regulations and laws. Advertisements and classifieds, too, were subject to the strictest censorship for everything from layout to content. Thus, published editions sometimes included entire blank columns. For example, it was initially forbidden to publish family notices; after the November pogrom's violence Propaganda Minister Goebbels's wanted to avoid a suspicious preponderance of obituaries listing dates close to one another.[6]

Even the smallest details of the text used in the advertisements were subject to censorship. Two years after Jewish lawyers and doctors had been stripped of their professional titles in 1938 and were forced to call themselves "*Konsulenten*" (advisors) and "*Behandler*" (caretaker), there were discussions in the Propaganda Ministry as to whether the titles *Justizrat* (legal advisor) and *Sanitätsrat* (health advisor) could appear in the classifieds. In this case, the decision was affirmative; the ministry classed the terms as informal rather than official titles.[7]

Any scope for freedom of expression depended on the authors' and editors' ability to convey news "between the lines," touching on themes that would mean more to Jewish readers than to the censoring authorities. Whatever the merits of such thought-provoking articles, however, they were of little practical help to the readers.

**Jüdisches NACHRICHTENBLATT**

Alle Zuschriften sind zu richten an: „Jüdisches Nachrichtenblatt", Berlin N 4, Oranienburger Str. 40/41 / Redakt.: Berlin N 4, Oranienburger Str. 40/41, Tel.: 42 55 21 / Bezugsgeld einschl. Bestellgeld je Monat RM 0,76, je Vierteljahr RM 2,28 / Anzeigenschluß jeweils Montag 17 Uhr / Für die Rücksendung unverlangt eingesandter Manuskripte kann keine Gewähr übernommen werden

Nr. 33    Berlin, Freitag, den 14. August 1942    Jahrgang 1942

## Aus den Gemeinden

**BERLIN:**

Gottesdienste in den Gemeinde-Synagogen in der Zeit vom 14. bis 21. August 1942

Freitag, 14. August, 19.30 Uhr: Alte Synagoge. — 19.15 Uhr: Münchener Str. 37. — 19.50 Uhr: Oranienburger Str. 31 (kleiner Betraum). — 19.30 Uhr: Betsaal Thielschufer 10/16; Schönhauser Allee 162. — 19 Uhr: Saal Oranienburger Str. 29; Weißensee, Lothringenstr. 22.

Sonnabend, 15. August, 8.30 Uhr, Alte Synagoge. — 9 Uhr: Münchener Str. 37. — 8 Uhr: Oranienburger Str. 31 (kleiner Betraum). — 9 Uhr: Betsaal Thielschufer 10/16; Schönhauser Allee 162. — 10 Uhr: Saal Oranienburger Str. 29; Weißensee, Lothringenstr. 22.

Mincha-Gottesdienste mit Tora-Vorlesung und Ansprache.

18 Uhr: Alte Synagoge; Schönhauser Allee 162 (Alexander).

Außerdem Mincha: Sonnabend, 15. August, 19.15 Uhr: Münchener Str. 37. — 17 Uhr: Thielschufer 10/16. — 18 Uhr: Oranienburger Straße 31 (kleiner Betraum).

Gottesdienst an den Werktagen. Morgens 7.30 Uhr: Alte Synagoge; Thielschufer 10/16; Schönhauser Allee 162. — 7 Uhr: Münchener Straße 37. — 6.30 Uhr: Oranienburger Str. 31. — 7.15 Uhr: Jagowstr. 38.

Abends 19.30 Uhr: Alte Synagoge; Thielschufer 10/16; Schönhauser Allee 162; Jagowstraße. [...] Uhr: Münchener Str. 37 [...]

# Aus den Verordnungen

**Haushaltsbesteuerung mit Bezug auf die Ehegatten**

Oberregierungsrat Dr. Oermann behandelt in einem Aufsatz in der Deutschen Steuer-Zeitung vom 1. August 1942 (S. 349 ff.) die Haushaltsbesteuerung mit Bezug auf die Ehegatten. Unter Ziffer 4 des Aufsatzes wird zur Ausscheidung der Einkünfte der Ehefrau aus nicht selbständiger Arbeit in einem dem Ehemann fremden Betrieb folgendes ausgeführt: § 19 Abs. 1 der Einkommensteuer-Durchführungsverordnung 1941, der diese Ausscheidung anordnet, bezweckt, den Arbeitseinsatz der Ehefrau während des gegenwärtigen Krieges auch steuerlich zu fördern. Die Vorschrift findet demgemäß auch auf Juden und auf Polen Anwendung.

**Schönheitsreparaturen im Kriege**

Zur Frage der Durchführung von Schönheitsreparaturen im Kriege beim Wohnungswechsel des instandsetzungspflichtigen Mieters hat der Reichsminister der Justiz im Einvernehmen mit dem Reichsarbeitsminister der Presse eine Verlautbarung zur Veröffentlichung zugeleitet (Deutsche Justiz 1942 Nr. 31/32 S. 515). Darin heißt es:

Die Kriegsverhältnisse bringen es mit sich, daß Schönheitsreparaturen in Wohnungen nicht oder nur in sehr beschränktem Umfang möglich sind. Hierbei handelt es sich aber um eine [...] vorübergehende Unmöglichkeit. [...]

gegenüber seinem bisherigen Vermieter als befreit betrachten. Der Anspruch auf künftige Ausführung der Schönheitsreparaturen bleibt vielmehr bestehen und damit auch das Recht des Vermieters, wegen dieses Anspruchs ein Pfandrecht an den eingebrachten Sachen des Mieters auszuüben. Die Geltendmachung dieses Anspruchs kann der ausziehende Mieter durch Sicherheitsleistung abwenden.

Die Ausübung des Pfandrechts oder später des Anspruchs auf Nachholung der Schönheitsreparaturen kann leicht zu Streitigkeiten führen. Es wird sich daher empfehlen, im Falle eines Wohnungswechsels eine gütliche Verständigung wegen der nicht ausführbar gewesenen Schönheitsreparaturen herbeizuführen. Hierfür dürfte der geeignetste Weg sein, daß sich der ausziehende Mieter mit dem Vermieter über die Zahlung eines angemessenen Betrages zur Abgeltung seiner Instandsetzungspflicht einigt.

**Beschwerdebegründung in Steuersachen**

Der Reichsminister der Finanzen hat am 24. Juli 1942 (Reichssteuerblatt vom 1. 8. 1942 Nr. 69 S. 801) eine Verordnung zur Durchführung des § 304 der Reichsabgabenordnung erlassen. Danach muß bei Beschwerden in Steuersachen der Beschwerdeführer die Beschwerde schriftlich begründen. Die Begründung geschieht, wenn sie nicht bereits in der Beschwerdeschrift enthalten ist, durch Ein-

rungen des Bescheides beantragt werden (Beschwerdeanträge); 2. die Beschwerdegründe. Diese sind im einzelnen anzugeben; 3. wenn der Beschwerdeführer zur Rechtfertigung der Beschwerde neue Tatsachen oder neue Beweismittel vorbringt: die bestimmte Bezeichnung der neuen Tatsachen oder der neuen Beweismittel. Die Behörde, die über die Beschwerde entscheidet, hat zu prüfen, ob der Beschwerdeführer die Beschwerde formgerecht und fristgerecht begründet hat. Ist das nicht der Fall, so ist die Beschwerde als unzulässig zu verwerfen.

**Veranlagung von Sozialrentnern mit Einkünften aus nicht selbständiger Arbeit aus einem gegenwärtigen Dienstverhältnis**

Regierungsrat Dr. Steinweg vom Reichsfinanzministerium Berlin erörtert in einem Aufsatz in der Deutschen Steuer-Zeitung vom 1. 8. 1942 (S. 365 ff.) Zweifelsfragen zu den Einkünften aus Kapitalvermögen, aus Vermietung und Verpachtung und zu den sonstigen Einkünften. Bei den sonstigen Einkünften wird unter Ziffer 13 des Aufsatzes die Veranlagung von Sozialrentnern mit Einkünften aus nicht selbständiger Arbeit aus einem gegenwärtigen Dienstverhältnis behandelt.

Nach einem Erlaß des Reichsministers der Finanzen vom 14. Mai 1942 (Reichssteuerblatt 1942 S. 507) erhalten Sozialrentner, die Einkünfte aus nicht selbständiger Arbeit aus [...]

**Figure 6.2** Front page, August 14, 1942. Included under the rubric "From the Regulations" are very specific legal details pertaining to "Household Taxes on [working] Marriage Partners," "Beautification Repairs [to rented residences] in Wartime"—which details problems encountered by renters changing residence, especially the difficulty of making required repairs before moving out and of recovering one's deposit, "Grounds for Compliant in Tax Matters," and the "Tax Assessment of Social Welfare Recipients (*Sozialrentner*) with Non-independent Income from Current Employment."

THE GENERAL GERMAN DAILIES, for their part, offered little information about—and even less public comment on—the many Nazi laws affecting the Jews. Most information about the anti-Jewish measures, regulations, and instructions was thus only available in the *Nachrichtenblatt*, which explained them and detailed their consequences. The paper also passed on information about judicial decisions to its Jewish readers. The *Nachrichtenblatt* was hugely important to regime and readers alike. Without adequate up-to-date information on the ever-changing landscape of repressive measures, people were liable to breach them out of ignorance, and in doing so, to put their survival at risk.

It is remarkably difficult to establish the outlines of the Propaganda Ministry's overall publication policy toward the newspaper. Although some 450 laws, regulations, orders, decrees and circulars, implementation provisions, and legal judgments in precedent cases were published in the *Nachrichtenblatt,* there are surprising gaps and inconsistencies.[8] Certain extremely repressive measures are not mentioned at all. For example, the *Nachrichtenblatt* contains no notice of the ban on Jews owning radios that was implemented on September 20, 1939. Nor is mention made of the 8 P.M. curfew implemented at the same time. When highly restrictive shopping hours for Jews were imposed in 1940, that regulation went unpublished as well. In the issue of June 26, 1942, however, the Reichsvereinigung printed a warning that these very rules had to be observed. The edition of December 6, 1938, draws attention to the introduction of *Judenbannbezirken*—areas and streets from which Jews were banned or were only allowed to enter in exceptional cases—while the order's extension by the Gestapo in May 1942 was never mentioned. A letter to the Berlin Gestapo in the Berlin Jewish Community correspondence for this month sheds some light on the matter; in it the Community confirms that it was expected to spread information among Berlin's Jews "by word of mouth in a suitable fashion" regarding which streets could no longer be entered. No "written announcement" was to be made.[9]

If, for reasons that are hard to understand today, the *Nachrichtenblatt* failed to publish a regulation, one may assume that other means of transmitting information were adopted. The Gestapo and the Propaganda Ministry controlled such publications according to their own specific criteria and had at their disposal other means of propagating information as well. These included circulars issued by the Reichsvereinigung to the Communities and local groups. From here the news would then be passed on by word of mouth. It was often the case, however, that regulations were made public both through circulars and via the *Nachrichtenblatt.*

One can see the Gestapo's motives at work in the case of one particular Nazi order—the ban on emigration—which went unpublished in the *Nachrichtenblatt.* Passed October 23, 1941, the measure was of tremendous importance to Jews since it brought a complete halt to all emigration (already severely restricted as a result of the war). It can be assumed that the Gestapo refrained from publicizing the law in order to avoid stirring up further unrest or panic among those still living in the country. Indeed, after the law was passed, the next edition of the paper actually included two articles about emigration.

THE *NACHRICHTENBLATT* DID MORE than merely list anti-Jewish regulations. It also served as the information engine for the Jewish Communities. The circulation was initially very high. A working report presented by the publisher to the Propaganda Ministry in July 1939 mentions 62,000 copies.[10] Subscribers to the now-defunct Jewish newspapers received the *Nachrichtenblatt* more or less by default[11]—at a cost, of course. It was, moreover, the only newspaper in which the Jews were still allowed to place advertisements and which reported on the circumstances of other Jewish Communities in Germany. The number of subscribers would fall rapidly, a downward spiral that is indicated by the paper's own calls for subscribers. Up to 1941, the drop in subscriptions could be explained by extensive emigration. In later years, it indicated both the increasing pauperization of Germany's remaining Jews (each copy of the *Nachrichtenblatt* tended to circulate among multiple readers) and the sad reality of deportation.

Based on the success of the Berlin-based *Nachrichtenblatt*, the regime soon set up corresponding publications in the two other large Jewish Communities within the sphere German influence: Vienna and Prague. The Viennese edition consisted of the first four pages of the Berlin edition,[12] with the addition of a *Wiener Mantel* (Viennese supplement) containing specific regulations and main themes.[13] Its editor-in-chief received instructions on content from the Reichsvereinigung. His direct supervisor, the head of the Kulturbund's Vienna branch, was sometimes summoned to Berlin by the Propaganda Ministry to receive instructions in person. He had served as a member of the Kulturbund's board on the order of the Propaganda Ministry since February 1939. The Viennese edition was not, however, censored by the Propaganda Ministry in Berlin but at the SS Security Service (SD) by Adolf Eichmann himself.[14]

Although there were relatively close links between the Berlin and Viennese editions, this was not the case for the bilingual Prague *Nachrichtenblatt*.

THE *NACHRICHTENBLATT'S* FORMAT WAS subject to constant change with respect to the header and typeface used. Regular columns also changed, with some added and others removed. Others changed their names, even as content remained the same. Hence, news about government regulations was published variously under the headings "Reich Association Announcements" (*Mitteilungen der Reichsvereinigung*), "From the Regulations" (*Aus den Verordnungen*), and "From Law and the Economy" (*Aus Recht und Wirtschaft*), as well as under the titles of the regulations themselves.

In its first three years, the *Nachrichtenblatt*, which was published on Tuesdays and Fridays, had between four and sixteen pages per edition and was thereby much more extensive than it was in later years (1941–43). From January 21, 1941, the paper eliminated its Tuesday edition, and by June 1943 the weekly edition consisted of a single page.

The paper's initial size was connected to the political framework of Jewish existence in the German Reich between 1938 and 1941. Although a good deal of emigration had taken place in the years prior to this, a large number of Jews remained within Reich territory. During this period, there was still some attention given to the cultural life and the cultural needs of the German Jews. These were officially supervised by the Jüdische Kulturbund in Deutschland e.V. (Registered Jewish Culture Organization), the *Nachrichtenblatt*'s official publisher until 1941. This organization, originally founded on the initiative of Jewish artists and the Communities, was later centralized by the Nazis and placed under the control of the Propaganda Ministry.

Because of this, the newspaper in these years offers a snapshot of the cultural life of German Jews, revealing the conditions at work in the Jewish "cultural ghetto." Reviews and programs of the Jewish Kulturbund initially formed a large part of the paper's editorial content. This ended when the Jewish Kulturbund was disbanded in September 1941. A month later, Jewish emigration from the Reich would come to a halt as well with the aforementioned ban. The *Nachrichtenblatt* thus lost another of its main themes: reporting on emigration.

SINCE ITS INCEPTION, the *Nachrichtenblatt* had served as a crucial source of information with regard to most of the issues associated with forced emigration. According to the Kulturbund's working report of July 1939, one of the paper's goals was to promote emigration, informing its readers of emigration possibilities and the respective laws in force. It carried information on potential immigration destinations and kept up with their corresponding legal regulations. The extensive classifieds section, moreover, gave details on retraining programs, passage, and tickets, among other things. Priority was given to information and announcements from the Reichsvereinigung and the Palestine Office—the emigration organization of the Jewish Agency in Palestine (see chap. 7).[15] The Propaganda Ministry had stipulated this editorial policy down to the last detail. A January 1939 letter to Eichmann from the Propaganda Ministry department responsible for overseeing the Kulturbund explicitly states that the *Nachrichtenblatt* should be primarily an instrument of expulsion.[16]

By mid-1940, it must have been crystal clear to the editorial staff and Kulturbund employees that the *Nachrichtenblatt* was designed, above all, to serve the purposes of the Propaganda Ministry. Minutes taken at meetings between Jewish staff and Propaganda Ministry representatives reveal the degree to which the ministry was, from the spring of 1940 on, critical of the paper. In Eichmann's opinion, the paper failed to fulfill its task of encouraging emigration. The Kul-

# Jüdisches NACHRICHTENBLATT

**Preis 15 Rpf.**

Verlag: Jüdischer Kulturbund in Deutschland e. V., Abteilung Verlag, Berlin W 15, Meinekestr. 10 / Zweigstelle Wien: Wien I, Marc-Aurel-Straße 5 / Erscheint zweimal wöchentlich. Redaktion für die Ausgabe Berlin: Berlin W 15, Meinekestraße 10 (Telefon 91 90 31); für die Ausgabe Wien: Wien I, Marc-Aurel-Straße 5 (Telefon U 22 2 11) / Einsendungen an die Redaktion, Berlin W 15, Meinekestraße 10 / In Fällen höherer Gewalt besteht kein Anspruch auf Nachlieferung oder Erstattung bereits gezahlter Bezugsgebühren / Bezugsgeld einschließlich Bestellgeld je Monat RM. 1,12, je Vierteljahr RM. 3,36 (einschl. Postzeitungsgebühr von 10 Rpf. je Monat); bei Abholung RM. 1,— bzw. RM 3.— / Postscheck-Konto: Berlin Nr. 173 605 Jüdischer Kulturbund

| Nummer 13 | Dienstag, den 13. Februar 1940 | Jahrgang 1940 |
|---|---|---|

## Leben in Brasilien  *Mitteilungen der Reichsvereinigung*

Mit diesem dem Material des Hilfs-vereins entnommenen Aufsatz setzen wir die Darstellung der wirtschaftlichen Voraussetzungen und des jüdischen Lebens in südamerikanischen Ländern fort (Red.).

Brasilien ist immer noch in erster Reihe ein Agrarland. Die fortschreitende Industrialisierung dieses Landes darf nicht darüber hinwegtäuschen, daß sein größter Reichtum in der Landwirtschaft liegt. Die 47 Millionen Einwohner Brasiliens ernähren sich vom Ertrage ihres eigenen Bodens; nur ein geringer Teil der Einfuhr (etwa 15 v. H.) besteht aus Lebensmitteln (hauptsächlich Weizen und Weizenmehl). Außer dem eigenen Bedarf erzeugt die Landwirtschaft Brasiliens aber auch noch den größten Teil — etwa 90 v. H. — der Ausfuhr. Dabei ist bisher erst nur etwa ein Drittel der Fläche Brasiliens landwirtschaftlich genutzt; der Rest ist entweder Urwald, der aber nach seiner Rodung dem Ackerbau fruchtbarste „rote Erde" bietet, oder „Camp", d. h. Grasland und Weiden.

Unter den landwirtschaftlichen Erzeugnissen Brasiliens steht der Kaffee weitaus an erster Stelle. Vom Weltbestande von rund 5 Millionen Kaffeebäumen stehen rund drei Millionen in Brasilien. [...]

über ein Drittel mit Mais bestellt ist, — aber die Erträge aus dem Kaffeeexport bildeten mehr als die Hälfte des gesamten brasilianischen Ausfuhrwertes. 1935/36 stammten fast zwei Drittel (62,4 v. H.) des Weltkonsums an Kaffee aus Brasilien, und vor einigen Jahren waren die Ziffern noch weit höher; sie gingen erst nach dem katastrophalen Fall der Kaffee-preise, nicht zuletzt infolge der brasilianischen „Kaffeevalorisation", auf das heutige Niveau zurück.

Während Brasilien der bedeutendste Kaffeeproduzent der Welt ist, steht es als Kakaoproduzent mit einer Ernte von 127 000 t (1935/36) an zweiter Stelle nach der afrikanischen Goldküste. 1936 wurden 122 000 t Rohkakao im Werte von 2,1 Millionen ausgeführt.

Nach Kaffee ist Baumwolle das wichtigste Ausfuhrerzeugnis Brasiliens. Bis 1933 wuchs die brasilianische Baumwolle überwiegend in den nordöstlichen Staaten von Maranhão bis Sergipe. Die Baumwollerzeugung wurde in den folgenden Jahren stark ausgebaut, ganz besonders im Staate São Paulo, wo die Kaffeepflanzer seit 1932 dazu übergingen, statt Kaffee Baumwolle anzubauen.

In den Jahren 1920/32 hatte die Baumwoll-produktion São Paulos durchschnittlich 15 000 [...]

und 392 000 in ganz Brasilien gestiegen. 200 000 Tonnen Baumwolle konnte Brasilien im Jahre 1936 ausführen.

Ein bedeutender Teil der brasilianischen Baumwollerzeugung wird im Lande selbst verarbeitet; die Textilindustrie nahm durch die gesteigerte Erzeugung von Baumwolle einen großen Aufschwung. Auch die Neben- und Abfallprodukte der Baumwolle (Oelsaat und Futterkuchen) wurden zu bedeutenden Ausfuhrartikeln.

Brasilien ist der drittgrößte Tabakerzeuger der Welt. Heute wird der Tabakanbau nur in Bahia, Rio Grande do Sul und São Paulo gepflegt, aber der Boden des ganzen Landes gilt als für Tabakkulturen geeignet. Zur Hälfte wird der Tabak in Brasilien selbst verbraucht, zur Hälfte ausgeführt.

### Landwirtschaftliche Produkte

Auch als Zuckerproduzent steht Brasilien an dritter Stelle; doch nahm die inländische Konsumtion schon den größten Teil der Erzeugung auf, so daß nur ein geringer Ueberschuß exportiert wurde und Brasilien nicht zu den wichtigsten Konkurrenten auf dem Weltmarkt gehörte.

Ein großer Teil des Zuckerrohres wird [...]

### Mazzothversorgung 1940

Die Reichsvereinigung der Juden in Deutschland, Gemeinde - Abteilung, gibt zur Frage der Mazzothversorgung folgendes bekannt:

Mazzoth können in diesem Jahre nur durch die Kultusvereinigung bezogen werden. Sie werden von der Mazzothfabrik der Jüdischen Gemeinde in Frankfurt/Main hergestellt und von Frankfurt aus zum Versand gebracht. Es soll in erster Reihe dafür gesorgt werden, daß die rituell lebenden jüdischen Familien versorgt werden. Es müssen diejenigen zurückstehen, die während der Pessachtage nicht ausschließlich Mazzoth essen. Es ist beabsichtigt, dem rituell Lebenden 2 Pfd. Mazzoth und ½ Pfd. Mazzothmehl pro Kopf zur Verfügung zu stellen. Die nicht rituell Lebenden werden sich mit einem geringen Quantum, voraussichtlich 350 g pro Kopf, begnügen müssen. Es wird darauf hingewiesen, daß Mazzoth durch die Kultusvereinigung nur gegen Vorabgabe entsprechender Abschnitte der Brotkarte ausgegeben werden. Für 2 Pfd. Mazzoth und ½ Pfd. Mazzothmehl müssen 1500 - g - Mehl-oder Brotabschnitte abgegeben werden. Da [...]

---

turbund and editor-in-chief Kreindler were told several times that they had to devote more depth to emigration-related topics at the expense of other columns. In the spring of 1940, Kreindler even went to Geneva with the Propaganda Ministry's permission in order to collect information about emigration possibilities and aid organizations operating there.[17]

ADVERTISEMENTS, NOTICES, AND CLASSIFIEDS were a critical part of the *Jüdisches Nachrichtenblatt*. Among the usual items listed in the section, which varied in size from year to year, were offers of various educational and service opportunities, requests for marriage partners, and family notices. This final group conveyed information about births, deaths, and marriages of friends and relatives to readers across Germany, helping to maintain links among the increasingly scattered Jewish population. For example, in the edition of April 14, 1939, an emigrating family gave news of the birth of their child en route. A baby girl was born "on the journey to our new home." According to the address

**Figure 6.3** Front page, February 13, 1940, with a lead story on "Life in Brazil." "With this material drawn from the [Jewish] Aid Association we continue to present the prerequisites for business in South American countries as well as Jewish life there." The section extracted here describes Brazil's agriculture and its main export crops.

**Figure 6.4** Classified from the edition of March 15, 1940, advertising a private household sale of "furniture, beds, to be bought at a bargain."

given in the advertisement, the family was on its way to Argentina. "A fond farewell," bade another family in the February 10, 1939, edition, "to all our relatives, friends and acquaintances—Julius Israel Alpern."

Another important element of the classifieds was the listing of items to be bought and sold. This section in particular reflected increased impoverishment and expulsion. Without sufficient work, many families were forced to sell the few possessions they still owned. Furniture and household goods were often offered for sale in bulk. Often, such classifieds were placed by people already in possession of an exit permit. Families needed to sell off everything, since stringent German emigration provisions made it extremely difficult to take such possessions with them. In the same April 14, 1939, edition, for example, a family sought a buyer for complete "hallway furnishings," including a grandfather clock and chest. During 1939 and 1940 most editions had items announcing the sale of pianos, sewing machines, furs, and items of furniture.

One notice advertising "doctor's equipment for sale" in the edition of February 3, 1939, was clearly related to the recent exclusion of Jews from the medical profession. On February 10, 1939, quantities of fabric were offered "at extraordinarily low prices!" because of a business closure, just as clearly connected to the recent ban on Jews running retail shops. Forbidden to earn a living professionally, Jews sought to provide for themselves by selling their possessions, almost always at prices far below the actual value of the items on offer.

Those few doctors and lawyers who were still allowed to practice used the *Nachrichtenblatt* to inform their patients and clients via an advertisement that they were still working.

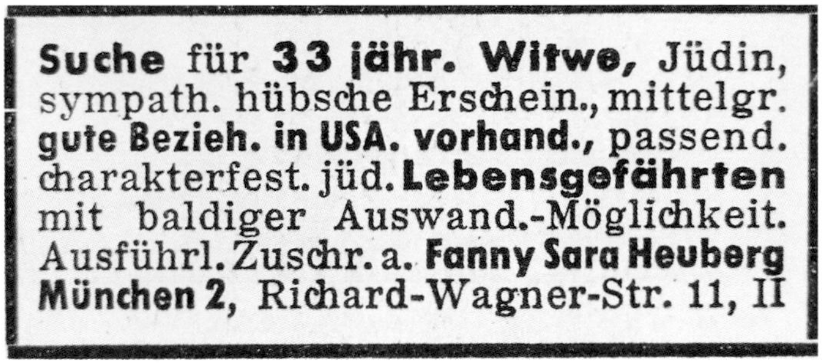
**Suche** für **33 jähr. Witwe,** Jüdin, sympath. hübsche Erschein., mittelgr. **gute Bezieh. in USA. vorhand.,** passend. charakterfest. jüd. **Lebensgefährten** mit baldiger Auswand.-Möglichkeit. Ausführl. Zuschr. a. **Fanny Sara Heuberg München 2,** Richard-Wagner-Str. 11, II

**Figure 6.5** Another classified from the March 15, 1940 edition. "Jewish widow, 33, pleasant, pretty, medium height, with good connections in the USA, seeks suitable, reliable Jewish life partner with prospects for emigration within a short period." Candidates were invited to send detailed descriptions to Fanny Sara Heuberg in Munich

The ranks of unemployed Jews rose steadily, a factor of the professional bans gradually extending into all areas of work, and the dismissal of Jews from an ever growing number of firms. Many tried via the *Nachrichtenblatt* to find new livelihoods. Women generally offered their services as secretaries, shorthand typists, caregivers, and housekeepers; men, for work in accounting, household clearance, window cleaning, and similar work.[18] As is well known, the new laws forced a large number of highly qualified professionals and academics into lower-skill jobs. It was thus normal to see advertisements for work as caregivers in which applicants indicated that they were trained medics or even doctors.

Jewish Community institutions, meanwhile were attempting to fill the gaps caused by the departure of staff members abroad. They published notices seeking doctors and other employees to work, for example, in Community hospitals. The same was true of the religious realm, where there was an urgent need for prayer leaders, rabbis, cantors, and synagogue directors.[19]

Emigration concerns often dominated the Marriage Partners Sought column, grim testimony to the desperation caused by the severely restricted emigration opportunities. From the *Nachrichtenblatt*'s first such column until the fall 1941 ban on emigration, there were—alongside the usual personal ads—a quantity of advertisements mentioning emigration possibilities, passage on ships, and the like. These often solicited people already in possession of the required papers for immigration to other countries: visas, sureties or affidavits (guarantees from residents of the country to which one wished to emigrate), and so forth. In other cases, those placing the ads already had these papers but sought partners with appropriate start-up capital. At the least, people tried to bring relatives to safety. In the edition of February 21, 1939, for example, a father sought to help his daughter find passage abroad: "Seeking suitable husband with secured emigration destination for my nineteen-year-old daughter . . . dowry and costs for double passage available."

Ich bin zum
# KONSULENTEN
bestellt, zugelassen nur zur rechtlichen Beratung und
Vertretung von Juden
## Dr. HANS ISRAEL FRIEDEBERG
Berlin-Schöneberg, Grunewaldstraße 44, I, Ruf 26 42 71

Ich bin durch Verfügung des Herrn Kammergerichts-
präsidenten von neuem als
## KONSULENT
für die Landgerichtsbezirke **Berlin** und Prenzlau
zur Vertretung und Beratung von Juden zugelassen.
Mein Büro befindet sich: **Nestorstr. 1.** Ruf: 97 26 29
### Dr. jur. et rer. pol.
## FRIEDRICH ISRAEL STAUB

**Figure 6.6** Advertisements for legal "advisors"—that is, lawyers—in the edition of February 13, 1940

Those wishing to emigrate to the United States who met the necessary criteria were given a number on a waiting list for entry permits by the embassy, and mention of these numbers became a recurrent theme in the marriage advertisements. Since those at the bottom of the list often waited in vain for their planned emigration, it was normal to want to join up with someone with the opportunity to emigrate sooner. "Businessman, electrical technician, film projectionist, . . . with affidavit for U.S.A., but low on the waiting list," noted a classified in the April 19, 1939, edition, "seeks marriage with young woman of good family with an opportunity to emigrate soon." There were of course also advertisements from marriage agencies promoting foreign marriages.

There were also many advertisements offering language lessons—mainly English but also Spanish, Portuguese, French, and Modern Hebrew; these were the languages of potential host countries like England, the United States, Central and South America, France, and Palestine.

When emigration was still legal, there were many advertisements offering "vocational retraining courses." Certain professions offered better prospects for a new start or to simply get a work permit. In 1939–40, private individuals often placed advertisements in the Lessons and Education column offering "crash courses" in all kinds of professions. These included sewing and tailoring, commercial art, fashion design, or further education in the chemical profession.[20]

THE TWIN FACTORS OF emigration and impoverishment dominated the *Nachrichtenblatt's* editorial content as well. The editorials, in particular, either focused on emigration issues or would call on readers to support the Jewish welfare institutions and the Reichsvereinigung.

From 1938 to 1941 the Jewish Communities in the Reich could submit specific information to the *Nachrichtenblatt* for publication. This included information on religious services, opening hours for cemeteries, consultation times, obituaries of well-known members of the Community, job notices, and so forth. This section, which was mainly found in the middle of the paper under the rubric From the Communities (*Aus den Gemeinden*), might be described as a "religious services" section. The subsection for Berlin was the largest. The notices suggest that at first the religious infrastructure was gradually recuperating from the decimations of the November 1938 pogrom. Later, however, they show the disintegration ultimately wrought by the Nazi's deportation policy. Some synagogues had reopened in 1939, but their number began to fall rapidly at the end of 1941.

From the first year of publication, the paper's Community section also contained the religious calendar, marking the dates of festivals according to the Jewish year and indicating which texts were to be read out for various services. This was standard in Jewish newspapers, and following the ban on other Jewish publications, it became an even more important part of the *Nachrichtenblatt*. The section provided information about the Community boards and bade farewell to its long-standing members when they emigrated. Obituaries were also frequently printed in this section.

In addition to religious matters, the section contained more mundane community service information such as the new telephone numbers for the Welfare Office or the Emigration Advice Center. It listed the names of Jewish doctors and lawyers still authorized to practice.

From February 1939, this service section was supplemented by a series of published language courses. For example, until the spring of 1940, English and Spanish language courses alternated in the paper.[21] From 1941, a series of eleven "accounting lessons" provided an introduction to American accounting, even though the possibilities for emigrating to the United States were already extremely limited.[22] In the case of both the English-language and accounting courses, the paper made explicit reference to the demand readers had made for such courses.

IN THE FIRST THREE years of publication, articles on emigration filled almost all of the front pages. Lead stories on emigration alternated with reports on routes, opportunities for passage abroad, regulations, and the prospects and successes German Jews had in particular countries. The lead stories, written without exception by editor-in-chief Kreindler, often had an admonishing or imploring tone. There were articles in which Kreindler begged those who had already emigrated not to forget those left behind and to do everything they could to allow them to follow.[23] Sometimes he would call on governments and foreign Jewish organizations to create more possibilities for immigration to their countries. Here it becomes painfully clear what the Jews remaining in Germany lacked: money (see chap. 3, which details laws restricting funds).

Kreindler continued to reproach foreign governments for hindering emigration, asserting that they had enough resources and space to take people in. "Ample Room Overseas,"[24] the headline of one of Kreindler's lead articles, is exemplary of the tone he set for the *Nachrichtenblatt*. The article criticized powerful countries and colonial powers—like Britain—asserting that they had large, previously unpopulated areas within their territories that could be made available to refugees by establishing linked settlement areas. The states and the emigrants, Kreindler went on, would profit from such an opportunity, especially as such a project would require just one concerted operation. Such a measure would be of greater benefit to the refugees and the target countries than immigration in dribs and drabs according to quotas.

It is uncertain whether Kreindler really saw this as a realistic option—whether he thought that any country in the world would be ready to take in tens of thousands of people—or if this article was simply dictated to him by the Nazi authorities. In these articles in particular, the warnings of Kreindler and the Reichsvereinigung converged with Nazi goals, even if the motives were different. At this stage, Jews and Germans alike sought to create as many opportunities for emigration as possible—for the Jews, because this would save human lives, and for the regime, because it could thereby expel as many Jews as possible.

Kreindler must have been under unbearable pressure when compiling such articles. He was of course forbidden to write about the true causes of emigration, and one searches in vain for a single word interpreting the Nazi policy of persecution or the actual circumstances of those concerned. Instead, one finds recurrent mention of "migration movements in the course of the last two centuries" or of a "tradition of migration"—as if the expulsion of hundreds of thousands of people was a perfectly natural historical process.[25] One can nonetheless read in those carefully chosen words the importance and the urgency that Kreindler attached to creating more opportunities for emigration.

OTHER ARTICLES ALSO COVERED the subject of emigration, some of which read, surprisingly, like standard foreign country reports. Thus, alongside a series of articles reporting on the fruitless international refugee conference at Evian in

# Jüdisches NACHRICHTENBLATT

Preis 15 Rpf.

Verlag: Jüdischer Kulturbund in Deutschland e. V., Abteilung Verlag, Berlin W 15, Meinekestr. 10 / Zweigstelle Wien: Wien I, Marc-Aurel-Straße 5 / Erscheint zweimal wöchentlich. Redaktion für die Ausgabe Berlin: Berlin W 15, Meinekestraße 10 (Telefon 91 90 31); für die Ausgabe Wien: Wien I, Marc-Aurel-Straße 5 (Telefon U 22 2 11) / Einsendungen an die Redaktion, Berlin W 15, Meinekestraße 10 / In Fällen höherer Gewalt besteht kein Anspruch auf Nachlieferung oder Erstattung bereits gezahlter Bezugsgebühren / Bezugsgeld einschließlich Bestellgeld je Monat RM. 1,12, je Vierteljahr RM. 3,36 (einschl. Postzeitungsgebühr von 10 Rpf. je Monat); bei Abholung RM. 1,— bzw. RM 3.— / Postscheck-Konto: Berlin Nr. 173 605 Jüdischer Kulturbund

Nummer 10 | Freitag, den 2. Februar 1940 | Jahrgang 1940

## Jüdische Auswanderung

L. I. K. Alle Fragen, die mit der Auswanderung zusammenhängen, sind den Juden längst vertraut. Die Sprachen, die in den verschiedenen überseeischen Ländern gesprochen werden, werden eifrig gelernt, viele Versäumnisse, die in der ersten Zeit begangen wurden, sind sehr schnell nachgeholt worden. Die Juden haben rasch begriffen, worauf es bei der Ausnutzung der Auswanderungschancen ankommt, nämlich auf Beruf und Sprache. So schwer es manchem unter uns geworden ist, sich auf neue Beschäftigung umzustellen, die Erfahrung hat gezeigt, daß die Umschichtung im guten Sinne den meisten geglückt ist. In einem Tempo, das vorher kaum für möglich gehalten wurde, haben sich die jüdischen Menschen den Forderungen der Wanderungstechnik angepaßt. Die Möglichkeiten, die in verwandtschaftlichen Beziehungen eingeschlossen sind, sind bis zum letzten Rest genutzt worden. Alles, was von den einzelnen jüdischen Menschen abhing, ist geschehen, um die Durchführung der Auswanderungspläne zu beschleunigen. Jeder hat begriffen, daß in der Schnelligkeit des Entschlusses ein wesentlicher Vorteil liegt, weil je früher man mit dem Umbau einer Existenz beginnt, desto größer die Chancen des Gelingens sein müssen.

### Schwierigkeiten der Einwanderung

Hätten sich die überseeischen Länder, die für die jüdische Auswanderung in Frage kommen, bereitwilliger geöffnet, es gäbe wahrscheinlich heute kaum noch ein mit der jüdischen Wanderung zusammenhängendes Problem. Die Erfahrungen zeigen jedoch, daß die Schwierigkeiten der Einwanderung es sind, an denen manche, die bereits auf dem gepackten Koffer sitzen, scheitern können. Die Einwanderungsbestimmungen der Länder in Uebersee sind dem Wechsel unterworfen, ein Staat, der heute noch jüdische Einwanderer einläßt, beschränkt unter Umständen schon morgen die Zulassung in ganz empfindlicher Weise oder hebt sie ganz auf. Ueberblickt man jedoch die Auswanderungsziffern der letzten sieben Jahre, dann läßt sich leicht feststellen, von welchem wesentlichen Erfolg die Auswanderungsbemühungen gewesen sind. Die Erkenntnis, daß jeder Ausgewanderte seine Angehörigen und Freunde nach sich zieht, hat in steigendem Maße Erfolge gebracht. Wenn auch gegenwärtig die jüdische Auswanderung nach Uebersee von erheblicher zahlenmäßiger Bedeutung ist, ist dies in erster Linie der Anforderung durch Verwandte zuzuschreiben. In manche Staaten jenseits der Meere kann der jüdische Auswanderer überhaupt nur gelangen, wenn er von nahen Verwandten angefordert wird. Die Auswanderungspläne, die in allen jüdischen Familien vorhanden sind, basieren zu einem großen Teile auf den Verbindungen, die mit Verwandten und Freunden angeknüpft sind.

Wenn manche überseeischen Länder sich vorübergehend der jüdischen Einwanderung verschließen, so liegt das zum Teil an der Ansammlung größerer Massen von Juden in den Zentren der betreffenden Staaten. Es ist eine alte Forderung, die hier erhoben wurde, daß mit der Auswanderung allein das Problem noch nicht gelöst ist, daß vielmehr der in ein überseeisches Land eingewanderte jüdische Mensch von sich aus einen wesentlichen Beitrag leisten kann, um die Einwanderungschancen der nach ihm kommenden Juden zu vergrößern. Jeder jüdische Einwanderer, der die großen Städte verläßt und aufs Land geht, vermehrt in dem betreffenden Ueberseestaat die Chancen der späteren Einwanderer. Der Eingliederungsprozeß mag in den großen Städten jenseits der Meere rascher vor sich gehen, dauerhafter sind jedoch die Erfolge, die in den kleineren Orten und auf dem Lande erzielt werden. Die normale Berufsstruktur der Juden, die bei uns nicht mehr zu erreichen war, läßt sich nach der Auswanderung unschwer erzielen, wenn jeder Wanderer sich der Tatsache bewußt bleibt, daß er nicht für sich allein steht, und daß von der Wahl seines Wohnortes und Berufes auch die Lenkung des gesamten Wanderungsstromes abhängt.

Wer sich trotzdem entschließt, die ersten Wochen nach der Landung in einer Großstadt zu bleiben, soll die Ratschläge der jüdischen Hilfsstellen befolgen und seine endgültige Niederlassung auf dem Lande suchen. Dort werden vornehmlich Handwerker und Landwirte willige Aufnahme finden.

### Produktive Einordnung

Um eine Erfahrung sind wir in den Jahren jedenfalls reicher geworden: wir haben erkannt, daß eine produktive Einordnung der jüdischen Einwanderer nur in den dünnbevölkerten überseeischen Ländern auf die Dauer möglich ist. Solchen Erwägungen sind die Anregungen zuzuschreiben, die an dieser Stelle in ununterbrochener Folge gegeben worden sind. Unermüdlich haben wir auf die Möglichkeiten hingewiesen, die in jenen Teilen der Welt gegeben sind, die noch der Erschließung harren und in denen jüdische Hände sich nutzbringend betätigen können. Daß solche Chancen nur in überseeischen Gebieten vorzufinden sind, braucht nicht erst bewiesen zu werden. Wir haben hier auf Alaska als eine Chance für Juden hingewiesen, wir haben die Philippinen genannt, ebenso sicher ist jedoch, daß auch die gering bevölkerten Staaten in USA. noch unerschlossene Möglichkeiten gewähren. Wir haben seinerzeit darauf aufmerksam gemacht, daß in den landwirtschaftlichen Distrikten der Vereinigten Staaten die Ansiedlung einer größeren Masse von jüdischen Wanderern vorgenommen werden kann. Die Projekte, die sich damals an diese Anregung knüpften, sind in den Anfangsstadien steckengeblieben, sie sind aber durchaus wert, weiter verfolgt zu werden. Wenn von einer Uebersättigung der Vereinigten Staaten von Amerika mit jüdischen Einwanderern gesprochen wird, dann können naturgemäß nur die großen Industrie- und Handelsplätze gemeint sein, abseits der Weltzentren gibt es in USA. noch Gebiete, die für Einwanderer noch nutzbar gemacht werden könnten.

## Am nächsten Sonntag „Haus-Sammlung"

**Das Opfer, das die ehrenamtlichen Sammler der Jüdischen Winterhilfe durch ihre unermüdliche Tätigkeit für unsere Bedürftigen bringen, muß allen Mitgliedern der jüdischen Gemeinschaft eine Mahnung sein, in den eigenen Opfergaben nicht zu erlahmen.**

**Wenn auch an jeden unter uns steigende Ansprüche gestellt werden, so dürfen zusätzliche Leistungen zugunsten unserer Betreuten keinesfalls fortfallen. Hängt doch hiervon die Fortsetzung unserer Arbeit ab.**

**Deshalb ergeht auch heute wieder der Ruf an alle: Helft und gebt weiter am nächsten Sonntag für die Jüdische Winterhilfe der Jüdischen Gemeinde zu Berlin e. V.**

**Postscheck: Berlin 934 46**

## Einwanderungspolitik in USA.

Bekanntlich ist eine Einwanderung nach den Vereinigten Staaten nur nach Maßgabe der feststehenden Quote möglich, die zwar an und für sich nicht sehr hoch ist, die aber auf die Dauer den größten Teil der jüdischen Auswanderer aus dem Altreich aufzusaugen geeignet ist.

**Um den Prozeß zu beschleunigen, hatten wir seinerzeit vorgeschlagen, allen denjenigen, die eine Quotennummer besitzen, jedoch erst nach einer gewissen Zeit zur endgültigen Einwanderung gelangen können, die Möglichkeit zu geben, sich in den dünnbevölkerten landwirtschaftlichen Staaten der USA. niederzulassen und dort den Aufruf ihrer Quotennummer abzuwarten.**

Eine solche Regelung hätte sowohl für die Auswanderer wie für das Einwanderungsland wesentliche Vorteile. Die Auswanderer könnten ihre Uebersiedlung beschleunigt durchführen, sie würden zwar des Vorteils verlustig gehen, sich ihren Wohnort frei wählen zu können und müßten damit einverstanden sein, sich zunächst dort niederzulassen, wo man sie haben will. Dieser Nachteil wäre jedoch nicht von Bedeutung, er würde für die Juden auf die Dauer zu einem Vorteil werden. Sie würden erkennen, daß die Siedlung auf dem Lande zwar höhere Anforderungen an den ganzen Menschen stellt, daß dafür jedoch die Siedler eine gesicherte Zukunft erwartet. Auf diese Weise würden wahrscheinlich viele der so Eingewanderten beim Aufruf ihrer Quotennummer kein Verlangen danach tragen, in die Weltstädte zu ziehen, sie würden sehen, daß eine Existenz als Landwirt oder Farmer, der in einem städtischen Beruf vorzuziehen ist.

Jedoch auch für das Einwanderungsland könnten und würden sich nicht zu unterschätzende Vorteile ergeben. Die Einwanderer hätten Gelegenheit, sich schneller in das Leben einzugliedern, sie würden rascher die Sprache und Gewohnheiten des Einwanderungslandes erlernen und da dieses ohnehin entschlossen ist, sie, wenn auch nur auf Jahre verteilt, aufzunehmen, so entstünden zahlenmäßig ganz gewiß keinerlei Veränderungen im Gesamteffekt. Für ein so großes Land wie die Vereinigten Staaten kann es ohne Belang sein, ob es in drei Jahren 150 000 Einwanderer aufnimmt, die sich über das ganze Land verstreuen, oder ob es in einem Zuge und zu gleicher Zeit derselben Zahl von 150 000 Menschen Einlaß gewährt, die zunächst an wenigen bestimmten Stellen gesammelt verbleiben und erst später die Freizügigkeit gewährt erhalten. Die Bedenken, die gegen die einmalige Zulassung einer größeren Zahl sprechen, mögen formell von Wichtigkeit sein, in tatsächlicher Beziehung sind sie ohne jeden Einfluß. Entschlössen sich die Vereinigten Staaten zu einer solchen Einwanderungspolitik, dann entspräche eine solche Haltung sowohl dem Vorteil der Einwanderer wie dem Interesse des Einwanderungslandes.

Neben den USA. kommen die südamerikanischen Länder als Zielstationen für die jüdische Einwanderung in Betracht. Manche dieser Staaten sind gegenwärtig für Juden ganz verschlossen, sie öffnen sich nur unter bestimmten Bedingungen für nahe Verwandte bereits in den Ländern ansässiger Personen, andere südamerikanische Staaten lassen nur wenige jüdische Einwanderer und auch diese nur unter erschwerten Umständen zu. Auch hier ließe sich eine Planung in der Weise denken, daß denjenigen Auswanderern eine gewisse Vorzugsstellung eingeräumt wird, die entschlossen sind, von Anfang an in der Landwirtschaft zu arbeiten. Manche Staaten in Südamerika gewähren in der Tat landwirtschaftlichen Siedlern eine Vorzugsbehandlung, aber diese ist an erschwerende Bedingungen geknüpft. Anzuregen wäre hier eine Ausweitung des Begriffes „Landwirte", die auch für solche Personen die Einwanderung erleichtert, die zwar nicht über landwirtschaftliche Vorkenntnisse verfügen, die aber doch ihrer ganzen Haltung nach für eine landwirtschaftliche Beschäftigung geeignet sind. Eine solche vorzugsweise Behandlung der Einwanderer, die auf dem Lande arbeiten wollen, würde dazu beitragen, die Nachteile zu verringern, die sich aus der Zusammenballung bereits eingewanderter Juden in großen Städten ergeben. Es unterliegt keinem Zweifel, daß die produktive Einordnung der Einwanderer erleichert würde, wenn das von uns vorgeschlagene Verfahren beobachtet würde, und damit würde die ganze Einwanderungsfrage ein ganz verändertes Gesicht bekommen.

Schließlich ist es ja das Ziel jeder vernünftigen Wanderungsplanung, nicht in den Anfängen steckenzubleiben, sondern erst dann von einem Erfolge zu sprechen, wenn die endgültige Einordnung des Ausgewanderten wirklich geglückt ist. Man muß bei den Problemen der Wanderung nicht nur von der Auswanderung an sich ausgehen, so dringend deren Beschleunigung ist, man muß auch an die spätere Zeit denken und dabei ist es von ungewöhnlichem Vorteil, sich um die Produktivierung der Eingewanderten zu bemühen, weil nur dadurch allein eine wirkliche und befriedigende Lösung der ganzen Frage gewährleistet wird.

Der produktiv eingegliederte Einwanderer wird ein Gefühl der Befriedigung empfinden, wenn er weiß, daß seine Arbeit ihm und noch mehr seinen Kindern dauerhafte Erfolge bringt, die sich mit der Zeit steigern.

**Figure 6.7** Front page, February 2, 1940. The lead story on "Jewish Emigration" is by Leo Kreindler. The last paragraph urges potential immigrants to consider the long-term possibilities afforded by "lightly populated lands overseas. . . . We have here pointed to Alaska as a place for Jews. We have named the Philippines . . . equally sure, however, are the less populated states of the USA, which still grant opportunities." Below the fold is a focus on "USA Immigration policy." Two small items in the lower left and upper right corners urge readers to donate to the "Jewish Winter Help" drive scheduled for the following Sunday.

1939 (Kreindler was present as a reporter), were articles describing individual countries in terms of topography, economy, and infrastructure, articles that assessed the possibilities of a new start.

Such articles give the impression that they could actually have been of practical use for an immigrant. Already beginning in 1939, headlines like "Bolivia as an Immigration Country: Facts and Opportunities for Jewish Immigrants from Germany"(Feb. 28, 1939) and "Upon Arrival in San Domingo" (June 7, 1940) began to appear. The winter of 1940–41 brought a string of reports on individual countries and regions under headlines such as "In the Tropics and Sub-tropics" or "Shanghai: A Fact File."

If anything, the articles make one thing particularly clear: that there were fewer and fewer places for the German Jews to escape to. More and more countries closed their borders and offered ever fewer people—usually just the affluent—the chance to enter. Jews still living in the German Reich started to opt for more "exotic" alternatives for immigration: "Working as a Farmer in Kenya" (May 3, 1939) and "Uruguay, the Smallest South American Country" (March 11, 1941).

The start of World War II drastically reduced opportunities for emigration. A blockade by the British Navy made it almost impossible to reach the Americas via the Atlantic. The *Nachrichtenblatt* now began to run articles on the last possible combined land-sea routes to North America across the Soviet Union, China, and Japan. Headlines such as "The Land Route Is Open" and "New Emigration Routes" (June 18, 1940) now appeared. Those who lacked immigration papers for the Americas failed to reach their goals via this route. Many were stranded in Japanese-occupied Mandschukuo. Others found a temporary safehaven in Shanghai.

The Asian experience triggered a new series of articles. The edition of October 10, 1940, printed a detailed report on the formalities involved in obtaining a certificate for Shanghai and soon thereafter a column of "Jewish News from the Far East" (November 22, 1940).

With the German attack on the Soviet Union in June 1941 this route, too, was blocked; Jews in Germany were now effectively trapped. In the edition of October 24, 1941—a day after the final ban on emigration became effective, Kreindler again summed up details of Jewish emigration in the article "Have They Done Enough?" It was the last of the *Nachrichtenblatt*'s articles on the subject.

A FEW MONTHS PRIOR to this, the *Nachrichtenblatt* was deprived of an important source of content when its publisher, the Kulturbund, was closed. The regime, seeing no further need for "Jewish art," banned the cultural organization on September 11, 1941. The *Nachrichtenblatt*, however, was still deemed to be useful. The Gestapo, which now took over supervision of the newspaper from Goebbels's Propaganda Ministry, explicitly exempted the newspaper from the ban.[26] A few months later the paper was granted status as an independent department within the Jewish Reichsvereinigung.

Prior to its banning, the Kulturbund's cultural events had featured prominently in the paper. Orchestral, theater, and film productions were announced in the *Nachrichtenblatt*, sometimes in advance, and they were often reviewed. School drama productions and performances by the Jewish music school, as well as cabaret performances, were mentioned in both short and lengthy articles.

There was, to be sure, little room for genuine criticism in these pages. Theater reviews generally ranged from positive to positively raving. What could the critics have written otherwise? Could they have criticized the remaining culture available to Jews and advised readers not to go to the performances? After all, even the least successful productions financed the Kulturbund's overall work through ticket sales. To most, this last Jewish cultural institution furnished the only possible entertainments left to them, and provided, moreover, a living to its staff, sparing them from forced labor. During a period when Nazis were systematically stripping Jews of all their rights, there was simply no question of a critic exercising his journalists' calling, possibly at the expense of the institution.

It is, furthermore, questionable whether negative comments would have made it past the censor anyway, especially during the *Nachrichtenblatt*'s first two years, when the Propaganda Ministry kept an eagle eye on how well the Kulturbund functioned (as well as on its surplus funds, which in the fiscal year 1939–40 amounted to some RM 20,000).[27]

One standard feature of the paper was its quite extensive book review section, of which only brief mention can be made here. Beginning in January 1940, the paper regularly ran reviews and printed extracts of books published by the Kulturbund's publishing arm, whose list of titles consisted of the collections of the now-defunct Jewish publishing houses. (The Kulturbund had been forced to buy these at extremely low prices.)[28] Its Book Talk column, along with small ads, were intended to promote these books. Here, too, it was a matter of income, theoretically intended for the Kulturbund and other Jewish organizations, although a portion of it likely went to the Propaganda Ministry as well.[29] It is thus plausible that the series was launched on direct orders from the Propaganda Ministry—even though the sale of the books would also benefit the Kulturbund.

The closure of the Kulturbund dealt a irretrievable blow to the *Nachrichtenblatt*'s editorial content; the paper withered to a mere two-page "regulations

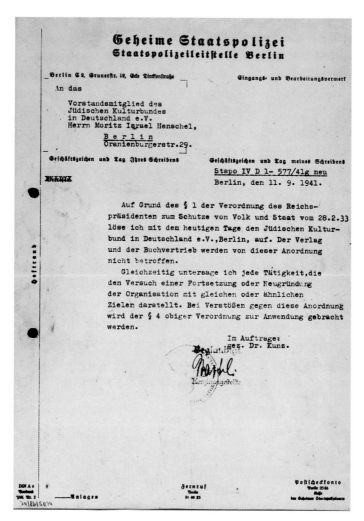

**Figure 6.8** This letter from the Gestapo dated September 11, 1941, orders the shutting down of the Jewish Kulturbund. Specific exception is made for its publishing activities.

sheet,"[30] a shadow of its former self. The content consisted entirely of regulations, housekeeping tips,[31] and short articles on religious matters.

The religious articles were nothing new—though now they were often little more than reprinted passages from the Bible and other religious writings. Already at Chanukah in 1938, a front-page article of December 16 called on its readers to celebrate the festival of lights by donating to Jewish aid organizations and giving Kulturbund-published books and *Nachrichtenblatt* subscriptions as presents. The February 10, 1939 issue inaugurated the column entitled Teachings (*Das Wort der Lehre*), which discussed and explained Talmudic passages. The column ran for almost a year and a half, until June 13, 1941.

Articles about the Jewish holidays and other religious issues grew more and more prevalent. The religious passages, which at first seemed to be taken out of context, often referred to present conditions. During the *Nachrichtenblatt*'s final years, citations from the apocryphal Book of Sirach, a collection of sayings, popular exhortations, and maxims, became more frequent. One motive was often the appeal for donations to keep the Community and welfare institutions going. Citations like "Let not your hand be open to receive and clenched when it is time to give," published on October 2, 1942, lent extra weight to such appeals. Other pearls of wisdom had a keener lesson to convey, as for example the aphorism printed in the same issue: "Take no counsel with a fool, for he can keep nothing to himself." At a time when the only alternative to deportation was often a precarious existence underground, this was nothing short of a warning: one thoughtless comment could lead to inadvertent—and deadly—betrayal.

The religious articles were intended to hearten and encourage during a time of mass deportations and profound despair. Thus the April 2, 1943, issue printed an extract from Psalm 90: "Thou turnest man to contrition; and sayest: 'Return, ye children of men.' For a thousand years in Thy sight are but as yesterday when it is past, and as a watch in the night. Thou carriest them away as with a flood; they are as asleep; in the morning they are like grass which groweth up. In the morning it flourisheth, and groweth up; in the evening it is cut down, and withereth."[32] Two months prior, Goebbels had delivered his notorious "Total War" speech, just after the fall of Stalingrad and the decisive turn in the war. The reader might have found comfort in lines from the Prayer of Moses reminding that even a "Thousand-Year Reich" would and must some day come to an end.

The hidden inferences and insinuations in such religious citations, of which there are many examples, bear witness to the attempt on the part of the paper's writers and editors to dodge the censor and offer more than a mere regulations sheet. Opinions are divided on the effect of such allusions and how desirable they were. What remains is the impression that throughout the entire period of publication the staff of the *Nachrichtenblatt* tried to exceed the scope of opportunities imposed by the censor and serve their readers, who would have been well aware that they were on very thin ice. On the one hand the paper was always in danger of becoming an executive organ of the regime. On the other hand, it did not want to endanger its function as a means of contact, exchange, and dissemination of information.

In its final years, moreover, when editorial content was virtually banned from the paper (or allowed only in a very restricted form), some of the *Nachrichtenblatt*'s articles and columns still sought to be of help to the readers, providing household tips, for example, or information about blackout times and points where one could pick up ration cards. None of this can disguise the fact that, because of its close supervision by the regime, the *Jüdisches Nachrichtenblatt* was primarily an instrument of persecution policy. It was a close to perfect—though not entirely effective—information and propaganda organ, devised by the National Socialists to control and drive out the Jews.

The last issue of the *Jüdisches Nachrichtenblatt* was printed on June 4, 1943, shortly before the closure of the Reichsvereinigung offices and the deportation of its directors. What little was left of the Reichsvereinigung was now transferred to the premises of the Jewish Hospital on Iranische Strasse and directed by Dr. Walter Lustig, a figure of no small controversy. Here a handful of people managed the association's remaining assets (see chap. 18).

Whether the paper would carry on seems at first to have been unclear. A letter dated July 19, 1943, typed on Reichsvereinigung stationary (Iranische Strasse address) testifies to the uncertainty. A subscriber to the *Nachrichtenblatt* had written to complain that the paper was no longer being delivered. The response informed him that the paper was no longer appearing at regular intervals and that it was still not certain at what intervals it would appear in the future.[33] On August 10, 1943, the German Library, too, complained that it no longer received reading copies.[34] Else Harnack, a survivor from Berlin, later claimed that Lustig had prevented the *Nachrichtenblatt* from being published further.[35] While it cannot be proven that this was the case, one thing is certain: from the summer of 1943 on, the Jewish press ceased to exist in Germany.

**1** The date cannot be stated exactly.

**2** This notice was printed in the first edition together with the censor's release. *Jüdisches Nachrichtenblatt*, 23 November 1938.

**3** Until the 30 December 1938 issue, the publisher's name was featured on the *Nachrichtenblatt*'s masthead. From the next issue on, the Kulturbund was mentioned. The address Meineckestr. 10 remained unchanged.

**4** Erich Liepmann, *Erinnerungen: Berlin, November 1938 to April 1939*, Yad Vashem Archives, Jerusalem, Documents, 01/135, p. 2. English translation in Saul Friedländer, *Nazi Germany and the Jews*, vol. 1, *The Years of Persecution, 1933–1939* (New York, 1997), p. 284.

**5** See "Consultation in the Reich Ministry for Public Enlightenment and Propaganda on June 3, 1940," file note, Stiftung Archiv der Akademie der Künste (SadK), Berlin, SadK/FWA, 74/86/5001, sheet 64. In this Fritz Wisten, head of the Kulturbund, was given the task of informing Leo Kreindler that the next day's edition was authorized.

**6** Katrin Diehl, *Die Jüdische Presse im Dritten Reich. Zwischen Selbstbehauptung und Fremdbestimmung* (Tübingen, 1997), pp. 240–41.

**7** "Meeting in the Ministry, September 23, 1940," SadK/FWA, 74/86/5001, sheet 83.

**8** Calculation by the author.

**9** Board of the Registered Association for the Israelite Religion in Berlin to the Gestapo, Berlin regional headquarters, department IV D 1, letter dated May 8, 1942, Bundesarchiv, Berlin (BArch), R 8150/18, sheet 10.

**10** "Working Report of the Jewish Kulturbund, e.V., October 1, 1938–June 30, 1939" [submitted to the Propaganda Ministry], SadK/FWA), 74/86/5042, p. 18.

**11** *Jüdisches Nachrichtenblatt*, 23 November, 1938, p. 2. Editor's notice: "Subscribers to the *Jüdische Rundschau*, the *C.V. Zeitung*, and other Jewish newspapers will from this point, with the authorization of the authorities, receive the *Jüdisches Nachrichtenblatt* with information about Jewish matters. [signed] The Editors."

**12** See "Working Report of the Jewish Kulturbund, e.V., October 1, 1938–June 30, 1939."

**13** Herbert Rosenkranz, *Verfolgung und Selbstbehauptung der Juden in Österreich, 1938–1945* (Vienna and Munich, 1978), pp. 203–4.

**14** "Meeting in the Ministry, October 25, 1939," file note, SadK/FWA, 74/86/5001, sheet 13.

**15** See "Working Report of the Jewish Kulturbund, e.V., October 1, 1938–June 30, 1939," pp. 18–19.

**16** RMfVuP, dept. IIA [Hinkel] to Adolf Eichmann, letter dated January 2, 1939, WL, Documents Section, 575), pp. 76–77. Cited in Reiner Burger, " 'Jüdisches Nachrichtenblatt' (1938–1943). Historischer Kontext, Entwicklung, Inhalte," undergraduate thesis at the Catholic University of Eichstätt (Eichstätt, 1996).

**17** "Consultation in the Reich Ministry for Public Enlightenment and Propaganda, department Be KA, March 18, 1940," file note, SadK/FWA, 74/86/5001, sheet 43.

**18** Representative of many issues is that of 30 December, 1938, p. 5.

**19** See for example, *Jüdisches Nachrichtenblatt*, 7 February, 1939, p. 5, and 2 June, 1939, p. 6.

**20** See, for example, the issue of 3 March, 1939, p. 13.

**21** The first English lesson was published in *Jüdisches Nachrichtenblatt*, February 3, 1939, p. 7. Spanish lessons began in the edition of November 24, 1939, p. 3.

**22** There were a total of eleven articles in the Accounting Lessons series, the first of which was published on January 24, 1941.

**23** "Appeal from the editors of the *Jüdisches Nachrichtenblatt*," *Jüdisches Nachrichtenblatt*, 22 March, 1940, front page.

**24** Leo Kreindler, "Viel Raum in Übersee," *Jüdisches Nachrichtenblatt*, 24 January, 1941, front page.

**25** Leo Kreindler, "Bahnet, bahnet den Weg—Renaissance der jüdischen Wanderungs-Bewegung," *Jüdisches Nachrichtenblatt*, 10 October, 1940, front page.

**26** The Gestapo, Berlin regional headquarters, IV D 1, to Moritz Henschel, member of the board of the Jüdisches Kulturbund in Deutschland, Berlin, letter dated September 11, 1941, SadK/FWA, 74/86/5074, n.p. (illustrated here).

**27** "Consultation in the Ministry for Public Enlightenment and Propaganda, June 3, 1940," file note, SadK/FWA, 74/86/5001, sheet 65.

**28** On this, see an essay by Chaim Nachman Bialik in *Jüdisches Nachrichtenblatt*, 26 January, 1940, p. 4.

**29** Volker Dahm, *Das Jüdische Buch im Dritten Reich*, 2nd ed. (Munich, 1993), p. 152.

**30** On May 21, 1943 the front page announced that the *Nachrichtenblatt* "is published as a regulations sheet for Jews."

**31** In the fifth year of publication (1943), almost every edition of the *Jüdisches Nachrichtenblatt* contained advice on how to make "tasty recipes" from the little that could still be obtained through meager food rations.

**32** Psalm 90: 3–6, English translation from the Jewish Publication Society's Hebrew Bible, 1917.

**33** Reichsvereinigung of Jews in Germany to William Fürst, letter dated July 19, 1943, BArch, R 8150/22, n.p.

**34** Postcard (preprinted) from the German Library to the *Jüdisches Nachrichtenblatt* publishing house, August 10, 1943, BArch, R 8150/22, n.p.

**35** "Testimony of Mrs. Else Harnack, née Brode, arrival with the July 1944 exchange," Yad Vashem Archives, Documents, 01/58, p. 1.

# 5

# Zionists

# Chapter Seven

# אף על פי כן (In Spite of Everything): Zionists in Berlin

CHANA C. SCHÜTZ

From the start, Zionism had trouble with German Jews, and German Jews had trouble with Zionism. Theodor Herzl, the movement's founder, had originally hoped to convene the first Zionist World Congress of 1897 in Germany. When the leading representatives of Munich's Jewish Community raised objections, however, he called Zionists to the Swiss city of Basel instead. At the turn of the century and well into the Weimar period, the problem hinged largely on a theoretical debate over Jewish identity and the best way to counter growing anti-Semitism. Herzl had called in 1896 for the establishment of a Jewish national homeland, preferably in Palestine. Even in later years, however, the majority of Germany's Jews—politically liberal, culturally assimilated, and German-speaking—thought that the situation would improve through reform efforts in Europe. Many remained not only proudly Jewish but patriotically German as well.

Even in later years, the overall number of *Schekelzahler* (dues-paying Zionists) was never very high in Germany. Nonetheless, a small minority of German-based Jews were intensely active in promoting the development of Jewish life in Palestine. Indeed, Berlin was for many years the world headquarters of the Zionist movement, with Otto Warburg, a professor and scientist at Berlin's university, serving as its president from 1911 to 1920. The organization flourished within the city's Jewish Community during the Weimar period, achieving considerable, if not spectacular, success in the 1926 elections to the Community's Assembly of Representatives. That year, the two Zionist parties won a combined eight of the assembly's twenty-one seats. In numerical terms, however, the national German Zionist Organization (Zionistische Vereinigung für Deutschland, ZVfD) was never particularly strong. In 1930, there were only about twenty thousand members nationally.

The proportion of German Jews to emigrate to Palestine was equally small. The numbers remained low until the first two years of the 1930s and were virtually insignificant in comparison with the influx to Palestine of Jews from Poland, Hungary, Romania, and other parts of Eastern Europe. Indeed, until 1933, Zionism in Germany remained, even among its most ardent supporters, more a matter of theory than practice.

## The Years 1933 to 1938

The situation changed with the National Socialist victory in 1933. The new government brought with it overwhelming state support for systematic, organized anti-Semitism. Suddenly, there was considerably more interest in Palestine among German Jews. Even so, the willingness to emigrate was far more frequent on the part of young people and emerged much more slowly among those who considered themselves firmly established in their German *Heimat* (home).

In many ways, the emigration statistics mirror the fluctuations of the Third Reich's "Jewish policy." German Jews were struggling to make sense not only of the uncertain situation in Germany but of conditions in Palestine as well. In 1933, 7,600 German Jews emigrated to Palestine; in 1934 and 1935 the figures were 9,800 and 8,600, respectively; some 8,700 German-Jews arrived in 1936; in the years 1937 and 1938, however, the figures fell to 3,700 and 4,800, respectively, before shooting up again to 8,500 in 1939.[1] For one thing, fluctuations in Nazi policy toward the Jews—particularly the cosmetic lessening of anti-Semitism during the 1936 Olympic games—gave some Jews false hopes. Moreover, reports from Palestine of economic recession and violent demonstrations by Arab residents (which even induced the British Mandate authorities to close the borders temporarily) cast deep shadows over the prospect of a future life in Palestine.

The old tension between Zionists and the German Jewish majority meant that the newcomers were not always welcomed in Palestine with open arms. Their motives for immigration were often considered suspect. Committed Zionists who had been in Eretz Israel (the land of Israel) for years would sarcastically inquire of newcomers, "Are you from Germany—or did you come here out of conviction?" No less a figure than Israel's future prime minister David Ben Gurion was to refer scornfully to the German-Jewish immigrants as "Hitler-Zionists."

If the Nazis made little secret of their policy of forcing Germany's Jews to emigrate in the first years after 1933, the reaction of the Jewish Agency in Jerusalem toward accepting them was more ambiguous. Established by the Mandate for Palestine in 1922, the agency's priority had always been the development of a "Jewish homeland" in Palestine. There was, naturally, awareness of the plight of German Jewry, and complaints and indignation about it were voiced throughout the world. Despite the drastically changed circumstances, however, the Zion-

**Figure 7.1**
The Theodor-Herzl school at Kaiserdamm 78 in Charlottenburg, after 1936. The number of pupils at this Zionist school tripled—from two hundred to six hundred—between 1933 and 1934. It was closed by the authorities in March 1939.

ist leadership in Jerusalem did not want, even for an instant, to lose sight of its original goal: to establish a thriving Jewish community in Eretz Israel. Moreover, because of immigration restrictions placed by the British Mandate, there was a limited number of entrance certificates available for European Jews.[2]

Above all, Jerusalem wanted immigrants who were young, strong, and willing to play a role in building the new homeland. Some committed Zionists thought the German Jews—because of their largely urban, middle-class backgrounds—were less than satisfactory candidates. Some considered them to be ill suited to proving themselves as pioneers on the land, indifferent toward Zionist ideology, and politically less than committed to the cause of the homeland.

Nobody, Zionist or otherwise, wanted unplanned emigration. To the extent that Jews left Germany, they had to do so within the framework of economic agreements with the German government and in a well-ordered fashion" (see chap. 3). The principle was that each instance of immigration had to be "legal" and in full agreement with the British Mandate authorities.[3]

## Certificates: Regulated Emigration

While other Jewish institutions called on Jews to remain in Germany—even years after the Nazis had come to power and despite heightened discrimination—the German Zionist Organization (ZVfD) had from the start worked with the sole goal of facilitating emigration. It alone organized the emigration of Jews from Germany to Palestine, in large part through its headquarters, the Palestine Office (Palästinaamt) at Meinekestrasse 10 in Berlin's Charlottenburg district. The ZVfD had been forced by Nazi law to work under the umbrella of the recently formed Reichsvertretung der Juden in Deutschland (Reich

**Figure 7.2** The Palestine Office at Meinekestrasse 10 in Charlottenburg, after 1933

Representation of Jews in Germany), which in July 1939 was forced to rename itself the Reichsvereinigung (Reich Association) der Juden in Deutschland.

AROUND 236,000 JEWS—roughly half of Germany's Jewish population—left the country between 1933 and 1939. Of these, 57,000 went to Palestine and 22,614 managed to get to Eretz Israel with the support of the Palestine Office.[4]

From 1933 on, the Palestine Office did its best to manage an increasing flood of applications, distributing a portion of the coveted immigration certificates that permitted legal emigration to the British Mandate territory. It advised people wishing to emigrate, provided training and other preparatory courses, and organized the journey. The office offered "retraining courses" in professions that would be useful in Palestine. For young people, in particular, the Zionists set up a large number of training centers (*Ausbildungsstätten*). Above all, the office had the extremely difficult task of selecting applicants according to their suitability.

With the exception of a few wealthy Jews who could apply directly to the British Consulate for "capitalist certificates" (*Kapitalistenzertifikat*), the Palestine Office looked after the vast majority of people emigrating to Palestine. The craftsman's certificate (*Handwerkerzertifikat*) only applied to certain professions and required applicants to prove that they had capital of at least 250 Palestine pounds. Even more stringent were the criteria for acquiring a worker's certifi-

**Figure 7.3** The hay harvest at the Ahrensdorf agricultural center, around 1938

**Figure 7.4** The carpentry workshop at Ahrensdorf, 1938

cate (*Arbeiterzertifikat*). Applicants had to be in perfect health and aged between eighteen and thirty-five. These younger candidates for emigration were known as *chalutzim*—pioneers—and had to be nominated for emigration by a youth organization.

The primary organization nominating such candidates was Hechalutz (the Pioneers), an international Zionist youth body that had had a German branch since 1921. Hechalutz had long targeted young Jews seeking to make a life in Palestine and sought to help them realize their goals of *Aliyah* (immigration to Palestine). Members received placement at *Hachshara* (preparatory) centers in Europe, which were organized much like kibbutzim and were intended to provide groundwork and vocational training for life in Palestine. Here young people were trained in the practical professions that would be useful in developing the new homeland.

Thirteen of the thirty-five *Hachshara* centers in Germany were situated in the countryside around Berlin—in Brandenburg villages like Ahrensdorf, Havelberg, Jessen, and Neuendorf. Here, on lands rented from local landowners, both Jewish and Gentile, young *chalutzim* from all over Germany were trained in agriculture as well as various types of manual work. Girls were primarily instructed in housekeeping. Hebrew courses and Palestine studies were also part of the curriculum for both sexes. If they could afford it, *chalutzim* and their families were responsible for their own tuition.

As more and more young people joined the Zionist youth organizations in the 1930s, and as the conditions for Jews in Germany grew more dangerous,

**Figure 7.5** Walter, Eva, and Lore Levin in their family home at Cäcilienallee 47 (now Pacelliallee 47) in Dahlem, around 1936. Later, in the United States, Walter Levin founded the LaSalle String Quartet and played first violin.

additional training centers were also set up in England, Belgium, Holland, and Scandinavia in order to get them out of Germany as quickly as possible. From here they waited to enter Palestine.

Often, they waited in vain. After 1933 there were never enough immigration permits (with the exception of the capitalist certificates) to go around. The situation grew even worse after 1936. In 1937 the Jewish Agency applied for over 11,000 workers' certificates from the British Mandate. Of these, a mere 220 (!) certificates were distributed to the Palestine offices throughout Europe.

## The Case of Alfred Levin

The decision to leave Germany was difficult for almost everyone, especially in the first years of Nazi rule. Some—including those who had actively supported the establishment of Jewish life in Palestine in the years prior to this—later realized that they had waited too long to prepare for their own departures. Alfred Levin, who owned a gentlemen's clothing factory on Klosterstrasse, was one such reluctant emigrant. After being forced to sell his factory at a ridiculously low price in the summer of 1938, Levin applied for a capitalist certificate for his wife Erna and himself and their three children Lore, Eva, and Walter.

**Figure 7.6** Erna and Alfred Levin during a stop in Munich on their way to Palestine, December 1938

The capitalist certificate application required one to prove to the British Mandate the possession of sufficient "immigration capital"—at least one thousand Palestine pounds, or about RM 15,000. The British Passport Control Office at Tiergartenstrasse 17 issued the Levin visas promptly. When it came time to apply to German authorities for a passport, however, the Levin family's applications were rejected without a reason. The passports were only distributed by the police headquarters on Alexanderplatz after the family had paid an additional RM 30,000—essentially a bribe—to a German lawyer. (Berlin's corrupt police chief, Count Helldorf, also figures in Beate Meyer's account of "Aryanization," chap. 4.) German authorities regularly forced wealthy Jews to make such payments in line with the extent of their assets. Finally, in December 1938 the Levin family was able to leave Berlin. They arrived in Haifa the following month.

What remained for those who could not buy their freedom? For all those who could not claim the "capitalist privilege," the only alternative was the Palestine Office.

*Emigration was now pushed forward at great speed. One had to apply for a visa—a so-called Kapitalistenvisum.*
WALTER LEVIN, 1999

## From 1939 to 1943

If the year 1938 was marked by a drastic intensification of the Third Reich's "Jewish policy," the pogrom of November 9–10, 1938, finally made it clear to all that there would be neither justice nor rule of law for German Jews in Nazi Germany.

The pogrom's state-sponsored terrorism only targeted institutions that were officially registered as Jewish. Thus, while the Palestine Office on Meinekestrasse was severely damaged during the pogrom and temporarily closed, the office of the Palestine Trust Company (Palästina Treuhandgesellschaft, or "Paltreu") on Potsdamer Strasse was spared. The Paltreu had been set up to transfer money and goods to Palestine, and it continued to operate without interference after the pogrom, despite the fact that only Jews were employed there. Owned jointly by the Anglo-Palestine Bank (which, as a foreign enterprise, was classed as neutral) and by the Wassermann and Warburg banks (both of which had already been "Aryanized"), the Paltreu had been saved by its ownership status.

By November 1938 at the latest, the ZVfD was officially banned. From this time on, the activities of the Zionists in Berlin thus elude comprehensive account. There are documents, but few of them are Jewish. There is also the testimony of survivors, but only the reports of and on the fate of a handful individuals remain.[5]

The Palestine Office was in fact able to continue its work under the auspices of the Reichsvertretung (after July 1939, the Reichsvereinigung). When its Meinekestrasse quarters reopened in mid-November 1938, the Palestine Office was immediately overwhelmed with a stream of applicants.

Also operating within the Reichsvereinigung as a department for vocational guidance was the Zionist youth organization Hechalutz, which recruited "pioneers" for emigration to Palestine. In the wake of November 9, it took on a new responsibility as well. Hechalutz worked to free some of the thousands of Jewish men who had been taken to concentration camps in the days after the pogrom (see chap. 1). Since the Nazis still hewed to a policy of forcing Jews into emigration, they were at that time willing to free those prisoners who could prove to the authorities that they had completed all emigration formalities. To this end, a "Release Department" within Hechalutz now worked to provide the authorities with confirmation of prisoners' acceptance to Zionist centers (as preparation for emigration to Palestine). Additional centers were now set up in Holland, Denmark, and England to help speed the process, and a significant number of prisoners were freed—or at least brought to temporary safety—through their efforts.

Meanwhile, as could be expected, a flood of people now approached all of the foreign consulates, including the British Passport Control Office, which was responsible for entry to Palestine as well as England. In response to the pogrom, the British government temporarily relaxed its entry restrictions for England

*Around 12:30 a mob broke down the door on Meinekestrasse. After consulting the [offices on] Kantstrasse, the leaders announced that all Jewish institutions had to be closed.*

BENNO COHN
(QUOTED IN
BALL-KADURI, *VOR
DER KATASTROPHE*,
P. 164)

*Captain Foley achieved amazing things at the time; not only in obtaining certificates and approval of certificates but also in sending news out of the country. [He] gave information to the foreign correspondents and made it possible for us to meet with these correspondents in his extraterritorial official apartment.*

FRANZ MEYER
(QUOTED IN
BALL-KADURI, *VOR
DER KATASTROPHE*,
P. 195)

and Palestine. Consulate staff was increased in the following weeks. Thanks to the Passport Control Officer Francis Ewald Foley, the administrative process of distributing visas was streamlined, and many additional entry permits were made available for both Palestine and England. Nonetheless, the consulate had to turn away a great many applicants.

## Youth Aliyah

A special category of immigration certificates was available for Youth Aliyah, an organization that worked for the group emigration of adolescents between the ages of fifteen and seventeen—without their parents. The Jewish Agency pledged to the British Mandate government that the accommodation and education of these young people would be provided for in Palestine (generally on kibbutzim). The youths, too, were prepared for life in Palestine while still in Germany.

Up to the outbreak of war, over 5,000 youths from Europe were able to enter Palestine, two-thirds of whom were from Germany. Preparatory centers for an additional 15,000 young people were set up in other European countries.[6] Working with groups such as Hechalutz, the Youth Aliyah training courses were financed on the one hand by the families of the young people and on the other hand by the German Jewish Communities and various international Jewish aid organizations. In view of the worsening situation in Germany, many parents wanted desperately to make it possible for their children to emigrate to Palestine, even if it meant that they themselves would have to stay behind.

Marianne Givol (née Marianne Henschel) was fifteen in September 1938. Her father, a lawyer, was active in the Jewish Community leadership and could not and did not want to leave Germany (see chap. 18). In November 1939 Marianne was sent to a Zionist preparatory camp in Rüdnitz near Berlin and was eventually able to emigrate with a Youth Aliyah group. Their train left Berlin's Anhalter station on January 31, 1939. Her parents, Moritz and Hildegard Henschel, remained behind, later surviving Theresienstadt. Her younger sister had been able to reach England with a *Kindertransport* in 1939.

Even where young people were concerned, however, the number of available emigration certificates was limited. Once again, the Palestine Office was in the terrible situation of having to decide who merited an immigration certificate. For most young people, registration with a Zionist association training camp was the only means of obtaining the coveted certificate. Hundreds registered, even as the majority of their parents remained reticent toward, or even opposed, Zionist ideology. Nonetheless, the Palestine Office made sure that not only

*There were some fifty or sixty youths from all over Germany. Most of them were from the Jewish youth movements. . . . We slept there in large rooms and did farm work in the mornings. . . . We didn't find it so easy, since we weren't used to it.*
MARIANNE GIVOL, 1999

*Some were not suited to community life or were not adaptable enough. They were not approved for Youth Aliyah.*
MARIANNE GIVOL, 1999

*My parents wanted nothing to do with it. But once [it became clear that] the emigration quotas for the U.S. and England meant waiting far too long, they agreed that I could register for Youth Aliyah.*
HERMANN WAGNER, 1999

I had no illusions
about it; why
should it be me [to
get the certificate]
when there were
so many Zionists
there? But—well, I
never!—I was the
tenth [one chosen]
and was then able
to sort everything
out that summer:
passport; getting
supplies. . . . Sum-
mer 1939. The
Anhalter station.
Farewell to my par-
ents. The last time
I saw them. Never
saw them again.
HERMANN WAGNER,
1999

First I asked for the
certificates for the
Polish Jews. That
was rejected, since
the German Jews
said that we had to
rescue the German
Jews first.
RECHA FREIER
(SFB TELEVISION
FEATURE)

children from Zionist families but also youths from "assimilated" families could emigrate. Parents, however, had to remain behind. Only a few were able to follow their children.

There were, furthermore, cases in which the Palestine Office did not recommend young people for emigration to Palestine, based on the results of the "trial period" spent in the *Hachshara* centers. And without acceptance for Aliyah, there was no emigration certificate.

## The Dispute over Recha Freier

Worsening general conditions for Jews in Berlin brought tremendous pressure on the staff of the Palestine Office. In the course of time, the decision to grant immigration certificates became a matter of life and death. A bitter dispute that took place between Recha Freier, the leading figure in Youth Aliyah, and the Reichsvereinigung offers a telling instance of this. Freier had chaired the Jewish Youth Aid (Jüdische Jugendhilfe) since its establishment in January 1933 by various Zionist youth organizations. In response to the infamous *Polen-Aktion* of October 1938—a Nazi round-up of male Polish Jews living in Germany—Freier sought to free some of the hundreds of Polish men who had been arrested in Berlin and taken to Sachsenhausen (see chap. 1). Her scheme was to provide them illegally with entry permits to Palestine.

With the assistance of a colleague in the Palestine Office, Freier managed to steal a hundred certificates, securing the release of some but not all of the Poles. The theft was discovered by the Reichsvereinigung, however. Denounced for giving certificates to Polish Jews that should have gone to German Jews, Freier was forced from her job in the Palestine Office and hurriedly left Berlin with her daughter Maayan in July 1940. Her husband the rabbi Moritz Freier and her sons were already in England. She managed to reach Zagreb via Vienna with the help of a smuggler, and from there she organized the exit of sixteen more girls from Berlin. The last transport of the Youth Aliyah left Berlin in early 1941.

## *Aliyah Beth:* Illegal Immigration

Beginning in October 1939, entry visas for Palestine could no longer be issued to German Jews in Germany, as Germany and Britain were officially at war. Henceforth emigration took place underground. From March 1939 to August 1940 the Palestine Office in Berlin organized illegal immigration—known as *Aliyah Beth*.[7]

With the Gestapo's knowledge—and sometimes right under its nose—emigrants were brought via Vienna along the Danube and into Yugoslavia, where they boarded Palestine-bound ships. About 1,700 Jews managed to leave Germany between March 1939 and September 1940. Travel documents, transit visas, and the ship's charter and equipment were organized by a German travel agent; payment was made in foreign currency through resources provided above all by the philanthropic American Jewish Joint Distribution Committee (known as the Joint). A total of six such illegal transports, or *Sonderhachshara* (special *Hachshara*) set sail for Palestine. The operation ended with the explosion of the ship *Patria* in the harbor of Haifa in November 1940. British authorities had forced 1,100 refugees to board the *Patria* to bring them to Mauritius for internment. The Jewish Resistance in Palestine tried to stop this operation with an explosion, but the *Patria* sank and 250 people perished.[8]

At first, the matter of illegal immigration to Palestine was a contentious one, not just among representatives of German Jews but also among the leading members of the Zionist movement. From Palestine, both Chaim Weizmann and David Ben Gurion feared that illegal immigration would annoy the British and thereby shatter their hopes of inducing Britain to return to a pro-Zionist Middle East policy. Ultimately, the opposite view won through. With time, these differences of opinion disappeared. From November 1938 on, the Jewish Agency in Jerusalem fully supported illegal immigration.

Two envoys, Pino Ginsburg and Max Zimels, were sent from Palestine to Germany in December 1938 with the mandate to dissolve the *Hachshara* farms in Germany and direct the young people working there to Palestine. Instead of closing them down, however, it was determined that that new *Hachshara* and training places should be set up, as more and more Jewish youth were clamoring to join. It was ultimately their last chance to leave Germany.

Yet now, at the beginning of 1939, the leading members of the Zionist movement in Germany had to ask themselves how long they themselves were to remain in Germany. Soon, they knew, it would be too late to get to Palestine. Kurt Goldmann, the head of the Palestine Office, left in March 1939. His successor was Efraim Erich Frank, who headed Hechalutz in Berlin until September 1940.

In the rising tide of Nazi decimation, Hechalutz was something of a Noah's Ark. Up to the last, when selecting candidates for emigration, Hechalutz insisted that three quarters of those bound for Palestine should be *chalutzim*—young "pioneers." This was true even of the *Sonderhachshara*. The young people bound for Palestine, it was said, had tiring journeys ahead of them and demanding,

*Recha went her own way. Neither Paul Eppstein nor Alfred Selbiger approved. One was typically German—that is, anxious to follow the instructions of the authorities. They felt that one risked everything by not doing so.*
JIZCHAK
SCHWERSENZ, 1999

*[I]t was still possible for transports to leave right under the noses of the Gestapo, for illegal transports still to depart in 1940. They were going to Vienna and from there along the Danube.*
JIZCHAK
SCHWERSENZ, 1999

*We were sixteen girls. I was the oldest at the time, and the youngest was nine. That was January 29, 1941, at the Anhalter station in Berlin. The farewell was awful—after all, we were leaving our mothers behind.*
TILLA OFFENBERGER
(NÉE TILLA NAGLER),
SFB FEATURE

**Figure 7.7**
Margot Edel (left) and Tilla Nagler (center) at the *Hachshara* agricultural center at Ahrensdorf, 1940

vital work to accomplish in the new homeland. Those assembling the transport lists thus considered it crucial that they be the brightest and the most highly skilled—in short, the fittest.

## Youth Work and Illegality

At the Youth Aliyah school in Berlin, young people were taught Hebrew, the history of the Jewish people, the history of Zionism, and Palestine studies as they awaited emigration to Palestine. From 1935 until the pogrom of November 9, 1938, the school had been housed in the youth center of the Berlin Jewish Community at Oranienburger Strasse 31. Only in May 1939 did it reopen, and then at two locations: on the premises of the Adass Jisroel high school in the Tiergarten district of Berlin, and at Choriner Strasse 74 in the Mitte district. There were a total of 280 pupils and 15 teachers. Jizchak Schwersenz became head of the Youth Aliyah school in 1938.

When war broke out in September 1939, a number of the school's pupils and teachers had already reached Palestine. The school continued on Choriner Strasse with 160 pupils and ten teachers. Its aim was to provide "preparatory

**Figure 7.8** Pupils with their teacher Jizchak Schwersenz during a Hanukkah party in the Youth Aliyah school, December 1940.

lessons for Jewish youths from the Berlin Jewish Community who have been dismissed from school." The school was officially closed in the fall of 1941 at the time of the first deportations of Jews from Berlin. But Schwersenz continued to teach, and for a short time he was able to use a few rooms in the Academy for Jewish Studies at Artilleriestrasse 14.

By 1941, most members of the Zionist youth groups and their leaders no longer had any hope of leaving Germany as emigrants. They continued, nonetheless, to maintain links with each other as comrades. Despite the official ban on Hechalutz, more and more young people joined the youth organizations. The sense of community was an important source of support to individuals. Hence, in a situation where there seemed to be virtually no chance of getting people to Palestine, the Zionist education of young Jews continued to spread.

In lieu of schools, small groups (*kwuzoth*) of six to eight members now formed, meeting regularly in secrecy to go on excursions, celebrate Jewish holidays together, study, and learn about life in Palestine. For the most part, youth leaders were already drafted to forced labor or auxiliary service within the framework of Nazi deportation programs, but they nonetheless tried to meet their groups two or three times a week in the homes of some of the *chaverim* (comrades). If

**Figure 7.9** Meeting of Zionist youth leaders in Alfred Selbiger's office at the Reichsvereinigung, Kantstrasse 158, August 1941. *Left to right*: Lotte Kaiser, Arthur Posnanski, Hans Wolfgang Cohn, Sonja Okun, Alfred Selbiger, Ludwig Kuttner, Kurt Silberpfennig, Jizchak Schwersenz, and Herbert Growald.

possible, they went to the synagogue together on the Sabbath, celebrating Oneg-Shabbat together after services. On Sundays they went on walks and hikes.

The teacher Jizchak Schwersenz, for example, was able to continue the Zionist education of some members of his former Youth Aliyah school group. For some time they would meet at Am Grossen Wannsee 46 and 76, on an estate that had previously belonged to the families Oppenheim and von Simson.[9] Since 1940 it had served as a Reichsvereinigung vocational center for gardening and forestry. In the fall of 1941 the Gestapo seized the plot and brought it under the control of an SS unit. Until 1943, the Gestapo permitted Jewish youths to stay on the land and work it agriculturally, with all produce handed over to the SS. The youngsters lived in Berlin and came to work in Wannsee in groups. Jizchak Schwersenz obtained permission to continue teaching agricultural subjects; secretly, however, he also taught the young people Hebrew, Jewish history, and Palestine studies.

## Alfred Selbiger and Jewish Youth Aid

Adolf Eichmann officially dissolved the Palestine Office in Berlin on May 21, 1941, on instructions from the Reich Ministry for the Interior. The offices at Meinekestrasse 10 were finally closed. Some of the leading employees were taken on by the Reichsvereinigung and maintained contact from their new posts with the young people on individual *Hachshara* farms. Alfred Selbiger, the last head of the Jewish Youth Aid and the last secretary of Hechalutz in Germany, was in charge of the Reichsvereinigung's department of "Vocational Training and Pro-

**Figure 7.10**
Tu BiShevat festival held by the Zionist members of the Reichsvereinigung at Kantstrasse 158, spring 1942

fessional Retraining." He thus managed all Jewish training centers—particularly the agricultural camps of Hechalutz, the Youth Aliyah, and manual training.

Within a few months, all Jewish schools would be closed, and all training centers officially banned. Selbiger was now transferred to the Reichsvereinigung's finance department. Here, too, he sought to continue his Zionist youth work. Although the youth organization was officially banned, he coordinated individual Zionist groups in Berlin and in the *Hachshara* farms around the city. However, the complete travel ban for Jews imposed on May 1, 1942, greatly hindered personal contact between the Berlin leadership and the individual kibbutzim. The farms were increasingly isolated.

The last major joint Zionist youth event in Berlin was Yom Hatzofim (Day of the Jewish Scouts) in March 1942, when thirty-five *chaverim* assembled to mark Tu BiShevat, the traditional "New Year of the Trees," or Arbor Day, which is held on the fifteenth day of the month of Shevat. The celebrants disguised the event at a Jewish school on Wilsnacker Strasse from the Gestapo by informing them that they had organized an educational event involving slides.

After all emigration was banned on October 23, 1941, the *Hachshara* farms were officially turned into camps for forced labor and came under the control of the local National Socialist employment offices. Remarkably, even under these circumstances, the young people lived relatively undisturbed on the farms in segregated Jewish communities, though they were forced to hand over their produce. They could no longer be supported financially by the Reichsvereinigung, however, and were only able to continue if they were self-sufficient. At the beginning of 1942, there were still six such communities with a total of

290 members in functioning centers. Once Jewish emigration was banned on October 23, 1941, preparation for emigration was no longer meaningful. In the course of 1942, these earlier *Hachshara* centers were gradually liquidated, and the youths working there and their teachers were deported to extermination camps.

Connections among individual Zionist groups in Germany almost completely broke down in late 1942. Alfred Selbiger and other leading members of the Reichsvereinigung were arrested as "hostages" during a Gestapo act of "retaliation" and subsequently shot (see chap. 18).

## Illegality: Chug Chalutzi

In the months that followed, all links to Palestine were cut off. There was, however, scattered contact with the world headquarters of Hechalutz in Geneva. Nathan Schwalb, who headed the office there, sent money, medicine, and food, along with reports on developments in Israel and encouragement to whomever he could. His primary goal was to encourage friends in Berlin to go underground or to cross the border to Switzerland illegally, organizing special escape routes for them. By this time, however, many of the leaders of individual youth groups in Berlin believed that they had to stay with their groups as long as possible, as only a small number of the young people had a chance of escaping and surviving illegally on their own.

Jizchak Schwersenz, the former head of the Youth Aliyah school, was one of the few who dared to go underground after being called up for deportation in August 1942. He did so with the help of Selbiger, who supported him with a sum of RM 100 per month. Schwersenz maintained contact with his Youth Aliyah group for many months to come.

Then came the Nazi *Fabrik-Aktion* on February 27, 1943, during which over 11,000 Berlin Jews were arrested, a majority of whom were deported directly to Auschwitz. That evening, a group of Jewish youths who had somehow managed to go underground founded one of the last known Zionist youth groups in Berlin, the Chug Chalutzi (Circle of Pioneers). They had assembled in the Friedenau district of Berlin in the home of a young woman named Edith Wolff who had already prepared hiding places and other means of assistance to help them survive. Along with two Jews living underground—Heinz Zwi Abrahamson and Leopold (Poldi) Jehuda Chones—the group consisted of *Mischlinge* who had up until the *Fabrik-Aktion* been protected from deportation because they had a non-Jewish parent. (Some of them had been arrested and held for several days on Rosenstrasse in an administrative building of the Jewish Community—see chap.

*We are living in truly difficult times. Many of us have been taken away already to face an uncertain future in Poland. But a Tzofeh, a Jewish scout, will never falter. And so one thing was certain for us: in spite of everything we will come together, this time, too, on this special day.*

ARJEH DAVIDOW-ITSCH, MARCH 1942

**Figure 7.11**
The Zionist group Chug Chalutzi in Grunewald forest, June 1943. Left to right: Gad Beck, David Billard, Jizchak Schwersenz, Zwi (Heinz) Abrahamson, Leopold (Poldi) Jehuda Chones.

9.) With Schwersenz as their leader, the group would meet regularly for lessons in Hebrew and Jewish history.

In the face of the overwhelming external pressure, Schwersenz and the members of Chug Chalutzi sought to create an alternative world through comradeship and "being there for one another." The young people not only helped one another survive underground but also consolidated their will not to expose themselves to their fate without a fight. True to their Zionist credo, they were determined to remain upright and proud Jews to the end.

In the face of obvious danger, Schwersenz continued to organize hikes through Berlin's Grunewald forest with his group as late as June 1943. They celebrated Jewish holidays in the families of some of the *chaverim*. Finally, in February 1944, Jizchak Schwersenz managed to escape to Switzerland, and leadership of the group passed to a young man named Gad Beck, who continued its resistance activities. Nathan Schwalb in Geneva gave support from afar, drawing, above all, on financial resources from Joint, organizing accommodations in Berlin for people living underground, and providing them with food. Money and messages were transferred by courier. As late as July 1944 Beck was still able to smuggle letters and even parcels containing food to people who had been deported to Auschwitz.

Not all members of the Chug Chalutzi escaped to Switzerland. Edith Wolff was arrested on June 19, 1943 (see chaps. 15 and 16). Schwalb had sent a document for her to Berlin declaring her to be a citizen of San Salvador, but it never reached her. The Americans liberated her from Lippstadt Prison in 1945. Poldi

*We said "No!" . . . One couldn't withdraw from Jewish fate—one had to support others within the framework of the Community.*

ANNELIESE-ORA
BORINSKI, MEMOIRS

7.12

**Figure 7.12** Schawuot-Fest of the Beck family, June 1943.

**Figure 7.13** Ahrensdorf agricultural center, 1937–38

**Figure 7.14** Anneliese-Ora Borinski and Akiba Levinski, representatives of the Jewish Agency in Geneva, 1946

7.13

7.14

Chones, who had been living underground since the deportation of his parents in February 1943, was captured in October 1943 and deported to Auschwitz. In the final months of the war, Gad Beck and the remaining members of the Chug Chalutzi also had to hide from the Gestapo. Their resistance activities had become known, and the group was denounced. Zwi Abrahamson had previously been arrested but managed to escape from the prison at the assembly camp on Grosse Hamburger Strasse on New Year's Eve 1943–44 with other members of Chug Chalutzi. He was arrested for a second time on March 5, 1945, and taken with Gad Beck to the Gestapo prison on Schulstrasse. It was here that the two young men experienced the end of the war, after having been liberated by camp leader Dobberke on April 22, 1945.

The last representatives of the Berlin Jewish Community and the Reichsvereinigung classed as *Volljuden* were deported from Berlin with the major wave of deportation that took place from January to June 1943. Among them were Zionists such as Alfred Selbiger who had worked throughout the period to get young people out of Germany.

The last remaining Zionist *Hachshara* farms near Berlin was the agricultural center at Neuendorf, which housed around sixty youths and a group of thirty older *chaverim*. They were led by Anneliese-Ora Borinski, Hans Wolfgang Cohn, and Herbert Growald. On April 7, 1943, the authorities ordered them to prepare for deportation. They gathered that evening for their final *Fahnenappell* (a roll call flag-raising ceremony). For the last time, the participants dressed in the Zionist colors of blue and white. The flags were brought in, including the *Degalim* (flags) of the *Hachshara* farms at Ahrensdorf, Havelberg, and Jessen, which had already been closed. Herbert Growald took the flag from Ahrensdorf and gave portions of it to twelve of the *chaverim* and *chaverot* present.

On April 8, 1945, the group was taken from the Neuendorf agricultural center to the assembly camp at Grosse Hamburger Strasse 26 in Berlin. Here they held the last joint Sabbath celebration for all of the detainees. The next Monday, April 19, 1943, they were deported to Auschwitz.

Ora Borinski, one of the three youth leaders at Ahrensdorf, survived Auschwitz. In 1947 she brought her piece of the Ahrensdorf flag with her to Palestine; she lived in the Maayan Zwi kibbutz in northern Israel until her death in 1997. The flag is now in the collection of the Centrum Judaicum in Berlin.

**Figure 7.15** Ora Aloni (Anneliese-Ora Borinski) on the Maayan Zwi kibbutz, spring 1976

[W]e were singing our songs, and the Gestapo heard us. And if they could understand, they may have laughed at these fools who in this situation were singing, "We are building a new, strong race! We demand Jewish honor! We stand up for freedom, equality, and justice!"

ANNELIESE-ORA BORINSKI, MEMOIRS

**1** Avraham Barkai, "Jüdisches Leben unter der Verfolgung," in *Deutsch-Jüdische Geschichte in der Neuzeit,* vol. 4 of *Aufbruch und Zerstörung, 1918–1945,* ed. Avraham Barkai and Paul Mendes-Flohr (Munich, 1997), p. 227.

**2** The British Mandate in Palestine had administered the area since 1920. As early as 1917, it was committed to aiding the cause of the Jewish homeland and fostering Jewish immigration there. At the same time, however, the number of Jews to be admitted was limited. British Mandate authorities set stringent requirements for entrance permits.

**3** Tom Segev, *The Seventh Million: The Israelis and the Holocaust* (New York, 1993), German edition, *Die siebte Million. Der Holocaust und Israels Politik der Erinnerung* (Reinbek bei Hamburg, 1995), pp. 46–51, 105–14.

**4** Shalom Adler-Rudel, *Jüdische Selbsthilfe unter dem Naziregime 1933–1939 im Spiegel der Berichte der Reichsvertretung der Juden in Deutschland* (Tübingen, 1974), pp. 85–86.

**5** Recha Freier, *Let the Children Come: The Early History of Youth Aliyah* (London, 1961); Kurt Jakob Ball-Kaduri, *Vor der Katastrophe. Juden in Deutschland, 1934–1939* (Tel Aviv, 1967); Anneliese-Ora Borinski, *Erinnerungen, 1940–1943* (Nördlingen, 1970); Jizchak Schwersenz, *Die versteckte Gruppe. Ein jüdischer Lehrer erinnert sich an Deutschland* (Berlin, 1988); Schwersenz, German typescript for the Hebrew edition and typescript on Alfred Selbiger, LBI Jerusalem, no. 152; Gad Beck, *Und Gad ging zu David. Die Erinnerungen des Gad Beck,* ed. Frank Heibert (Berlin, 1997). See also Gad Beck, *An Underground Life: Memoirs of a Gay Jew in Nazi Berlin,* trans. Allison Brown (Madison, 2000).

**6** Barkai, *Jüdisches Leben,* p. 289.

**7** Eliyahu Kutti Salinger, *"Nächstes Jahr im Kibbuz," Die jüdisch-chaluzische Jugendbewegung in Deutschland zwischen 1933 und 1943* (Paderborn, 1998), pp. 116–19 and 145–48; Ferdinand Kroh, *David kämpft. Vom jüdischen Widerstand gegen Hitler* (Reinbek bei Hamburg, 1988), pp. 22–33.

**8** Avraham Barkai and Paul Mendes-Flohr, *Deutsch-Jüdische Geschichte in der Neuzeit,* vol. 4, *Aufbruch und Zerstörung, 1918–1945* (Munich, 1997), p. 317.

**9** Salinger, *Nächstes Jahr,* pp. 209–11.

6

Forced Labor

# Chapter Eight
## Forced Labor

DIANA SCHULLE

The National Socialists launched their anti-Jewish policy as soon as they came to power in 1933, discriminating against the approximately 500,000 Jews then in Germany, isolating them, and driving them from the country. The "elimination" of Jewish Germans from economic life brought with it extensive demographic and social change. Because the majority of Jews who emigrated were youths or people of working age who could meet the stringent immigration provisions of host countries, the proportion of the elderly and women within the Jewish population in Germany increased considerably. So did the proportion of unemployed. Yielding to Nazi pressure, many firms now refused to employ Jews and hired non-Jews to replace those Jews they had fired. There were, moreover, ever fewer firms in Jewish ownership that would have employed the growing ranks of unemployed Jews.[1] "Legality is not the watchword but harassment," Joseph Goebbels had noted in his diary in June 1938. "The Jews must get out of Berlin."[2] The Reich Propaganda Minister, as Gauleiter of Berlin, played a key role in making the city unbearable for its Jewish population.

By the summer of 1938, a state of social misery had completely taken hold. Around a quarter of the city's Jews could no longer support themselves and had to rely on public charity.[3] The international conference at Evian that convened to address the Jewish refugee crisis had come to nothing, and the chance of emigrating was smaller than ever. Because the Nazi regime had heretofore made the expulsion of all Jews a priority, it had not made plans for employing the many out-of-work Jews who were unable to emigrate.

Up until then, forced labor (*Zwangsarbeit*), or "segregated labor deployment" (*geschlossener Arbeitseinsatz*), as it was officially known, had not featured in the Nazi policy of persecution. It was discussed as new legal possibility by the employment offices in the summer of 1938.[4] The interest corresponded with the wishes of local authorities to reduce or completely eliminate the financial burdens arising from the authorization of welfare payments to needy Jews. As early as 1937, Heinrich Himmler, Reichsführer of the SS, had deprecatingly described half of the Germans who were unemployed as "work-shy," declaring that their labor capacity could be exploited if they were grouped together in camps. Those defined as "work-shy" were "men of working age, whose capacity for labor deployment . . . has been established and in whose case it can be proven that on two occasions they rejected jobs offered to them without a justifiable reason, or accepted the jobs but gave them up again after a short time without a good reason."[5]

Previously, neither Nazi political propaganda nor the welfare system distinguished among the social categories of "work-shy" Germans, "asocials," and Jews. Only after the first three Nazi campaigns against "asocials" and the "work-shy" did the Jews appear as a distinct target group. In general, male Jews were to be transferred to concentration camps as soon as they were found to have a previous conviction.[6]

On October 14, 1938, Hermann Göring, director of the Four-Year Plan, attended a meeting to discuss how best to implement the "gigantic" goals of the war economy program ordered by Hitler. In the course of the discussions the necessary management of labor was set in motion along with the armaments industry. Road, canal, and railway building had to be pushed forward "with brutal means" and, if necessary, with "forced labor camps." Göring called for the "Jewish Question" to be solved by all possible means. The expulsion policy had, he claimed, come to a standstill and "required" new isolation measures such as the creation of ghettos in cities and the establishment of Jewish labor columns. Only then would "the people . . . emigrate on their own volition."[7]

Five days later, on October 19, 1938, Friedrich Syrup, president of the Reich Institution for Labor Provision and Unemployment Insurance (Reichsanstalt für Arbeitsvermittlung und Arbeitslosenversicherung), ordered that lists be made by the end of the month. The lists were to detail the names of all unemployed Jews registered with the labor administrations. In addition, Syrup asked the labor administrations to "check the extent to which the unemployed Jews registered in your district can be deployed to carry out useful work. In doing so, it should be assumed that unemployed Jews can generally only be deployed for work in small or fairly large groups in which they will not come into contact with non-Jewish workers. When presenting the . . . summary, please inform me at the same time of existing or potential possibilities for labor deployment . . . in your district."[8]

Employing out-of-work Jews was difficult, so thoroughly had they been excluded from their professions and barred from entering new ones. Ill and elderly Jews, were, moreover, unsuited to the physically strenuous work that the au-

**Figure 8.1**
Jewish forced laborers
in Berlin

thorities had in mind. The employment offices had made efforts to exclude Jews, refusing to place them or making such unattractive job proposals that those concerned refrained from using the employment offices again. Some employment office employees even refused to grant unemployed Jews the financial assistance due to them by law.[9]

IN THE WAKE OF the pogrom of November 9, 1938, special taxes were levied on the Jews as punishment, driving even more of them into poverty. Also, November 19, 1938, saw the start of Jewish segregation in terms of welfare. All state welfare obligations were thereafter to fall on the Jewish Community; needy Jews could only receive Jewish resources and could only draw minimum public benefits in an extreme emergency. Because the authorities counted even the most modest assets, needy Jews were unable to save money that would have been critical for emigration, thus ruling that option out entirely.

Four weeks later, on December 20, 1938, all unemployed Jews and Jews receiving social benefits on Reich territory were ordered to take part in "segregated labor deployment." On December 23, 1938, the Berlin labor administration set up a Central Jewish Service Department (Zentrale Dienststelle für Juden) at Fontanepromenade 15 in the Kreuzberg district. This institution was not staffed by employees of the Jewish Community but rather by "German-blooded" officials and employees. Government Inspector Alfred Eschhaus headed the Labor Deployment Office for Jews (Einsatzstelle für Juden) at the Berlin employment office. He made no effort to conceal his hostility and was consequently feared

*And he yelled at me, "Impertinent Jewish riff-raff!" I don't know what he said. It was a dreadful barrage of abuse . . . That was the Eschhaus then.*
MARIE SIMON, 1998

by Jewish workers. The employment office soon became known as "Bully Promenade" (*Schikanepromenade*).[10]

The authorities preferred to refer to forced labor with the euphemism *Dienstverpflichtung* (service duty). Among Jews, "it was generally common to speak of forced labor [*Zwangsarbeit*]. [But a] special vocabulary . . . among the Jews in their interaction with one another often served as camouflage so that a third party to their conversations would not know what they were talking about and could not therefore denounce them."[11]

Many unemployed Jews opposed the new policy by simply deregistering themselves from the employment office in question. On the one hand, this reduced the labor capacity available for deployment. On the other hand, it reduced the social welfare available to those unemployed Jews who had essentially relinquished their entitlement to unemployment benefits. It was thus technically impossible to register a portion of Jews. To fill the resulting gaps, many administrations consulted their registers of Jews (*Judenregister*), which they had set up on their own initiatives. The National Socialist administration also made use of the list compiled by Jewish institutions to track down those who had deliberately withdrawn from the official lists.

In this respect, special attention was paid to the records kept by the Reichsvereinigung der Juden in Deutschland (Reich Association of Jews in Germany). (see chap. 18). They consulted the records of the Jewish Communities themselves, which had to set up internal "labor deployment" departments.

More and more Jews—as well as "asocials"—were deployed as a result of the "Syrup Decree." They were not granted extra food rations and had to work under restrictive overtime and holiday regulations. In May 1939 all Jewish men in Germany between 18 and 55 and all women between 18 and 50 were ordered to register for labor deployment with the appropriate department of their respective Jewish Communities.

Eyewitness reports confirm that Jews were consistently deployed in work alien to their own profession. Doctors, lawyers, writers, and academics were often forced to perform the dirtiest tasks: trash collection, toilet cleaning for the Reich Railways, clearing snow in winter, cleaning jobs in the chemical and textile industries, and so forth. Or they were relegated to physically exhausting tasks such as quarrying and construction work or to strenuous and monotonous jobs in the metal and electrical industries.

THE START OF THE war brought fundamental changes for Germany's already persecuted Jewish population. The borders of the German Reich were all but sealed, trapping the Jews who remained.[12] "Because the National Socialist lead-

*Just to harass us they made us . . . wait in a really dark and narrow corridor. . . . It was very depressing, simply because we were so afraid of what was to come. We didn't know how long it would last and we felt that this unpleasant situation was being caused deliberately.*

MARIE SIMON, 1998

ership had to abandon the thought of deporting the Jews in groups to a territory beyond German control during the war," writes historian Wolf Gruner, "it concentrated its efforts after the occupation of Poland on examining the opportunities for forced resettlement within the new area of control."[13] After several deportations of Jews were made there, however, the German governor of occupied Poland, Hans Frank, protested vehemently. It was then stipulated that transports would no longer be sent to Poland "without proper registration within the assigned period."[14] Such arrangements meant that Jews would remain in the German workforce longer than originally intended.

At the beginning of April 1940 the Berlin employment office placed an announcement in the *Jüdisches Nachrichtenblatt* stating that "young, strong Jews wishing to work in the construction industry can be . . . placed immediately"[15] (see chap. 6). When the response did not match the employment office's expectations, staff members from the Jewish institutions were summarily fired and informed that they were to provide the required labor themselves. The operation was terminated after the Reich Security Main Office (Reichssicherheitshauptamt RSHA) objected. But new conditions required the Jewish Community to nominate "able labor forces" based on its tax register (*Kataster*).[16]

Both the employment office and the RSHA would hereafter draw on the Reichsvereinigung to obtain auxiliary forces for its own use. Surprisingly, the RSHA did not always prevail over its competitor, especially when it came to matters that were not of fundamental importance to the Gestapo. In November 1940, for example, the Berlin employment office requested—and received— "Jews" in order to manage the delivery of Christmas packages.[17] However, contact between both institutions intensified after armaments inspectorates were established. The deployment of Jews in the armaments industry had become important. When the deportations began, both authorities initially resisted, reluctant to lose labor forces that were vital to armaments production.[18]

The labor shortage in industry once again intensified beginning in September 1940. Despite the huge war machine there were relatively few foreign workers in Germany (from Poland, France, and other occupied countries). Since the numbers of Jewish forced laborers had to be increased, men as old as sixty and women up to fifty-five were now to be deployed as well. In fact, many of those recruited were considerably older than sixty; the industrial health and safety regulation of December 12, 1939, did not apply to Jews.

"More and more people are coming through the door," observed Edith Freund at the employment office. "One cannot imagine that there could still be so many Jews able to work. But are they really able to work? There are so many old people in this room, it seems that one is taking people up to seventy years of age. What

**Figure 8.2** Jewish forced laborers from the Hensel family on a lunch break from building the air-raid shelter for the Community school on Richard-Wagner-Strasse

*A terrific community developed. The pressure was great enough to bind us closely together. The pressure was awful. But it was not so extreme that one would steal the last crumb of bread from another, that one would betray another or—to put it crudely—that one had to kill another in order to survive.*

MARIE SIMON, 1998

do they want with these old people?"[19] From October 1940 on, the employment offices also recruited children under the age of 16, once again disregarding health and safety legislation.

Of the 41,000 Jews aged between 18 and 60 registered in Berlin, almost half were over 45 years of age and therefore not suitable for the assembly line work envisaged. To fill the gap of young labor, the labor administration increased its recruitment of Jews living in mixed marriages, including those who already held regular jobs. These people were then compulsorily drafted into a segregated labor reserve.[20] Problems arose almost immediately. As the labor ministry had not permitted any exceptions to segregated labor deployment, its discriminatory conditions thus affected many close relatives of "German *Volksgenossen* (fellow nationals)." The provision was soon relaxed in order to avoid social unrest. In the future, too, this group was generally protected from forced labor.[21]

While the decree of August 23, 1941, prevented the emigration of Jews, the potential for recruited Jewish forced labor was finally exhausted in the summer of 1941. From August 1941 the Berlin labor administration no longer released Jewish laborers for work in other areas, although the expansion of the war to almost the whole of Europe made the labor shortage close to immeasurable. "We also have so many sick women, who should really not be . . . working here," noted Edith Freund of the large laundry facility in the Köpenick district where she was forced to work. "The responsible company doctor, however, does not sign them off. . . . But the company only very rarely fires workers, and only when

**Figure 8.3** Forced laborers collecting garbage in Berlin, 1940. Left to right: Siegbert Weber, Max Jacobi, David Haller; on truck: Erich Lachmann.

there is a major reason, for the employment office sends no replacements for people who have been let go."[22] Of the 32,275 Jewish men and women in Berlin who were classed as fit to work, 28,000 were compulsorily drafted for forced labor and an additional 2,000 worked for the Jewish institutions. With this, labor capacity was fully utilized.

Some 19,000 Berlin Jews were employed in industries considered essential to the war effort, but their economic significance as workers continued to decline on account of the approximately two million "foreign workers" (*Fremdarbeiter*) within the German economy.[23]

Hitler, who expected Moscow to fall by October 15, 1941, at the latest, planned to deport "the Jews from German territory." Ostensibly to provide accommodation to "Aryans" whose apartments had been destroyed by air raids, some of the Jews were to be moved east, to the Lódz ghetto from the Altreich, Vienna, and the Protectorate (of Bohemia and Moravia). These families were "resettled" together, and Jews fit to work were forced into labor in the armaments firms "for payment"—though the payment went, in fact, to the firms. On October 3, Himmler demanded the collective confiscation of the entire assets of the "Jews to be deported."

In many firms, there was much agitation when the Gestapo assigned Jewish labor forces to the deportation transports without first consulting them. In some cases, firm proprietors managed just in time to reclaim Jews who were already awaiting deportation in assembly camps. The Gestapo continued to act on its own discretion, and in various regions there were disagreements between the

Gestapo and the labor authorities. The armaments commissions, for their part, called for the deportations to be postponed until a replacement workforce was available.

It soon became clear to the German Jews that their jobs were their lifelines—the only way to escape deportation. As a witness recalls, "the Jewish employment office on Rosenstrasse was . . . in constant contact with the employment office on Fontanepromenade and had often, before deportation loomed, . . . asked the Jews if they could work and what kind of work they could do. Unfortunately not everyone responded to the initial inquiries and paid dearly for this later. For with the constant increase in evacuations, the Fontanepromenade employment office was less and less inclined . . . to provide work, noting that the Jews looking for work at this stage mostly only did so to save themselves from evacuation."[24]

Soon it was said that no more Jews went voluntarily to Fontanepromenade, since they would have then been reported to the Gestapo.

By November 1941 the awaited contingent of Soviet prisoners of war had still not arrived. Jewish forced laborers continued to be deported even as those in charge of the war economy complained that substitute workers were not being recruited fast enough. The labor shortage was now acute, particularly in Berlin. The armaments inspectorate even called for a stop to the deportations—which in fact took place at the end of January. Authorities cited "insufficient railway capacity" for the halt. Indeed, according to Gruner, rail capacity had "never been so severe on account of the provision of winter supplies to the German army after its defeat outside of Moscow."[25]

*The nature of the work made it so wearing. The worst was, however, the monotony—the eternal repetition of a few hand movements and the feeling of senselessness, the conviction that we were not just doing something useless but also wrong—that is, serving the armaments industry.*

MARIE SIMON, 1998

IN EARLY 1942 JEWS were assigned to more than 230 firms in Berlin, a situation that could not have made hard-line Nazi ideologues very happy. On Hitler's birthday, Fritz Sauckel, the plenipotentiary general for labor deployment, announced the complete mobilization of all foreign labor forces for the German war economy. At the end of May, Hitler agreed with Goebbels that Jews employed in the armaments industry should be replaced with foreign workers as soon as possible.[26] June 1942 saw the start of deportation to Theresienstadt of Jews with war decorations, the elderly, and other previously "privileged" categories. Heinrich Stahl, the chairman of the Berlin Jewish Community, was among the first to be deported.[27] Additional transports followed. By early September 1942 there were just 46,658 Jews left in Berlin.[28]

In the meantime, companies and firms had to observe stricter guidelines with regard to the postponement of deportation for certain "essential" workers. The tightening of restrictions meant that an additional 3,000 Berlin Jews were deported that September. From November on, the transports from Berlin to the

**Figure 8.4**
Jewish forced laborers
unloading slag

east went only to Auschwitz and Theresienstadt (For the lists of deportations, see chap. 10.)

For all workers sent out "on a transport," the Gestapo on Burgstrasse kept the disability cards, tax statements, and *Arbeitsbücher* (work books—compulsory records of education and training). Any remaining wages due to the worker or his or her family were then transferred to a Gestapo account by the payroll office of the firm concerned. The Association for the Jewish Religion (Jüdisches Kultusvereinigung, as the Reichsvereinigung was known after April 1941) on Oranienburger Strasse received items of clothing and other belongings of the deportees.[29]

In October the armaments companies were informed that they would have to dismiss all of their Jewish laborers in the course of the next few months. They were, however, assured that the process would not burden the companies too much and, moreover, would allow enough time to find replacement labor. In mid-November, armaments commando III knew "that all of the Jews will be removed within the next half year and replaced by Poles."[30]

On November 26, 1942, Fritz Sauckel informed the labor administrations in each state (*Land*) that "Jews deployed in work essential to the war effort" would be exchanged "with Polish labor" that month. By December, however, far too few Poles had arrived in Berlin for the planned exchange of forced laborers to take place.[31] The RSHA gave the Reichsvereinigung the task of again registering all Jews for the next "deportation transports."[32]

In the first days of January 1943 Hitler called for more intensive recruitment of French and Dutch labor with the result that around 120,000 foreigners and prisoners of war were assigned to the war economy that month. By February their numbers had reached around 138,000.[33]

Despite continued objections from the armaments industry, the Gestapo stripped it of more and more Jewish workers. Goebbels feared that foreign laborers would forge dangerous links to the Jews if they were allowed to work alongside them. With this in mind, the Propaganda Minister embarked on his plan of "sudden" deportation—the so-called *Fabrik-Aktion* (see chap. 9).

This final campaign was aimed at removing the last working Jews from their jobs. Many of those who had until this point escaped deportation were living in mixed marriages. When this large number of forced laborers disappeared from the armaments industry, it caused operational difficulties in some areas, as no replacement labor could be found. Within a few days it was decided to return the "Jews taken from labor deployment essential to the war effort but not suitable for evacuation and resettlement" to a "segregated labor reserve that can be withdrawn at any time."[34] Jews from "privileged" mixed marriages were increasingly engaged in segregated forced labor—for example, for "service" with the Organisation Todt (OT), a state construction firm set up in 1938 to build military installations.[35] At the beginning of October 1943 Himmler ordered a second *Fabrik-Aktion*, "as there are still many Jewish *Mischlinge* in protected firms" who could be taken "to the OT for segregated labor deployment in construction battalions."

Himmler's final persecution campaign began a few months before the end of the war: "All male and female Jews living in a mixed marriage (including "Jews by definition" [*Geltungsjuden*])—both nationals and stateless people—who are able to work . . . are to be taken on collective transports to the old-age ghetto at Theresienstadt to join segregated labor reserves, if possible by February 15, 1945." Now, however, the prevailing chaos of war provided an opportunity for many of those concerned to escape. In the face of foreseeable defeat, the RSHA cancelled the operation in March 1945.[36]

**1** Dieter Maier, *Arbeitseinsatz und Deportation. Die Mitwirkung der Arbeitsverwaltung bei der nationalsozialistischen Judenverfolgung in den Jahren, 1938–1945* (Berlin, 1994), p. 18.

**2** Joseph Goebbels, diary entry dated June 11, 1938, in *Die Tagebücher von Joseph Goebbels*, ed. Elke Fröhlich, part 1, vol. 3 (Munich, 1993), p. 452.

**3** Wolf Gruner, *Der geschlossene Arbeitseinsatz deutscher Juden. Zur Zwangsarbeit als Element der Verfolgung, 1938–1943* (Berlin, 1997), p. 40. This article is largely based on Gruner's thorough and comprehensive account.

**4** Maier, *Arbeitseinsatz*, pp. 22–23.

**5** Ibid., p. 21.

**6** Gruner, *Der geschlossene Arbeitseinsatz*, p. 43. Jews were disproportionately affected by the *Juni-Aktion*, since more than 2,500 were taken to concentration camps. Of an estimated total of 9,000 to 10,000 people arrested, around 20 percent were Jews. In Buchenwald, the 1,256 Jews made up half of the "asocials" who had been brought there. In the concentration camp at Sachsenhausen, the 824 Jews made up 13 percent of the "asocials" (p. 44).

**7** Minutes of the meeting with Göring on October 14, 1938, in *Der Prozeß gegen die Hauptkriegsverbrecher vor dem Internationalen Militärgerichtshof, 14. November 1945–1. Oktober 1946*, Nuremberg 1948, vol. 27, doc. PS–1301, pp. 160–164.

**8** Maier, *Arbeitseinsatz*, pp. 23–24.

**9** Ibid., p. 26.

**10** Audio cassette account by Marie Simon (née Jalowicz), 1998, CJ; "Als Zwangsarbeiterin 1941 in Berlin. Die Aufzeichnungen der Volkswirtin Elisabeth Freund," edited with commentary by Carola Sachse (Berlin, 1996), p. 24.

**11** Marie Simon, "Zwangsarbeiterin 1941 in Berlin," audio cassette account, 1998.

**12** Gruner, *Der geschlossene Arbeitseinsatz*, pp. 107–13. This contains a detailed account of events. First the freedom of movement and food rations were restricted. The RFSS (Reichsführer SS Commando) imposed a curfew after 8 P.M. for Jews on September 6, 1939.

**13** Ibid., p. 110. On September 23, 1939, radios were confiscated throughout the Reich in order to prevent access to information.

**14** IMG, vol. 36, doc. 305–EC.

**15** *Jüdisches Nachrichtenblatt*, no. 29, April 9, 1940, p. 1.

**16** Note on the Gestapo summons of April 24, 1940, C Re 1, No. 45, Bl. 214, Bundesarchiv (BArch), Berlin.

**17** Maier, *Arbeitseinsatz*, p. 70.

**18** Ibid., p. 71.

**19** Sachse, *Als Zwangsarbeiterin*, p. 44.

**20** Gruner, *Der geschlossene Arbeitseinsatz*, p. 163.

**21** Ibid., p. 205.

**22** Sachse, *Als Zwangsarbeiterin*, p. 81.

**23** Gruner, *Der geschlossene Arbeitseinsatz*, p. 212.

**24** Eyewitness testimony quoted in Maier, *Arbeitseinsatz*, pp. 150–51.

**25** Gruner, *Der geschlossene Arbeitseinsatz*, p. 292.

**26** Ibid., pp. 298–300.

**27** Hermann Simon, "*Heinrich Stahl*," Vortrag von Hermann Simon, gehalten zur Gedenkfeier der Jüdischen Gemeinde zu Berlin am 22. April 1993 (Berlin, 1993), p. 24.

**28** Wolf Gruner, "Die Reichshauptstadt und die Verfolgung der Berliner Juden, 1933–1945," in *Jüdische Geschichte in Berlin. Essays und Studien*, ed. Reinhard Rürup (Berlin, 1995), p. 250.

**29** Payroll office of Schering AG to the regional headquarters of Gestapo Department 4 d, letters dated March 9, 1943, and March 24, 1943, Landesarchiv Berlin (LAB), Rep. 229, nr. 9/514.

**30** Maier, *Arbeitseinsatz*, p. 171.

**31** Gruner, *Der geschlossene Arbeitseinsatz*, p. 311.

**32** The Reichsvereinigung had an instruction printed in the *Jüdisches Nachrichtenblatt* of November 27, 1942, stating that "all Jews, thus also *Geltungsjuden* in Berlin" were obliged to hand in personal information to the Statistics Department of the Reichsvereinigung within three days. Four copies were required. This included details on "racial" classification—privileged/nonprivileged *Mischehe* [mixed marriage], *Rasse-/Geltungsjude* [Jew by race/by definition] as well as the address with the floor and section of the building. Discrepancies in the Reichsvereinigung's tax register led to a new registration of all Berlin Jews from November 27, 1942. Two editions later, on December 11, 1942, the *Jüdisches Nachrichtenblatt* published a "warning" that those who "turned out to be unregistered" upon checking, that is, on comparing the emigration and employment office files, would have "to reckon with punishment." This warning was above all addressed to Jews in mixed marriages. See also the "board matters" of November 22, 1942, p. 6, BArch, 75 C Re 1, No. 3, n.p.

**33** In addition, 15,000 men and 160,000 women were forced to go into industry as a result of the new registration order in February, BArch, R 41 (RArbM), no. 29, sheets 126–27. Quoted in Gruner, *Der geschlossene Arbeitseinsatz,* p. 314.

**34** Gruner, *Der geschlossene Arbeitseinsatz,* p. 322. See glossary for definitions of privileged and nonprivileged mixed marriages.

**35** Ibid., p. 327.

**36** Ibid., pp. 328–29.

# Chapter Nine

## The Rosenstrasse Protest

DIANA SCHULLE

Until the pogrom of November 1938 the Nazi regime had not differentiated between Jews living in so-called "mixed marriages" (*Mischehe*) and other "full Jews" (*Volljuden*) in terms of persecution and expulsion measures. After this date, a "period of exceptions and postponed repression" for those in mixed marriages began.[1] In 1942, however, the leadership began a more intense debate on how to deal with both Jews in "mixed marriages" and mixed-raced Jews, or *Mischlinge*. There were now rumors that first-degree Mischlinge would be treated as "full Jews," that they would have to wear the yellow star, and would be subject to "evacuation,"—that is, deportation.

In December 1942, officials in the Reich Security Main Office (Reichssicherheitshauptamt RSHA) began to coordinate the final wave of deportations. It was probably here that the guidelines emerged for a Reich-wide "concluding operation" (*Schluß-Aktion*).[2]

In 1941—nearly two years earlier—Joseph Goebbels had complained in a diary entry that Berlin's Jews could not be summarily "evacuated" because 30,000 of them were working (as forced laborers) in the armaments industry.[3] By February 1943, however, he was exultant: "Now the Jews of Berlin will finally be deported. On February 28 they are to be assembled, first, in camps and then deported in groups of up to 2,000 per day. My goal is to make Berlin completely free of Jews [*judenfrei*] by mid-March, or by the end of March at the latest."[4]

Nazi morale could not have been particularly high when the Reich Propaganda Minister was writing this diary entry. German and Italian troops had been in retreat from British and American forces in North Africa since November 1942. Then came extraordinarily heavy losses at Stalingrad. On January 31—the day after the Reich had duly celebrated the tenth anniversary of the Nazis' rise to power—the Sixth Army capitulated in the southern part of Stalingrad.

*Then came the last major operation in February 1943. I went downstairs. I wanted to take my book back to Thorbeck's lending library. . . . Then a policeman came and said, "You're a Jew." "So what?" I replied. "I've got to take you with me, you can't go back home," he said.*
HANS ISRAELOWICZ, 1999

THAT FEBRUARY THERE WERE 35,246 Jews living in Berlin, some 17,000 of whom were deployed as forced laborers.[5] Among these were members of Jewish families as well as single men and women (including those who had previously been married to non-Jews)[6] and had not yet been deported. There were also a substantial number of Jews in existing mixed marriages who had up until then enjoyed a certain degree of protection. The majority of Berlin's Jewish forced laborers worked in industries vital to the war effort, such as armaments production. Many mistakenly thought that the Nazis would spare them in the interests of production.[7]

An RSHA decree announcing the imminent *Fabrik-Aktion* revealed a different logic. The document, discovered a few years ago by historian Wolf Gruner, declared that the Jews "who had lived in the Altreich have virtually all been resettled, with the exception of Jews living in German-Jewish mixed marriages [*Mischehe*]." It went on to state its aim of removing "all Jews still working from their firms" in order to register them. "Those primarily targeted by this operation," it continued, "are Jews living in mixed marriages."

The decree went on to state that the operation was "to be carried out suddenly at the beginning of the work day" and that "impudent behavior" would be punished by protective custody followed by an application for transfer to a concentration camp.

The operation, it continued, would be carried out "on a generous scale," although it could not promise to resolve the mixed marriage problem "thoroughly." The goal was, rather, to remove Jewish members of such marriages from the workforce and register them. Jewish spouses living in a mixed marriage were to be allowed home afterward, though they would subsequently "under no circumstances to be reemployed in this or another firm."[8]

The arrests took place on February 27, 1943, a Saturday. For most of those affected, the assault was a swift and devastating surprise. Fritz Wundermacher recalled:

> On the morning of February 27, 1943, trucks of plain-clothed Gestapo officials drove into the factory yard. A civilian told the Jewish workers to gather in the yard. . . . We were first taken . . . to a building on Grosse Hamburger Strasse, where we were registered. . . . At any rate, I was taken with many fellow sufferers to the former Hermann-Göring barracks, where we had to spend several days camped out on the bare floor. There were women and children among us. I can still remember that we were housed in a very large room with several hundred people and I therefore assume that it was a vehicle shed. . . . I only recall that the Berlin Jewish Community prepared and distributed a fairly large package of provisions to each person on the deportation.[9]

*And then came February 27, 1943, and the Fabrik-Aktion, when the Jews were deported, including my mother. Someone came to pick me up three days later. Our former housekeeper was in the flat and they said to her, "We don't want to collect him at all, we'll shoot him right here."*

ERNST LUDWIG
EHRLICH, 1999

THE CAMPAIGN, INTENDED TO remove all Jews from industry, went on for several days and covered the whole of the Altreich. It was later named the *Fabrik-Aktion,* as most were arrested at their places of work, the factories. Jews were not only arrested at their workplaces but also in the streets and squares, at the employment office, at ration card distribution centers, and even at home. Only those working in segregated labor camps were initially spared.

Hilde Kahan, who worked at the time in the Jewish hospital, offered a description in her memoirs: "It was the end of February 1943. The board of the Association for the Jewish Religion in Berlin (Jüdisches Kultusvereinigung) telephoned in instructions to provide a number of shorthand typists for the next morning; more precise instructions would be given the following day."[10] Kahan explained, "The Jewish hospital on Iranische Strasse had to allocate staff for five to six emergency wards, equipped with medication and first aid provisions."[11] As early as 9 A.M. the next day, Kahan says that she received telephoned reports of numerous arrests. At the same time the instruction came to provide typists, marshals (*Ordner*), doctors, and nursing staff for hastily erected assembly camps and to prepare food for about ten thousand people.

THE ORDER TO KEEP the *Fabrik-Aktion* secret was not obeyed, as Goebbels noted in his diary: "That the Jews were supposed to be arrested on one day turned out to be . . . a washout. All in all, we failed to catch four thousand." These were now at large in Berlin, and Goebbels saw them as "quite a public danger."[12] The arrests, he wrote, had been thwarted "in huge numbers" by "industrialists." Moreover, many of those arrested were not workers at all but members of the elite, especially from "artistic circles."[13]

The *Fabrik-Aktion* was a departure from usual Gestapo procedure, first because of the extensive bureaucratic preparations and second because it involved the large-scale forced cooperation of the Jewish Communities. Under "usual" circumstances, *Mischlinge* and mixed-marriage partners were arrested on charges of some kind of infringement of regulations or police instructions. Proof was obtained in advance through apartment searches. Jews detained in this way were not "deported" immediately but rather sent to a labor camp for punishment. From there, they would be put on a collective transport to Auschwitz or Theresienstadt. In general, the public only got wind of what was happening when the Jews were taken to the station.

On this occasion, however, the procedure came closer to the approach implemented in the occupied eastern territories. The operation was prepared on very short notice; it was carried out by armed SS men, many of whom acted brutally (in defiance of orders);[14] and the subsequent deportations were conducted in

*For a twelve-year-old child, the experience of seeing a gun held up like that and another SS man running up the stairs . . . that's something one cannot forget. And then they took me to the camp on Rosenstrasse.*

EVA FRANK-KUNSTMANN, 1999

broad daylight for all to see.[15] It is said that Jews were chased through the streets as well.[16]

*The SS men said they could not send us to Auschwitz yet—unfortunately.*

EVA FRANK-KUNSTMANN, 1999

Jewish Berliners were initially detained in special assembly camps on the premises of the Levetzowstrasse synagogue and the former Jewish home for the elderly at Grosse Hamburger Strasse 26. The two locales soon proved insufficient, and further "auxiliary reception camps" had to be set up. These included the Hermann-Göring barracks in the Reinickendorf district and the riding stables of the barracks on Rathenow Strasse in the Moabit district. In Mitte, additional camps were established at the Café Clou on Mauerstrasse and in two Jewish Community buildings—a former Jewish home for the elderly on Gerlachstrasse and the administrative building on Rosenstrasse—as well as in Berlin's oldest synagogue on Heidereutergasse.

The people crammed together in the assembly camps were informed by the Gestapo that they would be "evacuated" very soon and that the only exceptions would be made for the Jews living in mixed marriages, *Mischlinge,* and those few Jews in possession of the "yellow certificate"—generally, employees of the Jewish Community and the Reichsvereinigung (Reich Association of German Jews).[17] Other Jews were forced to work as marshals and had, among other tasks, to draw up inmates' Declarations of Assets forms (*Vermögenserklärungen*) in the presence of financial officials.[18]

The deportations to Auschwitz began on Monday March 1, 1943, "although there were still many cases waiting to be dealt with in the assembly camps." In the assembly camp on Grosse Hamburger Strasse, according to witness Alfred Wagner, "the procedure was that the marshals would go to the rooms and from the lists call out the names of the people who had to prepare for the transport. Those whose names were called had to go down to the passage and were then taken off in a furniture truck."[19]

THE *FABRIK-ACTION* LAUNCHED a new wave of deportations—the biggest to take place since the previous September.[20] The armaments inspectorate in Berlin, reluctant to lose a substantial portion of its workforce, registered a loss of around 11,000 Jewish workers,[21] of whom the Gestapo deported 8,658 that March.

In November 1968, twenty-five years after the event, Fritz Gross recalled his arrest on February 27, 1943, "along with my Jewish work colleagues at my former workplace in Neuenhagen near Berlin." The seventy-four-year-old spoke of how he had been "put on a heavy goods vehicle and transported to Café Clou. We were guarded by SS men. . . . In the Clou young women took down our par-

**Figure 9.1** The administrative building on Rosenstrasse in the mid-1930s

ticulars such as [our country of] origin, marital status, profession and so on. . . .
After this came a so-called sorting [*Aussortierung*] according to privileges. In
the process, cards of various colors . . . were distributed, and those concerned
had to attach these cards to their clothes. It could thus be seen who was in a full
Jewish marriage or who was part of a mixed marriage or in a privileged mixed
marriage."[22]

Rudolf Schwersensky recalled a similar experience at the Levetzowstrasse assembly camp, where "the conditions were indescribable. Hundreds of women and children were lying horribly close together on the floor of the hall. . . . After a certain time we new arrivals were instructed to line up and to show our identity papers. . . . We were then sorted according to various aspects; the purpose was to ascertain who was a so-called *Mischling* and which Jews were living in mixed marriages."[23]

Both Gross and Schwersensky were boarded onto a heavy goods vehicle and taken to Rosenstrasse. After four or five days, the Gestapo sent "around 150 to 200 more spouses in mixed marriages"[24] on foot from the assembly camp at Grosse Hamburger Strasse to nearby Rosenstrasse.

IT THUS CAME ABOUT that most of the arrested *Mischlinge* and mixed-marriage Jews—about 1,700 of them—were concentrated by the Gestapo in the building on Rosenstrasse. The building soon became the site of a singular event, subsequently known as the Rosenstrasse protest.[25] "Women of German blood" assembled in front of the building in a spontaneous demonstration, calling loudly for the release of their Jewish husbands. For a whole week, the women were there day and night, trying again and again to make contact with their detained relatives inside the building. Some of them managed this in very different ways. New women joined the protest as others went home to attend to family business or to work. In the face of grave danger—and even when it seemed that machine guns would be used by the authorities against them—the women persisted, interrupting their demonstration only briefly.

The multistory administrative building on Rosenstrasse was packed with prisoners, mainly male.[26] Women were detained in a few rooms, and children were in another. Intolerable conditions prevailed throughout the building. Alfred Wagner recalled that people had to "share one room of about 5 by 4 meters with around thirty to forty men. We had to take turns sitting down or standing up. We were looked after by members of the Jewish Community."[27]

*And on Rosenstrasse there was one room containing seven children and one mother, since her child was just two.*
EVA FRANK-KUNSTMANN, 1999

The prisoners had to attend a roll call every day in the yard. Each day, members of "full-Jewish" families were deported to Auschwitz.[28] Then, on March 6 three hundred prisoners were released. Those who were set free belonged to privileged groups. Their "registration" with the Gestapo was complete. More releases followed the next day.

NOT ALL THE MEN living in mixed marriages and held at Rosenstrasse were immediately released. It was a different story for a group of twenty-five men who were deported "accidentally" from Rosenstrasse. Though these men, too, were "related to Aryans by marriage," they were nonetheless put onto the deportation wagons. One of those affected was Günther Rosenthal, who had been employed in the Reichsvereinigung's emigration department. In 1941 he had to carry out forced labor on a coal barge and as a transport worker in the German Weapons and Armaments Factory (DWM). Here he was arrested on February 27, 1943. "At around 8 A.M.," he says, "we were told to get ready. The cars were already waiting outside. The whole Jewish workforce—there were several hundred at DWM—was crammed into cars. The SS escorts encouraged us with hints that our last hour had come." Upon arrival at the assembly camp on Levetzowstrasse,"we were sorted. Those related to Aryans by marriage were put on one side, the [full] Jews on the other. I was in the first group. We were all registered again and then put onto wagons. . . . We were taken to Rosenstrasse."[29]

Then, during roll call in the yard on March 5, his name was called. "I reported and had to step forward. More names were called out. We lined up in the corridor. Those who had already been registered for work [with the Gestapo] went past us. We saw them joyfully heading home and consoled ourselves with the thought that we would soon be in the same situation." Finally the desired number was achieved: twenty-five people born between 1902 and 1905. "We then had to leave the building, quickly board the waiting truck, and then we were off. We had all kinds of worries." When the truck turned into the Putlizstrasse station the men saw a long goods train—an evacuation train—already packed with people of all ages. One of the wagons was opened up and they were pushed inside with the others. "We drew the commissioner's attention to the fact that we were in mixed marriages—a group of people to be released. He said, 'What do you want? You'll be neither shot nor hanged.' "[30]

The twenty-five men boarded the transport and were deported to Auschwitz-Birkenau, where they witnessed the selection process that awaited all arrivals. Their own group was taken by truck to Auschwitz-Monowitz to work for the Buna factory. Remarkably, these men returned from Auschwitz. After a fortnight of forced labor under extreme conditions there, an order apparently arrived to return them to Berlin. After what they had seen, it was of course unthinkable to simply release them in the manner of the other Rosenstrasse prisoners. The fear was that as they could have reported on the circumstances in Auschwitz.[31]

During questioning after the war by the public prosecutor's office, Kurt Blaustein, one of Rosenthal's fellow prisoners, recounted that "an SS leader informed us that we had been involved in spying and treason but that they were to be lenient and bring us back to Berlin. We all had to sign a corresponding declaration [of silence]." The men were brought back under the escort of an SS corporal and arrived at the Gestapo offices on Burgstrasse. The same night, fifteen of them

*An elderly couple, aged well over seventy, lived in the adjacent house. And my father said, "Run over there and tell them." . . . While I was there, there was banging on the door . . . SS men came in and said that they were guards at Sachsenhausen and that Berlin was now to be made free of Jews and [their] bones made into soap. . . . They hit the old people with rifle butts . . . until they discovered me. "Hey, are you a Jewish boy too?" they asked. I was so shocked that instead of saying "No" I said "Yes." "Let's take him now, too," they said. My parents were of course completely unprepared because nothing was supposed to happen to us during this Fabrik-Aktion as the head of the household was . . . an Aryan.*

HORST GESSNER, 1999

underwent individual interrogations. The next day, all of them arrived at the Grossbeeren forced labor camp, where they were deployed in railway construction. In July 1943 they were sent on to Wartenburg (now in the Czech Republic). The Reich Security Main Office had moved its files there, and the men were to sort and store them.[32]

Kurt Blaustein was brought back to Berlin on account of illness and interned in the Schulstrasse assembly camp from September 1944 until the end of the war. Günter Rosenthal, however, remained in Wartenberg. He found the working and living conditions there bearable in comparison to Auschwitz and Grossbeeren, particularly as an SS man had helped him to make contact with his wife. He survived. His brother and parents were murdered.

THE PROTEST HELD IN front of the building on Rosenstrasse in the first week of March 1943 was unique. As the American historian Nathan Stoltzfus points out, it was "the only instance of mass German opposition against the National Socialist destruction of Jewry."[33] The fact that mixed marriages even continued to exist up until this time—and beyond the end of the war—is itself noteworthy. Their perseverance was due in large part to the steadfastness and devotion on the part of the non-Jewish spouses. As Beate Meyer has pointed out, those marriages "in which the man was Jewish faced greater repression than those in which the wife was Jewish."[34] Mixed marriages faced pressure from all sides: neighbors, friends, relatives, superiors, landlords, employers, the police, the Gestapo, and so on. If it could withstand such forces, however, a mixed marriage generally represented a certain degree of protection for the Jewish partner.[35]

Some scholars have interpreted the Rosenstrasse protest as an indication that a greater degree of public opposition would quickly have put effective pressure on the responsible National Socialist institutions and eventually caused them to give way. In his book *Resistance of the Heart: Intermarriage and the Rosenstrasse Protest in Nazi Germany*, Stoltzfus suggests that a critical mass of protesting German civilians could possibly have slowed down, or even stopped, the Nazi genocide. According to his argument, had the isolation of Jews met with protests on a mass scale, the political stakes for the perpetrators would have been raised to such an extent that the Nazis would have had to back off.[36]

The Gestapo decree recently brought to light by historian Wolf Gruner and cited earlier in this chapter suggests a different interpretation of events.[37] Rather than yielding to pressure of demonstrators, the authorities had clearly planned, even in early phases of the *Fabrik-Aktion*, to release the men. The document suggests that, regardless of the protests, the deportation of mixed-marriage partners had never been part of the plan. The arrests of *Mischlinge* and Jews living

*We were taken on the bus to the assembly camp on Grosse Hamburger Strasse. [Walter] Dobberke now looked at the bus which was emptying, and there were people on it who were not even wearing a Jewish star. He naturally asked, "What kind are they, then?" "Why, those are Aryans who are married to Jewish pigs." He duly massacred them in front of the assembled men. My father was able to leave immediately.*

HORST GESSNER, 1999

**Figure 9.2** Rosenstrasse 2–5 after the liberation

in mixed marriages had been undertaken for a purpose other than deportation: registration.

When, on March 6, the first group of Jews from "protected" mixed marriages were released, 302 people were chosen from among them to replace a group of "unprotected" Jews who had until then been employed in the Jewish Communities and the Reichsvereinigung.[38] Having secured replacement labor for the Jewish institutions, the Gestapo was now free to deport the fully Jewish staff members and employees. They left on March 12 in a large transport "to the east" and a smaller one to Theresienstadt.

As Gruner writes, "those who had so far been spared now saw themselves faced with impossible tasks. Worn down by the events that had passed, . . . [they now had to fill] all necessary posts with Jews who through marriage to Aryans were protected from evacuation—people who up to now had made up only a fraction of those working in Jewish organizations. They had to be made familiar with the work so that, despite the complete elimination of the 'full Jews,' the machinery of the Jewish institutions would continue to run smoothly."[39] A much smaller number of *Mischlinge* and mixed-marriage partners had thus to be trained in new tasks. "One was aware that there was only limited time to familiarize them with the work . . . and that in a few months all full Jews . . . would be gone from Berlin."[40]

The theory that the Nazis needed such people in order to keep the Jewish institutions running smoothly suggests that the deportation of this group of Rosenstrasse inmates had not been planned—at least not at that stage.[41] Rather, they were arrested in order to be registered and subsequently deployed as replacements for the "full Jews"—presumably until the day when their services would no longer be needed—the day, that is, when all Jews would be gone from both Berlin and the entire Reich.

It seems in retrospect that the protests of the Rosenstrasse women, however courageous, were not as influential as they have previously been regarded. Indeed, to regard the existence of mixed marriages in Nazi Germany as "acts of political opposition"[42] and the Rosenstrasse protest as an act of "life-threatening civil disobedience"[43] may be to stand the matter on its head. The revised interpretation of events, however, in no way reduces the civil courage shown by those who took part in the demonstration. Nor does it diminish its importance as a unique and powerful political statement in the history of the Third Reich.

**1** See Beate Meyer, "*Jüdische Mischlinge.*" *Rassenpolitik und Verfolgungserfahrung, 1933–1945* (Hamburg, 1999), p. 25. Meyer cites an evaluation of the "census of population, professions, and firms" carried out in 1939 by the Reich Office for Statistics in which a registered 56,327 "full Jewish" married couples are recorded, with 20,454 mixed marriages. See also Beate Meyer, "The Mixed Marriage: A Guarantee of Survival or a Reflection of German Society during the Nazi Regime?" in *Probing the Depths of German Anti-semitism: German Society and the Persecution of the Jews, 1933–1941,* ed. David Bankier (Jerusalem, 2000), pp. 54–77.

**2** Wolf Gruner, *Der geschlossene Arbeitseinsatz deutscher Juden. Zur Zwangsarbeit als Element der Verfolgung, 1938–1943* (Berlin, 1997), p. 311.

**3** Josef Goebbels, diary entry dated 1941, in *Joseph Goebbels Tagebücher, 1924–1945,* ed. Hans Georg Reuth, vol. 4, (Munich, 2003), p. 547.

**4** Goebbels, diary entry dated February 1943, in *Die Tagebücher von Joseph Goebbels: Sämtliche Fragmente,* ed. Elke Fröhlich, part 2, vol. 7 (Munich, 1993), p. 369.

**5** Reichsvereinigung statistics from June 6, 1943, Bundesarchiv (BArch), Berlin, 75 C Re 1, no. 69, sheet 144.

**6** "Single" here also refers to people whose Gentile spouse had died or to whose marriage to a Gentile had ended in divorce.

**7** Gernot Jochheim, *Frauenprotest in der Rosenstrasse* (Berlin, 1993), p. 24.

**8** Pr. Br. Rep. 41 Grossräschen, no. 272, sheet 84–85; circular from the head of district administration (*Landrat*) in Calau, February 25, 1943; and copy of the decree from the Gestapo in Frankfurt/Oder, February 24, 1943, all from Brandenburgisches Landeshauptarchiv (BLHA).

**9** Landesarchiv (LAB), Berlin, (Fritz Wundermacher).

**10** Hilde Kahan, *Chronik deutscher Juden, 1939–1945* (LBI-Archive 207), p. 18.

**11** Quoted in Hildegard Henschel, "Aus der Arbeit der Jüdischen Gemeinde Berlin während der Jahre 1941–1945," in *Zeitschrift für die Geschichte der Juden* 9 (1972): 33–52, quotation from p. 46.

**12** Goebbels, diary entry dated March 11, 1943, cited in Wolf Gruner, "Die Reichshauptstadt und die Verfolgung der Berliner Juden, 1933–1945," in *Jüdische Geschichte in Berlin,* exhibition catalog, ed. Reinhard Rürup (Berlin, 1995), p. 253.

**13** Goebbels, diary entry dated March 11, 1943, in *Die Tagebücher,* part 2, vol. 7, p. 528.

**14** The RSHA decree specified that attacks were on no account to come from the officials, "especially not in public or in the firm itself." See note 10.

**15** Christof Dipper, "Schwierigkeiten mit der Resistenz," in *Geschichte und Gegenwart* 3 (1996): 410–11; and Meyer, "*Jüdische Mischlinge,*" p. 57.

**16** Henschel, *Aus der Arbeit,* p. 47.

**17** This "yellow certificate" did not provide permanent protection but only delayed deportation until employees of the Jewish institutions were no longer needed. See Henschel, *Aus der Arbeit,* p. 45.

**18** LAB, Sta LG Berlin, 1 Ks 1/69 (Bruno Goldstein), p. 6.

**19** LAB, no. R 34/32 (Alfred Wagner), p. 4.

**20** Statistics from the Reichsvereinigung, April 6, 1943, BArch, 75 C Re 1, no. 69, sheet 57; Gruner, "Die Reichshauptstadt," p. 253.

**21** Gruner, "Die Reichshauptstadt," p. 317.

**22** LAB, R 34/20, no. 257–01 (Fritz Gross), pp. 2–3.

**23** LAB, Sta LG Berlin, 1 Js 1/67 (Rudolf Schwersensky), p. 4.

**24** LAB, Sta LG Berlin, J 57–01, no. R 34/32 (Alfred Wagner), p. 4.

**25** See Kurt-Jakob Ball-Kaduri, "Berlin wird judenfrei. Die Juden in Berlin in den Jahren 1942/43," in *Jahrbuch für die Geschichte Mittel- und Ostdeutschlands* 22 (1973): 196–241, quotation from p. 214; Jochheim, *Frauenprotest,* pp. 122–33; and Nathan Stoltzfus, *Resistance of the Heart: Intermarriage and the Rosenstrasse Protest in Nazi Germany* (New York, 1996).

**26** Jochheim, *Frauenprotest,* p. 34

**27** LAB, R 34/32 (Alfred Wagner), p. 5.

**28** Ibid.

**29** Report from Günther Rosenthal/ Jewish section, Berlin Museum, copy in Centrum Judaicum Archive, Berlin, p. 2.

**30** Ibid, pp. 4 ff.

**31** See also LAB, Rep. 0507–01, No. 385 (Johanna Heym), 16.6.1966, p. 16.

**32** LAB, Rep. 0507–01, R 34/21 (Kurt Blaustein), pp. 1 ff.

**33** Nathan Stoltzfus, "Der Protest in der Rosenstrasse und die deutsch-jüdische Mischehe," in *Geschichte und Gegenwart* 2 (1995): 218–47, quotation from p. 218.

**34** For detailed information, see Meyer, *"Jüdische Mischlinge,"* pp. 91–94, quotation from p. 92. See also Meyer, "The Mixed Marriage."

**35** Dipper, *Schwierigkeiten,* p. 415.

**36** Meyer, *"Jüdische Mischlinge,"* p. 57.

**37** See note 10.

**38** Dipper, *Schwierigkeiten,* p. 415; Gruner, *Der geschlossene Arbeitseinsatz,* p. 319.

**39** Gruner, "Die Reichshauptstadt," p. 253.

**40** Henschel, *Aus der Arbeit,* p. 50.

**41** Gruner, "Die Reichshauptstadt," p. 253.

**42** Stoltzfus, *Der Protest,* p. 221; Dipper, *Schwierigkeiten,* p. 415.

**43** Stoltzfus, *Der Protest,* p. 223.

# 7

# Deportation

# Chapter Ten

## The Deportations

BEATE MEYER

Beginning late in the summer of 1941, various Nazi Gauleiter began pushing Hitler for a special order that would allow them to deport Jews from their respective districts. Prominent among these were Joseph Goebbels in Berlin, Karl Kaufmann in Hamburg, and Baldur von Schirach in Vienna. These were the cities in which most of the Jews in the Grossdeutsches Reich (greater German Reich) resided. Although Hitler duly promised this to his Gauleiter in August 1941, he wanted to postpone the deportations until after the anticipated quick victory over the Soviet Union. The scarcity of trains had to be alleviated before deportations could begin.

Following a discussion of the matter with Hitler, Gauleiter Goebbels dictated this note in the middle of that month: "The Führer has, furthermore, promised me that the Jews will be deported from Berlin to the east as soon as possible, once the first transport opportunity arises. There they will be dealt with under harsh circumstances."[1] When Karl Kaufmann in Hamburg formulated the same request in mid-September, however, Hitler agreed to an immediate deportation.[2] Goebbels noted this in his diary: "The Führer believes that the Jews must gradually be removed from throughout Germany. The first towns to be made free of Jews [judenfrei] will be Berlin, Vienna, and Prague. Berlin will be first, and I hope that in the course of this year we will succeed in deporting a major part of the Berlin Jews to the east."[3]

Hitler himself stipulated the deportation destinations for the first transports: "Twenty-five thousand Jews will go to Minsk; 25,000 to Riga; and 20,000 Jews and 5,000 gypsies to Litzmannstadt [Lódz]. The deportation will be carried out according to no special procedure . . . 11,000 . . . will be deported from Berlin. . . . The operation has the approval of the Führer; he has personally stipulated the destinations to which the Jews will be deported."[4]

The Reich Security Main Office (Reichssicherheitshauptamt [RSHA]) now took over the coordination of deportation. It secured (that is, it forced) the cooperation of the Reichsvereinigung der Juden in Deutschland (Reich Associa-tion of Jews in Germany) in organizing the deportation transports in the home-towns or villages of those to be deported.[5] In Berlin, the Jewish Community had to set up an assembly camp on the premises of the former Levetzowstrasse syna-gogue. Here "persons participating in the emigration transports," as they were called, were to be held for two to three days. During this time, their remaining assets were registered, and the transports were coordinated.

The first train left the capital of the Third Reich on October 18, 1941. It brought over a thousand Berlin Jews to Lódz. Five days later, the Nazis imposed a ban on emigration. From now on, the policy of "forced emigration" was to become the policy of extermination.

Until the end of January 1942 the transports went, in keeping with Hitler's specifications, to "Litzmannstadt" (Lódz), Minsk, and Riga.[6] More than ten thousand Jewish Berliners were thus deported. From the fall of 1942 on, the trains went directly to Auschwitz—a name that at the time meant little to most Berlin Jews. Theresienstadt, in contrast, was better known. Constructed by Czech Jews beginning in June 1942, the camp had been lauded as a "privileged camp" (*Vorzugslager*). Among those "resettled" there were World War I veterans, the elderly, Jews who had been in "mixed marriages," and the so-called "Jews by definition" (*Geltungsjuden*).[7]

In December 1942, Paul Eppstein at the Berlin headquarters of the Reichs-vereinigung received a report from a Jewish Elder named Edelstein regarding the construction of the Theresienstadt "ghetto." Reading between the lines gives an insight into reality at the camp:

> We had to contend with unbelievable difficulties. There was virtually nothing to assist us. . . . There is, moreover, great variation in the mix of people, in terms of age, origin, as well as overall mentality. The fact that, in spite of everything, the tasks could be more or less completed is due to the following factors: 1. The un-derstanding of the commanding authority. [Nazi] Command has shown a degree of expertise and realizes the necessity that its instructions and orders within the ghetto must serve as a guideline for the work on the part of the Jewish self-administration. 2. Our workers' readiness for action. One can scarcely believe how willing and able our ten thousand male and female workers are. Perhaps you can gain an impression if I tell you that, over these twelve months, there has not been a single case of someone refusing to work, though day and night our workers have had to give their utmost. 3. The [Jewish] organization, which was set up in good time and functions well. Our organization is like a cross between a town ad-ministration, an administrative council of a large firm, and a religious community association. . . . A central accommodation office takes care of housing. . . . Despite

the many technical obstacles, each participant who arrives on the transports has been fitted in. Everyone is looked after, although all arrivals must be aware that our possibilities are limited, and we can only offer what we ourselves have at our disposal![8]

The letter goes on to suggest that nutrition was sparse but sufficient, that health care was difficult but successful, that conditions were "scrupulously clean," that "the Jewish workers" could relax in a coffeehouse, and that the problems between the Czech and German Jews had been ironed out. It is interesting to speculate how Paul Eppstein would have interpreted this letter, which—even while glossing over matters—contained many hints of the harsh reality of life in the camp.

The Reichsvereinigung was forced to assume the costs of funding Theresienstadt. To this purpose, the deportees to be sent there filled out contracts while they waited in the assembly camps. The contracts gave the impression that applicants were "buying" a place in a home (*Heimeinkaufsverträge*) for themselves—that is, that they were moving to a home for the elderly. The contracts specified that the remaining assets of those concerned would be transferred to the Reichsvereinigung, with a subtraction 250 Reichsmarks to cover the cost of their stay in the assembly camp.[9]

Only later was there talk among Berlin's remaining Jews that, for many deportees, Theresienstadt was merely a transit camp on the way to an extermination camp. In total, almost 15,000 Berlin Jews were deported to Theresienstadt. Over 14,000 others were transported further "to the east"—and to near certain death.[10]

Until late 1942 and the beginning of 1943, the forced labor system spared many of those working in firms essential to the war effort, as well as their families. The firms provided their Jewish laborers with "protection letters" (*Schutzbriefe*) to be presented to the Gestapo on demand. Employment in the Reichsvereinigung also initially provided protection from deportation. Reichsvereinigung employees carried "yellow certificates" designating their status. In addition, the basic principle applied that families should only "emigrate" together.

These protections for the most part ceased to apply on February 27, 1943, the date of the so-called *Fabrik-Aktion*. In late February and early March 1943, Jews working in the Berlin munitions factories were arrested and deported, along with all Jews that the Gestapo, the police, and the SS could get their hands on—in the streets, in the "Jewish houses," in homes and institutions, or anywhere else (see chap. 9). Only those living in "privileged mixed marriages"—provided those marriages had not been dissolved through death or divorce—were spared for the time being. A few *Geltungsjuden,* too, were kept behind as "cases needing clarification." They had applied to the authorities for background checks with the aim of proving their "Aryan" origins. Even members of these groups, however, could not be sure that they would be spared. The deportation of the respective Jewish partners in "nonprivileged mixed marriages" had been underway since 1943; finally, in the first months of 1945, the deportation of all Jews in "privileged mixed marriages" was ordered.

In all, more than 50,000 Jews were deported from Berlin in the course of sixty-five transports "to the east" and 122 transports to Theresienstadt. If one counts those emigrants who had the misfortune of subsequently being picked up by German troops and becoming victims of Nazi persecution, the total comes to more than 55,000.[11] In 1933, over 160,000 Jews were living in Berlin. Of these, 90,000 had emigrated, 55,000 were murdered, and 7,000 committed suicide by the time of the deportations. A mere 8,000 survived the National Socialist regime: 4,700 in mixed marriages, 1,900 in concentration camps, and 1,400 in hiding.

**Table 10.1** Deportations from Berlin to the "East"

| No. | Date | Location | Number of Deportees | | |
|---|---|---|---|---|---|
| | | | From Kruglov[1] | From Kempner[2] | From Scheffler and Schulle[3] |
| 1 | 10/18/1941 | Litzmannstadt (Lódz) | 1,013 | 1,013 | |
| 2 | 10/24/1941 | Litzmannstadt (Lódz) | 1,146 | 1,146 | |
| 3 | 10/27/1941 | Litzmannstadt (Lódz) | 1,009 | 1,009 | |
| 4 | 11/01/1941 | Litzmannstadt (Lódz) | 1,033 | 1,038 | |
| 5 | 11/14/1941 | Minsk | 1,030 | 1,030 | |
| 6 | 11/17/1941 | Kovno/Kaunas | 942 | 942 | 1,006 |
| 7 | 11/27/1941 | Riga | 1,000 | 1,000 | 1,053 |
| 8 | 01/13/1942 | Riga | 907 | 1,037 | 1,035 |
| 9 | 01/19/1942 | Riga | 579 | 1,006 | 1,002 |
| 10 | 01/25/1942 | Riga | 905 | 1,051 | 1,044 |
| 11 | 03/28/1942 | Piaski | 972 | 974 | |
| 12 | 04/02/1942 | Warsaw | 1,025 | — | |
| 13 | 04/02/1942 | Warsaw | 642 | 654 | |
| 14 | 04/14/1942 | Warsaw | 211 | 65 | |
| 15 | 06/02/1942 | to the "east" | — | 758 | |
| 16 | 06/13/1942 | Majdanek/Sobibor | 748 | — | |
| 17 | 06/26/1942 | Majdanek/Sobibor | 201 | 202 | |
| 18 | 07/11/1942 | Majdanek/Sobibor? | 210 | 210 | |
| 19 | 08/15/1942 | Riga | 1,004 | 1,004 | 938 |
| 20 | 09/05/1942 | Riga | 790 | 790 | 797 |
| 21 | 09/26/1942 | Reval | 816 | 811 | 812 |
| 22 | 10/19/1942 | Riga | 944 | 963 | 959 |
| 23 | 10/26/1942 | Riga | 800 | 791 | 798 |
| 24 | 11/29/1942 | Auschwitz | 980 | 1,011 | |
| 25 | 12/09/1942 | Auschwitz | 1,000 | 997 | |
| 26 | 12/14/1942 | Auschwitz | 811 | 811 | |
| 27 | 12/01/1943 | Auschwitz | 1,190 | 1,210 | |
| 28 | 01/29/1943 | Auschwitz | 1,000 | 1,000 | |
| 29 | 02/03/1943 | Auschwitz | 952 | 952 | |
| 30 | 02/19/1943 | Auschwitz | 1,000 | 1,000 | |
| 31 | 02/26/1943 | Auschwitz | 913 | 1,100 | |
| 32 | 03/01/1943 | Auschwitz | 1,862 | 1,736 | |
| 33 | 03/02/1943 | Auschwitz | 1,592 | 1,758 | |
| 34 | 03/03/1943 | Auschwitz | 1,732 | 1,732 | |
| 35 | 03/04/1943 | Auschwitz | 1,143 | 1,143 | |
| 36 | 03/06/1943 | Auschwitz | 657 | 662 | |

**Table 10.1** *(continued)*

| No. | Date | Location | From Kruglov[1] | From Kempner[2] | From Scheffler and Schulle[3] |
|-----|------|----------|-----------------|-----------------|-------------------------------|
| | | | | Number of Deportees | |
| 37 | 03/12/1943 | Auschwitz | 946 | 947 | |
| 38 | 04/19/1943 | Auschwitz | 338 | 688 | |
| 39 | 06/28/1943 | Auschwitz | 319 | 297 | |
| 40 | 08/04/1943 | Auschwitz | 99 | 99 | |
| 41 | 08/24/1943 | Auschwitz | 50 | 50 | |
| 42 | 09/10/1943 | Auschwitz | 53 | 53 | |
| 43 | 09/28/1943 | Auschwitz | 74 | 74 | |
| 44 | 10/14/1943 | Auschwitz | 74 | 74 | |
| 45 | 10/29/1943 | Auschwitz | 49 | 50 | |
| 46 | 11/08/1943 | Auschwitz | 50 | 50 | |
| 47 | 12/07/1943 | Auschwitz | 55 | 55 | |
| 48 | 01/20/1944 | Auschwitz | 48 | 48 | |
| 49 | 02/22/1944 | Auschwitz | 32 | 32 | |
| 50 | 03/09/1944 | Auschwitz | 32 | 32 | |
| 51 | 04/18/1944 | Auschwitz | 30 | 30 | |
| 52 | 05/03/1944 | Auschwitz | 27 | 30 | |
| 53 | 05/19/1944 | Auschwitz | 24 | 24 | |
| 54 | 06/15/1944 | Auschwitz | 29 | 29 | |
| 55 | 07/12/1944 | Auschwitz | 30 | 30 | |
| 56 | 08/10/1944 | Auschwitz | 38 | 38 | |
| 57 | 09/06/1944 | Auschwitz | 39 | 29 | |
| 58 | 10/12/1944 | Auschwitz | 31 | 31 | |
| 59 | 11/24/1944 | Auschwitz | 28 | 28 | |
| 60 | 12/08/1944 | Sachsenhausen/ Ravensbrück | 15 | 15 | |
| 61 | 01/05/1945 | Auschwitz | 14 | 14 | |
| 62 | 02/02/1945 | Sachsenhausen/ Ravensbrück | — | 25 | |
| 63 | March/April 1945 | Sachsenhausen/ Ravensbrück [planned only] | — | 24 | |

[1] A. I. Kruglov, "Die Deportation deutscher Bürger jüdischer Herkunft durch die Faschisten nach dem Osten 1940 bis 1945," in *Zeitschrift für Geschichtswissenschaft* 32 (1984): 12: 1,086–1,091.

[2] Robert Maximilian Wassili Kempner, *Die Ermordung von 35,000 Berliner Juden. Der Judenmordprozeß in Berlin schreibt Geschichte, Gegenwart und Rückblick* (Berlin, 1970).

[3] Wolfgang Scheffler and Diana Schulle, editors, *Buch der Erinnerung. Die ins Baltikum deportierten deutschen, österreichischen und tschechoslowakischen Juden*, 2 vols. (Munich, 2003).

**Table 10.2** Deportations from Berlin to Theresienstadt

| No. | Date | Number of deportees |
|---|---|---|
| 1 | 06/02/1942 | 100 |
| 2 | 06/05/1942 | 100 |
| 3 | 06/06/1942 | 100 |
| 4 | 06/07/1942 | 100 |
| 5 | 06/08/1942 | 69 |
| 6 | 06/09/1942 | 50 |
| 7 | 06/11/1942 | 50 |
| 8 | 06/12/1942 | 50 |
| 9 | 06/16/1942 | 50 |
| 10 | 06/18/1942 | 50 |
| 11 | 06/19/1942 | 50 |
| 12 | 06/24/1942 | 50 |
| 13 | 06/25/1942 | 50 |
| 14 | 06/26/1942 | 50 |
| 15 | 06/30/1942 | 50 |
| 16 | 07/02/1942 | 50 |
| 17 | 07/03/1942 | 50 |
| 18 | 07/06/1942 | 100 |
| 19 | 07/07/1942 | 100 |
| 20 | 07/08/1942 | 90 |
| 21 | 07/09/1942 | 100 |
| 22 | 07/10/1942 | 100 |
| 23 | 07/13/1942 | 100 |
| 24 | 07/14/1942 | 100 |
| 25 | 07/15/1942 | 100 |
| 26 | 07/16/1942 | 100 |
| 27 | 07/17/1942 | 99 |
| 28 | 07/20/1942 | 100 |
| 29 | 07/21/1942 | 100 |
| 30 | 07/22/1942 | 100 |
| 31 | 07/23/1942 | 100 |
| 32 | 07/24/1942 | 100 |
| 33 | 07/27/1942 | 101 |
| 34 | 07/28/1942 | 100 |
| 35 | 07/29/1942 | 100 |
| 36 | 07/30/1942 | 100 |
| 37 | 07/31/1942 | 100 |
| 38 | 08/03/1942 | 100 |

**Table 10.2** (*continued*)

| No. | Date | Number of deportees |
|-----|------|---------------------|
| 39 | 08/04/1942 | 100 |
| 40 | 08/05/1942 | 100 |
| 41 | 08/06/1942 | 100 |
| 42 | 08/07/1942 | 100 |
| 43 | 08/10/1942 | 100 |
| 44 | 08/11/1942 | 100 |
| 45 | 08/12/1942 | 100 |
| 46 | 08/13/1942 | 100 |
| 47 | 08/14/1942 | 100 |
| 48[1] | 08/17/1942 | 1,003 |
| 49 | 08/19/1942 | 100 |
| 50 | 08/20/1942 | 100 |
| 51 | 08/21/1942 | 100 |
| 52 | 08/24/1942 | 100 |
| 53 | 08/25/1942 | 100 |
| 54 | 08/26/1942 | 100 |
| 55 | 08/27/1942 | 100 |
| 56 | 08/28/1942 | 100 |
| 57 | 08/31/1942 | 100 |
| 58 | 09/02/1942 | 100 |
| 59 | 09/02/1942 | 100 |
| 60 | 05/09/1942 | 100 |
| 61 | 05/09/1942 | 100 |
| 62 | 09/07/1942 | 100 |
| 63 | 09/08/1942 | 100 |
| 64 | 09/09/1942 | 100 |
| 65 | 09/10/1942 | 100 |
| 66 | 09/11/1942 | 103 |
| 67[2] | 09/14/1942 | 1,000 |
| 68 | 09/21/1942 | 100 |
| 69 | 09/22/1942 | 100 |
| 70 | 09/23/1942 | 100 |
| 71 | 09/24/1942 | 100 |
| 72 | 09/25/1942 | 100 |
| 73 | 10/03/1942 | 692 |
| 74[3] | 10/14/1942 | 948 |

[1] First large transport.
[2] Second large transport
[3] Third large transport

**Table 10.2** (continued)

| No. | Date | Number of deportees |
|-----|------|---------------------|
| 75 | 10/28/1942 | 100 |
| 76 | 10/29/1942 | 100 |
| 77 | 10/30/1942 | 100 |
| 78 | 11/04/1942 | 99 |
| 79 | 11/05/1942 | 99 |
| 80 | 11/06/1942 | 102 |
| 81 | 11/19/1942 | 80 |
| 82 | 11/23/1942 | 61 |
| 83 | 12/13/1942 | 100 |
| 84 | 12/16/1942 | 100 |
| 85 | 12/17/1942 | 100 |
| 86 | 01/12/1943 | 100 |
| 87 | 01/13/1943 | 100 |
| 88 | 01/14/1943 | 100 |
| 89 | 01/26/1943 | 100 |
| 90 | 01/28/1943 | 100 |
| 91 | 01/29/1943 | 100 |
| 92 | 02/02/1943 | 100 |
| 93[4] | 03/17/1943 | 1,159 |
| 94 | 04/19/1943 | 100 |
| 95 | 05/17/1943 | 100 |
| 96 | 05/18/1943 | 100 |
| 97 | 05/19/1943 | 100 |
| 98 | 05/28/1943 | 327 |
| 99 | 06/16/1943 | 443 |
| 100 | 06/29/1943 | 100 |
| 101 | 06/30/1943 | 100 |
| 102 | 07/01/1943 | 100 |
| 103 | 08/04/1943 | 70 |
| 104 | 09/10/1943 | 63 |
| 105 | 10/15/1943 | 51 |
| 106 | 11/15/1943 | 50 |
| 107 | 01/10/1944 | 351 |
| 108 | 01/21/1944 | 63 |
| 109 | 02/09/1944 | 100 |
| 110 | 02/23/1944 | 74 |
| 111 | 03/10/1944 | 56 |
| 112 | 04/19/1944 | 50 |

[4] Fourth large transport

**Table 10.2** (continued)

| No. | Date | Number of deportees |
|---|---|---|
| 113 | 05/04/1944 | 26 |
| 114 | 05/26/1944 | 30 |
| 115 | 06/16/1944 | 28 |
| 116 | 07/13/1944 | 27 |
| 117 | 08/11/1944 | 32 |
| 118 | 09/05/1944 | 27 |
| 119 | 10/13/1944 | 30 |
| 120 | 10/27/1944 | 50 |
| 121 | 11/24/1944 | 37 |
| 122 | 12/08/1944 | 22 |
| 123 | 01/05/1945 | 19 |
| 124 | 02/02/1945 | 38 |
| 125 | 03/27/1945 | 19 |

Primary source: *Die Grunewald-Rampe/ Die Deportation der Berliner Juden* (Berlin, 1993), pp. 77–78.

**1** Joseph Goebbels, diary entry dated August 18, 1941, *Die Tagebücher von Joseph Goebbels*, part 2, *Diktate 1941–1945*, ed. Elke Fröhlich (Munich, 1987), p. 266.

**2** See Frank Bajohr, "Hamburgs 'Führer.' Zur Person und Tätigkeit des Hamburger NSDAP-Gauleiters Karl Kaufmann (1900–1969)," in *Hamburg in der NS-Zeit. Ergebnisse neuerer Forschungen*, ed. Frank Bajohr and Joachim Szodrzynski (Hamburg, 1995), pp. 59–91, quotation on p. 81; Peter Witte, "Zwei Entscheidungen in der 'Endlösung der Judenfrage.' Deportation nach Lódz und Vernichtung in Chemno," in *Theresienstädter Studien und Dokumente*, ed. Miroslav Kárny et al. (Prague, 1995), pp. 38–68.

**3** Goebbels, diary entry dated September 24, 1941, p. 485.

**4** Zeitler Deutscher Gemeindetag (DGT) Berlin to Eichler in Munich, teletype message dated October 28, 1941 (spelling altered), Landesarchiv Berlin (LAB), Rep. 142/7, 1–2-6/Nr. 1, Bd. 2, quoted in Wolf Gruner, "Die NS-Verfolgung und die Kommunen. Zur wechselseitigen Dynamisierung von zentraler und lokaler Politik 1933–1941," in *Vierteljahreshefte für Zeitgeschichte* 48 (2000): 75–126, quotation on p. 75.

**5** See my chapter on the Reichsvereinigung (Reich Association of Jews in Germany), chapter 18 in this volume.

**6** On the deportations—the figures not entirely accurate—see Robert W. Kempner, "Die Ermordung von 35,000 Berliner Juden. Der Judenmordprozeß in Berlin schreibt Geschichte," in *Gegenwart und Rückblick. Festgabe für die Jüdische Gemeinde zu Berlin 25 Jahre nach dem Neubeginn* (Heidelberg, 1970), pp. 180–205. On the bureaucratic development of the deportations, see Hans Günther Adler, *Der verwaltete Mensch. Studien zur Deportation der Juden aus Deutschland* (Tübingen, 1974).

**7** See Miroslav Kárny, ed., *Theresienstadt in der 'Endlösung der Judenfrage'* (Prague, 1992).

**8** Schreiben Ghetto Theresienstadt, Der Aeltestenrat an Paul Eppstein, Reichsvereinigung, December 8, 1942, pp. 1–2, Bundesarchiv (Barch), Berlin, 75 C Re1, Nr. 2.2.1/480/1.

**9** Heimeinkaufsvertrag blanko, p. 252, BArch, 75 C Re1, Nr. 2.2.1/480/3; on the fee for the assembly camp, see Lustig instructions, dated July 10, 1943, BArch, 75 C Re1, Nr. 1.1.1./9/9.

**10** See Wolf Gruner, *Judenverfolgung in Berlin, 1933–1945. Eine Chronologie der Behördenmaßnahmen in der Reichshauptstadt* (Berlin, 1996), pp. 98–99.

**11** See Wolf Gruner, "Die Reichshauptstadt und die Verfolgung der Berliner Juden, 1933–1945," in *Jüdische Geschichte in Berlin. Essays und Studien*, ed. Reinhard Rürup, (Berlin, 1995), pp. 229–66, quotation on p. 255.

# Chapter Eleven

## Every Person Has a Name

RITA MEYHÖFER

There are many ways to remember the six million murdered European Jews. Memorial books (*Gedenkbücher*) present the names and biographical data of the victims in such a way that real people—with names, addresses, and biographies—reemerge from abstract numbers. Such books attempt to restore the identities of those whom the Nazis wanted to relegate to "a grave in the air" (in the words of the poet Paul Celan).[1] In the summer of 1989 a working group at the Central Institute for Research in the Social Sciences at the Freie Universität Berlin began preparatory work on a memorial book for the city of Berlin. In May 1995, to mark the fiftieth anniversary of the city's liberation, Berlin's then Senator for Culture, Ulrich Roloff-Momin, presented the first edition of the Berlin memorial book to Jerzy Kanal, chairman of the Berlin Jewish Community, at the Centrum Judaicum.[2] Today, over a decade after work on this book began, it is clear that future editions will require revisions.

The working group benefited to a large extent from the preparatory work carried out by the Federal Archive (Bundesarchiv), located in Koblenz at the time. The archive made available to us a set of data from the 1986 memorial book that had been compiled for the former West Germany, including West Berlin.[3] Using additional sources we made additions, corrections, and thoroughly expanded this information. Unlike the Federal Archive project, we also included the names of those Jews who were deported from Berlin but officially had another place of residence.[4] We considered anyone who had lived in Berlin between 1933 and 1945 to be a resident of Berlin. In the cases of emigrants to the city, we noted the place of birth.

Both the memorial book and the database, which was given to the Berlin State Archive (Landesarchiv Berlin) and the New Synagogue Berlin/Centrum Judaicum Foundation, have since been used extensively by many different people and institutions. Among users are the relatives of those who were deported and murdered, official departments, academics, and interested individuals.

## Sources

The research into the names and biographies was based on three categories of sources: existing publications, evaluation of the most important sources, and finally, the written and oral questioning of eyewitnesses.[5]

### Existing Memorial Books and Publications from Germany and Abroad

In 1986, after years of research, the Federal Archive in Koblenz published the *Gedenkbuch. Opfer der Verfolgung der Juden unter der nationalsozialistischen Gewaltherrschaft in Deutschland, 1933–1945* (Memorial Book. Victims of the Persecution of the Jews under the National Socialist Tyranny in Germany, 1933–45). Produced in close cooperation with organizations including the Missing Persons Tracing Service of the International Red Cross in Arolsen, *Gedenkbuch* contains the names, dates of birth, and biographies of more than 52,000 Berlin Jews who were either deported from the city, committed suicide, or were deported from the country to which they had emigrated. Over the past few years, regional and local memorial books have also been produced for many regions, towns, and communities of the Federal Republic of Germany, based on information, for example, contained in local archive resources.

The memorial center located on the site of the former Sachsenhausen concentration camp north of Berlin compiled the names and dates of birth and death of Jewish prisoners (drawing mostly on documents from the Oranienburg registry office) for its exhibition Jüdische Häftlinge in Sachsenhausen (Jewish Prisoners at Sachsenhausen). This information, which the memorial site kindly made available in copy, enabled us to establish the dates of death of a further 222 of the total of 720 Jewish prisoners from Berlin who died in Sachsenhausen and who are documented in the Berlin memorial book. Most of them were Berlin Jews of Polish nationality who instead of being "deported" to Poland were imprisoned at the camp in 1938.

Another source is the documentation of over 6,500 Jews who were deported from the Baden and Rheinpfalz regions to the Gurs camp in the south of France in October 1940. In 1980, on the fortieth anniversary of this deportation, Barbara Vormeier produced a list on behalf of Soldarité—Association des réfugiés israélites en provenance d´Allemagne et d'Autriche (Solidarity: The Association of Israelite Refugees from Germany and Austria).[6] The project included, among others, the names of 6,258 German and 1,746 Austrian Jews deported from France to Auschwitz, Majdanek, and Sobibor. Among them were around five hundred Berlin Jews, most of whom had left Germany for France in the 1930s.

In his book on the deportation of Jews from Norway, the Norwegian historian Kristian Ottosen also published the names and biographies of 157 Jews who had been transported via Stettin to Berlin and were deported from there to Auschwitz on March 2, 1943, together with 1,650 Berlin Jews. Only seven of the Norwegian Jews survived.

In addition to the existing publications, there is also a whole range of biographical works and handbooks. One example is the *Biographische Handbuch der deutschsprachigen Emigration nach 1933* (Biographical Handbook of German-speaking Emigration after 1933) published by the Institute for Contemporary History, which contains the names and biographies of prominent figures and their relatives, including many people of Jewish origin from Berlin.[7]

Using its archive, the Dutch Red Cross was able to draw up a list of previously unknown names of Berlin Jews who had found refuge in the Netherlands and were subsequently deported from there to Auschwitz and Sobibor.[8]

## The Evaluation of Sources

From the outset it was considered essential that the preparatory work for a Berlin memorial book be grounded in an academic assessment of the sources. Significant in this respect were, above all, the National Socialist files and documents remaining from Jewish institutions of the period. Also important were postwar documents produced with regard to compensating victims of racial persecution (*rassisch Verfolgter*) as well as in the course of subsequent research. Much of the time spent on preparatory research was devoted to work with sources. Similar projects—for example, compiling and reconstructing data on Auschwitz and Theresienstadt prisoners—were taking place at the same time as, or even later than, the research for the Berlin memorial book. Thus it was not possible for the first edition to incorporate data that subsequently emerged. Nor was it initially possible to carry out a systematic overview of the East European archives and the archives found in the concentration and extermination camps themselves.

## Sources from the National Socialist Bureaucracy

Existing sources from the files of the German Nazi regime have made it possible to gain a deeper insight into the mass murder that it bureaucratically organized and implemented. For our purposes, the most important in both qualitative and quantitative terms have been the files and documents from the Department for the Utilization of Assets (*Vermögensverwertungsstelle*), which was under the control of the former head of finance in Berlin-Brandenburg. The associated files and card indexes have been stored in the Federal Archive in Berlin for several years.

From the end of 1941, the Department for the Utilization of Assets had to confiscate and "utilize" the remaining property of Jewish Berliners up until the time of their deportation. This final confiscation marked the completion of the Nazi regime's material plunder of the Jews. With the eleventh supplementary decree to the Reich Citizenship Law of November 25, 1941, the regime created for itself a pseudo-legal framework for this unprecedented confiscation procedure.[9] The regulation stated that all Jews who had "their usual residence abroad" would lose German nationality. In this way, the Nazi regime gave itself the "right" to seize and confiscate the property of the "expatriated." The fact that expatriation generally coincided with deportation to an extermination camp was stated in pseudo-legal terms by the ministerial bureaucracy following the Law on Registration (*Meldegesetz*): "Usual residence abroad" applied if a Jew was living abroad in circumstances that made it evident "that he is not just living there temporarily."

All Jews, including small children, had to fill out a sixteen-page Declaration of Assets (*Vermögenserklärung*) prior to deportation. The form required detailed personal information and, especially, exact details on financial circumstances, assets, and property. Those who gave inaccurate or incomplete information were threatened with immediate deportation to a concentration camp and seizure of assets.

The signed and dated Declaration of Assets is often a Jewish Berliner's last sign of life. Directly before deportation the document had to be submitted to Gestapo officials, who passed it on to the Department for the Utilization of Assets. This body then ensured that bank credit, profits from the sale of property, furniture, household goods, and so on were transferred to the finance office. Debts were settled and arrears collected. The department haggled with Berlin armaments firms—where a large number of Berlin Jews had to carry out forced labor before their deportation—for wages in arrears. It calculated down to the last *pfennig* the gas and electricity bills of those who had already been deported. The authorities carried out endless correspondence in dispute with landlords, who generally demanded compensation for shortfalls in rent and renovation costs.

Of the entire archive at the Department for the Utilization of Assets—which held an estimated total of 90,000 to 100,000 files—about 40,000 files remain,

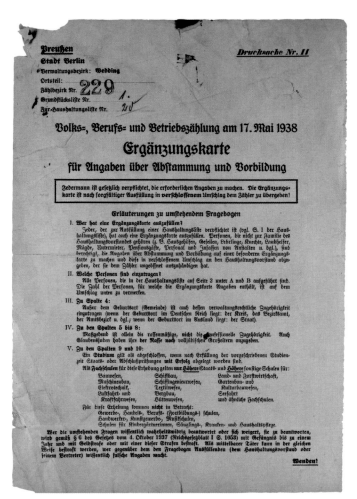

**Figure 11.1**

The "Supplementary Form for Details on Origin and Background" included in the May 17, 1938, census

along with about 100,000 record cards. Some of these contain names, addresses, and details of the time and destination of deportation; in all probability, however, the latter information was not entered until after the war. In some cases, cards contain only the names of emigrants.

The Gestapo also provided the Department for the Utilization of Assets with copies of the deportation lists.[10] However, lists do not remain for all of the transports—for the first four transports to Lódz (Litzmannstadt), for example. Here it was possible for us to check the record card details against the lists provided by the Frankfurt am Main city archive, which lists those people who were sent to the Lódz ghetto.

Another important source consists of the Supplementary Form for Details on Origin and Background (*Ergänzungskarte für Angaben über Abstammung und*

Figure 11.2 Reverse side of the supplementary form. Columns five through eight are for answering the question "Are or were any of the four grandparents full Jews [*Volljuden*] in racial terms (yes or no)." (There follow boxes—"paternal grandfather, paternal grandmother," etc.) Section 4 of the instructions on the other side of the form clarifies the racial definition of the term *Volljude*: "Of Relevance is only racial, not religious belonging. Jews by religion [*Glaubensjuden*], too, must list their full Jewish grandparents according to race."

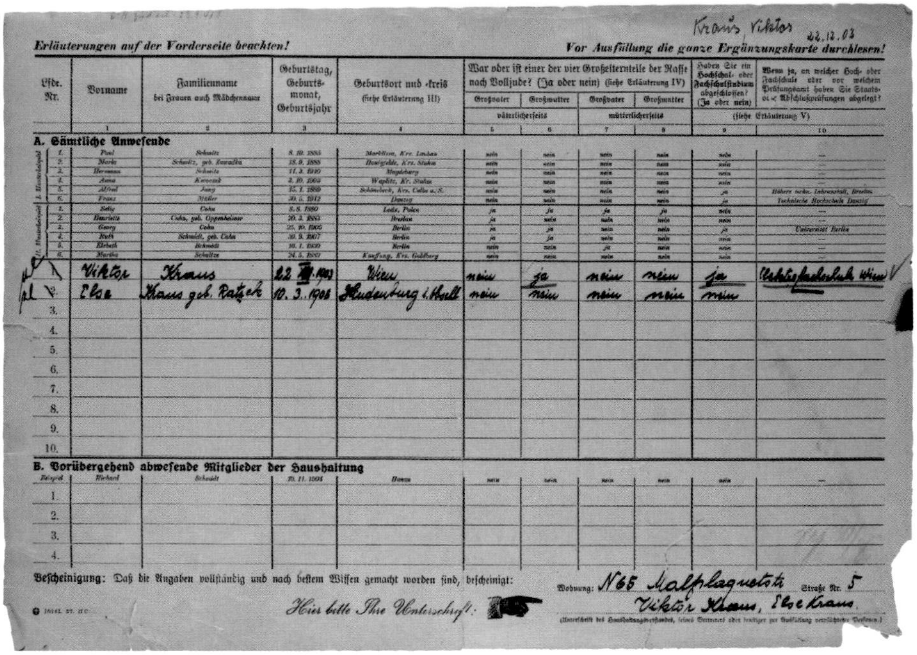

Kraus, Viktor 22.12.03

*Erläuterungen auf der Vorderseite beachten!* *Vor Ausfüllung die ganze Ergänzungskarte durchlesen!*

| Lfde. Nr. | Vorname | Familienname bei Frauen auch Mädchenname | Geburtstag, Geburtsmonat, Geburtsjahr | Geburtsort und -kreis (siehe Erläuterung III) | War oder ist einer der vier Großelternteile der Rasse nach Volljude? (Ja oder nein) (siehe Erläuterung IV) — Großvater väterlicherseits | Großmutter väterlicherseits | Großvater mütterlicherseits | Großmutter mütterlicherseits | Haben Sie ein Hochschul- oder Fachschulstudium abgeschlossen? (Ja oder nein) (siehe Erläuterung V) | Wenn ja, an welcher Hoch- oder Fachschule oder vor welchem Prüfungsamt haben Sie Staats- o. Abschlußprüfungen abgelegt? |
|---|---|---|---|---|---|---|---|---|---|---|
| | 1 | 2 | 3 | 4 | 5 | 6 | 7 | 8 | 9 | 10 |
| **A. Sämtliche Anwesende** | | | | | | | | | | |
| I. Musterbeispiel 1. | Paul | Schmitz | 8. 10. 1885 | Marklissa, Kr. Lauban | nein | nein | nein | nein | nein | — |
| 2. | Maria | Schmitz, geb. Zawadka | 18. 9. 1888 | Honigfelde, Kr. Stuhm | nein | nein | nein | nein | nein | — |
| 3. | Hermann | Schmitz | 11. 3. 1910 | Magdeburg | nein | nein | nein | nein | nein | — |
| 4. | Anna | Kowczak | 3. 10. 1903 | Waplitz, Kr. Stuhm | nein | nein | nein | nein | nein | — |
| 5. | Alfred | Jung | 15. 1. 1889 | Schönbeck, Kr. Calbe a. S. | nein | nein | nein | nein | ja | Höhere techn. Lehranstalt, Breslau |
| 6. | Franz | Müller | 30. 5. 1912 | Danzig | nein | nein | nein | nein | ja | Technische Hochschule Danzig |
| II. Musterbeispiel 1. | Selig | Cohn | 8. 8. 1880 | Lodz, Polen | ja | ja | ja | ja | nein | — |
| 2. | Henriette | Cohn, geb. Oppenheimer | 20. 3. 1883 | Breslau | ja | nein | nein | nein | nein | — |
| 3. | Georg | Cohn | 25. 10. 1905 | Berlin | ja | ja | nein | nein | ja | Universität Berlin |
| 4. | Ruth | Schmidt, geb. Cohn | 30. 9. 1907 | Berlin | ja | ja | nein | nein | nein | — |
| 5. | Elsbeth | Schmidt | 10. 1. 1930 | Berlin | nein | nein | ja | nein | nein | — |
| 6. | Martha | Schultze | 24. 5. 1889 | Kauffung, Kr. Goldberg | nein | nein | nein | nein | nein | — |
| 1. | Viktor | Kraus | 22. XII. 1903 | Wien | nein | ja | nein | nein | ja | Welthandelshochschule Wien |
| 2. | Else | Kraus geb. Ratzek | 10. 3. 1908 | Judenburg i. Stmk. | nein | nein | nein | nein | nein | |
| 3. | | | | | | | | | | |
| 4. | | | | | | | | | | |
| 5. | | | | | | | | | | |
| 6. | | | | | | | | | | |
| 7. | | | | | | | | | | |
| 8. | | | | | | | | | | |
| 9. | | | | | | | | | | |
| 10. | | | | | | | | | | |
| **B. Vorübergehend abwesende Mitglieder der Haushaltung** | | | | | | | | | | |
| Beispiel | Richard | Schmidt | 21. 11. 1904 | Hamm | nein | nein | nein | nein | nein | — |
| 1. | | | | | | | | | | |
| 2. | | | | | | | | | | |
| 3. | | | | | | | | | | |
| 4. | | | | | | | | | | |

**Bescheinigung:** Daß die Angaben vollständig und nach bestem Wissen gemacht worden sind, bescheinigt:

Wohnung: N65 Malplaquetstr. Straße Nr. 5

*Hier bitte Ihre Unterschrift:* Viktor Kraus, Else Kraus

(Unterschrift des Haushaltungsvorstandes, seines Vertreters oder sonstiger zur Ausfüllung verpflichteter Personen.)

*Vorbildung*) used in the census of May 17, 1939. A Reich-wide census had been conducted as early as June 1933, and in 1936, the Reich Office for Statistics published the detailed results of the "Special Count of Jews by Religion in the German Reich" (*Sonderauszählung der Glaubensjuden im Deutschen Reich*), carried out within the framework of the 1933 census.[11] Already, there was a clearly anti-Semitic basis for the work. As the statisticians wrote in their report, "a new count is urgently needed for official purposes" in view of the "fundamental reorganization in the status of Jewishness in German society brought about by the National Socialist government."

For the May 1939 census, the Reich Office for Statistics had prepared and distributed a supplementary form along with the Household List form (*Haushaltungsliste*), also used in 1933. The supplementary form (see illustration) had to be returned in a special envelope that the Office for Statistics alone was entitled to open. The aim was twofold: to achieve greater acceptance of the questionnaire as well as to obtain more accurate results. The form asked for name, date, and place of birth, and if "any of the four grandparents were or are *Volljuden* [full Jews] in racial terms." Such details enabled the Nazi authorities to produce a virtually complete list of all people classed by the 1935 Nuremberg racial laws as "Jewish," "non-Aryan," or "of non-German-blood."

At a later stage, such information would determine life or death in "border-line cases." If any question on the supplementary form had been answered with a "yes," the form would later be passed on to the Reich Office for Genealogical Research (Reichsstelle für Sippenforschung)—after 1940, the Reich Office for Genealogy (Reichssippenamt). This body decided on descent in questionable cases and played a role in connection with the deportation of the Jews to the extermination camps. The "experts" in its employ produced certificates on descent relating to the racial classification of a person drawing on the supplementary forms, along with church records and documents in Jewish Community archives (see chap. 20).

Such Nazi-era census documents make it possible to reconstruct an almost complete list of Berlin's Jewish population for a certain period. The supplementary forms are invaluable for establishing biographical details. The police stations, in their capacity as registration authorities, often noted in the files such details as marriage, death, cancellation of residence for the purposes of emigration, and so on. Comparing these documents with other sources, however, also made it clear that if police registration was cancelled for the purposes of emigration to another country, this did not necessarily mean that emigration had been successful. In a range of cases, people who had cancelled their residency with the police were later deported from Berlin. The supplementary forms, for their part, contain very little information on deportations to extermination camps.

In the postwar period, this compilation of sources was initially administered by the Jewish Community in East Berlin and housed from 1981 in the former Central State Archive of the GDR.[12] It is now located in the Federal Archive in the Berlin district of Lichterfelde.

## Sources from Jewish Institutions during the National Socialist Period

The Jewish cemetery in Weissensee opened in 1880, and its register of deaths provides a valuable list of names of the Berlin Jews who died in the 1930s and 1940s. The register includes names, dates of birth, the address at time of death, the dates of death and burial, and in some cases also the place of death. Unfortunately at the time of the publication of this book, it was only possible to examine a small number of the associated files, since these are in the process of being thoroughly restored. In the case of many of the files examined, the corresponding details indicate that the person committed suicide or had died in one of the German concentration camps such as Sachsenhausen, Buchenwald, or Dachau.

The card index kept by the Reich Representation of Jews in Germany (Reichs-vertretung der Juden in Deutschland), now located in the Federal Archive, contains the names and addresses of male and female pupils who attended Jewish schools in Berlin as well as details pertaining to their parents. This archive also contains files detailing internal migration, notices of death from the early 1940s, and files on emigration from Berlin in the years 1940 and 1941.

Additionally, there are files on cancellation of membership in the Jewish Community, now located in the Centrum Judaicum Archive. These made it possible to note the names, dates of birth, addresses, and professions of those who had officially withdrawn from the Jewish Community. Unfortunately, the Jewish Community's membership register, which was used by the Nazi Office for Genealogy at least through February 1944, has "disappeared without a trace."[13]

*Postwar Sources*

The Berlin Senate's files on "victims of racial persecution" document the biographies of Berlin Jews who survived the National Socialist period and later applied for some degree of compensation. It also contains a smaller number of files on the few survivors of the concentration and extermination camps as well as those who were able to survive in hiding in Berlin and surrounding areas. Some of the record cards and files also contain information on murdered family members and relatives. The majority of these concern Berliners who were in some degree protected from persecution: Jewish spouses in "mixed marriages," for example, and men and women classed in Nuremberg terminology as "first- and second-degree *Mischlinge*." (Applications for compensation by "second-degree *Mischlinge*" were often rejected on grounds that these individuals had not suffered such severe persecution.)

From the summer of 1945 on, when the extent of Nazi atrocities against the Jews became known worldwide, the Jewish newspaper *Aufbau* published lists of names of survivors from the concentration and extermination camps. It also published the names of Jewish emigrants who had died in the city of Shanghai. Immediately after the liberation of Theresienstadt, lists of survivors were produced. They were published soon afterward in a book.

At the same time that our research group was evaluating the sources, we made intensive efforts to establish contact with survivors and eyewitnesses. The project was announced in various newspapers, magazines, and notices, both in Germany and abroad, with the request for those involved to contact the research group. Hundreds of former Jewish residents of Berlin responded, reporting on their experiences as well on those of their friends and relatives.

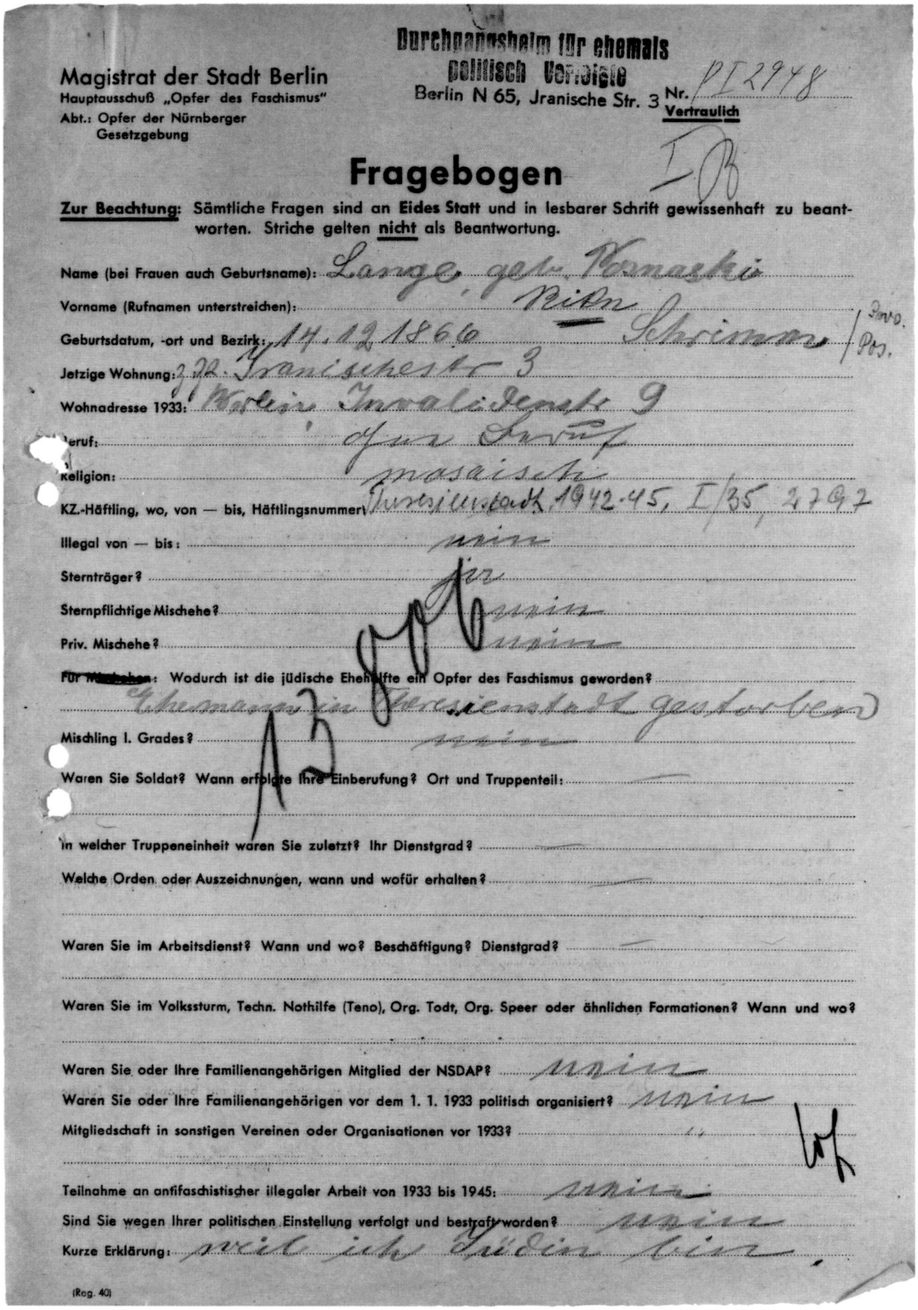

Durchgangsheim für ehemals politisch Verfolgte
Berlin N 65, Jranische Str. 3

Magistrat der Stadt Berlin
Hauptausschuß „Opfer des Faschismus"
Abt.: Opfer der Nürnberger Gesetzgebung

Nr. PI 2948
Vertraulich

**Fragebogen**

Zur Beachtung: Sämtliche Fragen sind an Eides Statt und in lesbarer Schrift gewissenhaft zu beantworten. Striche gelten nicht als Beantwortung.

Name (bei Frauen auch Geburtsname): Lange, geb. [illegible]
Vorname (Rufnamen unterstreichen): [illegible]
Geburtsdatum, -ort und Bezirk: 14.12.1866 — Schrimm / Prov. Pos.
Jetzige Wohnung: z. Zt. Jranischestr. 3
Wohnadresse 1933: Berlin Invalidenstr. 9
Beruf: ohne Beruf
Religion: mosaisch
KZ.-Häftling, wo, von — bis, Häftlingsnummer: Theresienstadt 1942-45, I/35, 2797
Illegal von — bis: nein
Sternträger? ja
Sternpflichtige Mischehe? nein
Priv. Mischehe? nein
Für Mischehen: Wodurch ist die jüdische Ehehälfte ein Opfer des Faschismus geworden?
Ehemann in Theresienstadt gestorben
Mischling I. Grades? nein
Waren Sie Soldat? Wann erfolgte Ihre Einberufung? Ort und Truppenteil: —
In welcher Truppeneinheit waren Sie zuletzt? Ihr Dienstgrad? —
Welche Orden oder Auszeichnungen, wann und wofür erhalten? —
Waren Sie im Arbeitsdienst? Wann und wo? Beschäftigung? Dienstgrad? —
Waren Sie im Volkssturm, Techn. Nothilfe (Teno), Org. Todt, Org. Speer oder ähnlichen Formationen? Wann und wo?
Waren Sie oder Ihre Familienangehörigen Mitglied der NSDAP? nein
Waren Sie oder Ihre Familienangehörigen vor dem 1. 1. 1933 politisch organisiert? nein
Mitgliedschaft in sonstigen Vereinen oder Organisationen vor 1933? „
Teilnahme an antifaschistischer illegaler Arbeit von 1933 bis 1945: nein
Sind Sie wegen Ihrer politischen Einstellung verfolgt und bestraft worden? nein
Kurze Erklärung: weil ich Jüdin bin.

(Reg. 40)

**Figure 11.3**
Postwar questionnaire for "Victims of Fascism" issued by the Berlin magistrate

## Limitations of the Memorial Book and the Database

It was foreseeable from the outset that the memorial book could be neither complete nor fully accurate.[14] The book's epilogue describes the limits and shortfalls of the research.[15] Following publication, the Berlin Federal Archive, the New Synagogue Berlin/ Centrum Judaicum Foundation, and the Free University in Berlin received many corrections and additions. Above all, the corrections clarified biographies and provided additional information from emigration countries and countries from which the victims were deported. Additional sources were subsequently discovered. Employees of the Federal Archive, for example, discovered in documents from the women's prison on Barnimstrasse details about deportees that had not been included in the Gestapo deportation lists.[16]

As research progressed and further sources were added, it was necessary to add to the database and to standardize it so that users in the Federal Archive and the archive of the Centrum Judaicum could refer to a common database.

At the time of this project's completion, the database contained a solid base of documentation on Jewish residents in Berlin from the May 1939 census through the end of the war. Since our priority was to document those who were murdered, there are still major gaps for the 1933–39 period. Thus, it is not yet possible to carry out representative studies on Berlin's Jewish population by referring solely or primarily to this database.[17]

In particular, the names and biographies of those Polish Jews who had resided in Berlin and were deported to Poland in 1938–39 are only minimally documented.[18] As the German army entered Poland shortly after this, one can presume that many of them were subsequently murdered. Other non-German Jews who had resided in Berlin were affected by deportation as well. Also undocumented are the majority of the approximately 100,000 Berliners who succeeded in leaving the city for other countries.[19] Those who had emigrated to countries later occupied by the Nazis were, for the most part, deported and murdered.


## Some Methodological Problems

Although there was some criticism that the research process was taking too long, data collection had to be much more extensive than what was included in publication. Often people only planned emigration without being able to carry it out; people left Berlin for other cities within Germany as well as abroad. Only an intensive assessment of a wide variety of sources could provide plausible and substantiated statements on the biographies of Berlin Jews in a way that appropriately evaluated sources and considered these according to a hierarchy of importance. In doing so, we encountered several fundamental methodological problems.

It is to be expected that problems continually arise in using a wide range of sources. The more sources are considered, the more inconsistencies will become apparent. In the case of this project, this pertained not only to biographical details, but also to the spelling of names and discrepancies in dates of birth.

A general problem for a large city like Berlin is that of clarifying personal identity. Certain names appear with frequency; even in the case of a rare name, there is no guarantee that it refers to the same person. Only when we could find at least two coinciding details did we assume that the name referred to one and not two separate people. The name Martin Cohn, for example, appears forty-two times in the database. Without details of the date of birth it is impossible to identify the person. Addresses are not as reliable for identification, since people were often obliged to move many times in the course of Nazi persecution.

Even when the date of birth is available, problems can arise. For example, the memorial book lists a man named Leo Gabriel, born on December 29, 1873, in Wreschen in the district of Posen (now Poznan in Poland) and deported to Theresienstadt on March 17, 1943. Other sources relating to Leo Gabriel state the same place of birth but gave the date of birth as December 5, 1873. Since the name Gabriel is an infrequent one, it was initially assumed that both records referred to the same individual. When the sources on which the 1986 Federal Archive's memorial book was based were compared with information from the residents' registration card index, however, it became clear that there were indeed two Leo Gabriels. Both were born in December 1873 in Wreschen and died in 1943. One was "the owner of a gentlemen's clothing store," the other a "banker."[20] One was married and lived on Kalckreuthstrasse in Schöneberg, the other was divorced and lived on Schwäbische Strasse in the same neighborhood.

In cases where various dates of birth are given for the same person, the origin of the mistake cannot always be clearly determined and often goes very far back in time. Registry offices did not exist in Prussia until 1875, nor for the German Reich until the following year, and in Eastern European countries they often did not exist at all. Until the second quarter of the nineteenth century, births, marriages, and deaths had been registered with the district courts in the larger towns; in rural areas they were noted in the parish registers or in the documents of the respective Jewish Community.[21] Where information was passed down orally, the risk of inconsistencies is inherent from the outset.

Name changes entailed further problems.[22] Many Jewish families had "Germanized" their names in the course of acculturation. The name Meir, for example, might have been changed to any number of forms, including Meyer, Maier, Mayer, or Meier. During the Nazi years, as Jews were increasingly excluded and persecuted, the documents began to reinclude the Hebrew forms of the names, and sometimes various names were given. Hence, for example, in non-Jewish sources a person was recorded as Adolf Wolff and in Jewish sources as Salomon Wolf. Based on the address given and the name of his wife, it is clear that Adolf and Solomon were the same person. Different spellings of names should also be taken into account, particularly in the case of Jews of Eastern European origin. (Kantorowicz, for example, would become Kantorowitz.)

Under such circumstances, errors in interpreting sources were bound to occur despite years of experience on the part of researchers. The 1986 Federal Archive memorial book, for example, states that Dr. Hugo Tischler died at Theresienstadt on July 25, 1943. In his files from the office of the head of finance (*Oberfinanzpräsident*), however, we found a note dated September 30, 1948, from the lawyer Berl Coper that mentioned a "Dr. Hugo Tischler, formerly of 17 Essener Str. in Berlin, now at 1838 North-Wells-Street 14 Chicago USA." From this information we assumed that he had survived and that the entry in the memorial book was incorrect. When the Theresienstadt memorial project initiative informed me of the date of death, which was the same as the one found in Federal Archive's memorial book, it was necessary to carry out further research. Our inquiries to the authorities dealing with compensation payments to former forced laborers and the reparations offices revealed that the details given by both the Federal Archive and the Theresienstadt initiative were correct.[23] It was not Dr. Tischler but his daughter who was living in Chicago in 1948. A very busy postwar lawyer was responsible for the error when providing the addresses of descendants in connection with details on deportees.[24] In this case, an otherwise accurate methodological approach that gave greater weight to postwar details than to earlier information, proved incorrect.

Often the names of deportees are included on several deportation lists. If the dates of deportation are far apart, then we considered the last mentioned date to be the decisive one. (Deportation was sometimes postponed on account of illness or in the case of forced laborers deemed "indispensable" by a company.) It was not always possible to state clearly whether someone had been deported to Theresienstadt or to Auschwitz. Hence, an employee of the Reichsvereinigung reported that Mr. and Mrs. Marx of Cologne were to be deported to Theresienstadt on account of the husband's severe illness. Only during transport to the station was it apparently ordered that Mr. Marx be sent to Auschwitz. The couple was ultimately deported to Auschwitz via Berlin.[25] In this case the deportation destination was determined from the Berlin Gestapo's deportation lists.

In other cases, however, we had to refer to the lists of Theresienstadt arrivals for clarification. For instance, Erna Herrmann (born on April 5, 1898), the head of the Jewish home for the elderly on Brunnenstrasse, was down on the list for the 88th old-age transport to Theresienstadt on May 18, 1943. Her name is also on the list for the 38th transport to Auschwitz on May 17, 1943, one day prior. According to documents from the Czech memorial book project, she was actually deported to Auschwitz but only after first being taken to Theresienstadt.

## New Sources

With funding from the New Synagogue Berlin/Centrum Judaicum Foundation in the summer of 1998, I had the opportunity to incorporate three additional elements into the database: 1) the collective guardianship files of the Jewish Community, 2) the files for the state of Brandenberg from the Department for the Utilization of Assets, and 3) most of the emigration files from the foreign exchange office at the office of the head of finance. These have helped to fill in information for the period 1933 to 1935.

### The Collective Guardianship Files of the Jewish Community

The files on collective guardianship[26] held at the Department for Welfare and Youth of the Jewish Community in Berlin provided biographical information on adopted children, mothers and "biological parents," and sometimes on foster parents and others as well.[27]

This is by no means the entire holding of the Department for Welfare and Youth. Rather, the files were from the Jewish Community's final phase in Nazi Berlin. Most of the wards were deported. Some of them survived in the care of an "Aryan" parent; in some cases the biographies could not be established. These files contain barely any information on wards who were able to emigrate.

With respect to the memorial book database, these files proved useful for making additions and corrections. This was above all the case when it came to ascertaining the identity of certain people. In some cases the mothers married shortly before deportation, and the child was listed under the mother's maiden name as well as under the name of the new stepfather. Klara Jablonski and Karl-heinz Klobach, for example, did not marry until October 30, 1944. They were deported to Theresienstadt on November 24, 1944, along with a child listed as Joab Nathan Jablonski. The parents survived, but the fate of their son was unclear. A story about him was published in the newspaper *Aufbau* on October 12, 1945 naming him as Joel Klobach.

**Figure 11.4**
Guardianship file for Mirjam Kleinhändler

In some cases foster parents gave the child their own name using a so-called Child Adoption Agreement (*Kindesannahmevertrag*). For instance, the child Ruth Tannenbaum, born in 1937, was given the name of her foster parents, Lewin, in 1942.[28] According to information from the Jewish registration office, the whereabouts of Ruth Tannenbaum were thus "not in the file of the Jewish registration office or the emigration file." Indeed, Ruth Lewin had been deported on March 4, 1943.

A further problem was posed when parents had been married according to Jewish ritual but not at the registry office. An example is the case of Bihri Schäfer, the child of Marie Schäfer and Jakob Geber. Because the head of finance for Berlin-Brandenburg had a file on both Bihri Schäfer and Bihri Geber, both names were later entered in the memorial book database as well as the published memorial book. The girl's name was in fact Bihri Schäfer, since the marriage of her parents could not take place in the registry office due to missing papers.[29] Since variants of names were involved, the problem was not recognized by the memorial book working group. The fact later came to light when a letter from the father was located in the files.[30]

Subsequent additions to the database mainly concerned further details on Berlin addresses, nationality, and other such matters. In the case of adopted children, later details pertained above all to those "biological parents" who emigrated before the 1939 census and had therefore not been listed in the original database.

New information was also taken down for children who were born after the 1939 census and were not deported. As the files end in 1944 at the latest, they cannot tell us about postwar biographies. The fate of a woman named Vera E., for example, has still not been established, apart from the fact that she was living in Berlin at the time of the 1939 census. We now know, however, that in 1940, 1942, and 1944 she gave birth to her children Michael, Thomas, and Franziska. It is not known whether she survived. Classified by Nazi racial law as a "*Geltungsjüdin*" (Jew by definition)[31] she, too, would have been threatened with deportation.

## The Brandenburg Files from the Department for the Utilization of Assets

After the war, the files kept by the Department for the Utilization of Assets were divided up, and the Brandenburg files were given to Brandenburg in the German Democratic Republic (GDR). The holdings contain deportation files on Jews whose final place of residence was that state of Brandenburg. They also contain documents on pupils at Berlin schools who were taken back to their parents for the purposes of deportation. The same holdings also contain files from a register of real estate,[32] in so far as estates in the state of Brandenburg were concerned.[33]

The fate of the various sources in the postwar period reflects the different ways in which Nazi crimes were subsequently addressed in East and West Germany. In the Federal Republic of Germany the files for West Berlin were initially kept by the financial administration in order to settle restitution claims. Only after this process had largely been concluded were the card indexes and files transferred to the Berlin Federal Archive. At the time, it could not be predicted that these holdings could also be of relevance for reparations in East Berlin. It is still not possible to reconstruct what happened to the files in the former GDR, or for what purposes—let alone when they were handed over to the Brandenburg Central State Archive (Brandenburgische Landeshauptarchiv [BLHA]).

The Department for the Utilization of Assets holding in the Brandenburg State Archive comprises 1,363 files, of which around 50 percent were relevant to Berlin for three reasons. First, in the years 1939 to 1942–43 there were movements of people between Berlin and the surrounding state of Brandenburg. Because the census data allow a full list of the Jewish population of Berlin in May 1939, it was possible to determine some additional biographies. Second,

Brandenburg pupils attended Jewish schools in Berlin after 1938, when they were forced from state schools. Pupils from other parts of Germany—for example, Pomerania—were also in Berlin while some of their parents were deployed as forced laborers in the Jewish labor columns in Brandenburg. If they were deported from Brandenburg, there are also files on them. Finally, there were several Zionist-sponsored training centers in Brandenburg (*Hachshara* centers), which later became labor camps (see chap. 7). These included the agricultural center at Neuendorf and the forestry centers at Boossen, Kersdorf, Neumühle, and Radinkendorf, among others. Young Berlin Jews made up the largest group in these centers, and most were deported via Berlin in 1943.

Like the Berlin files, the Brandenburg files are not complete. Nonetheless, the evaluation of files relating to the deportees from the Neuendorf agricultural camp revealed that Declarations of Assets" documents and so on were available for 80 percent of the deportees.

The files, moreover, showed that one of our basic assumptions had been incorrect—that is, that all Brandenburg deportations were carried out by the Berlin Gestapo. There are barely any deportation lists remaining from Brandenburg.[34] However, one can find evidence of deportations from the original file referencing, as well as individual official documents in the files.[35] The activities of the Gestapo regional headquarters in Potsdam and Frankfurt an der Oder also affected Berlin Jews.

### Sources and Publications Not Yet Assessed

It has not yet been possible to assess a range of newly available sources and new publications. These include the card index from the residents' registration office; documents from Berlin prisons (card indexes and files); files at the district court (divorces); the holdings on *Opfer des Faschismus* (Victims of Fascism) in the Berlin Federal Archive; criminal proceedings on tax affairs and Reich emigration tax documents; documents from the finance office in the district of West Moabit; further files from the foreign exchange office; documents from the police headquarters with applications to change names; files and further documents from the Reichsvereinigung; the letter archive from the Berlin memorial book project; the office of the head of finance files on enemy assets; documents from the *Haupttreuhandstelle Ost* (Central Privatization Office for the Occupied Eastern Territories—an organization that confiscated land, property, businesses, etc.); the index of expatriated people; the Reich film archive in the Federal Archive; new memorial books being published in Germany and abroad; documents on the money that the Jews had to raise after the pogrom of November 9, 1938, to finance the repairs (*Judenvermögensabgabe*); the index of baptisms from the baptism register for Old Berlin; and new research findings from the memorial sites at Sachsenhausen, Ravensbrück, Bergen-Belsen, Yad Vashem in Jerusalem, the Holocaust Memorial Museum in Washington, and the Theresienstadt initiative, among others.

## Perspectives

The wide range of new research findings alone shows that, as before, there is a great deal of interest in this topic. The move of parts of the Federal Archive to Berlin and—here, above all—the availability of sources it used for its 1986 memorial book have decisively improved research possibilities. The value of the new access to the documents of the Nazi chief finance office should not be underestimated, for example, in determining the fate of Berlin's Polish Jews. Moreover, the Federal Archive in Berlin and the Centrum Judaicum Archive have received new holdings.

Anyone who deals with the history of Jewish victims cannot ignore the perpetrators. The lack of a sense of injustice with regard to expulsions from 1933 onward formed a basis for the administrative mass murder in the 1940s. Memory of these crimes is not an end in itself. To use the apt formulation by Herbert A. Strauss, "It is not about accusation or guilt. It is about understanding, responsibility, and the future."[36]

**1** Paul Celan, "Deathfugue" in *Selected Poems and Prose of Paul Celan*, translated by John Felstiner (New York, 2001), p. 31.

**2** Zentralinstitut für sozialwissenschaftliche Forschung, Freie Universität Berlin, editor (on behalf of the Senator for Cultural Affairs), *Gedenkbuch Berlins der jüdischen Opfer des Nationalsozialismus* (Berlin, 1995).

**3** Bundesarchiv Koblenz, editor (in cooperation with the Missing Persons Tracing Service of the International Red Cross in Arolsen), *Gedenkbuch. Opfer der Verfolgung der Juden unter der nationalsozialistischen Gewaltherrschaft in Deutschland, 1933–1945* (Frankfurt am Main, 1986).

**4** Because Jews from areas that are no longer in Germany were also deported from Berlin, it seemed unjustifiable not to include them. It is unlikely, at least for the foreseeable future, that Poland and Russia will produce their own memorial books. These Jews were present in Berlin at least during their time in the assembly camps. It is preferable for a name to appear in several different memorial books than for it to go undocumented.

**5** What follows is based on a revised version of the epilogue to the Berlin memorial book, p. 1410 ff.

**6** Barbara Vormeier, *Die Deportierungen deutscher und österreichischer Juden aus Frankreich* (Paris, 1980).

**7** Institut für Zeitgeschichte (Munich) and the Research Foundation for Jewish Immigration (New York), editors, *Biographisches Handbuch der deutschsprachigen Emigration nach 1933*, vols. 1–2 (Munich, New York, London, and Paris, 1980, 1983).

**8** The revised Dutch memorial book, *In Memoriam. Sdu Uitgeverij Koninginnegracht* (The Hague, 1995), appeared at the same time as the Berlin memorial book, and the list could therefore not be incorporated at this stage.

**9** *Reichsgesetzblatt (RGBl)*, 1, 1941, p. 414 f. Because many Berlin Jews committed suicide before deportation, the thirteenth supplementary decree to the Reich Citizenship Law stipulated that after the death of a Jew, his assets would go to the Reich. In the cases of "mixed marriages," it was possible to obtain compensation for relatives. See *RGBl*, 1, 1943, 1, p. 372.

**10** Copies of the lists are located in the Berlin State Archive as well as the Federal Archive.

**11** *Statistik des Deutschen Reichs: Volkszählung. Die Bevölkerung des Deutschen Reichs nach den Ergebnissen der Volkszählung 1933, no. 5, Die Glaubensjuden im Deutschen Reich*, revised by the Statistisches Reichsamt (Berlin, 1936).

**12** The transfer document and the associated legal foundations are located in the Centrum Judaicum Archive (CJA). See also Gerlinde Grahn, "Der Teilbestand des Reichssippenamtes im Bundesarchiv, Abteilungen Potsdam," in *Archivmitteilungen* 6 (1991): 269–74.

**13** The director of the Reichssippenamt to the head of finance for Berlin-Brandenburg, letter dated February 17, 1944, in Rep. 92, Ac. 3924, no. 10217/43, Landesarchiv Berlin (LAB). On the disappearance of the register see Grahn, "Der Teilbestand," p. 271. This reports on a letter of July 6, 1943, from the Reichssippenamt to the head of finance, according to which the Reichssippenamt had taken over the register from the Reichsvereinigung. According to a note made by the Reichsvereinigung on July 9, 1943, the administration of the tax register (*Kataster*) of the Jewish residents registration office, which was based on Grosse Hamburger Strasse, was taken over by the Reichssippenamt. See 75 C Re 1, Nr. 640, sheet. 9, Bundesarchiv (BArch), Berlin.

**14** *Gedenkbuch Berlins*, p. 7.

**15** Ibid., p. 1411.

**16** The evaluation of files from the city council already showed that the deportation lists do not cover all of those who died in Auschwitz. I also found details of additional victims in the compilation of corrections for the Federal Archive's 1986 memorial book. I would like to thank Ms. Brachmann-Täubner for pointing this out.

**17** For example, the results of a study on lawyers by Ladwig-Winters, *Anwalt ohne Recht* still has to be put in perspective. This study established the biographies of the lawyers mainly using the database (p. 9) and described these results (not the biographies of the lawyers together) as representing the whole. Because of the sources considered, the deportees and those who died are thereby overrepresented. The proportion of those for whom they could not establish any further information apart from the lists of lawyers—that is, those who were no longer living in Berlin at the time of the 1939 census—was nonetheless 32 percent.

**18** The men were to be deported first; the women generally followed in 1939. According to the 1939 census's analysis, in 1939 there were still 5,669 Jews of Polish nationality living in Berlin. In 1933 the number was said to be 48,075. See *Statistik des Deutschen Reichs . . . 1933*, no. 5, p. 15; and *Statistik des Deutschen Reiches: Volkszählung. Die Bevölkerung des Deutschen Reichs nach den Ergebnissen der*

*Volkszählung 1939*, No. 4 (*Die Juden und jüdischen Mischlinge im Deutschen Reich*), revised by the Statistisches Reichsamt (Berlin, 1944), p. 72.

**19** From the average figures on migration to and from Berlin, which naturally vary widely in practice, it emerges that between 1933 and October 1941—when deportations began—around 100,000 Berlin Jews moved *away* from Berlin, while about 54,000 moved *to* the capital. There are exact figures for the period of August 1935 to March 1936. See BArch, R 58, Nr. 994, sheets 15 ff. On the months January to November 1938, see Sonderarchiv Moskau (Moscow), 500, RSHA, -3, Nr. 316, sheet 677.

**20** In this case, profession proved the best way of distinguishing one Leo Gabriel from the other. The entry "owner of a gentlemen's clothing store" comes from 1933. The persecution of Jews during the period makes it highly unlikely that he later became a banker. It is a different case, for example, for such entries as "trader" (sales invoiced to one's own account) and "representative" (sales invoiced to a different account). Here there were more frequent changes of profession or status, which means that these details are not very useful.

**21** At the turn of the eighteenth to nineteenth century, records pertaining to baptized (i.e., converted) Jews sometimes provided the age of the person in lieu of date of birth.

**22** Due to the large number of countries involved, this problem concerns the staff of the memorial site at the Yad Vashem Archive in Jerusalem more than ourselves. See Alexander Avraham, "The Pages of Testimony. Ein Verzeichnis der Zeugenaussagen zum Gedenken der Opfer des Holocaust und die Computerisierung ihrer Namen," in *Theresienstädter Studien und Dokumente* (Prague, 1996), pp. 250–64, especially from p. 259 on.

**23** Letter of March 18, 1998, from the Compensation Authority and letter of April 23, 1998, from the Berlin Reparations Office. I would like to thank Mr. Bogdahn from the Authority for Compensation to Former Forced Laborers and Ms. Recknagel from the reparations office for this information.

**24** Dr. Alexander Berl Coper (born on October 17, 1891, in Tuchel, West Prussia) was in a mixed marriage. His wife died on June 21, 1944. He was subsequently deported to Theresienstadt on October 27, 1944. He survived the camp and after liberation practiced again as a lawyer in Berlin.

**25** Letter of February 25, 1943, from the Reichsvereinigung, with the subject heading "*Heimeinkaufsvertrag*" (Agreement to Purchase Accommodation in a Home) Rudolf Isr. Marx, Köln-Müngersdorf, Fort V, in BArch, 75 C Re 1, Nr. 480, sheet 67; Berlin memorial book database.

**26** I would like to thank Ms. Welker, archivist at the Centrum Judaicum, for her knowledgeable introduction and supervision during the work on the memorial book. See Stefanie Schüler-Springorum, "Elend und Furcht im Dritten Reich. Aus den Akten der Sammelvormundschaften der Jüdischen Gemeinde zu Berlin," in *Zeitschrift für Geschichtswissenschaft* 7 (1997): 617–41.

**27** I use this term because the "biological parents" often acted in a nonpaternal way.

**28** Her mother, Debora, was expelled from Germany in 1938 and went to Great Britain, where she was unable to care for her child.

**29** This was a frequent problem for stateless people and Jews from East European countries.

**30** Centrum Judaicum Archive (CJA), 1, 75 A Be 2, no. 456. The family was deported to Auschwitz on March 3, 1943.

**31** Vera E. had two Jewish grandparents and, since her children were cared for by the Jewish Community, she was presumably a member. For more on the racial definitions of the Nuremberg Laws, see Andreas Rethmeier, "*Nürnberger Rassegesetze" und Entrechtung der Juden im Zivilrecht* (Frankfurt am Main, 1995).

**32** This files were stamped "real estate register." I am not aware of a corresponding source for Berlin. It was possibly only added to the files after the war. In the office of the head of finance collection at the Berlin State Archive the "Aryanizations" of properties and businesses are an integral part of the files.

**33** It is still not clear what happened to the files in the state of Brandenburg. There were obviously considerations with regard to reparations up to the start of 1949, but the matter was no longer relevant in the following decades. The East German government declined to pay reparations, and the files remained closed. It is not known when they were transferred to the current Brandenburg Central State Archive. The collections have been accessible to the public for the last few years. For reasons of time, they could not be incorporated into the memorial book project, which lasted from 1989 to 1995.

**34** There are at least two lists for Frankfurt. See BArch, Zsg 138/63, sheets 995–96: letter dated September 2, 1942, from the Gestapo, regional headquarters Frankfurt/Oder:

"From August 26–27, 1942, 92 Jews were evacuated from the Frankfurt/Oder administrative district to the Protectorate of Bohemia and Moravia. I enclose the declarations of assets handed in by the Jews for further attention. . . . I also enclose a transport list of the current whereabouts of all evacuated Jews." There is also a transport list for 1943 containing fourteen names. See letter dated June 22, 1943, from the Berlin Gestapo to the office of the head of finance: "Please find enclosed the registers of assets with confiscation orders for those Jews who have been evacuated by the Gestapo regional headquarters in Frankfurt/Oder. The Jews mentioned were deported with the 91st old-age transport. The Frankfurt transport list is enclosed." For Potsdam there are merely indications that lists must have existed. See BArch, Zsg 138/60, sheet 364 (356).

**35** It should be stated that the course of deportation in Brandenburg has yet to be worked through sufficiently.

**36** Herbert A. Strauss, "Der Holocaust. Reflexionen über die Möglichkeit einer wissenschaftlichen und menschlichen Annäherung," in *Antisemitismus. Von der Judenfeindschaft zum Holocaust,* ed. Strauss and Kampe (Bonn, 1984), p. 227.

# Chapter Twelve

## The Opera Singer
## Therese Rothauser

ALEXANDRA VON PFUHLSTEIN

In August 1942, a seventy-seven-year-old former opera singer named Therese Rothauser was awaiting deportation at the assembly camp at Grosse Hamburger Strasse 26.[1] There she met Martha Mosse, who was at the time in charge of the Department of Housing Advice and Emigration Preparation at the Reich Association of Jews in Germany (Reichsvereinigung). Mosse, because of her administrative position, was allowed to enter and leave the assembly camp. She later recalled Therese Rothauser's account of being arrested in her Berlin apartment. "She told the Gestapo officials who had come to take her away that she wished to bid her grand piano farewell. She sat down at the piano; behind her a large picture of the Kaiser hung on the wall. The two Gestapo officials removed their hats and stood to attention at the other side of the grand piano. Then she sang the [folk]song 'Teure Heimat, lebe wohl.'"[2]

This short account, which so ingrained itself in Martha Mosse's memory that she was able to write it down years later, suggests that Therese Rothauser was highly charismatic. Inspired by this vivid anecdote, I set out in search of more evidence about her life and artistic career.

Therese Rothauser was born in Budapest on June 10, 1865, the daughter of a trader.[3] No records have been found regarding her childhood and youth, but there are details about her beginnings as a singer. She studied with Emmerich Bellovicz in Budapest and gave her first public concert in 1886 at the age of twenty-one. One year later she moved to Leipzig, where she made her debut at the opera house there as the winegrower in Max Bruch's *Loreley*. After two years there she moved on to Berlin's Königliches Opernhaus (Royal Opera House), known today as the Staatsoper Unter den Linden.

Berlin became her new home. She was accepted into the opera ensemble, where she was a member for twenty-five years.[4] On November 20, 1894, the artistic director of the Royal Theater Count Bolko Hochberg recommended her in warm terms: "During her six years at this opera ensemble, Miss ROTHAUSER has firmly established herself. A woman of interesting appearance and with a distinguished musical training, she has a beautiful, warm, and appealing voice. The roles of Carmen, Mignon, and Hänsel seem to have been written for her, and she interprets them splendidly. She has become a popular member of the Royal Opera, and it can only be considered a major advantage for her to remain there."[5]

The success Therese Rothauser enjoyed as an opera singer in Berlin was considerable. She was lavishly praised by press and public alike for her interpretation of the title role of *Carmen* and received particularly high honors from the Kaiser, who, after a performance in 1890, had her presented with a valuable sapphire brooch.[6] In 1911 she sang Annina in the memorable Berlin premiere of *Rosenkavalier* before an audience that included Richard Strauss himself.[7]

It was not always easy to work with Therese Rothauser, a fact not inconsistent with her status as a celebrated opera diva. Her personal files show ample evidence of this. Among other things, her letters complain vociferously about the poor condition of her costumes, with suggestions for alteration and improvement. Since her suggestions were not always followed, she would sometimes wear her own costumes for performances, which caused regular disputes with the opera's artistic director; singers were not permitted to choose their own costumes.[8]

In addition to her work in the opera house, Therese Rothauser also made frequent appearances as a singer in Berlin society—something which did not always produce an enthusiastic response. The famous diarist and social commentator Alfred Kerr, complaining about the new trend in Berlin society of introducing artistic performances at all sorts of events, singled her out. "At the home of a parliamentary lawyer," wrote Kerr, "Miss Rothauser of the opera house launches into a pompous aria of French origin."[9] (Kerr would rather have skipped this artistic interlude and gone directly in to dinner.)

Retiring from the stage in 1914, Therese Rothauser, like many former singers and actors in Berlin, supported herself by giving voice lessons.[10] The pleasure of teaching her craft to a new generation may indeed have played a role, but other reasons were at work as well; her pension was simply insufficient. Collecting her modest *Gnadenpension* (artists' pension) was apparently a matter of constant struggle,[11] as evidenced by a reminder she sent in December 1924 claiming missing pension payments for the year of 1923–24.[12] Under the Nazis, further cuts to her pension were made for racist reasons. She tried in vain to oppose these.[13]

Even after withdrawing from active artistic life, Therese Rothauser continued to maintain close ties to the opera. In March 1924 she appeared once more on the stage as a guest performer in the role of Agnes in Bedrich Smetana's

**Figure 12.1** Therese Rothauser as Carmen, 1903   **Figure 12.2** Therese Rothauser as Hänsel, 1903

*The Bartered Bride*.[14] Nor was she forgotten by the public or her colleagues, who awarded her with a number of honors for her long service as an artist.[15] On her seventy-fifth birthday in 1940—at a time when contact between Germans and Jews had to take place under conditions of utmost secrecy and could lead to severe punishment—Fritz Soot, a Staatsoper singer of outstanding merit, appeared at her home and presented her with a bouquet of flowers, along with the "sincerest greetings" of Heinz Tietjen, the opera's former artistic director.[16]

Therese Rothauser never married. She lived until the time of her deportation with her unmarried sister Katalin Rothauser in the Wilmersdorf district of Berlin. The sisters briefly took in their brother Dr. Eduard Rothauser and his wife Ida until the pair emigrated to Spain in January 1934. Eduard was an actor who, until being banned from the profession, had worked at various Berlin theaters.

In October 1933 the former Hungarian was stripped of his German naturalization, which he had acquired years earlier.[17] Stateless, he was forced to leave Germany. Therese Rothauser supported him and his wife as best she could and gave him the necessary funds to emigrate.[18] The couple survived the Nazi period in fascist Spain.

By 1939, Therese Rothauser and her sister were sharing their five-room apartment with four lodgers.[19] In retrospect it is not clear whether the two sisters "voluntarily" rented out the flat in order to improve their financial situation or whether the lodgers were assigned to them as part of a Nazi order to concentrate Jews in a certain number of houses. By August 1942 seven people, including the two sisters, were living in the apartment at Konstanzer Strasse 11. All of them were single Jewish women, approximately the same age as the sisters. When she was arrested, Therese Rothauser listed details pertaining to the women with whom she shared her apartment in the "Declaration of Assets" (*Vermögenserklärung*)—the sixteen-page form that all Jews in Germany had to complete prior to deportation (see chap. 11).[20]

Following the form's instructions, Therese Rothauser thus provided Berlin's financial authorities with the minutest details of her remaining assets—her furniture, art, valuables, table linen, and even the clothing in her possession. As a rule, the Declaration of Assets form required precise information on salary and pension entitlements. If financial circumstances were disclosed and comprehensible—as in Therese Rothauser's case—the entire assets were "confiscated for the benefit of the German Reich."[21] Hans Günther Adler, chronicler of Theresienstadt, has described the Declaration of Assets as the "bureaucratic peak of the administrative procedures connected with deportation."[22] Indeed, it embodied the perfect organization of total robbery, forcing those being robbed into full cooperation with those who robbed them.

A few days after submitting her Declaration of Assets, Therese Rothauser and her sister were arrested and taken to the assembly camp on Grosse Hamburger Strasse. Presumably she was required to settle all outstanding bills and other debts before her arrest. The value of her furniture and other personal effects was then calculated by the office of the head of finances (*Oberfinanzpräsident*), and her entire possessions were sold to trading firms. The apartment was cleared on November 27, 1942.[23]

It appears that all the other women who lived in the apartment at number 11 Konstanzer Strasse died in concentration camps.[24]

Therese Rothauser had sought in vain to deter her impending deportation. In December 1941 she directed a personal letter to Hermann Göring asking him to intervene for her and her sister. Göring, who controlled all state theaters, had

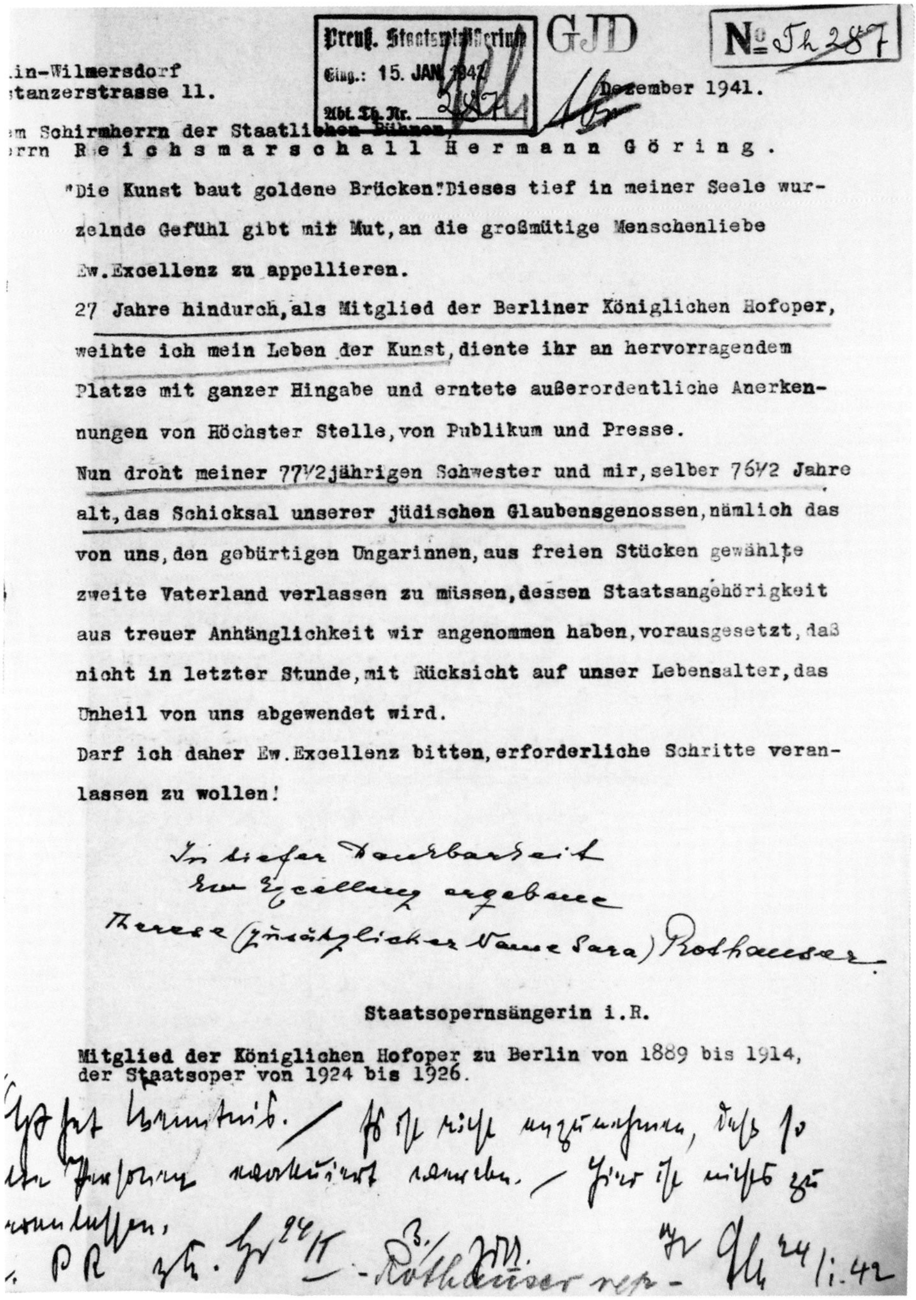

Preuß. Staatsministerium
Eing.: 15. JAN 1942
Abt. Th. Nr. 287

GJD

No. Th 287

.in-Wilmersdorf
:tanzerstrasse 11.

December 1941.

:m Schirmherrn der Staatlichen Bühnen,
:rrn Reichsmarschall Hermann Göring.

"Die Kunst baut goldene Brücken!" Dieses tief in meiner Seele wurzelnde Gefühl gibt mir Mut, an die großmütige Menschenliebe Ew. Excellenz zu appellieren.

27 Jahre hindurch, als Mitglied der Berliner Königlichen Hofoper, weihte ich mein Leben der Kunst, diente ihr an hervorragendem Platze mit ganzer Hingabe und erntete außerordentliche Anerkennungen von Höchster Stelle, von Publikum und Presse.

Nun droht meiner 77 1/2 jährigen Schwester und mir, selber 76 1/2 Jahre alt, das Schicksal unserer jüdischen Glaubensgenossen, nämlich das von uns, den gebürtigen Ungarinnen, aus freien Stücken gewählte zweite Vaterland verlassen zu müssen, dessen Staatsangehörigkeit aus treuer Anhänglichkeit wir angenommen haben, vorausgesetzt, daß nicht in letzter Stunde, mit Rücksicht auf unser Lebensalter, das Unheil von uns abgewendet wird.

Darf ich daher Ew. Excellenz bitten, erforderliche Schritte veranlassen zu wollen!

In tiefer Dankbarkeit
Ew. Excellenz ergebene
Therese (zusätzlicher Name Sara) Rothauser

Staatsopernsängerin i.R.

Mitglied der Königlichen Hofoper zu Berlin von 1889 bis 1914,
der Staatsoper von 1924 bis 1926.

[illegible]

**Figure 12.3** Letter from Therese Rothauser to Hermann Göring, December 1941

a reputation of protecting not only former Jewish air force comrades but also cherished artists.[25] He had drawn up a list of "protected Jews" (*Schutzjuden*) who were to be released immediately from the assembly camp in the case of arrest.[26] Therese Rothauser made her plea in the name of art:

> "Art builds golden bridges." This belief, so deeply embedded in my soul, has given me the courage to appeal to Your Excellency's magnanimous love of mankind.
>
> Throughout my twenty-seven years as a member of the Berlin Royal Court Opera, I lived for art; I served its cause with utter devotion in that extraordinary place.
>
> . . . Now my sister (aged seventy-seven and a half) and I (aged seventy-six and a half) face the same fate as our fellow comrades of Jewish faith. In short, we will be forced to abandon our second fatherland, which we, two Hungarian-born women, chose of our own free will . . . unless we are spared at the last minute from this misfortune out of respect for our advanced age.
>
> I implore Your Excellency to find the will to take the measures necessary![27]

The letter remained unanswered, though a note was written on it in an unknown hand: "It is unlikely that such elderly people will be evacuated. No action is required here."[28]

Sadly, this assumption was not borne out. Therese and Katalin Rothauser were deported to Theresienstadt on August 21, 1942, in the forty-seventh old-age transport (*Alterstransport*). Therese Rothauser died there in April 1943, Katalin the following year.

**1** A writ of summons for Therese Rothauser dated August 20, 1942, wrongly states the recipient's address as "Kl. Hamburger Str. 26."

**2** Martha Mosse, "Ergänzungen zu meinem Bericht vom 23/24 Juli, 1958," Rep. 235, MF 4170–4171, Landesarchiv Berlin (LAB).

**3** K. J. Kutsch and Leo Riemens, editors, *Großes Sängerlexikon,* 3rd ed., vol. 4 (Bern and Munich, 1997), p. 2982.

**4** Genossenschaft Deutscher Bühnen-Angehöriger, *Deutsches Bühnenjahrbuch* (1915): 139.

**5** Letter dated  November 11, 1894, personnel file, Rep. 119, Neue Generalintendanz Nr. 3407, Geheimes Staatsarchiv Preußischer Kulturbesitz (GStPK), Berlin.

**6** Kutsch and Riemens, *Großes Sängerlexikon,* 3rd ed., vol. 4, p. 2983.

**7** Ibid.

**8** See letters dated May 31, 1902 and November 4, 1913, personal file, Rep. 119, Neue Generalintendanz, no. 3407, GStPK.

**9** Alfred Kerr, *Wo liegt Berlin? Briefe aus der Reichshauptstadt, 1895–1900* (Berlin, 1997), p. 37.

**10** LAB, Karteikarte zu A Rep. 167 (Therese Rothauser).

**11** See personnel file cited in note 5. Kaiser Wilhelm to the minister of the Königlichen Hauses and the General Director of the Königlichen Schauspiele, letter dated June 3, 1914.

**12** Letter from Therese Rothauser to the Geheimrat, December 1, 1924, personnel file.

**13** Ibid. Correspondence between Therese Rothauser and the General Director, letters dated March 18, 21, and 31, 1941.

**14** See note 10.

**15** Genossenschaft Deutscher Bühnen-Angehöriger, *Deutsches Bühnenjahrbuch 1928,* 39 Jg., pp. 92 and 1940, 52 Jg., p. 98.

**16** Notice dated June 3, 1940; letter from Generalintendanten Tietjen to Therese Rothauser. See note 5.

**17** The basis for this was the July 14, 1933, law on the revocation of naturalization and the removal of German nationality. On this see, for example, Joseph Walk, editor, *Das Sonderrecht für die Juden im NS-Staat. Eine Sammlung der gesetzlichen Maßnahmen und Richtlinien—Inhalt und Bedeutung* (Heidelberg, 1996).

**18** Eduard Rothauser to the reparations authorities, letter dated November 22, 1953, Brandenburgisches Landeshauptarchiv (BLHA), Pr.Br. 36A OFP, Devisenstelle A 3620.

**19** Therese Rothauser's "supplementary form" (Ergänzungskarte zur Volks-, Berufs- und Betriebszählung), dated May 17, 1939, BArch, R 15.09.

**20** Therese Rothauser, Declaration of Assets (*Vermögenserklärung*), LAB, OFP O 5205—XXVII 14308, sheets 2–12.

**21** Rothauser, Declaration of Assets, sheet 11.

**22** Hans Günther Adler, *Der verwaltete Mensch. Studien zur Deportation der Juden aus Deutschland* (Tübingen, 1974), p. 560.

**23** Adler, *Der verwaltete Mensch,* pp. 26–28.

**24** Zentralinstitut für Sozialwissenschaftliche Forschung, Freie Universität Berlin, editor (on behalf of the Senator for Cultural Affairs), *Gedenkbuch Berlins der jüdischen Opfer des Nationalsozialismus* (Berlin, 1995). The names of the other lodgers were Natalie Fridländer (née Wiener), born April 27, 1870; Adele Loewy (née Winter), born on October 7, 1877; and Sophie Guttsmann (née Tietz), born May 2, 1861.

**25** Joseph Wulf, *Theater im Dritten Reich* (Frankfurt am Main, Berlin, and Vienna, 1983), p. 17.

**26** Beate Meyer, *"Jüdische Mischlinge." Rassenpolitik und Verfolgungserfahrung,* (Hamburg 1999), pp. 152–57.

**27** See note 5. Therese Rothauser to Hermann Göring, letter dated December 1941.

**28** Ibid.

# Chapter Thirteen

## Sad Experiences in the Hell of Nazi Germany: The Scheurenberg Family

CHRISTIAN DIRKS

"Papa! Have been picked up. Come to Gr. Hamburger immediately—Klaus and Mama." This brief note, hastily scribbled on the back of a bill, was all that sixteen-year-old Klaus Scheurenberg could tell his father after being captured by Berlin Gestapo officials. Lucie Scheurenberg and her son had been found at Elsässer Strasse 54 in the Mitte district and brought to the assembly camp at Grosse Hamburger Strasse 26. Mother and son had already been "collected" on several occasions. But because Paul Scheurenberg was employed by the Jewish Community, he and his family were temporarily exempt from deportation. He had thus been able to get them out of the camp a number of times. The Scheurenberg's daughter had recently married. In the late 1930s Paul Scheurenberg had worked for the Jewish Winter Relief and was a caretaker of the Jewish Community building at Elsässer Strasse 54.[1]

Beginning with the first deportation of Berlin's Jews on October 18, 1941, the Gestapo had forced the Jewish Community employees to assist. At that time, Philipp Kozower, deputy chairman of the Jewish Community, gave a speech before the approximately two hundred assembled Community employees who had been selected to serve as "marshals" (*Ordner*). "The Jewish Community," he announced, "sees it as an honor to alleviate through personal commitment the circumstances of our emigrating comrades of Jewish faith."[2]

At the onset of the Berlin deportations, Paul Scheurenberg noted, "the emigration of the Jews is starting. The word 'emigration' is pure irony. Why do you Nazis keep lying? Just tell the truth; the extermination of the Jews has started." He would put together his account during his time in Theresienstadt.

The synagogue on Levetzowstrasse in the Moabit district was the first Community structure to be misused as an assembly camp. The building held prisoners awaiting deportation. Once the required number of about one thousand had been assembled, the deportees were led in long convoys on foot from the

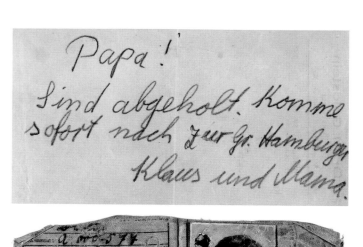

synagogue to Grunewald station (several kilometers away) or to Putlitz-/Quit-zowstrasse station in Moabit.

"The most terrible thing," Scheurenberg recounts, "is that the Jewish Community itself had to arrange the transport. I have encountered acquaintances [here] who helped with the first transport. The way people were deported was simply awful. They had no money, no valuables, only what they could carry. . . . At first, they were given a few days' notice. But later they were not even granted this. Now two Gestapo officials would simply arrive and tell the people to get ready; some would give them half an hour, others an hour. They had to leave the apartment, which was then sealed up. . . . People took what they could; and those last belongings were searched through in the Levetzo[w]strasse camp and everything 'superfluous' was stripped away. Alas, anything that the Jews were not carrying on their very backs was considered superfluous."

Scheurenberg was deployed as a marshal at the Levetzowstrasse assembly camp for the first time on November 17, 1941, at the time of the sixth transport

**Figure 13.3**
Paul Scheurenberg

to Riga, which was supposed to go to Riga but ended up in Kovno.[3] He distributed food among the detainees and piled up the luggage at the station. "Working in Levetzo[w]str. was nerve-wracking. One wants constantly to help, but this is very dangerous since the Gestapo are everywhere. People arrive, exhausted from carrying their luggage. There are two Gestapo officials for each person delivered up. This [arrival] takes place from 4 to 12 in the evening. Then about twenty Gestapo officials rummage through the luggage and steal the largest pieces. This is called 'sifting through' (*schleusen*). The people themselves are individually searched, along with their hand luggage. They are forced to strip naked, and their last belongings are taken away from them. This lasts until four in the morning. Then the people must spend three days in the synagogue without being able to sleep properly."

Up to mid-June 1942, Scheurenberg worked as a marshal on many of the transports that departed from Levetzowstrasse. Assisting the Gestapo placed a tremendous psychological burden on him, and he had several nervous breakdowns. Because the Gestapo made marshals responsible for the smooth running of the deportation, they were under particular pressure. Draconian punishments threatened even the smallest misdemeanor, and marshals themselves risked deportation if they did not comply with orders or were caught assisting escapees. "Two cases come to mind in which the 'marshals' . . . let a young girl run off [*flitzen*]. These two colleagues were immediately put on a transport to the east as 'replacements.'"[4] The marshals were also responsible if any of the detainees' possessions disappeared. One day, when a Persian carpet was reported missing, all of the luggage porters were called together and threatened with immediate

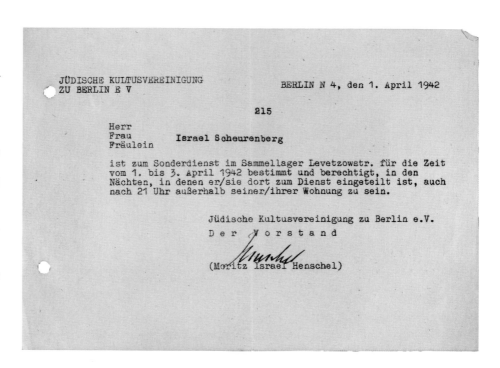

**Figure 13.4** The Jewish Community had to provide staff to assist in the assembly camp. This form, dated April 1, 1942, declares that "Israel" Scheurenberg (Israel was the official name forced upon all Jewish males after 1939) "is summoned to the Levetzowstrasse assembly camp for special service between April 1 and April 3, 1942, and is thereby authorized to be outside his/her home after 9 P.M. [curfew] on such nights in which he/she is appointed there for service." It is signed by Moritz Israel Henschel.

deportation. It soon turned out, however, that a Gestapo official had put aside the rug for his own use.

It was a matter of course that with regard to Jewish possessions Gestapo officials would be corrupt and involved in profiteering. Baskets of valuables—gold, silver, jewelry, cash, and so on—destined for the Gestapo headquarters on Burgstrasse were pilfered along the way. "The rascals fell on it like vultures," reported Paul Scheurenberg, who had been assigned to transporting the valuables. The practice had assumed such proportions by the fall of 1942 that the top authority of the Berlin Gestapo headquarters, the Reich Security Main Office (Reichssicherheitshauptamt [RSHA]) intervened. A group from Gestapo headquarters was arrested. "A whole hoard of Jewish possessions" was found in the possession of Gerhard Stübs, who as head of the Department for Jewish Affairs (Judenangelegenheiten) was responsible for the deportations.[5]

The embezzlement affair left the department temporarily dysfunctional, a situation untenable for the RSHA. To remedy the situation, a group of Austrian deportation experts was called to Berlin under the command of SS captain Alois Brunner. Brunner was asked to implement his "Vienna method" in the Reich capital.[6] Such methods involved cutting off entire blocks of houses and streets according to a specially drawn-up map and surrounding them with SS and police. Whole families and households could thus be arrested and brought to the

M E R K B L A T T

<u>für die Helfer in der Levetzowstraße</u>

Es wird nochmals mit aller Eindringlichkeit auf Folgendes hingewiesen:

1. Jeder hat über die Vorkommnisse im Sammellager Levetzowstraße
strengste Verschwiegenheit zu beobachten!

2. <u>Es ist strengstens verboten</u>, den im Sammellager befindlichen
Abwandernden Geld, Briefmarken, Wertgegenstände oder andere
Dinge zu übermitteln!

3. <u>Es ist strengstens verboten</u>, Briefe, Postkarten oder andere
Schriftstücke von den Abwandernden entgegenzunehmen oder zu
befördern!

4. Jeder Helfer muß Disziplin halten und sich die notwendige
Zurückhaltung auferlegen!

5. Den Anordnungen der Aufsichtsführenden und den Leitern der
Gruppen ist unbedingt Folge zu leisten!

6. Die Gruppeneinteilung: "Ordner, Gepäck- und Technischer
Dienst" stellt keine Klassifizierung dar, sondern umreisst le-
diglich die Hauptaufgabengebiete. Es ist selbstverständlich,
daß Jeder, falls erforderlich, auch andere Arbeiten verrich-
ten muß.

7. Ein erteilter Auftrag ist unbedingt auszuführen!

8. Die Helfer haben sich in allen Dienstobliegenheiten ausschließlich an die Leiter ihrer Gruppen zu wenden!

9. Das Telefon darf von den Helfern nicht benutzt werden!

10. Zuwiderhandlungen haben schärfste Maßnahmen zur Folge!

Die Ausweise sind bei Dienstbeginn den Leitern der jeweiligen
Gruppe auszuhändigen. Bei Dienstbeendigung erhält jeder Helfer
seinen Ausweis durch den Leiter zurück.

Die Leiter der einzelnen Gruppen sind:

<u>Gepäck:</u> Werner Israel Simon          <u>Ordner:</u> Max Israel Lichtwitz
Hans Israel Marcuse                      Walter Israel
Hermann Israel Grünbaum                  Löwenthal

<u>Technischer Dienst:</u>                 <u>Sanitätsdienst:</u>
Paul Israel Cohen                        der diensttuende
                                         Krankenbehandler

**Figure 13.5** "Urgent Guidelines for the Levetzowstrasse Helpers," distributed to the marshals in 1942. The document "once again" reminds the marshals to mark "the following urgent instructions." Ten points follow. "1. Each must observe the strictest secrecy with regard to all that occurs at the Levetzowstrasse assembly camp; 2. *It is strictly forbidden* to convey money, stamps, valuables, or other things to the emigrants in the assembly camp; 3. *It is strictly forbidden* to forward letters, postcards or other pieces of writing on behalf of the emigrants; 4. Each helper must maintain discipline and maintain the appropriate reserve; 5. The orders of supervisors and group leaders are to be followed unconditionally; 6. The division into "Marshals, Luggage, and Technical Service" is not a classification but only outlines the main areas [of work]. It is to be understood, of course, that each, when required, must devote himself to other work; 7. An order must be undertaken unconditionally; 8. Helpers must report to their group leader upon completing each of task of service; 9. The telephone may not be used by helpers!; 10. Those who resist will suffer the severest consequences!"

The notice goes on to explain that "at the start of service, passports are to be handed in to the leaders of each group. At the end of service, each helper will apply to the leader to get his passport [back]." It then names the leaders of the four divisions: Luggage, Technical Services, Marshals, and Sanitary Services.

**Figure 13.6**
Lisa Scheurenberg

newly established assembly camp at Grosse Hamburger Strasse 26, a former Jewish home for the elderly.

The Viennese officials behaved toward their victims with even greater brutality and ruthlessness than their Berlin colleagues. "The whole process was extremely violent, doors were broken down and apartments were broken into and so forth. . . . The rooms had to be overcrowded, twenty people to a room. The doors had to be locked day and night, the sanitary conditions defied description."[7] Brunner's express commands included rules dictating that inmates of the assembly camp stand "when a German-blooded man [*Deutschblütiger*] enters. They must walk at a distance of two steps behind him. 'Running off' is to be prevented at all costs; the functionaries are personally responsible for this."[8]

Also on Brunner's orders, the marshals were obliged to accompany the arresting commandos and help the victims pack and load their possessions. Paul Scheurenberg witnessed the Viennese SS methods firsthand when his own daughter Lisa was picked up on December 13, 1942:

Suddenly, without warning, all of the Jewish houses were cleared. . . . SS-Corporal Slawik stood in a yard with a riding whip.[9] (This Slawik was more like an animal—more like a monster. I have no words for what he was.) The marshals ran through the house. They had to prepare everything for evacuation. The terror was indescribable. . . . Around a hundred of our dear, good neighbors (we all got on well in the house) were forced to pack in impossible speed. The Viennese SS Captain Brunner had come from Vienna to Berlin with more inhuman creatures to solve the "Jewish question" in Berlin. In his view, the Berlin Gestapo was too ineffectual. Oh, you brutal Austrian pimps! Are you humans or animals? . . . My daughter and my son-in-law, who lived downstairs, had to go, too. They had been married for one year, and their apartment was so nicely done up, so clean. My daughter—a tender, frail person, still a child despite her twenty-two years. I had to comfort them, although my heart was so heavy it felt like it would break. The furniture van came at one in the morning. It made four journeys. The house was empty. I lay on my bed and cried like I had never cried in my life. My son was already gone. Now my daughter was, too.

Paul Scheurenberg was, in fact, able to release his relatives after a short period. He was helped by the Gestapo official Ernst Sasse.[10] Sasse headed a camp

at Auguststrasse 17, which detained various Jews who had been "laid claim to."
Here, for example, were Jews who had been marked for deportation but had
been designated as "indispensable" by their employers. Paul Scheurenberg had
been deployed as caretaker in this camp beginning in December 1942, the same
month that Brunner sought to deport his daughter.[11]

By May 1943, however, even his good relations with Sasse could not save
him and his family. On May 7, 1943, the Gestapo picked him up, together with
wife and son, at their home and took them once again to the Grosse Hamburger
Strasse assembly camp. They were to be deported to Theresienstadt. The Berlin
Transport Company (then and still known as the BVG) provided special trams to
bring deportees from the assembly camps to the Anhalter station—the point of
departure for all trains to Theresienstadt. At half past four in the morning they
boarded the tram at Monbijouplatz (on Oranienburger Strasse) and were taken
across Berlin to the station. Jewish marshals brought their luggage by horse and
buggy.[12] "Thus came the last night in Berlin. We had to get up at 2:30 on May 18
and were taken by tram to the Anhalter station at 4:30. The last two carriages
of the Dresden train were reserved for us. They were small passenger carriages,
and we were crammed in like sardines."

The former Czech fortress of Theresienstadt had served from June 1942 on
as a deportation destination for German and Austrian Jews. Inmates of this so-
called "old age ghetto" included elderly and frail Jews with their spouses; Jewish
veterans who had been decorated in World War I (Paul Scheurenberg was a
veteran), together with their wives; and Jewish partners from mixed marriages
that had dissolved through death or divorce. The real Theresienstadt was very far
from the "home for the elderly" lauded in Nazi propaganda. For most, it was but
a transit camp on the way to the extermination centers further east. The living
conditions there were wretched.[13]

**Figure 13.8**

The Wulkow labor camp, as sketched by the former prisoner Eli Leskly.

Site plan:
1. Main entrance,
2. barracks,
3. barracks of the head of construction,
4. supplies hut,
5. barracks,
6. sick room,
7. latrine,
8. women's barracks,
9. kitchen,
10. camp commander's garage,
11. bunker.

Immediately upon arrival the Scheurenbergs were put to work. Lucie Scheurenberg was forced to do washing up in the children's home in the ghetto; Paul Scheurenberg was again appointed as a marshal. He had to make sure that fire did not break out in the barracks and was in charge of wake-up duty. "We work for 24 hours and have 24 hours off," he wrote. "The worst thing is reveille. From midnight to 6 in the morning, each of us has about two hours to wake around two hundred men, who are allocated various jobs. You have to know the barracks exactly, writing the number of the plank bed of the man concerned on a slip of paper. We set off with a stub of candle. You hold the candle in one hand and, with the other, pluck off the fleas that accumulate on your body. After two hours of reveille I've always caught 150 to 200 fleas."

Young Klaus Scheurenberg, too, worked in the camp—as a carpenter. In the end, because of his manual skills, he was deployed on a special labor unit outside the ghetto. Under increasing threat of Allied air raids, Heinrich Müller, head of the RSHA's Department IV, planned the construction of reserve quarters some sixty kilometers east of Berlin. These had the cover name "Badger" (*Dachs*), or "Zossen barracks."[14] The site was not far from the village of Wulkow, in the middle of an extensive forest area in the Seelow hills. Klaus Scheurenberg was among the Jewish manual labor and construction workers sent there on Au-

eli 1983
FRANZ
STUSCHKA wie
ICH IHN HEUTE NOCH
SEHE...

**Figure 13.9** Portrait of SS-First Lieutenant Franz Stuschka "as I still see him today." Drawing by former prisoner Eli Leskly in 1983

gust 25, 1944. In exchange for their work, the Jews forced to work in Wulkow received protection from deportation "to the east" and the promise that their families would be protected as well. The families of the "Wulkowers" served as hostages in Theresienstadt, "securing the obedience of those in the labor commando. The latter's sense of responsibility for the lives of their close relatives in the ghetto meant that the commander of the labor commando could control the prisoners allocated to him with a small number of men, or prevent them from escaping."[15]

Heading the labor commando was SS First Lieutenant Franz Stuschka, one of the SS officials from Vienna. He was universally described as an excessively brutal and sadistic man.[16] From March 1944 on, the prisoners were at work constructing offices, barracks, catering facilities, garages, and special bunkers for files and documents. Considering the circumstances, some of the barracks were done out ostentatiously. Klaus Scheurenberg described Müller's reserve quarters as visibly "larger and more expensive than the others. When I entered it, my surprise stopped me in my tracks. . . . A massive desk commanded the entire room from the middle. An oil painting hung resplendent behind it—a life-size portrait of Hitler. On the side walls were hung in a close succession a series of clearly valuable pictures depicting Jewish motifs."[17]

With the advance of the Red Army, the fate of the Wulkow barracks camp was sealed. At the end of January 1945 the prisoners left the camp under SS guard and returned to Theresienstadt. Klaus Scheurenberg saw only his parents there. His sister Lisa and her husband had been taken to Auschwitz in October 1944, just before the crematorium ceased to operate. Both perished there.

Paul, Lucie, and Klaus Scheurenberg were liberated by Red Army troops on May 8, 1945, and returned to Berlin. Both parents were seriously ill when they left the ghetto. Klaus Scheurenberg, went on to become chairman of the Berlin Society for Christian-Jewish Cooperation from 1981 until the time of his death on June 14, 1990, in Berlin.

**1** The chapter title is drawn from the first volume of Paul Scheurenberg's memoirs, *Tagebuch. Traurige Erlebnisse aus der Nazi-Hölle Deutschland* in the Centrum Judaicum Archive (CJA), Scheurenberg Archive, unpaginated. Unless otherwise specified, all further quotes are Scheurenberg's and stem from this source.

**2** From the interrogation of Günther Abrahamson on November 1, 1947, Braunschweig City Police, Special Division. Copies of these files are found in the Berlin District Court (StA LG Berlin), *Criminal Proceedings against Otto Bovensiepen et al.*, StA LG Berlin, 1 Js 9/65, ZH 28, sheets 3–4.

**3** This deportation transport went to Kovno in occupied Latvia. The 1,006 people from the Berlin transport were shot dead in Fort IX in Kovno by an *Einsatzkommando* (special commando) of *Einsatzgruppe* A (SS mobile killing squad A) on November 25, 1941, along with roughly a thousand Jews from both Frankfurt am Main and Munich. See Wolfgang Scheffler and Diana Schulle, editors, *Buch der Erinnerung. Die ins Baltikum deportierten deutschen, österreichischen und tschechoslowakischen Juden* (Munich, 2003); and Kurt Schilde and Martina Voigt, "Überleben im Untergrund—auf der Flucht vor den Nachbarn," in *Versteckt in Tiergarten. Gedenkbuch für die im Bezirk in der Zeit des Nationalsozialismus Untergetauchten,* ed. Schilde and Voigt (Berlin, 1995), p. 27.

**4** See statement by Manfred Fackenheim, sheet 113; December 30, 1966, sheets 147–48; and statement by Martha Mosse, sheet 148.

**5** Statement by former detective Adolf Heiland in *Proceedings against Otto Bovensiepen*, 1 Js 9/65, PSt h 55, StA LG Berlin; Ermittlungsvermerk der StA, December 12, 1966, ibid., pp. 150–51; statement by Martha Mosse, March 16, 1959, ibid., Beistück no. 30, sheet 135. See also Winfried Meyer, *Unternehmen Sieben* (Frankfurt am Main, 1993), pp. 377–78.

**6** See Hans Safrian, *Eichmann und seine Gehilfen* (Frankfurt am Main, 1997), pp.189–90; and Mary Felstiner, "Alois Brunner: Eichmann's Best Tool," *Simon Wiesenthal Center Annual* 3 (1986): 10.

**7** Statement by Max Reschke, May 11, 1959 in *Proceedings against Otto Bovensiepen*, 1 Js 9/65, Beistück no. 30, sheet 165, StA LG Berlin; statement by Bruno Goldstein, ZH 34, StA LG Berlin; Hildegard Henschel, "Aus der Arbeit der Jüdischen Gemeinde Berlin während der Jahre 1941–1943," in Yad Vashem 01/52, p. 43. See also the anonymous report by a Berlin nurse on the course of the deportations, reproduced by Mira und Gerhard Schoenberner in *Zeugen sagen aus. Berichte und Dokumente über die Judenverfolgung im Dritten Reich* (Berlin, 1988), p. 325.

**8** "Aktennotiz einer Besprechung mit der Gestapo von Moritz Henschel," November 14, 1942, CJA, Fasanenstrasse Collection; Handakten RA Rolf Loewenberg in *Proceedings against Otto Bovensiepen*, n.p.

**9** Alfred Slawik was born on October 20, 1913, in Vienna. He worked with Adolf Eichmann in Department IV B 4 of the RSHA.

**10** Ernst Sasse was born on February 21, 1909, in Bernburg. He was detective secretary in Department IV D 1 of the RSHA.

**11** This camp existed until the *Fabrik-Aktion* (Factory Action) of February 1943. Those still detained there were transferred to Grosse Hamburger Strasse. Around one hundred Jews living in "privileged mixed marriages" were then moved to Augustrasse. Their task was to find Jews in hiding. "Some were indeed decent and did not find any, but the others were archetypal Gestapo spies. We would have nothing to do with it. . . . After two weeks, the "also-Jews" [*auch-Juden*]—whom we hated—were sent home." Scheurenberg, CJA. See also Regina Scheer, *Ahawah. Das vergessene Haus* (Berlin and Weimar, 1992), pp. 210–11.

**12** Testimony by Harry Schnapp from June 20, 1967, 1 Js 9/65, ZH 134, sheet 28, StA LG Berlin.

**13** See Miroslav Kárny et al., *Theresienstadt in der "Endlösung der Judenfrage* (Prague, 1992).

**14** Miroslav Franc, "Arbeitskommando Wulkow," in *Theresienstädter Studien und Dokumente* (1998): 239–40; and Andreas Seeger, *"Gestapo-Müller." Die Karriere eines Schreibtischtäters* (Berlin, 1996), pp. 64–65.

**15** Franc, "Arbeitskommando Wulkow," p. 241.

**16** See, for example, Klaus Scheurenberg's account, *Ich will leben!* (Berlin, 1982), as well as Paul Karalus's documentation, "Gesucht wird . . . Franz Stuschka," WDR 1985. A trial pending against the former commander of Wulkow in Vienna's District Court was terminated in 1969. *Mitteilung des Dokumentationszentrums des Bundes jüdischer Verfolgter des Naziregimes.*

**17** Scheurenberg, *Ich will leben!* p. 195.

# Chapter Fourteen

## Ruth Schwersenz's *Poesiealbum*

KARIN WIECKHORST

In May 1999 Ruth Recknagel (née Schwersenz, born in 1930), told me about a *Poesiealbum*—a "poetry" or keepsake album—that she had circulated among her friends as a schoolgirl in Berlin. She generously allowed me access to it. I set out to establish what had happened to the children and teachers who signed the book.[1] By consulting the Berlin memorial book (see chap. 11) and other sources as well as well as through contact with survivors of the Shoah, it has been possible to reconstruct quite a few biographies.[2] In the process, the survivors sometimes heard about each other for the first time in sixty years and were able get in touch with one another.

With the help of many, Ruth Schwersenz's *Poesiealbum* has become a kind of *Gedenkbuch* (memorial book) in its own right, a small testimonial to the murdered Jewish children.

How did a simple *Poesiealbum,* an unpretentious document of everyday life, become a historical document? The conventional "poetry album" format—in which schoolchildren inscribe all manner of rhymes, ditties, well-meaning bits of advice, wishes, and small maxims in one another's books—suggests a perfectly normal childhood. This was the world from which Jewish children in Germany were violently torn at the beginning of the Nazi onslaught.

Reconstructing the biographies of those who wrote in Ruth's book provides an unusual glimpse into the economic, educational, and cultural condition of the German Jews under the National Socialists. The lives of Jewish schoolchildren were of course profoundly effected by the host of anti-Jewish laws passed by the Nazis. In April 1933 Jewish teachers were dismissed from their posts in German schools as part of the ban on Jews in the civil service. Jewish fathers who had worked as lawyers and judges were disbarred. Doctors were stripped of their licenses to practice. Five years later, in November 1939, Jewish shops and artisanal trades were forced to close.

**Figure 14.1** An undated entry in *Jutta Pickardt's Poesiealbum* with a photograph of Ruth Schwersenz: "In allen vier Ecken soll GLÜCK drin stecken" (Good luck should be hiding in each of the four corners)

As a result, children were often obliged to change schools many times during the course of their education. Public school became less and less bearable, particularly after the compulsory classes in "race science"(*Rassenkunde*), and "genetics" (*Vererbungslehre*) were introduced. The children suffered untold degradations, neglect, and bullying. Finally, in the end of 1938, Jewish pupils were prohibited from attending German schools, and in mid-1942, they were barred from attending school altogether. After the ban, many children over age fifteen were made to work as forced laborers until they were deported.

Ruth Schwersenz's *Poesiealbum* has sixty entries and includes many photos. The entries span from June 1, 1939, to November 18, 1941. At the time, Ruth Schwersenz was a pupil at the Jüdische Grund- und Oberschule (elementary and high school). Teachers and a total of 45 children—23 girls and 22 boys, mostly between the ages of 10 and 12—wrote entries in the album. So did her parents and other members of her family.

The biographies of the children who signed the book show the whole spectrum of ways in which Jewish families sought to survive. Some children (like Hannelore Litten Adler and Anneliese Simson) emigrated directly to the United States; others (Ilka Neuhaus and Ellen Salomon) emigrated to the U.S. via the

open port of Shanghai; others tried to survive illegally at home, although only a few survived (Siegbert Landau, Ralf Moses, and Victor Trevor). Others—Renate Hammerschmidt, for example—failed in their attempt to escape deportation and murder. Generally, the children of mixed marriages—known in bureaucratic Nazi language as "first-degree *Mischlinge*"—had a better chance of survival. However, the biographical reconstruction also shows that many of Ruth's schoolmates were unable to escape deportation.

The biographies below focus on the children; it also includes personal memories of people from the album and others who are still able to remember them, and draws considerably on discussions I had with Ruth Schwersenz Recknagel, Jutta Pickardt Duniec, and Siegbert Landau.

RUTH SCHWERSENZ was born on April 26, 1930, in Berlin to a Jewish father and a Gentile mother. She was not raised in the Jewish faith. She started at a German elementary school in the Neukölln district in 1936 but was later barred as a result of the circular prohibiting Jewish pupils from attending German schools. She spent the next half a year out of school on account of illness. Ruth received private English lessons in Neukölln from the receptionist of the pediatrician Dr. Lassen, who was a member of the Nazi party. It was considered necessary that she learn English in view of possible emigration.

**Figure 14.3** Thomas Munderstein's November 1941 entry in Ruth Schwersenz's album: "Wo ein Wille ist / da ist ein Weg! Zur freundlichen Erinnerung an Deinen Mitschüler Thomas Munderstein" (Where there's a will there's a way! A friendly memento from your classmate . . .)

For about a year, between April 1939 and March 1940, Ruth then attended the Joseph-Lehmann School. Then from Easter 1940 to December 1941 she attended the Jewish Oberschule. This school changed its location frequently during the period. Hence, while Ruth took an entrance exam on Wilsnacker Strasse, lessons were already being held elsewhere in Berlin, at the Siegmundshof. Finally, in 1941 all of the city's Jewish schools were merged together at Joachimstaler Strasse 13.

Ruth was classified as a "first-degree *Mischling*" based on an official *Abstammungsbescheid* (declaration of origin). Her parents' marriage was classed as a "privileged mixed marriage," because her Gentile mother and Jewish father had not raised their children in the Jewish faith. This status entitled Ruth to attend the Luise-Henriette Oberschule in the Tempelhof district beginning in December 1941. On March 8, 1944, however, she was obliged to leave the school; *Mischlinge* were only permitted through the eighth grade. From September 1944 to April 1945 Ruth held an apprenticeship in industrial management in an "Aryanized" firm.

After the liberation of Berlin, she returned to Oberschule in the summer of 1945, this time in the Neukölln district, where she met her future husband. She graduated from high school in June 1948 (having passed an exam known as the *Reifeprüfung*). Both Ruth and her husband later became involved in the founding of the Free University in West Berlin and studied law. From March 1958 Ruth worked as a judge in the restitution offices of Berlin. She was later a judge in

Berlin's county, district, and superior courts. While holding these posts, she was for a long time director of the restitution offices, a position she continues to hold in her retirement.

Ruth, her father Alfred, and her younger brother Klaus all survived the Nazi period thanks to their relation to non-Jewish Lucie. The grandparents on her father's side, Julius and Minna Schwersenz, were deported on August 31, 1942, to Theresienstadt with the fifty-third transport. Ruth's grandfather died there on February 17, 1943. Her grandmother informed the family of his death. On May 16, 1944, Minna Schwersenz was taken to Auschwitz, where she was murdered. Ruth's uncle, her father's younger brother Fritz Schwersenz, was deported to the Warsaw ghetto and murdered at Trawniki. Her aunt Elisabeth emigrated in 1938, spent the war in Japan, and settled in the United States in 1947.

FROM THE *POESIEALBUM* entries themselves, it is often difficult to grasp all that happened to the children after they wrote the entries; often the notes were written but a few weeks, or even a few days, before emigration—or deportation and murder. This is the case with Thomas Munderstein.

Klaus Thomas Munderstein, born on January 5, 1930, in Berlin, lived with his mother Margarete Munderstein and his grandmother Elisabeth Nacher at Hohenzollerndamm 184 in the Wilmersdorf district of Berlin. His mother, a former legal secretary, became a forced laborer in the Heinrich Schelken leather factory in the Kreuzberg district. Thomas attended the Joseph-Lehmann School, and on June 3, 1941, changed to the Jewish Oberschule. Thomas Munderstein was a model pupil, as his friend Werner Jacobsohn reports, something of a teacher's pet.[3] His classmate Jutta Pickardt recounts how Thomas bade farewell to the children in his class before he and his family had to go to the Levetzowstrasse assembly camp on November 25, 1941.

The entries he wrote in the albums of both girls, Jutta and Ruth, were almost identical: "Where there's a will, there's a way! A friendly memento from your classmate Thomas Munderstein."

On November 27, 1941, the almost twelve-year-old Thomas was transported to Riga on the seventh transport. He was murdered there three days later, on November 30, 1941.[4]

HANNELORE MUSZKATBLATT, born on May 22, 1930, in Berlin, met the same fate. She and her parents were deported to Riga, also on the seventh transport, and were murdered there on November 30, 1941. The family had lived on Dahlmannstrasse in the Charlottenburg district. Her mother Frieda (née Levi), came from Nuremberg. Hannelore's father Richard, born in Berlin, was a doctor. Hannelore's parents were forced laborers before their deportation from the Levetzowstrasse assembly camp.

At a time when other children were still signing entries in the album, Siegmund Stillmann, Ruth Wollenberg, and Hella Buxbaum, were among the first children to be deported.

Siegmund Stillmann was born on November 25, 1929, in Berlin, the youngest child of Hanna Stillmann (née Auskerin), and Josef Stillmann, a trader in bed linen. His brother Wolfgang was born on November 21, 1925, and his sister Sonja on December 17, 1927. Siegmund attended the Jewish Community boys' school and later the Jewish Oberschule. In the beginning of January 1941, just months before his family's deportation, he signed Ruth's book with a well-known ditty: "Wenn Hass und Neider / Dich umringen, / Dann denk' an Götz von Berlichingen!" ( When you are surrounded / By hate and jealous men /Then just stop and think / of Götz von Berlichingen!)[5]

Helga Ruth Usherenko, who was deported with members of the Stillmann family and later lived through years in Siberia with Siegmund, reported that his older brother, Wolfgang, was deported at the beginning of July 1941 with his mother and sister to Zittau, an auxiliary camp of the concentration camp at Gross-Rosen.[6] Both fathers—Helga's and Siegmund's—had already been murdered.

Helga herself was also imprisoned in this camp with her mother and sister. She relates that there were about fifty Jewish families at Zittau. The women and children remained there for a long time and were one day taken from the camp to the station. Helga recalls:

> We were put on a cattle truck and traveled in it through countries that were already occupied by the Nazis. The last country was Turkey, from which we were [expelled into] Armenia. There, the [Russians] assumed we were German spies and put us in prison. Of the people that came from Germany with us, no one could speak a word of Russian. From the prison we were taken in cattle trucks to Siberia. No one had anything to wear. It was bleakest winter; many people who had come with us from Germany died on the way. Siegmund's sister [Sonja] died during the journey. His mother died soon after we arrived in Siberia. All of those who had come with us from Germany died there of hunger and cold. And that was why no one had heard anything from us. We were not liberated from [Siberia] until 1955, we had been there since 1942 and had been hungry more times than we had eaten. It was dreadful. Only my sister Toni and I are still alive. Apart from Siegmund, who also made it through that difficult time, no one else survived. We went through so much, no one can believe it. A really strange fate.

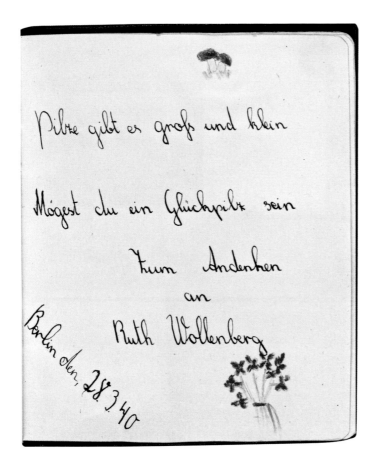

**Figure 14.4** Ruth Wollenberg's entry in Ruth Schwersenz's album, March 28, 1940: "Pilze gibt es groß und klein / Mögest du ein Glückspilz sein" (Mushrooms can be big or small / May you be the luckiest mushroom of them all)

Sage nie: 'Das kann ich nicht,' / Vieles kannst Du, will's die Pflicht, / Alles kannst Du, will's die Liebe / Darum Dich in schweren übe. / Viel erfordert Lieb und Pflicht / Drum sag' nie: 'Das kann ich nicht'!!! Zum Andenken an Deinen Schulkameraden Wolfgang Aschkenasi. Berlin, den 8.1.1941. (Never say: "I can't do it," / You can do many things if duty requires it, / You can do anything if love desires it / So learn to take on difficult responsibilities. / Love and duty demand a lot / So never say: "I can't do it"!!! To remind you of your classmate . . . January 8, 1941.)

It is presumed that Siegmund Stillmann later emigrated to Israel, to be with his brother Wolfgang, who also managed to survive. According to the cousin of both brothers, Mary Auskerin Hochberg, Wolfgang worked as a courier for the Israeli government; he later served as a consul in Denmark.

RUTH WOLLENBERG, born on April 5, 1930, in Berlin, lived with her parents on Kaiserallee in the Wilmersdorf district. Her mother came from Constance, her father from Thorn in West Prussia. On October 18, 1941—about a year and a half after signing her friend's *Poesiealbum*—she was deported with her mother on the first transport to Lódz. They were murdered there. Her father was deported "to the east" on June 26, 1942, with the sixteenth transport.

Hella Buxbaum was born in Berlin on April 28, 1930. Her father Ludwig, who had served in an infantry regiment in World War I, taught history, German, French, and Latin at the graduate level. He was forced to give up work as a

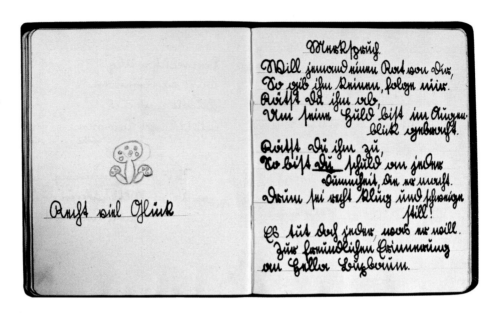

**Figure 14.5** Hella Buxbaum's entry (undated): "Merkspruch. / Will jemand einen Rat von Dir, / So gib ihm keinen, folge mir. / Rätst Du ihm zu, / So bist *Du* schuld an jeder Dummheit, die er macht. / Drum sei recht klug und schweige still! / Es tut doch jeder, was er will." (Something to remember. / If someone asks for your advice / Don't give it to him, believe me. / If you advise him / Then *you* will be to blame for every stupid thing he does. / So be smart and hold your tongue! / After all, everyone ends up doing what he wants.)

teacher in early 1939. Hella and her parents were deported on the fifth transport to Minsk on November 14, 1941, where they were murdered.

HANNELORE LITTEN survived the war. She was born on August 10, 1929, in Berlin and lived in the Charlottenburg district until emigrating at the end of September 1939. Her mother, Margarethe, came from Poznan and her father, Conrad, from Pomerania. She, too, attended the Joseph-Lehmann School. A little more than a month after signing Ruth's book, Hannelore emigrated:

> I emigrated to America with my parents in December 1939. We moved to Pittsburgh, Pennsylvania, where I had an uncle and an aunt. I was ten years old at the time. I went to school there and then to the University of Pittsburgh. In 1950 I married Alfred Adler, who had also come to America as a child in January 1939. In August [2000] we will have been together for fifty years. We have four children and nine grandchildren.
>
> We were lucky to get out on the last ship from Berlin via Amsterdam. Since the pogrom night [November 9, 1938] my father had been in hiding with old aunts. My father died in 1974 at the age of eighty-five. My mother is one hundred years old and lives in a home for the elderly.

Marianne Cohn was born on March 31, 1931, in Breslau, the daughter of the lawyer Conrad Cohn and Leonore Henriette. Her mother worked as a shorthand typist for the Reichsvereinigung ; her father was a board member of the Jew-

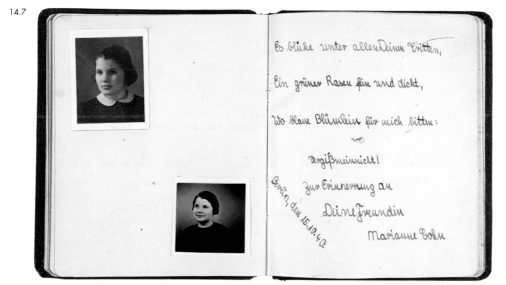

**Figure 14.6**
Hannelore Litten's entry, November 2, 1939: "Zwischen heut und morgen liegt/e ine lange Frist, /lerne schnell besor-gen, da Du /noch munter bist. . . . Berlin das Datum weiß ich nicht / Ich glaube es heißt Ver-gißmeinnicht." (It's a long time between today and tomorrow /Learn quickly to take care of your life /while you are still in good spirits. [oppo-site page:] Berlin, the date I've quite forgot /I think that means Forget-me-not.)

**Figure 14.7**
Marianne Cohn's entry, October 15, 1940: "Es blühe unter allen Deinen Tritten, /Ein grüner Rasen fein und dicht, /Wo blaue Blümlein für mich bitten: / Vergißmeinnicht!" (May a fine, thick lawn flourish /Under your feet /Where small blue flowers make the plea /on my account /Forget-not-me!)

ish Community in Berlin, where he was responsible for welfare. On June 26, 1942, Marianne Cohn and her mother were sent "to the east" on the sixteenth transport. They were murdered. Her father died in the Mauthausen concentration camp.

Ilse Baer was born on January 4, 1930, in Berlin. Her father, Siegbert Baer, worked as an administrative assistant at the Jewish Community in Berlin after

**Figure 14.8** Ilse Baer's inscription, October 29, 1940: "Sei deiner Eltern Freude, / Beglücke sie mit Fleiß. / dann erntest Du im Alter / den allerschönsten Preis." (Bring your parents joy / Make them happy through your hard work / Then, with age, you'll reap the best prize of all)

being dismissed from public service as a secondary school teacher. He was later forced to work as a helper in the assembly camp at Grosse Hamburger Strasse. Ilse Baer's mother, Gertrud, carried out forced labor at the Elektrika company in the Schöneberg district. Ilse, her brother Heinz Hermann, and both of her parents were deported to Auschwitz on January 29, 1943.

Jutta Pickardt, born to a Jewish father and a Gentile mother in Berlin on January 14, 1930, lived with her parents Johanna and Hans Pickardt and her siblings Bernd and Lore at Grunewaldstrasse 31 in the district of Schöneberg. Jutta's father was a manager at the famous KaDeWe department store and a World War I veteran. Her paternal grandfather was an extremely patriotic German, who had volunteered for the front in World War I, been awarded the Iron Cross Second Class, and belonged to the German Alliance of Frontline Soldiers. A family relation, Willy Pickardt, was the director of the German Cable Company. Another was a medical officer. Another, Albert Ballin, was the founder of the shipping company Hamburg-Amerika-Linie and had served as an advisor to the Kaiser.

Jutta's older sister Lore worked for a tinned food wholesaler whose proprietor was arrested and who subsequently managed to emigrate with his wife to Paraguay. Later she had to carry out forced labor at the firm of Siemens & Schuckert doing office work. Her brother, Bernd, apprenticed in carpentry as a lathe operator in the Jewish Training Workshop. In his free time he sang in the Lützowstrasse synagogue choir up until the night of the pogrom. He was initially assigned as a forced laborer to an armaments firm and later, up to liberation, to the Organisation Todt—a large-scale construction organization set up by the Nazis, particularly for military projects.

Jutta first attended school at the Jewish elementary school on Prinzregentenstrasse in 1937 and, later, the Joseph-Lehmann School. She skipped fourth grade and moved to the Jewish Oberschule on Wilsnacker Strasse on March 29, 1940, where she became one of Ruth Schwersenz's classmates. After she was officially designated a "first-degree *Mischling*" on her mother's initiative, she transferred from the Jewish school to the German Karoline-von Humboldt School for Girls.

"My earliest memory of Jewish childhood in the Nazi period is the following episode," Jutta Pickardt Duniec recalls.

A playmate from the building I was living in at the time came to see me with her brother, who told us that he had a Jewish classmate and was forbidden from playing with him. My mother responded, "We're Jews too, and you're still good friends." Shortly afterward I was suddenly abandoned by the children at the playground. My "friend" had told them that I was Jewish. I ran home sobbing and didn't understand why my mother had broadcast the fact. It was 1936. In 1937 I started at the Jewish elementary school, which was located on the premises of the [Prinzregentenstrasse] synagogue. . . . It must have been November 8, 1939, when an acquaintance came to us and wanted to speak to my father. My father told us that the man had advised him not to stay at home but rather to spend the night on the circle line of the S-Bahn, which is what he did. I could not really understand that, and the next morning I went to school as usual. The [synagogue] was ablaze. The neighbors called the fire brigade, who looked on without doing anything as the building burned. Many people were dumbstruck as they witnessed the event, and the mother of a classmate broke out in loud sobs. Two whippersnappers were standing next to us and one of them said loudly, "Look how that Jewish sow is blubbering." I was really shocked and went home. It was then I noticed that the windows of all the Jewish shops had been smashed. My mother was really agitated when I met her; a neighbor had told her what had happened that night.

Jutta recounts how conditions worsened:

All of the Jewish shops were either closed or Aryanized. Yellow-painted benches were put in the parks with JEWS ONLY written on them in black. I mostly went to Bayrischer Platz, where we were often attacked and mocked by "Aryan" children. However, there was one lady who always gave us a ration of sweets when there was a special allocation of food. Many of my [Jewish] classmates emigrated or were sent to England on Kindertransports. . . . In the meantime Jews were not

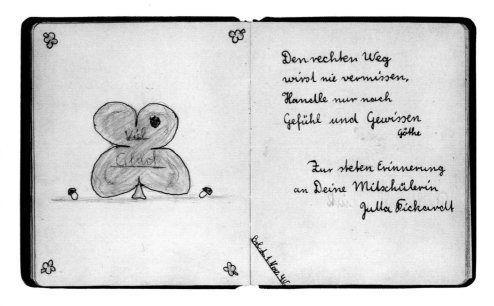

**Figure 14.9** Jutta Pickardt's entry, November 1, 1940, decorated with four-leaf-clovers, "lucky mushrooms," and ladybugs: "Den rechten Weg / wirst nie vermissen. Handle nur nach / Gefühl und Gewissen—Göthe / Zur steten Erinnerung an Deine Mitschülerin Jutta Pickardt" (You'll never stray from the right path / Just act according to your heart and your conscience—Goethe / To remind you always of Your classmate . . .)

allowed to go to cinemas, theaters, concert halls, beaches and so on. My father worked a lot on an honorary basis for a Jewish café and at events [sponsored by] the Jewish Cultural Organization [Kulturbund].

At the time, Jews did not yet have to wear the yellow star and they could still use public transportation. As Jutta remembers,

We went on a school trip to the Müggelberge hills with our gym teacher, Mr. Arndt, who later committed suicide. The sports field at Grunewald was still there for a while longer. Jews could only shop from 4 to 5 P.M. with Jewish ration cards. My mother, who had started work in the meantime and did not have to wear a Jewish star, ordered bread early at the baker's, and when I went to collect it at lunchtime a customer said: "That's outrageous, the Jews are now coming into the shops before 4 P.M." From then on I couldn't get into a shop before 4 P.M. for love or money. [Later, when] marked with the "Jewish star" we were—just like at the playgrounds—subject to constant attacks and abuse, mostly from other children but also from adults.

I should mention one curious thing. In Berlin instead of saying "Heil Hitler" one could still get away with the normal "Good day" and "Good-bye" in shops and still be served. That was impossible in the Rhineland or southern Germany. It comes back to me that around 1938 our landlord wanted to evict us from the apartment, which my family had lived in for twenty-four or twenty-six years. He collected signatures [of complaint] throughout the building along the lines that the other tenants did not want to live under the same roof as Jews. Everyone signed, apart from the music director Zickel and his French-born wife, who lived below us and surely often had to suffer the noise made by the three of us children. *The court threw out the complaint!*

The first deportations began; rooms and apartments were sealed up. Our lodger Jacob Braunschweiger was also deported.[7] One evening there was a knock on the door and when my mother opened it there were two Gestapo men standing on the doorstep. They asked, "Does Braunschweiger live here?" They took him away then and there and bolted up his room. He was an academic and up to then had been forced to work as a dustman. He was taken to Poland, and we received one last card from him from Lódz.

In the meantime, it was 1941, and Mother made efforts to get us officially recognized as "first-degree *Mischlinge*"; up to then we had been classed as *Geltungsjuden* [that is, treated like full Jews without any privileges, in contrast to first- or second-degree *Mischlinge*.] After a nerve-wracking wait of many months, during which my mother broke down on several occasions, we received the notice at the end of 1941 that our applications had been approved. Before and after, some other classmates were saved in this way, and today I think that it happened because of a personal initiative on the part of the official concerned. [Our new status] meant removing the star, leaving the Jewish school, and starting at a German school, which I could, however, only attend until age fourteen. *Mischlinge* were not allowed [by law] to pursue an academic career or to marry. My older sister was denounced by some of her "dear colleagues" and ended up in the Rosenstrasse assembly camp during the major operation [the so-called *Fabrik-Aktion* of February] 1943. A truly decent colleague let my mother know, and she searched in all the assembly camps until she found her on Rosenstrasse. . . . When we were still [considered] *Geltungsjuden* we were not allowed to go into the air-raid shelter. Now "only" my [Jewish] father was barred. They had also tried to persuade my [Gentile] mother to divorce him, which she absolutely refused to do. As she said, "In 1917, I had a war wedding with my husband who was in uniform and had just returned from battle. No one minded that he was a Jew then."

When the Russians conquered Berlin and we said that we were Jews they wanted to arrest us as spies, and we kept our mouths shut until the Americans arrived in Berlin. Later, neighbors would ask my mother: "Why does your daughter always creep along the walls of the building?" They did not know that I was unconsciously always searching for cover at least from one side.

My former Jewish classmates and friends were all deported and murdered, apart from two who had been living underground.

After the war's end Jutta rejoined the Jewish Community. In June 1948 she was recruited by the Israeli Army and emigrated to Israel that autumn.

WOLFGANG JAKOB ASCHKENASI was born on January 15, 1930, in Berlin. He had been a pupil at the Joseph-Lehmann School since 1939, and in 1940, at the age of ten, started at the Jewish Oberschule. His father, Salo Aschkenasi, born on June 9, 1888, in Warsaw, was a chemist and received his doctorate from Leipzig University in 1910. He later had to carry out forced labor as an auxiliary at Fromm's rubber factory in the Köpenick district. Wolfgang's mother, Käthe, born on September 27, 1899, came from Posen. Wolfgang's older sister, Eva Mirjam, was born on February 1, 1926, in Berlin. She also had to carry out forced labor—in the Daubnitz rubber factory in the Rudow district. Wolfgang's younger brother Abel was born on May 11, 1939. The entire family, which lived at Regensburger Strasse 14 in the Wilmersdorf district, was deported on October 19, 1942, on the twenty-first transport to Riga. All were murdered there on October 22, 1942.[8]

SIEGBERT LANDAU, who survived the Nazi terror, was born on December 24, 1929, in Berlin. His mother Salomea, born on May 3, 1908, came from Lemberg (Lvóv) in Galicia. His father Moszek was born in Lódz on October 19, 1899. Siegbert started at the Jewish elementary school on Klopstockstrasse in April 1936, and at Easter 1940 he moved to the Jewish Oberschule, where he remained until all Jewish schools were closed on June 30, 1942. Siegbert's father was deported in March 1941 and murdered at the Ravensbrück concentration camp in summer 1942.

*Ordnung, lerne liebe sie! / Ordnung spart dir Weg' und Müh.' / Zur freundlichen Erinnerungan Deinen Schulkameraden Siegbert Landau / Berlin, den 14.1.41.* (Learn to love order! / For order spares you work and effort. A friendly memento from your classmate . . . January 14, 1941.)

In a letter he wrote to me, Siegbert (today Simcha) Landau recounted how he survived underground with his mother from late summer 1942 to the end of the war in a room cut off from the outside world. In October 1945 he left for Palestine with a friend; they arrived in Haifa in April 1946. His mother joined them at the end of 1946. He calls himself not an eyewitness but an "earwitness" to the events of the period, since he was obliged to live in almost total silence for close to three years. He and his mother could not leave their hiding place, and their existence was marked by long days during which they could at best gain only an impression of what was going on around them. Only, as Siegbert Landau states, when "something went wrong" was the monotony of their lives broken. Today he sees it as pure chance that someone can tell his story. But how did the world look at the time from the perspective of an adolescent?

Siegbert grew up in an Orthodox household and received a traditional Jewish upbringing. He realized at an early age that as a Jew he was different from other people but he only understood the negative connotations of being different slightly later. The Nazi debasement of the Jews and concomitant elevation of the German *Volk* brought with it a series of prohibitions, which seen from a child's eyes amounted to, "You can't do that because you are a Jew." From now on, this rule determined his existence and excluded him from things that he had taken for granted up until then. Simcha Landau sums up with bitter humor how Judaism's critical spirit was powerless in the face of the murderous prejudice of the day. "Why the cyclists? Why the Jews?" he asks, pointing out that it would have made as much sense to designate all cyclists as scapegoats as to insist on the guilt of the Jews.

PETER MACHOL was born on May 1, 1930, in Berlin. He lived in the Charlottenburg district, where he initially attended the elementary school. After Jewish children were banned from German schools from November 1938, Peter was enrolled in the Joseph-Lehmann School and later attended the Jewish Oberschule. Werner Jacobsohn describes him as a very nice and intelligent boy who was relatively small for his age, which did not, however, hold him back.

**Figure 14.10**
Photograph of Peter Machol, who on November 9, 1941, wrote the following in Ruth's book: Lerne schweigen, ohne zu platzen / Zur frdl. Erinnerung an Deinen Schulkameraden Peter Machol (Learn to keep a secret without bursting / A friendly reminder of Your classmate . . .)

On March 6, 1943, the twelve-year-old Peter was deported on the thirty-fifth transport to Auschwitz together with his mother Lilly and his brother Gert, who was almost fifteen years old. There they were murdered. His father Heinz Joseph was deported to Auschwitz a few days earlier, on March 1, 1943. It is not known what happened to his brother Ernst, who was born on October 21, 1921.

HEINZ GROSS, the son of Ilsa and Iwan Gross, was born on March 31, 1930, in Berlin. He also lived in Charlottenburg and attended the Joseph-Lehmann School from 1936, later attending the Jewish Oberschule. He was deported with his parents to the Theresienstadt ghetto on the eighty-seventh Old-Age Transport of May 17, 1943. Heinz was sent on to Auschwitz, where he was murdered. His mother but not his father survived Theresienstadt. Like some of his classmates Heinz had worked as a helper for the Reichsvereinigung. His parents had been forced laborers in Berlin.

A classmate, Werner Jacobsohn, recalls: "Heinz Gross was a good friend, and we spent a lot of time together. After the war my mother and I met Mrs. Gross at a service held at the Joseph-Lehmann School.[9] She recognized me although I did not recognize her at first. She said that Heinz and his father had died. She looked at me and must have wondered what Heinz would have looked like. I did not know what to say to the poor woman. It was a devastating meeting that I could not get out of my head for a long time."

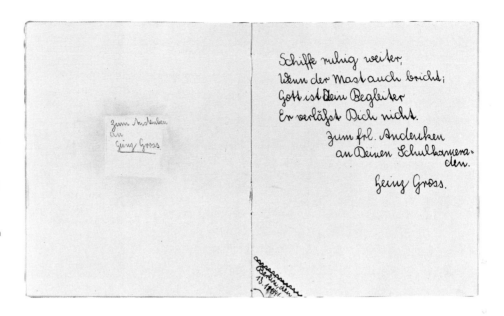

**Figure 14.11**
Heinz Gross's entry,
November 11, 1941:
"Schiffe ruhig wei-
ter, / wenn der Mast
auch bricht. / Gott ist
Dein Begleiter, / Er
verlässt Dich nicht."
(Sail calmly on / Even
if the mast breaks. /
God is your com-
panion, / He won't
leave you.)

WALTER IMMERWAHR, born on May 4, 1930, in Berlin, was the son of the jurist Dr. Kurt Immerwahr and his wife Käte. Kurt Immerwahr was barred by Nazi law from practicing as a lawyer and notary in spring 1933. He died on February 7, 1942, in Berlin. After his parents' divorce Walter Immerwahr lived at Sybelstrasse 66 in the Charlottenburg district with his mother and her sons, Wolfgang und Hans Ludwig Wolff, from her first marriage (to the lawyer Willy Wolff). He was deported with his mother and half-brother Wolfgang from the assembly camp at Grosse Hamburger Strasse 26 to Auschwitz on the thirtieth transport on February 26, 1943, and was murdered there. His half-brother Hans Ludwig ended up on the fortieth transport to Auschwitz of August 4, 1943, together with Willy Wolff. His brother Erich Immerwahr was able to emigrate to Great Britain.

Willy Wolff, the father of Walter's half-brothers, was a forced laborer for Siemens. He tried to save himself by going underground but was deported to Auschwitz after eight months.

RENATE FELICITAS HAMMERSCHMIDT, born on November 22, 1928, in Berlin to Stefanie and Martine Hammerschmidt, attended the Jewish elementary school on Klopstockstrasse and the Jewish Oberschule from September 1, 1941. Her mother was a receptionist in her father's dental practice. From November 1942, after it was no longer possible for them to emigrate to England, the family attempted to go underground. They were caught—the family's dec-

**Figure 14.12** Walter Immerwahr's entry, with photograph. November 18, 1941: "Wer zuletzt lacht, lacht/ am besten!" (He who laughs last laughs longest!)

**Figure 14.13** Left to right: Eva-Ruth Lohde, Klaus-Manfred Rosenthal, Lilli Wechselmann, and Ruth Schwersenz. Eva-Ruth Lohde, b. 1929 in Berlin, ninety-third old-age transport to Theresienstadt (June 30, 1943), d. Stutthof; Klaus-Manfred Rosenthal, b. 1929 in Berlin, thirty-ninth transport to Auschwitz (May 17, 1943), d. Auschwitz; Lilli Wechselmann, b. 1929 in Breslau, forty-forth transport to Auschwitz (October 14, 1943), d. Auschwitz; Ruth Schwersenz, b. 1930 Berlin.

laration of assets (*Vermögenserklärung*, a document that inevitably preceded deportation) dates from July 31, 1943. The family was transported to Auschwitz with the fortieth transport of August 4, 1943, and murdered there.

*Lerne leiden / ohne zu klagen / Zur frdl. Erinnerung an Renate Hammer-schmidt / Berlin, d. 4.12.41. (Learn to suffer in silence. / To remind you in friendship of Renate Hammer-schmidt / Berlin, December 4, 1941.)*

RUTH SCHWERSENZ'S *Poesiealbum* poses questions that can help give a realistic picture of the life of Jewish children under National Socialism. Does the album not reflect the need for a community life, particularly in view of the social deprivation of rights and isolation of German Jews? Do the entries not express a confidence in the world that may seem incredible in view of the undisguised aggression and exclusion with which the Jews were confronted in Nazi Germany? Does the marking of a childish everyday ritual serve to escape the difficult and gloomy present or to counter it with an intact element of life in the album?

There are no clear answers to these questions. Yet what can be said is that this *Poesiealbum* becomes a very special kind of historical document on account of the function of poetry albums in general. The personal content of the entries and the associated appeals to "note" and "remember" them serve as witnesses and traces. The empty spaces between the entries speak for themselves.

**1** This project was undertaken as part of the research project "Deutsch-jüdische Kindheit und Literatur für deutsch-jüdische Kinder im Nationalsozialismus" (German-Jewish Childhood and Literature for German-Jewish Children in the National Socialist Period) conducted by Tel-Aviv University, Goethe University in Frankfurt, and the Humboldt University in Berlin. My role in the project involved seeking literary evidence of people who had experienced or survived the Nazi state as children and young adults.

**2** I was able to establish contact with several people by placing advertisements. This research has led, in turn, to the discovery of new sources. For example, Jutta Pickardt Duniec and Hannelore Litten Adler sent me the personal albums that they had kept as girls. I would like thank all three owners of the *Poesiealbums*, as well as all of the others who sent information to me.

**3** Werner Jacobsohn, who lived underground with his mother, responded to one of my advertisements.

**4** Wolfgang Scheffler and Diana Schulle, editors, *Buch der Erinnerung. Die ins Baltikum deportierten deutschen, österreichischen und tschechoslowakischen Juden* (Munich, 2003).

**5** The sixteenth-century knight immortalized by Goethe was—to the delight of all schoolchildren—famous for telling an emissary of the commander of the forces to "kiss his ass."

**6** This was probably a transit camp that was assigned to various concentration camps. Although it was an auxiliary camp of Gross-Rosen in 1941 it later belonged to the concentration camp at Auschwitz.

**7** Jacob Braunschweiger, born on June 4, 1885, in Würzburg, was taken to Lódz on the first transport of October 18, 1941, where he died on March 26, 1942.

**8** See Scheffler and Schulle, *Buch der Erinnerung*.

**9** "The Lehmann school was the only private school to be taken over by the Reichsvereinigung in 1939 and was then run as the eighth elementary school of the Jewish Community. In June 1942 it had to close along with other schools. The former sports hall now houses the orthodox synagogue of the Jewish Community." Jörg H. Fehrs, *Von der Heidereutergasse zum Roseneck. Jüdische Schulen in Berlin, 1712–1942* (Berlin, 1993), p. 290.

# 8

# Betrayal

# Chapter Fifteen

## Snatchers: The Berlin Gestapo's Jewish Informants

CHRISTIAN DIRKS

## Origins of the Search Service

"The headquarters of the network of Jewish informants run by the Gestapo is located on Iranische Strasse. Some of the Jews are allowed to roam the streets without the yellow star and look for Jews who are in hiding, in disguise, or who have false papers. These patrols roam through the city streets and look for people they know. If they meet such and such a person they seem really delighted [to see them], but in the hours that follow—or the next day at the latest—the victims have already been picked up by the Gestapo and taken to Iranische Strasse, where there is a camp and where [deportation] transports are organized."[1]

This statement is probably the first written account of the ring of Jewish spies set up and supervised by the Berlin Gestapo: the Search Service (*Fahndungs-dienst*). It was founded after the *Fabrik-Aktion*, the last large-scale campaign to round up and deport all of Berlin's remaining "non-privileged" Jews. The events of February 27, 1943, had driven a mass of Jews into hiding. From this point onward, only three groups of Jews remained in Nazi Berlin: those deemed first-degree *Mischlinge* in the official race terminology, those in "privileged mixed marriages" to non-Jewish partners, and those living underground illegally. In the language of the persecuted, these were known as *U-Boote*—submarines.

When Propaganda Minister Joseph Goebbels declared Berlin to be officially *judenfrei* in June 1943, several thousand Jews had already gone underground in the city. They now became a chief target for the Berlin Gestapo. According to various estimates, there were three to four thousand people living underground in the summer of 1943. By the start of February 1944 there were some two thousand left. Other estimates from the postwar period refer to a total of five thousand Berlin Jews who were at least temporarily forced underground.[2] About 1,400 of them survived the National Socialist period living illegally in the capital of the Third Reich.[3]

## Previous Institutional Arrangements

Rumors of the mass murder in Wehrmacht-occupied territories to the east had reached Berlin as early as the turn of 1941–1942, and Jews were already living underground before the *Fabrik-Aktion*.[4] The Berlin Gestapo had long sought an effective means of tracking them down. A precursor to the Search Service—a search patrol (*Suchtrupp*)—was apparently set up at the end of 1942, a short time after the Viennese SS arrived in Berlin (see chap. 18).

(see chap. 18)

The Viennese SS had experience with Jews in hiding. Many Viennese Jews designated for the first wave of deportations, alerted by the summons they had received, simply disappeared from their apartments. In response, Alois Brunner, head of the Viennese Central Office for Jewish Emigration (Zentralstelle für jüdische Auswanderung), set up a force composed of Jews—the Jewish Police (*Judenpolizei*, or JuPo). The JuPo group leaders were also known as "levyers" (*Ausheber*) or "grabbers" (*Packer*). They were initially drawn from among the appointed marshals (*Ordner*) from the city's Jewish religious association, the Wiener Kultusgemeinde. In Vienna, the JuPo was forced to help in the course of the deportations, to supervise the "grabbers," and to make sure that no one tried to escape. They were also responsible for establishing the whereabouts of those Jews listed for deportation who had disappeared. In exchange, JuPo members were exempt from wearing the yellow star and granted special papers issued by Brunner. When, at the turn of 1942–43, the Viennese SS Oberscharführer Ernst Brückler and Josef Weiszl came to Berlin to implement "Viennese methods," three JuPo members—Robert Gerö, Walter Lindenbaum, and Wilhelm Reisz—came with them to initiate the staff of the Berlin Jewish Community.[5]

In Berlin, the search patrol was apparently set up on the Auguststrasse premises of a Jewish home for children and the elderly. "One hundred Jews who were living in privileged mixed marriages had been driven under threat [of deportation] to search for Jews in hiding," recounts Paul Scheurenberg.[6] In the mornings they received lists of the people whom they were to turn over to the Gestapo. The arrangement was short-lived, and three weeks later the operation came to a halt.

The Viennese JuPo member Robert Gerö is said to have undertaken some helpful acts while he was in Berlin. Viennese opponents of National Socialism had given him the address of a man named Otto Weidt, and through him, Gerö was able to warn numerous Jews—including a young woman named Inge Deutschkron—of their impending deportation.[7] Other reports do not portray the Viennese JuPo marshals in such a favorable light.[8] Nonetheless, the fact remains that as "senior marshals" (*Oberordner*), the three men had been forced

---

*One hundred Jews who were living in privileged mixed marriages had been driven under threat [of deportation] to search for Jews in hiding.*
PAUL SCHEURENBERG

*His very words to me were 'If you keep bringing me Jews, you and your family can stay here and you can take your [yellow] stars off right away.' I replied that I could not reconcile this with my conscience. . . . Dobberke retorted that he had not expected anything different from me.*
HARRY SCHNAPP

---

to work as auxiliaries for the SS. At the end of January 1943, Gerö, Lindenbaum, and Reisz left Berlin along with the Viennese SS officials. The role Alois Brunner played in setting up the subsequent Search Service is not entirely clear. There is much to support the view that he was responsible for setting up the network, based on his Vienna experiences.[9]

## Tasks and Members of the Search Service

The Search Service was originally housed in the assembly camp on Grosse Hamburger Strasse in the Mitte district, a former Jewish Community home for the elderly. The building mostly held Berlin Jews awaiting deportation. The entire operation, including the Search Service, was run by Gestapo official Walter Dobberke.[10] In addition to assigning duties to his Jewish informers, Chief Commissioner Dobberke continually sought new recruits from among the camp's inmates. His promise to potential informers was a powerful one: that he would make sure that they their families would go to Theresienstadt instead of Auschwitz.[11] Members of the Search Service had their own rooms on the premises, which were furnished rather luxuriously, according to eyewitness accounts. They were granted green permanent certificates of passage that allowed them to leave the camp day and night, unsupervised and without the yellow star.

Harry Schnapp recounts how Dobberke summoned him to his office and asked him "if I would like to stay in Berlin and be spared from evacuation. I had, after all, worked for the Jewish Community before and must know many Jews living in hiding." Many of those who received such offers refused to be corrupted. Some committed suicide. Others, however, accepted the offer, hoping that in doing so they could improve their chances and protect their families.[12] The Search Service comprised eighteen people, according to a Jewish Community list from 1946.[13] The Jews living underground called them *"Greifer"*—"catchers" or "snatchers."[14]

Günther Abrahamson was one of the first Jews assigned to the new spying machine. After the *Fabrik-Aktion,* Dobberke ordered the Jewish head of the camp, Max Reschke, to assign him two people for special tasks.[15] Abrahamson's task was to locate the addresses of underground Jews. He had to look into some fifteen addresses a day, produce short memos for Dobberke, and to report orally to Dobberke each day. That summer Heinz Gottschalk, a "first-degree *Mischling*"

**Figure 15.1**
Gestapo officer Walter Dobberke, head of the assembly camp at Grosse Hamburger Strasse and of the Search Service

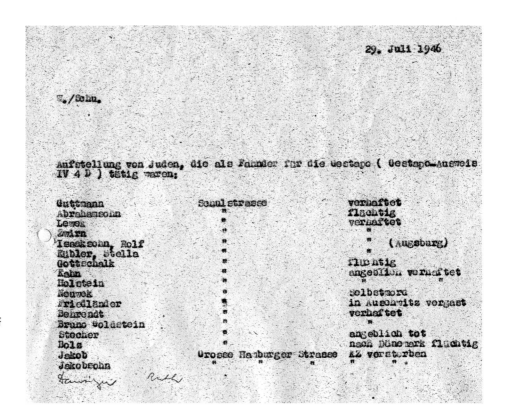

**Figure 15.2** "List of Jews Who Acted as Searchers for the Gestapo" drawn up by the Jewish Community, 1946

*I seized [the offer] immediately, firstly because I saw it as the chance to get out of the hell of the camp system. But secondly [because] I had the instinctive feeling that here, in contrast to having to look on powerlessly as usual, there would be a chance to do something positive against the Gestapo.*

GÜNTHER ABRAHAMSON

and former World War I flak officer, was assigned to work with him. Shortly afterward, a woman named Stella Kübler also arrived at the camp.[16]

Detained in the assembly camp's prisonlike conditions, some prisoners were prepared to yield to Gestapo pressure and betray other Jews. Ruth Danziger, for example, turned in Fedor Friedländer; Friedländer in turn became an informer, allegedly betraying several hundred people to the Gestapo. Danziger and Fritz Neuweck worked as a "snatcher pair."[17] Other Jews or *Mischlinge* deployed in the spying service were Fritz Behrendt, Kurt Bolz, Bruno Goldstein, Manfred Guttmann, Heinz Holstein, Rolf Isaaksohn, Dr. Jakob, Dr. Jakobsohn, Eugen Kahn, Adolf Alphons Leweck, Harry Stecher, and Kurt Zwirn.[18]

## Stella Kübler: The "Blonde Phantom"

Undoubtedly the most famous and notorious *Greiferin* was Stella Kübler, née Goldschlag, who with her (later) husband Rolf Isaaksohn roamed Berlin's streets looking for Jews in hiding and handing them over to the Gestapo. The couple

**Figure 15.3**
Stella Goldschlag in
the mid-1930s

**Figure 15.4**
Rolf Isaaksohn in
the 1930s

**Figure 15.5**
Stella (center) with
family, 1936

was generally known by the abbreviation "Mr. and Mrs. Iskü" among the city's
*U-Boote*.[19] Witnesses consistently describe Stella as unscrupulous and cruel but
also as extraordinarily attractive and intelligent, qualities that soon made her a
legend among *U-Boote*.

Stella Goldschlag, born on July 10, 1922, grew up in Berlin and attended the
Feige-Strassburger fashion design school on Kurfürstendamm. Like many others, her family wanted to leave Germany after the pogrom of November 9, 1938,
and apparently tried to get authorization to go to the United States. In November 1941, when several thousand Jews had already been deported from Berlin,
Stella's father Gerhard Goldschlag sent news via a Red Cross letter to relatives
in Palestine: "In good health. Possible change of residence!! Stella's marriage

*Her example
became the norm.
And so the system
emerged that
became known as
the Search Service.
Its development
meant that there
were eventually
only a few people
delivered to the*

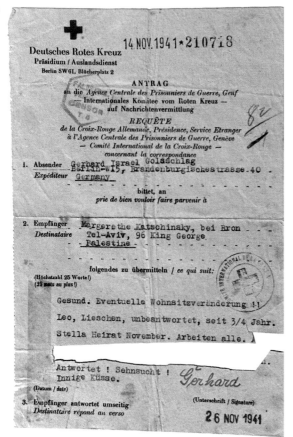

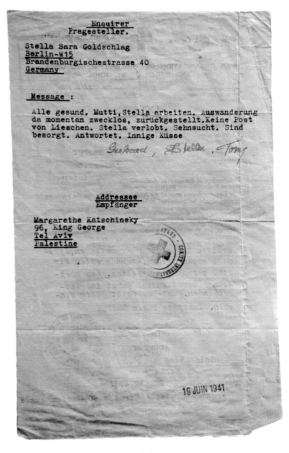

**Figure 15.6** Red Cross letter from Gerhard Goldschlag to a relative in Tel Aviv, November 1941

**Figure 15.7** Red Cross letter sent by Stella Goldschag to a relative in Tel Aviv, June 1941. The note reads: "All are healthy. Mummy, Stella working. Emigration put off for the time being . . . Stella engaged. Longing. Worried. Answer! Affectionate kisses, Gerhard, Stella, Tony."

*assembly camp who did not 'blow the whistle'—that is, disclose the where-abouts of other former fellow suf-ferers. In this way the aforementioned Search Service kept growing in size.*

GÜNTHER
ABRAHAMSON, 1947

November. All working. [The next sentence was censored out.] Respond! Longing! Many kisses, Gerhard." [20] All too obvious in the euphemism "change of residence" was the reference to the feared deportation "to the east."

Stella meanwhile married Manfred Kübler, her boyfriend of many years. After completing her training at the end of 1941 she was called up for "service duty"—forced labor—at the Siemens-Schuckert firm in Fürstenbrunn. Manfred Kübler was likewise deployed, working at the Wilhelm Banzhaf firm in the Pankow district, as were her parents, who were forced to work at the firm of Ehrich & Graetz in the Treptow district. [21] Stella was transferred there in early 1942 and, as a forced laborer, received about half the normal pay for her shift work. The Goldschlag family worked in Treptow until the *Fabrik-Aktion* of February 1943.

**254** CHRISTIAN DIRKS

Just one year earlier—on February 28, 1942—Gerhard Goldschlag had written in another Red Cross letter to Palestine: "Not too bad. Hope all will turn out all right. Unbelievable amount of work. Hope to see you again. Kisses, write again soon, Gerhard."[22]

Because he worked the night shift, Gerhard Goldschlag was not at the firm on the morning of the raid, but Stella and her mother were there. The two women hid under a large cardboard box in the cellar and managed to escape the wave of SS arrests. Stella and her parents went underground immediately, first hiding with family friends in the Wedding district. Stella's husband, however, had been arrested. He was deported to Auschwitz on the thirty-third transport to the east and died there a few weeks later.[23]

In the period following the *Fabrik-Aktion,* anyone who decided to go underground had certain priorities: organizing an illegal existence, obtaining food and false papers, and renting some halfway safe accommodation. While searching for false identity papers for herself and her parents, Stella came into contact with Rolf Isaaksohn, who was also living underground in Berlin and conducting a brisk trade in false documents. Isaaksohn gave Stella forged papers for her parents to protect them from SS arrest. She herself received a fake identity card from him with the name "Inge Proeck," issued by the "Oberkommando of the Wehrmacht."[24] Samson Schönhaus, a former fellow student of Stella's and himself a talented forger and *U-Boot,* produced a police registration document for her, also using the name "Proeck."

Isaaksohn and Stella had arranged to meet on July 2, 1943 at noon in the Bollenmüller Pub near Friedrichstrasse. The locale was a favorite meeting place for *U-Boote.* "I wanted to avoid this pub, since I thought it was too much of a focal point, and my parents had warned me against going there," Stella later recounted.

We had barely ordered when the door opened and a girl I knew came in, I recognized her as Inge Lustig. She went past the table to Rolf . . . but was noticeably nervous and pale. She did not seem to have recognized me, since I turned to her and said, "Don't you remember me, Inge?" She was very distant and said, "Oh, yes, of course, you're Stella." Then I said I was Manfred Kübler's wife. She looked at me closely and hurried out of the pub. Rolf and I remained at our table. Suddenly two men in plainclothes appeared at the table, showed their ID, and said to Rolf, "Gestapo come with us." . . . When we were outside, one of them took hold of Rolf and the other got me. . . . I knew that my parents were nearby and I had arranged to meet them at the table. So out of desperation, I wanted to free myself and tore myself away. They got me and started to hit me at random. . . . A Gestapo patrol van turned up immediately. We were packed into the truck together, and it was not till then that I realized that Inge Lustig was standing by the truck. I thought that she had been arrested, too, through this unhappy coincidence, and I said, "Inge, you too!" She did not answer.[25]

At the Gestapo regional headquarters on Burgstrasse, Stella was brutally interrogated by the Gestapo officials Greinert, Schwöbel, and Kurz. The next morning she was taken to the women's prison on Bessemerstrasse in the Tempelhof district. On July 10, 1943, Stella's twenty-first birthday, she was able to escape during treatment at the dentist's ward and went to her parents' in the Weissensee district. It was not possible for Stella to stay there either, and so they decided to rent a room for the night at a boarding house they knew on Rankeplatz. The decision had serious consequences. The house was being watched by the Gestapo, and all three were rearrested and taken to the police prison on Alexanderplatz. Stella was once again brutally interrogated.[26]

During her questioning, the Gestapo found a slip of paper containing names and addresses. Once Stella and her mother were transferred back to the Bessemerstrasse barracks, officials from the Gestapo regional headquarters again questioned her, this time about the whereabouts of a passport forger on her list named Mikki Hellmann.[27] He was a friend of the forger Samson Schönhaus and had also attended the design school with them. The Gestapo then forced Stella to write a card to Hellmann, inviting him for a rendezvous. "On the designated day, Kurz, Schwöbel, and another Gestapo official picked me up in the car. They drove me to the arranged location. I wish the earth could have swallowed me up—I had never been forced to do anything so terrible. Hellmann stood to one side, but Schwöbel and Kurz jumped out of the moving car and arrested Hellmann."[28]

Hellmann's arrest was Stella Kübler's first "successful" cooperation with the Gestapo, a mere foretaste of her later activities.

On August 24, 1943, the Bessemerstrasse prison was completely bombed out during an air raid, and Stella was able to escape. She went to her parents, who were being held at the assembly camp on Grosse Hamburger Strasse. She planned to share their fate. Instead, Stella would become fully caught up in the search for underground Jews.

During one of her subsequent interrogations by the Gestapo, Stella revealed that Samson Schönhaus had produced false passports for her.[29] Working under the assumed name of Günter Rogoff, Schönhaus had become one of the most notorious passport forgers in Berlin and was frantically sought by the Gestapo regional office. Chief Commissioner Dobberke headed the preliminary investigations.[30]

Schönhaus aka Rogoff had been traced in the course of an inquiry into a Jewish-Christian resistance network based in the Dahlem district. This "circle of traders," led by the lawyer Dr. Franz Kaufmann, obtained papers and documents to help Jews in hiding, housed them in private accommodation, and procured food ration cards through bribery. Schönhaus-Rogoff carried out forgery work for the group. He also had contact through a woman named Edith Wolff with Zionists led by Jizchak Schwersenz, for whom he forged identity papers.[31]

Meanwhile, forty of Schönhaus-Rogoff's fake documents had turned up in the assembly camp, and Dobberke, learning of Stella's connection to the forger, saw her as a means of getting to him.[32] According to Dobberke's investigation report, "a statement by Ruth Pontow revealed that Stella Sara Kuebler, née Goldschlag . . . currently in the assembly camp, was one of Schönhaus' close acquaintances."[33] Stella had, after all, already been very useful in the case of finding Hellmann, another passport forger. Perhaps she could lead them to the man they were looking for this time.

Shortly before the date on which Stella was to be deported, Dobberke had her questioned again, this time to establish the whereabouts of Schönhaus. "During my interrogation by the Gestapo I was asked where Samson Schönhaus might be. I saw a range of forged and genuine papers from Schönhaus lying on the desk."[34] Stella recalled that "Mr. Dobberke first interrogated me, and then the searchers (*Fahnder*) Abrahamson and Gottschalk dealt with me. I was to consider how I could get hold of Schönhaus. I then asked Gottschalk what I would gain from helping them to get Schönhaus. He did not say exactly, but just said that it would be possible to be exempted from this transport."[35] Finally, Dobberke made her an offer. He would spare her and her parents from the next transport if she produced Schönhaus. "Dobberke announced that, starting the following day, I would be in the external service of the Gestapo. He said that he had already consulted Sturmbannführer Stock about it . . . and that written approval would follow."[36]

From this point on—probably the end of August 1943—Stella worked for the Search Service. Her Gestapo papers read something like: "Mrs. Kübler is permitted to take measures in Jewish matters. The authorities are asked to support her in this."[37] The reverse side had a photo and stamp from the Berlin Gestapo's regional office. Stella's parents remained "citizens" of the assembly camp. Dobberke was holding them as hostages.[38]

**Figure 15.8**
Dr. Franz Kaufmann

*We gave him all kinds of documents, personal papers, Postausweise [identity documents for picking up mail], work certificates, identity cards with a photo, and so forth. He was able to change these with admirable skill, putting in new names, false dates, other photos, etc. Finally, all of this had to be assembled very carefully and also stamped with a fake*

When the search for Schönhaus came to nothing, Dobberke gave Stella a list of names and addresses of other Jews for her to investigate. She was also supposed to supply new addresses. She worked on this for about three months.[39] She was also deployed to accompany other "searchers" without herself intervening in the operations. In the event of Jews being "picked up" she traveled along in the infamous van that brought the captured victims to the assembly camp.[40]

In the meantime, Rolf Isaaksohn had also been transferred to Grosse Hamburger Strasse at the end of 1943. He had previously been detained at the worker's educational camp (*Arbeitserziehungslager*) in Wuhlheide, a training and indoctrination camp for people released from concentration camps. Isaaksohn knew that, as a forger, his name would down for one of the next transports.[41] He soon proved willing to collaborate.

Dobberke now made Stella a further offer. He "proposed another task to me, working in full cooperation with the Gestapo, which consisted of establishing which Jews were living in Berlin. I worked on this until November 1943, and afterward I began to work with Rolf Isaaksohn. . . . Our work with the Gestapo differed from what I had done previously in that I was now taking part in arrests."[42] As Max Reschke, the Jewish leader of the assembly camp, later recalled, Dobberke instructed him that Kübler could "go to the camp leadership at any time without disturbance and may not be stopped by any camp marshals." Reschke understood immediately what this "extraordinary instruction" meant. "After that, we knew the score."[43] Stella was allowed to enter and leave the camp at all times, had constant access to the SS, and a special room on the premises.

After this, Stella and Rolf operated individually and in cooperation with other "searchers" to hunt down Jews throughout Berlin. Rolf's preferred districts were

**Figure 15.10**
*Left to right*, Bruno Goldstein (?), Stella Kübler, and Rolf Isaaksohn on the Kurfürstendamm, 1940s

Mitte, especially around the Börse station (now Hackescher Markt) and Prenzlauer Berg. Stella was most familiar with the area around Kurfürstendamm in the western part of the city. The Gestapo received tips from various informants, both within and outside of the assembly camp.[44] It also maintained an index file on illegals at its regional headquarters on Burgstrasse.[45]

Stella and the other *Greifer* were authorized to check the papers of passersby. They would then point out individuals to be bundled into a bogus furniture van that lurked in a nearby street. The *Greifer* were the last to get in the van, which then went directly to the assembly camp.[46] In some cases, Stella would approach people whom she suspected of being Jews and would offer to obtain food or accommodation for them. If they took her bait, Stella would bring the Gestapo along to the rendezvous.[47]

*The doors of the furniture van were open at the back, flanked by two marshals, who had to prevent the victims from escaping.*
CURT NAUMANN, 1965

**Figure 15.11**
Werner Scharff

**Figure 15.12**
Alexander Rotholz
with his daughter
Helga

*Since there was
going to be another
batch of transports,
and because Rolf
had to face the pros-
pect of evacuation,
he did all that he
could through me to
find a way to enter
this service, too. . . .
Subsequently, Dob-
berke summoned
Rolf and [Rolf] said
. . . that he could
assemble a whole
transport for him.*
STELLA KÜBLER-
ISAAKSOHN, 1946

Since the "searchers" had themselves lived illegally, they were familiar with the special difficulties faced by the *U-Boote.* It was precisely this intimate knowledge of the living conditions of underground Jews that made them so useful as informants.

Many Jews spent the days and evenings in public places, blending into the crowd. In particular, they went to cinemas, theaters, and opera houses. Stella knew very well where she could find her prey. On December 16, 1943, for example, there was an arrest in the Staatsoper Unter den Linden, where Stella and Rolf regularly "made the rounds." Earlier that evening, after being interrogated by Dobberke in the assembly camp, Gerda Kachel and Elly Lewkowicz overheard the Gestapo man ask Stella, "So where are you off to today?" To which she replied, "To the theater."[48] During the performance, Rolf recognized members of the Zajdman family in the orchestra. They arrested Abrahm Zajdman and his son Moritz immediately after the performance. Moritz tried to tear himself away. "Keep him! Jew!" Stella shouted after him. Passersby caught him in the street, and he was dragged back to the Staatsoper by his hair. The Gestapo was already waiting. Stella, who had recognized Mrs. Zajdman in the audience, then threatened her husband. "I saw your wife. She must be here, too!"[49] Father and son were taken to Grosse Hamburger Strasse.

It was normal for *Greifer* to line their own pockets with the possessions of Jews in hiding. It was sometimes even possible for Search Service staff to exempt certain people from the transports on account of their good relations with the camp leadership. And so *Greifer* and Gestapo officials alike received food, tobacco, and money as bribes.[50]

## Resistance

By the end of 1943, Stella was already known as a Gestapo spy among those living underground. These warned one another of the extremely attractive blonde Jewish woman. There was even a photo of her circulating. Stella is described as a "blonde specter" or "blonde poison" in many reports.[51] The *Greifer* continually faced potential acts of revenge. At the beginning of 1944, the threat became very tangible for Stella. A resistance group, the Society for Peace and Reconstruction (Gemeinschaft für Frieden und Aufbau [GFA]), led by Werner Scharff, was very well informed about the Search Service activities. Information came in via various people employed and interned at the assembly camp.[52]

One informant for this group was Alexander Rotholz, who worked for Lothar Hermann's painting company. The Jewish Community's building management assigned various painting and repair jobs to Hermann's firm, and Rotholz thus had an excellent overview of conditions on Grosse Hamburger Strasse. Every day he saw *Greifer* appearing before the Gestapo with the people they had caught. According to Rotholz, the GFA decided "to stop Isaaksohn and Stella in their tracks, too."[53]

Several attempts were made to entrap the pair. Members of the GFA rented a room and hoped to lure Stella and Rolf there under the pretext that illegal Jews were living in it. The plan was to kill them when they arrived, but neither materialized. On two occasions, a GFA member named Hans Winkler followed Stella into a restaurant with the intention of pouring poison into her coffee. He was foiled both times. Another attempt to liquidate her took place when Stella

**Figure 15.13**
Hans Winkler

*We are not criminals, we are Jews!*
ABRAHM ZAJDMAN

*[As] a warning, we sent them both a death sentence by post. . . . The last part read, "The sentence will be carried out after the end of the war."*
ALEXANDER ROTHOLZ, 1956

KJ F 5 Berlin, den 1o. 3. 47

Auf Vorladung erscheint der Lagerist

Willi I s r a e l ,
geb. 17. 12. 96 in Filehne,
Berlin - Pankow,
Telleborgerstr. 62 wohnhaft

und sagt zur Sache folgendes aus:

Ich lebte während der Nazizeit vom 18. 11. 41 bis Kriegsende
illegal in Berlin. Aus dieser Zeit ist mir bekanntgeworden,
dass Bruno G o l d s t e i n mit dem bekannten Rolf Isaksohn
und B ö l z für die Gestapo tätig waren. Der Standort von I. + B.
war Rorenthalerplatz+und Schönhauser Tor. Auf das Konte des Goldstein kommen m. W. ca. 300 - 400 Verhaftungen von Juden, die ebenso
wie ich in Berlin getaucht lebten.

Durch irgendeinen Zufall wurde es der Gestapo bekannt, dass ich
mit einem Teil anderer Juden in Müggelheim aufhältig bin. Die Gestapo setzte eine Groß-Aktion an, bei der zugegen waren:
SS - Hauptscharführer D o b e r k e , G o l d s t e i n,
F r i e d l ä n d e r , I s a k s o h n und Andere. Im Ganzen
waren es ca. 14 Personen, die nach dort kamen und uns verhaften
wollten. Es gelang mir, mit einer Frau Fanny S c h o t t , z. Zt.
wohnhaft Berlin - Pankow, Hallandstr. 44, zu flüchten, aber ca. 18
Personen wurden bei dieser Aktion verhaftet. Späterhin wurde auch die
S c h o t t durch Isaksohn verhaftet und der Gestapo ausgeliefert.

Bruno G o l d s t e i n war als berüchtigter Fahnder bekannt
und wir illegal lebenden Juden mussten uns sehr vorsehen, um von
ihm nicht gefasst zu werden. Mir ist noch weiter bekannt, daß Goldstein
wenn er seine Glaubensgenossen verhaftet hatte, sich an deren Eigentum
bereicherte. Aus diesem Grunde hatte er sich auch als Fahnder gemeldet
Juden, die verhaftet waren und Goldstein reichliche Geldzuwendungen
machte, hatte er begünstigt, indem er den Abtransport nach Auschwitz verzögerte. Wenn die Geldzuwendungen seiner Schützlinge aufhörten
hörte auch sein Einspruch zum Abtransport auf.
Weitere Zeugen, die über Goldstein Auskunft geben können, sind:
Gerda R o t h e r , Berlin - Pankow, Trelleborgstr. 53

**Figure 15.14** Testimony given by Willi Israel at the trial against Bruno Goldstein, 1947 in which he describes a raid:"During the Nazi era, I lived illegally in Berlin until the end of the war. At the time it became known to me that Bruno Goldstein was active with . . . Isaksohn [sic] and Bolz in the Gestapo. . . . For this Goldstein was able to [bring in] ca. 300–400 arrests of Jews who, like me, were living underground in Berlin.

Through some coincidence it became known to the Gestapo that a number of other Jews and I were staying in Müggelheim. The Gestapo launched a large operation [involving] SS Chief Dobberke, Goldstein, Friedländer, Isaksohn, and others. There were 14 people in all, who came there and wanted to arrest us. I was able to flee with a woman named Fanny Schott . . . but ca.18 people were arrested through this campaign. Later even Schott was, through Isaksohn, arrested and handed over to the Gestapo."

Willi Israel goes on to describe Goldstein as a "notorious searcher" who "enriched himself" by taking bribes from his victims. Jews who had been arrested and paid Goldstein "abundantly" could avoid deportation. If payments "by his protectees [Schützlinge] stopped, then he also stopped objecting to their deportation."

sought dental treatment at the Jewish hospital. The plan was to bribe the dentist into poisoning her. In exchange, the dentist demanded that the GFA organize his immediate escape abroad—something the GFA was unable to do—and the scheme had to be abandoned.

By early 1944 it seemed unlikely that there would ever be an opportunity of gaining direct access to Stella. That February the GFA sought a new tactic: intimidation. Using a form from the Luckenwalde district court, they prepared a phony death sentence for her "in the name of the German people" to be carried out by hanging. She was anonymously warned about continuing to work for the Gestapo and told that if she was seen on the street, she would be killed instantly. Hans Winkler and Hildegard Bromberg sent the letter by registered mail, with a copy to the Gestapo.[54] The "death sentence" had an immediate effect; Dobberke banned his agents from leaving the assembly camp for fourteen days. In late 1944, in response to the increased danger faced by members of the Search Service, the Gestapo apparently issued them pistols.[55]

The transport to Theresienstadt of February 23, 1944, included many who had worked in the Search Service as well as several employees of the Jewish Community. This last transport from the Grosse Hamburger Strasse camp (*lager*) also included Stella's parents, Tony and Gerhard Goldschlag. At the beginning of March 1944 the assembly camp (*Sammellanger*) and with it the Search Service were moved to the grounds of the former Jewish hospital in the district of Wedding.[56] Stella tried in vain to get her parents struck off the list or to have them moved from Theresienstadt to Bergen-Belsen. She pleaded with Obersturmbannführer Möller to intervene on their behalf. Möller refused but led her to understand that he would make sure that she would be appointed an "honorary Aryan" (*Ehren-Arierin*) after the Germans won the war.[57] Despite Stella's efforts, her parents were deported to Auschwitz soon afterward and perished there.

Her parents' deportation, accompanied by the fear that she would be blamed as a Gestapo informant at the war's end, brought about a change in Stella's attitude toward the Search Service. Friends of hers had suggested "that the surviving Jews would take revenge on her after the collapse of the regime."[58]

Her situation became increasingly tense. That summer saw serious, sometimes violent disputes between Stella and Rolf at the Schulstrasse assembly camp.[59] Stella told Dobberke that she was having no success finding people and clearly wanted to put an end to the collaboration. Rolf, for his part, categorically denied her statements and claimed to be operating very "successfully." He wanted to bind her permanently to him—both personally and as a partner in the Search Service. The two were married with special Gestapo permission in October 1944 at the registry office in the Wedding district. Rolf continued meanwhile to "make the rounds" with fellow "snatchers" Bruno Goldstein and Kurt Bolz. As she later testified, Stella was henceforth regarded with suspicion by her colleagues.[60] In the postwar period, she tried to save herself through her association with Heino Meissl, who had been detained in the assembly camp on Schulstrasse. [61] The two were in a relationship, and Stella was expecting his child.

## The End of the Search Service

Rumors began to circulate among detainees in mid-April 1945 that the Schulstrasse assembly camp would be "liquidated" by Gestapo officials from Ravensbrück. Dobberke had apparently received orders by phone from *Obersturmbannführer*Möller, and a fourteen-year-old detainee whom Dobberke used as his shoe-shine boy allegedly overheard the call. Some of the prisoners now tried to persuade Dobberke that, considering the imminent German defeat, it was pointless to carry out the order. In return for release certificates and the release of all prisoners they promised to intervene on Dobberke's behalf after regime's collapse.[62]

Günther Abrahamson had meanwhile been denounced to Dobberke by another *Greifer* and was now in confinement in a darkened cell at the camp. He, too, tried to turn his fate around by making promises. On the evening of April 19, 1945, a guard informed him that he was to be shot the next day. Dobberke was to oversee the execution. In a few lines, Abrahamson warned Dobberke not to do anything hasty. He proposed a deal in view of the military situation: Abrahamson had good connections and would intercede for Dobberke at the end of the war. "I was brought upstairs the same night," Abrahamson later stated, "but everyone was under the influence of alcohol, and no negotiations took place." The next morning Dobberke sent for him and asked if the deal was still on.[63]

Finally on April 21, 1945, Dobberke summoned the inmates of the Schulstrasse assembly camp and personally signed their release papers. "He held them out to us without comment," recounts former detainee Gad Beck. Then, "almost as an aside remarked, 'now I need a bit of peace for the next few days.' . . . Dobberke exited our cells and left the door open."[64]

A few days earlier, on April 17, 1945, Stella and Rolf Isaaksohn and Kurt Bolz had fled the Schulstrasse camp, fearing a bloodbath. Isaaksohn forged some papers for the escape stating they were couriers and were granted permission to travel unrestricted by train. The passports were issued in the names of dead senior Gestapo officials. Stella and Rolf saw each other for the last time at the Zoo railway station. He told her that he wanted to flee to Denmark via Lübeck and

Figure 15.15 Stella, her shorn head concealed by a headscarf, at the time of her arrest in 1946

Figure 15.16 Stella during questioning at the police headquarters on Alexanderplatz, 1946

to go underground there. Dobberke had offered unsuccessfully a high reward for their capture.[65]

Heino Meissl had in the meantime arranged accommodation for Stella with an acquaintance in Bad Liebenwalde right outside Berlin. She was to wait there until Berlin was captured and give birth to their child. He himself headed south.[66] That October "Mrs. Meissl" gave birth to a daughter, Yvonne Meissl, in the hospital there. That December 1945 Stella applied in Liebenwalde for recognition as a "victim of fascism" (*Opfer des Faschismus* [OdF]). Her cover was blown during a check by the Berlin Jewish Community in Berlin. The person responsible for processing OdF applications in the Jewish Community was Alexander Rotholz, the very man who had once been commissioned by the GFA to observe Stella in the assembly camp and had been involved in drawing up the bogus death sentence against her.

A large crowd had assembled when Stella Kübler-Isaaksohn was brought by the Bad Liebenwalde police to the Berlin Jewish Community on Oranienburger Strasse. News that the notorious *Greiferin* had herself been caught had spread among survivors at lightning speed, and Community staff had difficulty protecting her from vigilantes. After various interrogations at the police station on Alexanderplatz, she was handed over to the Soviet secret police and immediately tried before a Soviet military tribunal.[67] The trial took place in May 1946 at a court at the garrison in the district of Lichtenberg. Stella was charged with crimes against humanity and for distributing anti-Soviet propaganda and sentenced to ten years in prison.[68]

*When I read in the papers that I had allegedly brought tragedy to so many men, women, and children, that really disturbed me. Then I spoke to my own conscience and I came to the conclusion that my only crime and the only thing I was guilty of was to have let myself be engaged*

Der Polizeipräsident in Berlin
Kriminal-Inspektion Fahndung zbV.
KJ F 2 - Fahndungsnachweis

Berlin, den 19. März 1946
C 2, Dirchsenstraße 13-14

# Großfahndung

nach dem flüchtigen Gestapoagenten **Rolf Julius Isaaksohn,** geb. 9. 5. 22.

J. hat während der Nazizeit gemeinsam mit seiner Mithelferin **Stella Ingrid Kübler,** geb. Goldschlag, alias Meisel - alias Isaahsohn, etwa 2000 Juden der Gestapo verraten.

Isaaksohn hält sich vermutlich in Lübeck auf. Das Ermittlungsergebnis und die bereits angestellte Kleinfahndung weist auf Groß-Berlin hin.

Personenbeschreibung: 1,68 bis 1,70 m., etwas untersetzte Figur, Haare blauschwarz, Augen grün, Nase durch Bruch etwas borerähnlich, Teint brünett, rundes Gesicht, Narbe am Mittelfinger, auffallend gute Haut, weiße Zähne.

Alle Polizeidienststellen sowie die gesamte Bevölkerung werden um Mitfahndung ersucht. Festnahme und Nachricht - die auf Wunsch auch streng vertraulich behandelt werden - an das Polizeipräsidium Berlin, Abteilung KJ F - zbV. - Zimmer 7, Telefon 42 53 21, Apparat 55.

Im Auftrage: Born

**Figure 15.17**
Stella during her trial at the Berlin district court,1957

**Figure 15.18**
Wanted poster for Rolf Isaaksohn,1946. "Betrayed about 2,000 Jews during the Nazi period with his helper Stella Ingrid Kübler, née Goldschlag, alias Meisel [sic]—alias Isaaksohn."

*as a Jew in an external service of the Gestapo. But I note that I entered this Gestapo service against my will.*

STELLA KÜBLER-ISAAKSOHN (K147, J 31 SHEETS 16–17, BARCH), MARCH 15, 1946

In the years that followed Stella was first imprisoned in Torgau, then Sachsenhausen, Hoheneck, and Waldheim. Sanitary conditions in the camps were dreadful, and she contracted tuberculosis. She was released in January 1956 and went to West Berlin, where efforts were made to initiate a new trial against her. Many witnesses contacted the Jewish Community expressing their desire to testify against her, and a trial took place in 1957 at the court in the Moabit district. Stella was convicted of serving as an accessory to murder as well as wrongful deprivation of personal liberty resulting in death. Another ten-year sentence resulted, but her time served in the prison in the Soviet Occupation Zone and her time in custody were taken into account. Stella was now free again. An 1972 appeal reconfirmed the 1957 guilty verdict.

Until she committed suicide at the age of seventy-two in 1994, Stella Kübler-Isaaksohn showed no particular signs of guilt or remorse. Rejecting reproaches that she had unscrupulously betrayed her fellow Jews and given them up to the Gestapo, she sought to portray herself as a victim.[69]

## Conclusion

Between 1943 and 1945 some twenty Jews carried out spying duties for the Gestapo in Berlin in return for promises that they and their families would receive preferential treatment. Stella Kübler-Isaaksohn, who betrayed several hundred Jews to the Gestapo, was the best-known and most feared among them.

In some cases the Gestapo partly kept the promises that had been made to the *Greifer*. Family members were deported to the Theresienstadt ghetto rather than directly to Auschwitz. Perhaps the informants did not realize that Theresienstadt was but a "waiting room of death," a through-station on the way to the extermination camp. In other cases, the spies were themselves deported once they had fallen out of favor. Often, they too, went first to Theresienstadt, then Auschwitz.[70] Only a small number of *Greifer* avoided deportation and remained under Gestapo protection until the end of the war. Only three were subsequently tried—either immediately after the war or later, in the Federal Republic. Others, including Rolf Isaaksohn, disappeared without a trace, and it is unlikely that they will ever be brought to justice.[71]

One can only speculate about the complex motives of such collaborators. They were themselves subject to Nazi persecution, and certainly, many sought to improve their own situations by working with the Gestapo. But a whole range of other motives may have applied as well. The "searchers" enjoyed some power in the camps and may have been able to influence the Gestapo's persecution policy in certain areas. They could, moreover, warn people of impending arrest and were even in a position to strike the names of some camp detainees from the transport lists. At the same time, they were authorized to make arrests on their own initiative; in most cases, this amounted to nothing short of the power to issue death sentences. An insidious feature of National Socialist persecution was its ability to turn victims into the agents of their own destruction.[72]

*The Jews said, furthermore, that they would much rather be picked up by Jews than by the Gestapo, since the Gestapo was far more drastic.*
STELLA KÜBLER-ISAAKSOHN, 1995

**1** "Report from Berlin, summer 1943, to the Jewish World Congress in Geneva," document no. 219, reproduced in H. G. Adler, *Die verheimlichte Wahrheit. Theresienstädter Dokumente* (Tübingen, 1959), p. 303. The 1943 date given to the report cannot be correct, since the Gestapo did not use the former Jewish hospital as an assembly camp until March 1, 1944. When activities were moved from Grosse Hamburger Strasse to Iranische Strasse, the Search Service moved as well—to Schulstrasse, an adjacent part of the Jewish hospital complex. See Dagmar Hartung-von Doetinchem and Rolf Winau, *Zerstörte Fortschritte. Das jüdische Krankenhaus in Berlin* (Berlin, 1989), p. 196; and Rivka Elkin, *Das jüdische Krankenhaus in Berlin zwischen 1938 und 1945* (Berlin, 1993), p. 130.

**2** Report to the Jewish World Congress cited in note 1; Kurt Jakob Ball-Kaduri, "Berlin wird judenfrei. Die Juden in Berlin in den Jahren 1942/43," in *Jahrbuch für die Geschichte Mittel- und Ostdeutschlands* 22 (1973): 237; Stefi Jersch-Wenzel, "300 Jahre jüdische Gemeinde in Berlin," in *Leistung und Schicksal. 300 Jahre Jüdische Gemeinde zu Berlin* (Berlin, 1971), p. 25.

**3** Siegmund Weitlinger, *Hast Du es schon vergessen?* (Berlin, 1954), p. 7.

**4** Jizchak Schwersenz, *Die versteckte Gruppe* (Berlin, 1988), pp. 83, 89.

**5** Harry Schnapp, report, in *Criminal Proceedings against Otto Bovensiepen et al.*, 1 Js 9/65, Staatsanwaltschaft beim Landgericht Berlin (StA LG Berlin), accompanying document no. 30, pp. 3–4; account of a discussion with Max Reschke, 1 Js 9/65, StA LG Berlin; ZH 27 (Robert Gerö), ibid.; interrogation report of the StA at Berlin District Court in the Bovensiepen case, vol. 25, sheets 147–48, StA LG Berlin; also testimony of Curt Naumann in *Criminal Proceedings against Fritz Wöhrn et al.*, 1 Js 1/67, no. R34/33, vol. 2, Landesarchiv Berlin (LAB).

Other sources on the Viennese Gestapo: Hildegard Henschel, "Aus der Arbeit der Jüdischen Gemeinde Berlin während der Jahre 1941–1943," in Yad Vashem (YV) O1/52, p. 43; Herbert Rosenkranz, *Verfolgung und Selbstbehauptung. Die Juden in Österreich, 1938–1945* (Vienna and Munich, 1978), pp. 299–300; Walter Lindenbaum, *Von Sehnsucht wird man hier nicht fett. Texte aus einem jüdischen Leben*, ed. Herbert Exenberger and Eckart Früh (Vienna, 1998); Hans Safrian, *Eichmann und seine Gehilfen* (Frankfurt am Main, 1997), pp. 175–176; Inge Deutschkron, *Sie blieben im Schatten. Ein Denkmal für "stille Helden"* (Berlin, 1996), p. 104; and Simon Wiesenthal *Recht, nicht Rache. Erinnerungen* (Berlin, 1988), pp. 288–289. My thanks to Doron Rabinovicz, who is writing a history of the Jewish Religious Community in Vienna, 1938–1945, for giving me important information.

**6** Paul Scheurenberg, "Traurige Erlebnisse aus der Nazi-Hölle Deutschland," Centrum Judaicum Archive (CJA), Scheurenberg archive (unpaginated); see also Klaus Scheurenberg, *Ich will leben!* (Berlin, 1982), p. 94; and Regina Scheer, *Ahawah. Das vergessene Haus* (Berlin, 1997), pp. 210–211.

**7** Otto Weidt's *Blindenwerkstatt* (workshop for the blind) manufactured brushes for customers that included the Wehrmacht. Weidt made use of many Jewish laborers, claiming that their deployment was "essential to the war effort." He meanwhile supported underground Jews with false papers. He hid several people in his Rosenthaler Strasse workshop, some of whom were later turned over to the Gestapo by Stella Kübler and Rolf Isaaksohn. See statement by Else Weidt, March 31, 1956, in *Criminal Proceedings against Stella-Ingrid Isaaksohn*, 1 PKs 1/57 (42/72), vol. 1, sheet 10, StA LG Berlin, and the June 29, 1957, sentence from the trial by jury, vol. 2, sheets 26–27. See also Deutschkron, *Sie blieben im Schatten*, p. 104, and idem, *Outcast: A Jewish Girl in Wartime Berlin*, trans. Jean Steinberg (New York, 1989).

**8** See Henschel, *Aus der Arbeit*, p. 43. "[T]he saddest thing that Jews experienced from other Jews . . . relates to the Jews who did not have to wear the star and truly became the right hand of the Gestapo. Indeed they were sometimes quite rightly feared more than the Gestapo."

**9** See statement by Ms. Wüstenberg, former secretary to Erich Möller, head of the "Jewish Department" in the Reich Security Main Office (Reichssicherheitshauptamt [RSHA]), in *Criminal Proceedings against Bruno Goldstein*, (500) PKs 9/48 (80/48), vol. 2, sheet 5, StA LG Berlin.

**10** Walter Dobberke (1906–1946) had risen from the post of mere detective commissioner in the vice squad to chief commissioner of the SS and head of the assembly camp. His resumé is in Bundesarchiv (BArch), BDC, no. 600501/6090; BA-ZA, ZR 760, ZR 274, ZR 590; and Brandenburgisches Landeshauptarchiv (BLHA), Rep. 030, 198-5, nos. 14 and 105.

**11** Documents from Office of the Berlin State Prosecutor (StA LG Berlin) concerning Stella Kübler: her questioning, April 17, 1956, 1 PKs 1/57, vol. 1, sheet 25; her questioning, May 28, 1956, vol. 2, sheet 142; and statement by Herbert Tietze (former SS official from the Gestapo regional headquarters in Berlin), April 18, 1956, vol. 1, sheets 28–29.

**12** StA LG Berlin, PKs 9/48, vol. 1, sheets 67–68. Gerda Kachel refused similar offers from Dobberke, which Dobberke accepted without argument. Gerda Kachel's statement, 1 PKs 1/57, vol. 1, sheet 121, StA LG Berlin. Hugo Röhmann committed suicide on February 8, 1943, after being forced to work as a marshal at the assembly camp on Grosse Hamburger Strasse. Documents on Röhmann, 5 C 2, CJA; See also video interview with Rolf Joseph, CJA.

**13** "List of Jews who acted as searchers for the Gestapo (identity papers issued by Gestapo department IV 4 D)," dated July 29, 1946, CJA, 2A1 (reproduced in this chapter). In a report of summer 1944, Else Hannach mentions "around twenty" Jewish spies and names Stella Kübler ("the worst of the whole bunch"), Rolf Isaaksohn, Manfred Guttmann, Fedor Friedländer, and Fritz Neuweck. Her report is found in YV 593/55, p. 2.

**14** In addition to trials that took place after the war, a series of internal "tribunal proceedings" (*Ehrengerichts-verfahren*) were held within the Jewish Community to determine whether people had "acted against the interests of the Jewish Community" during the Nazi period. Following interrogations of witnesses and examinations of evidence, rulings were made by a committee consisting of a chairman, a legal assessor, and a lay assessor (see chap. 18).

**15** Abrahamson had been a sports instructor at the Auerbachsche orphanage run by the Jewish Community. He was forced to work as a marshal during the first deportations in October 1941. From the beginning of 1943 Abrahamson had to work twenty-four-hour shifts at the Grosse Hamburger Strasse assembly camp. On his assignment to the Search Service, see his questioning of November 1, 1947, Braunschweig City Police, special division, copies of which are on file in *Criminal Proceedings against Otto Boven-siepen* (Günther Abrahamson), 1 Js 9/65, ZH 28, sheets 3–4, StA LG Berlin. Abrahamson was tried before a Berlin district court in 1952. *Criminal Proceedings against Günther Abrahamson* (510) 1 PKls 7/52 (47/52), StA LG Berlin.

**16** On Gottschalk, see 1 Js 9/65, ZH 28, sheets 3–4, StA LG Berlin. See also Stella Kübler, statement, March 12, 1946, in the Berlin criminal police department's personal files on "Stella-Ingrid Kübler," K 147, J31, BArch. For a general biography of Stella, see Peter Wyden, *Stella: One Woman's True Tale of Evil, Betrayal, and Survival in Hitler's Germany* (New York, 1992). Wyden writes that Gottschalk

was later deported to Theresienstadt, where fellow prisoners allegedly drowned him in a vat of cleaning fluid (289).

**17** On Friedländer, see the testimony of Martin Rosen and Rachil Rosa, whom he betrayed, 1 PKs 1/57, vol. 1, sheet 74, StA LG Berlin, as well as 4.1., no. 581, CJA. See also Stella Kübler, statement, March 13, 1946, K 147, J31, sheets 9, 10, and 12, BArch; Leonard Gross, *Versteckt. Wie Juden in Berlin die Nazi-Zeit überlebten* (Hamburg, 1983), pp. 81 and 198. On Ruth Danziger and Neuweck, see Stella Kübler, statement, March 13, 1946, K 147, J31, sheet 12, BArch; Johanna Heym, statement, June 14, 1965, Rep. 057–01, no. 385 (Wöhrn case), sheet 1,266, LAB. See also Auguste Meder, audio interview, 1999, CJA. For the Jewish Community's tribunal proceeding (*Ehrengericht*) against Fritz Danziger, see 1 Js 9/65 ZH 21, StA LG Berlin, as well as his statement from April 14, 1969, in the trial against Bovensiepen, also in the same file. Neuweck killed himself and his family in late 1944 when his name was placed on the deportation list for Auschwitz (Wyden, *Stella*, p. 204). See also card index and files of the Jewish cemetery in the Weissensee district of Berlin, CJA, 2.0.

**18** See note 13. Another document from the immediate postwar period that names the searchers is the "List of *Belastet* and '*Unbelastet*' Jews [Part] 1. Official Searchers." The term *belastet* refers to Jews who were activists, militarists, perpetrators of war crimes, or profiteers during the regime. CJA.

On Fritz Behrendt, see Scheurenberg, *Überleben* (Berlin, 1990), p. 49. On Bolz, see statements by Rudolf Wolf and Hertha Eichelhardt, 1 PKs 1/57, vol. 1, sheets 80–81, StA LG Berlin, and, in the same volume, Stella Kübler, statement, April 17, 1956, sheet 30. On Goldstein, who was sentenced to seven years' penal servitude for his activities, see PKs 9/48, StA LG Berlin. See also 1 Js 9/65, ZH 34 (Bruno Goldstein), StA LG Berlin, and, in the same source, ZH 92 (Alfred Metz), sheet 10.

On Guttmann, see the Jewish Community tribunal (*Ehrengericht*) against him, in 1 Js 9/65, accompanying documents nos. 17–22, StA LG Berlin. On Holstein, see Stella Kübler, statement, March 13, 1946, K147, J 31, BArch. On Rolf Isaaksohn, see his personal file in the Berlin criminal police headquarters, K147, J 34, state criminal police, BArch.

On Jakob, see Stella Kübler, statement, May 28, 1956, in 1 PKs 1/57, vol. 1, sheets 140–41, StA LG Berlin, and in the same file, Elly Lewkowicz, statement, April 18, 1956, sheet 38, and Gerda Kachel, statement, May 2, 1956, sheets 121–22. On Jakobsohn, see Bruno Blau (doc. 37) in *Jüdisches Leben in Deutschland*, ed. Monika Richarz (Stuttgart, 1982), p. 463. On Stecher, see Stella Kübler, March 13, 1946, K 147, J31, sheets 9, 10, and 12, BArch; and the questioning of Günther Abrahamson, November 1, 1947, cited in note 16. On Zwirn, who was tried for his work as a spy by the Berlin district court in 1947 and found not guilty, see 1 PKls 157/47, StA LG Berlin. See also 1 Js 9/65, ZH 92 (Alfred Metz), StA LG Berlin, as well Charlotte Hoffmann, statement, November 3, 1966, Rep. 057–01, no. 385, sheets 3–4, LAB.

**19** Carl-Hermann Salomon, statement, April 1, 1946, K147, J 31, sheets 77–78, BArch.

**20** Australia and England were Stella's preferred destinations. See correspondence from Stella and Gerhard Goldschlag to relatives in Palestine in the CJA, unpaginated, some of which is quoted in this chapter.

**21** For Siemens, see Stella Kübler, statement, April 17, 1956, 1 PKs 1/57, StA LG Berlin. For Banzhaf, see Manfred Kübler file, Rep. 092, no. 20685, LAB.

**22** See note 20.

**23** Zentralinstitut für sozialwissenschaftliche Forschung, Freie Universität Berlin, ed., *Gedenkbuch Berlins der jüdischen Opfer des Nationalsozialismus* (Berlin, 1995).

**24** Questioning of Stella Kübler, April 17, 1956, 1 PKs 1/57, vol. 1, sheet 4, StA LG Berlin; questioning of March 8, 1946, K147, J 31, sheet 5, BArch.

**25** Ibid., sheet 6.

**26** Questioning of Stella Kübler, March 14, 1946 BArch, K147, J 31, sheet 10.

**27** Minutes of the questioning of Stella Kübler by Chief Guard Nissenbaum, March–April 1946, operations group No. 6 of the Soviet military administration, in MfS-HA IX/11, PA 3472, vol. 6, here sheets 166–67, Der Bundesbeauftragte für die Unterlagen des Staatssicherheitsdienstes (BStU; former GDR).

**28** See note 26.

**29** In her description of the living conditions of and risks faced by "submarines" in Berlin, Else Hannach in the summer of 1944 mentioned the brisk trade in forgeries. "You can get anything if you know the right way to do it. . . . Some of the forgeries are quite artificial. A Jew called Schönhorst [sic] stood out in particular." YV, 593/55, p. 3. On Schönhaus- Rogoff, see also Helene Jacobs's description cited in Gerda Szepansky, *Frauen leisten Widerstand, 1933–1945* (Frankfurt am Main, 1994), pp. 74–75.

**30** See the so-called "Hallermann case" at the Berlin special court III of January 1944 and Dobberke, 31, 1943 reports on this case, August 31, 1943, 1 Gew. KLs. 203/43, sheets 119–20, StA LG Berlin. The files are now in the Berlin State Archive. See also the eyewitness testimony of Johanna Heym from June 21, 1966, Rep. 057–01, no. 385, sheets 22–23, LAB.

Other relevant sources include Gedenkstätte Deutscher Widerstand (GDW), editor, *Widerstand in Steglitz und Zehlendor* (Berlin, 1986), pp. 192–93; GDW, editor, *Widerstand in Kreuzberg* (Berlin, 1996), p. 259; Christine Zahn, "Nicht mitgehen, sondern weggehen!' Chug Chaluzi: Eine jüdische Jugendgruppe im Untergrund," in *Juden im Widerstand. Drei Gruppen zwischen Überlebenskampf und politischer Aktion. Berlin, 1939–1945*, ed. Wilfried Löhken und Werner Vathke (Berlin, 1993), pp. 168–69; and Ferdinand Kroh, *David kämpft. Vom jüdischen Widerstand gegen Hitler* (Berlin, 1988), pp. 92–93.

**31** Schwersenz, *Die versteckte Gruppe*, p. 94. The "circle of traders" was raided that August after denunciation. Some members were able to go underground. Others were arrested and taken to concentration camps. As a "non-Aryan," Dr. Kaufmann ended up at Sachsenhausen, where he died after severe abuse. Following a Nazi trial in January 1944, eleven more members of the "circle of traders" were sentenced to several years in prison. Although he was on the wanted list, however, Schönhaus-Rogoff managed to escape to Switzerland after an eventful journey by bicycle. Szepansky, *Frauen leisten Widerstand*, p. 78.

**32** On the fake documents, see MfS-HA IX/11, PA 3472, vol. 6, sheet 166, BStU.

**33** See note 30 (Dobberke's reports on the Hallerman case.)

**34** Questioning of Stella Kübler, April 17, 1956, 1 PKs 1/57, vol. 1, sheet 25, StA LG Berlin. See also K 147, J 31, sheets 7–8, BArch.

**35** Stella Kübler questioning, March 12, 1946 K 147, J 31, sheet 8, BArch.

**36** Stella Kübler questioning, March 15, 1946, K 147, J 31, sheets 15–16, BArch. See also MfS-HA IX/11, PA 3472, vol. 6, sheet 166, BStU.

**37** Margarete Gottschalk, statement, April 18, 1956, 1 PKs 1/57, vol. 1, StA LG Berlin.

**38** See note 34.

**39** MfS-HA IX/11, PA 3472, vol. 6, sheet 168, BStU.

**40** Curt Naumann, statement, July 14, 1965, in Rep. 1 Js 1/67, no. R 34/33, sheet 9a, LAB.

**41** See sheet 9 cited in note 34.

**42** MfS-HA IX/11, PA 3472, vol. 6, sheet 183, BStU.

**43** Max Reschke, statement, June 11, 1965, 1 PKs 1/57, vol. 1, sheets 212–13, StA LG Berlin.

**44** Stella Kübler, statement, April 17, 1956, 1 PKs 1/57, vol. 1, sheet 26, StA LG Berlin.

**45** Ibid. See also 1 Js 9/65, ZH 89 (Heinz Paul Meissl), sheet 9, StA LG Berlin: "The file was pretty extensive. It consisted of several thousand index cards, which were located in four to six long file card boxes." The files were stored in Dobberke's outer office and were maintained by his Jewish secretary Martha Raphael and detective secretary Herbert Tietze. The store of files was probably burned along with other documents in the Schulstrasse yard in late April 1945. Bruno Blau was an eyewitness to this event (Blau, *Jüdisches Leben in Deutschland*, p. 471, see note 18). As Alfred Slawik, a colleague of Adolf Eichmann's, reported, "Wherever I found anything written, I was to burn it. Documents had already been burned in the central heating system. I had myself set up a provisional furnace outdoors. I burned all the files that I found." See statement by Alfred Slawick, September 28, 1967, sheet 6, reproduced in Henry Friedländer and Sybil Milton, *Archives of the Holocaust,* vol. 22 (New York and London, 1993), pp. 284–85; see also the Jewish Community tribunal proceedings against Martha Raphael, Rep. 020, no. 4860–4861, LAB.

**46** Robert Zeiler, statement, April 27, 1956, Berlin, 1 PKs 1/57, vol. 1, sheets 113–14, StA LG Berlin.

**47** Eva Ronsfeld, statement, April 25, 1956, in 1 PKs 1/57, vol. 1, sheet 74, StA LG Berlin; and in the same file, Gertrud Rosenau, statement, February 29, 1956, vol. 1, sheet 11.

**48** Charge by jury of April 10, 1957, 1 PKs 1/57, sheet 15, StA LG Berlin.

**49** Ibid., vol. 1, sheet 142 f.; and from the same file, 1972 sentence by jury, sheet 45; and Moritz Zajdman, statement, April 18, 1956, vol. 1, sheet 42.

**50** Herbert Tietze, statement, April 18, 1956, 1 PKs 1/57, vol. 1, sheet 36, StA LG Berlin. File on Arnold Gerson, State Administrative Office, Dept. III, Berlin restitution authority. Gerson reports that he paid sums of RM 15,000, 35,000, and 60,000 as bribes to Möller and Dobberke. The "searchers" operating as intermediaries had set aside RM 10,000 for themselves. See also the decision of a trial by

jury (*Schwurgericht*) against Stella from October 9, 1972, which mentions how Rolf Isaaksohn enriched himself, 1 PKs 1/57, vol. 5, sheet 46, StA LG Berlin.

**51** Examples are cited in Konrad Kwiet and Helmut Eschwege, *Selbstbehauptung und Widerstand. Deutsche Juden im Kampf um Existenz und Menschenwürde, 1933–1945* (Hamburg, 1986), p. 158.

**52** The GFA was founded in the fall of 1943 on Scharff's initiative with the goal of enabling Jews to go underground and encouraging resistance to the regime. See Barbara Schieb, "Gemeinschaft für Frieden und Aufbau," in *Juden im Widerstand,* ed. Wilfried Löhken and Werner Vathke (Berlin, 1993), pp. 36–37.

**53** As manual workers for the Jewish Community, Rotholz (1904–74) and Scharff had unrestricted access to the assembly camp. Rotholz was thus often able to put the detainees in contact with the outside world. After liberation and until to his death he served as a legal adviser in compensation cases. A member of the assembly of representatives of the Jewish Community, Rotholz played a decisive role in the postwar tribunal proceedings and trials against the *Greifer.* See Rep. 020, no. 4860–4861 (decisions of the tribunal of the Jewish Community in Berlin), LAB; Scheurenberg, *Überleben,* p. 34; Schieb, *Gemeinschaft,* pp. 75–76, and interview with Rotholz's daughter, Helga Isvoranu.

On Hermann, who was apparently active in supporting GFA activities, see statements by Alexander Rotholz in 1 PKs 1/57, vol. 1, StA LG Berlin, for the following dates: February 3, 1956 (sheet 6), June 8, 1956 (sheets 207–8), and April 28, 1956 (sheets 115–16). See also CJA 1, 75 A Be 2, no. 318, sheet 160.

On Rotholz, see the above-mentioned statements. See also Stella Kübler, statement, April 17, 1956, 1 PKs 1/57, vol. 1, sheets 29, 33, StA LG Berlin; Alfred Metz, 1 Js 9/65, ZH 92, StA LG Berlin; Hans Winkler, statements, March 14 and 15, 1946, K147, J 31, sheets 43 and 79, BArch; Hildegard Bromberg, statement, K147, J 31, sheet 44, BArch; *Berliner Zeitung,* 31 July, 1947; *Der Weg,* 18 March, 1946; and Eugen Hermann-Friede, *Für Freudensprünge keine Zeit* (Berlin, 1991), p. 125.

**54** Hildegard Bromberg (1921–51) was the first GFA member to be arrested by the Gestapo, on April 18, 1944. Her statement, from March 20, 1946, is located in K147, J 31, sheet 44, BArch. See also Schieb, *Gemeinschaft,* p. 71. On the registered letter, see the indictment made during the

Nazi trial against Winkler et al., February 21, 1945, p. 10, Hans Winkler Collection, GDW.

**55** Stella Kübler, statement, March 13, 1946, K147, J 31, sheet 12, BArch.

**56** This was the 102nd old-age transport. Rita Meyhöfer, "Berliner Juden in Theresienstadt," in *Theresienstädter Studien und Dokumente* (1997): 42.

**57** Wyden, *Stella*, pp. 315–16. Although the plan to appoint an "honorary Aryan woman" seems farfetched, it was not plucked out of thin air. The legal basis was section 7 of the first supplementary decree on the Reich citizenship law, which stipulated indispensability or particular services "to the movement" as criteria. In the eyes of the Berlin Gestapo, such a "promotion" was justified on account of Stella's "services." See Beate Meyer, *"Jüdische Mischlinge." Rassenpolitik und Verfolgungserfahrung, 1933–1945* (Hamburg, 1999), pp. 96–97; and John M. Steiner and Jobst von Cornberg, "Willkür in der Willkür. Hitler und die Befreiungen von den antisemitischen Nürnberger Gesetzen," in *Vierteljahreshefte für Zeitgeschichte 2* (1998): 143–187.

**58** On her change in attitude, see Stella Kübler, statement, April 17, 1956, vol. 2, sheets 23–24, sheets 80–81. The warning came from a married couple, 1 Js 9/65, ZH 89 (Heinz Paul Meissl) sheet 15, StA LG Berlin.

**59** "There were often unpleasant scenes in the camp between the Isaaksohns," according to a statement by Martha Ehrlich, given April 25, 1956, 1 PKs 1/57, vol. 1, sheet 76, StA LG Berlin.

**60** On Isaaksohn, Goldstein, and Bolz, see Rudolf Wolf and Hertha Eichelhardt, statement, 1 PKs 1/57, vol. 1, sheets 80–81, StA LG Berlin; and Erica Niehoff, statement, February 23, 1947, PKs 9/48, vol. 1, sheet 109, StA LG Berlin. Those suspicious of Stella included her fellow *Greifer* Heinz Gottschalk and Günther Abrahamson as well as Gestapo official Felix Lachmuth. Stella Kübler, statement, April 17, 1956, 1 PKs 1/57, vol. 1, sheets 25–26, StA LG Berlin.

**61** Meissl had been detained because the Reichssippenamt (Reich Office for Genealogy) thought his "racial" background needed "clarification." As a graphic designer and media artist he worked for various newspapers until he was captured by two *Greifer*, Lewek and Zwirn, in mid-March 1942 and taken to the assembly camp. He was, however, released soon afterward. Following another denunciation in October 1944 he was arrested again and taken this time to Schulstrasse, where he was liberated by

Soviet troops on April 21, 1945. At the time of the Centrum Judaicum exhibition (2000) Meissl was ninety-one and lived in southern Germany. See note 58 (Meissl).

**62** See note 58 (Meissl).

**63** Günther Abrahamson, statement, 1 Js 9/65, ZH 28, sheets 3–4, StA LG Berlin.

**64** Gad Beck, *Und Gad ging zu David. Die Erinnerungen des Gad Beck*, ed. Frank Heibert (Berlin, 1997), pp. 218–19. Beck reports that in return Dobberke received confirmation from all those set free that he had opposed Möller's order to liquidate the camp. A few days later, on May 9, 1945, Dobberke was arrested at a refugee camp by Pichelsdorf by the Soviet secret police (GPU) as he sought entry to the western occupied zone. Gerda Lewinnek, a former inmate of the Schulstrasse assembly camp, and her boyfriend and later husband Bulli Schott gave the vital information regarding Dobberke's whereabouts.

Some of his former *Greifer* were captured at the same time: "One week after the end of the war, my husband, who is concentration camp [sic] told the GPU where . . . Dobberke was, [along with] four Jewish spies who worked for the Gestapo." Questionnaire filled out by Gerda Schott, née Lewinnek, August 6, 1945, CJA, 5A 1. Dobberke and the *Greifer* Heinz Holstein and Manfred Guttmann were put in a camp for Nazi criminals in Posen. Dobberke allegedly died of diphtheria in winter 1945–46. Wyden, *Stella*, p. 231.

**65** Stella Kübler, statement, April 17, 1956, 1 PKs 1/57, vol. 1, sheets 28–29, StA LG Berlin. See also Ferdinand Kroh's radio interview with Stella, "Stella K. Die Greiferin" (Ostdeutscher Rundfunk Brandenburg [SWR]/ Ostdeutscher Rundfunk Brandenburg [ORB], 1995).

**66** Wyden, *Stella*, p. 224.

**67** An incidental detail: the investigating commissioner and head of department with special responsibilities at the Berlin criminal police was one Jean Blomé (alias Johannes Blome). Shortly afterward, he was subject to criminal investigation and suspended from office. He had been detained in the Buchenwald concentration camp from 1942 to 1945, initially as a *Berufsverbrecher* (professional criminal). During the 1947 trial, fellow prisoners accused him of working as an SS spy. The Berlin district court sentenced him to four years' penal servitude and a fine. See reports in *Die Neue Zeit*, 7 February and 12 February, 1947; *Der Tagesspiegel*, 7, 8, and 12 February, 1947.

See also the following two publications: *Berlin. Kampf um Freiheit und Selbstdarstellung 1945–1946*, edited on behalf of the Berlin Senate (Berlin, 1961), p. 414; and *Berlin. Behauptung von Freiheit und Selbstverwaltung, 1946–1948*, edited on behalf of the Berlin Senate (Berlin, 1959), p. 146. The minutes of the first questioning of Stella on March 9, 1946, are found in the German Radio Broadcasting Archive, Berlin, shelf B 203–01–01/0350.

**68** See note 27. The minutes of Stella's March 1946 questioning by the Soviet military administration were not requested by the Soviet departments responsible until 1975, during an investigation into the past of an unnamed "prominent citizen of the Federal Republic."

**69** See Kroh radio interview cited in note 65.

**70** This is borne out by the statement of Adolf Exner, the detective secretary in IV D 1 of the RSHA. See the questioning of Julia Schneeberger, 1 Js 9/65, ZH 136, sheet 4, StA LG Berlin.

**71** The search for Rolf Isaaksohn that began immediately after the war came to naught. His colleague in the Search Service, Kurt Bolz, had an address in Copenhagen, but a search by the Danish police was fruitless. See personnel file on Rolf Isaaksohn, BArch, K147, J 34, Berlin state criminal police.

**72** This method was prevalent in the locations where the so-called "Eichmann-men" were deployed: Vienna, Berlin, Greece, France, Slovakia, and Hungary. The methods were continuously refined and developed. See, for example, the April 14, 1944, communication classed as a "Secret Notice" by SS Colonel Dr. Helmut Knochen and SS Captain Alois Brunner, reproduced in Friedländer and Milton, *Archives of the Holocaust*, vol. 20, doc. 147. See also Gideon Greif, *"Wir weinten tränenlos" Augenzeugenberichte des jüdischen "Sonderkommandos" in Auschwitz* (Frankfurt am Main, 1999).

# 9

Survival

# Chapter Sixteen

## How the Frankenstein Family Survived Underground, 1943–45

BARBARA SCHIEB

Since the 1950s, historians, sociologists, psychologists, writers, and film directors have dealt with the subject of Jews living underground during the Nazi period as well as the people who helped them. The topic continues to be of great interest, because there are no conclusive answers to many of the questions posed by the phenomenon. Up to now, German approaches have focused on the helpers, rescuers, and supporters with a view toward establishing the motives of people who voluntarily put themselves and their families at risk. The main aim was to ascertain what distinguished these people from those who did not help. In the course of time, the following picture became fixed: on one side were the active rescuers and, on the other, the powerless Jews, who could only survive thanks to the protection of these rare non-Nazis. The study of the history of the Jewish Community in Berlin in its time of crisis from 1938 to 1945 invites a long overdue change of perspective.

Although the personal testimony of Jews who lived underground has been accessible for a long time,[1] the emphasis has long been placed on their German saviors.[2] The monstrosity of genocide has its origins in the places where Jews were living in 1941. They had already been terrorized for eight years, segregated from the German majority, impoverished in economic terms and traumatized psychologically. From the fall of 1941, the Jewish Community was forced by the local "Jewish departments" (*Judenreferat*) of the Gestapo to assist in the deportation process. The official letters that it sent to individual members of the Community who had been marked out for deportation called for them to let themselves be "evacuated." At the time, no one knew what these operations— euphemistically termed "resettlement"—actually entailed. Yet those left behind soon became suspicious: news was rare that confirmed that the people deported were still alive, and some deportees were never heard of again. However, if the "evacuated" relatives were able to send short messages, it was clear that the living conditions and provision of food were catastrophic. Smuggled messages spoke a clear language; some soldiers quietly communicated their knowledge of the murder operations against the Jews "in the east"; Reich Railway employees mentioned unusual deportation trains. Today it is hard to determine how large a circle would have heard these frightening rumors. It is certain, however, that by 1942, all Jews would have heard them. But they had to decide for themselves and with close friends whether to believe them. As for their truth, no one had the faintest chance of investigating them.

By the end of 1941, there were already a few Jews who did not want to follow the prescribed route to some kind of labor camp "in the east." The only way to escape the fate mapped out for them seemed to cut themselves off completely from their former identities and begin new lives under false names. The decision to take this step could not have been easy. One withdrew from a group that provided the last protection possible; one had to consciously place oneself outside the law, which often seemed inconceivable to most assimilated Jews; and one had to become dependent on a vast number of people. Despite these serious disincentives, more and more Jews took this step in the hope of saving themselves. The phenomena intensified around the time of the final roundup of Jewish forced laborers—the *Fabrik-Aktion*—on February 27, 1943 (see chap. 9). Whoever closed the door on his former life for the foreseeable future had taken this decision consciously.

The stance within the Jewish Community and other Jewish institutions toward members who attempted to escape changed in the course of 1942. The teacher and Zionist Jizchak Schwersenz describes the change as follows: "Alfred Selbiger, our association leader at the time, believed that [the Zionist organization] Hechalutz had a 'holy duty' . . . to lead the way for the Jews, even in the case of the deportation. Dr. Eppstein[3] had also warned of illegal actions. In the course of heated discussions, the majority of the *chaverim* (comrades) adopted this standpoint, and only a small minority was prepared to consider escaping or going underground."[4] This was how things stood in the first half of 1942. This line was, moreover, consolidated in the aftermath of the arson attack on the Nazi propaganda exhibition "Soviet Paradise." In retribution for the May 28, 1942, attack initiated by Herbert Baum's circle, some 250 Jewish men from Berlin and Sachsenhausen prisoners had been randomly singled out and shot.[5] Many Jewish Community officials, among them Heinrich Stahl and Paul Eppstein, were well informed about the Nazi retribution campaign and held that it was better to keep a low profile rather than trigger further brutal intervention. Along with open resistance, Eppstein considered deliberate "withdrawal from deportation" to be one such greatly feared "illegal action."

**Figure 16.1**
Walter Frankenstein
in Berlin, 1939

**Figure 16.2**
Leonie Rosner in
Leipzig, 1939

Schwersenz was summoned for deportation on August 28, 1942. Convinced by his close friend Edith Wolff that going underground was the right thing to do, he sought advice and something akin to "authorization from above" for his plan. "In an extreme state of agitation I went to Alfred Selbiger to talk about my situation. I did not want to act without the approval of the association and the Hechalutz. Friends were shocked by the news, since I was the first in our movement's leadership to be marked out for deportation. We again discussed going underground at length, and this time Alfred agreed with my plan. In addition, he declared himself willing to provide me with one hundred marks per month from the 'black money' of the Hechalutz" (see chap. 7).[6]

Clearly, the Jewish institutions were torn. The Jewish Community was firmly under the control of the Reich Security Main Office (Reichssicherheitshauptamt [RSHA]), which was planning the systematic murder of the Jews and using it to organize this more efficiently. Nonetheless the Community's abiding goal should have been to protect its members. Aware of the Community's dilemma, those who decided to go underground did not seek its authorization. Most embarked alone on a lonely and risky route, not knowing how and where it would end.

LEONIE AND WALTER FRANKENSTEIN had married in Berlin on February 20, 1942.[7] Walter was not yet eighteen at the time and had to get his mother's permission. Leonie Rosner was twenty. Both had grown up under the terror of the Nazi regime and had decided despite their youth to spend the rest of their lives together. Leonie was from Leipzig. Walter came from Flatow on the

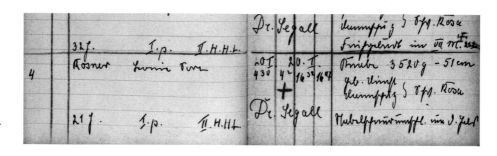

**Figure 16.3** Entry
for the birth of a
boy on January 20,
1943, to Leonie
Rosner, who was
registered at the
Jewish hospital under
her maiden name.

Petziner lake, northeast of Schneidemühl. His father had died in 1929. From 1933, he had major problems at school because of Nazi persecution. As a result, his uncle and guardian secured a place for him at the Auerbachsche orphanage in Berlin in 1936. Up to 1938 he attended the Jewish Volksschule (elementary school) on Rykestrasse in the Prenzlauer Berg district. Knowing that he was forbidden to study his chosen field, architecture, in secondary school, he decided to continue at the Jewish Bauschule (school for construction) on Fruchtstrasse, near the Ostbahnhof. When the school was closed in 1941, he and two of his teachers were taken on as construction workers by the Jewish Community.

After separating from her first husband, Leonie Rosner's mother married Theodor Kranz, a Gentile and a leftist, in the mid-1920s. Her mixed marriage to an "Aryan" protected her. Leonie went to Berlin, where she trained to be a kindergarten teacher. She then worked as an intern at the Jewish institution for deaf-mutes in the Weissensee district of Berlin and moved with the last charges to the Auerbachsche orphanage in 1941. It was here that she met Walter Frankenstein.

Theodor Kranz had told Leonie and her mother about Auschwitz. "My stepfather worked in the construction industry and had a colleague who had worked in Auschwitz, and he had talked about the terrible things that happened there."

Both of the young newlyweds had to work as forced laborers. As a handyman for the Jewish Community, Walter Frankenstein was under the control of the Gestapo, which deployed the Community's construction workers for its own purposes. He had the task of converting the cellars of various RSHA buildings into air-raid shelters. He worked on Emser Strasse (Wilmersdorf district) on the premises of a Masonic lodge that had been closed down,[8] then, briefly, at Kurfürstenstrasse 116 (Adolf Eichmann's office), and finally near Bayerischer Platz.

Leonie Frankenstein was assigned to a factory that produced balloons for military use. During her pregnancy in 1942 she often fainted on the job. "My forewoman said that it was no good that I kept fainting, and I said that I was pregnant and couldn't stand the smell of glue. 'Yes, but that's not acceptable. I have to dismiss you.' 'If you get rid of me I'll be sent to Auschwitz the next day,' I said. 'Well, I can't be held responsible for that,' she said. 'I'll give you a letter for the employment office stating that you can't endure the work here.' From then on I wound coils for transformers."

Around New Year 1942–43 the couple had to move from Treskowstrasse in Prenzlauer Berg to an assigned apartment at Linienstrasse 7 in the Mitte district. Their son Peter was born on January 20, 1943, in the Jewish hospital.[9] On February 24, just before the *Fabrik-Aktion*, the notorious trucks stopped outside their building to pick up the inhabitants. "I said, 'My baby isn't even six weeks old. They won't take me; they'll keep me back for now.' Indeed the man went down and made a phone call and inquired with his superior. He came back and said that he had to take me, after all. I then went down with the pram, and the others said how terrible it was with the little baby and so on, and I just said, 'I'll sleep in my own bed at home tonight.' We were taken to [the assembly camp at] Grosse Hamburger Strasse, and I did not join the back of the queue but rather stayed at the front, and there were around eight women who said they had a certificate from the Gestapo saying that they were to be kept back and I said, 'Me, too.' 'Where is it then?' 'Well, the SS locked it up in my apartment.' Then they wanted to know where my husband worked. The marshal [*Ordner*] then said that these eight women could go, and I asked what about me. 'Don't ask such stupid questions!' came the reply, and so I did not ask any more stupid questions, and I went too."

On February 28, the day after the *Fabrik-Aktion*, Walter Frankenstein went to work as usual near Bayerischer Platz but no one from his labor column was there. "The foreman came up, saw me, and asked: 'What are you doing here?' 'Well, I'm here for work.' 'Don't you know that all the others were picked up last night?' 'Not me.' He went into the building to ask what he should do with me. Then I went home quickly and thought: 'Now the time has really come.'" Leonie Frankenstein was distraught and packed some small items in the pram as well as diapers, and it was Walter's idea that his wife should travel first to her "protected" mother in Leipzig. Walter's spontaneous plans were to "wait here today and then I'll try and take something else from the apartment."

"I was sitting on the train," recounts Leonie Frankenstein of the journey. "I still had no idea about illegality, my baby was lying on a pillow next to me, and the controller came in. A woman in my compartment did not have her identity card, just her clothing ration card, and the controller said: 'You can buy one of

*We hadn't planned anything. We just knew that we would not go with them.*

those on any street corner in Berlin,' stumbled over my feet, went out and didn't check me. I don't think that I could have lied, I don't know what I would have said."

Walter Frankenstein followed a few days later and had similar luck on the train. "I was standing outside a compartment and looking out of the window, the compartment door behind me opened and six men came out. You could tell that they were Gestapo men from the leather coats, the hats with the brim turned downward. Three went to the right, three to the left, and they carried out checks in each compartment. I stood outside the compartment and they didn't check me!" Leonie did not leave her mother's house in Leipzig for almost six months.

For the whole time neither had false papers. Rather, they assumed false names according to the circumstances. Only Walter carried with him his real birth certificate, on which no religion was marked. He could not live in the apartment of his mother-in-law, but he was helped by some Jehovah's Witnesses with whom Leonie's mother and stepfather had good contacts. They supported the family with food rations coupons. Walter was housed in the workshop of an old left-wing carpenter, Mr. Koch: "He took me in out of pure idealism, but then there were rumors in the neighborhood, and I had to disappear."

Leonie Frankenstein still has a vivid memory of one occurrence during her time in Leipzig, when she did not leave the apartment for months: "I had a dream. I was sleeping on the sofa in the living room with my child next to me, and I dreamt that I was on a country road. It was pitch black. I was also in a house and everything was pitch black, dark, and I did not know how to get out. And then in my dream I climbed out of a window. And in reality—there were two windows, one was open, the other had black-out curtains in it—I removed the flower pots, lifted up the black-out curtains, opened the window, and jumped out. From the first floor. My mother heard noises and came to see what was happening. I was gone [from the room] and lay below. I only had a concussion. I was black and blue but hadn't broken anything and didn't need a doctor. I couldn't even have gone to a doctor. What would I have said?"

In August 1943 Leonie's mother was denounced, and Leonie had to abandon her hiding place.

My mother's name was Beate, and she had a *Postausweis* [the card required to collect mail] with just "Beate Kranz" on it, which she had to show at the post office. And someone denounced her on account of the missing [Jewish name] 'Sara.' The Gestapo came and told her that she was going to be arrested. They did not take her with them right then but they told her to report there. She was not to go to the Gestapo, however, but to the police, which [she thought] wouldn't be so dangerous. We never said our last farewells. We thought that she would have to stay there for a while but would get out again. And the terrible thing is that mummy was taken to Auschwitz and knew beforehand what was to happen to her there. She was not there for long; she was arrested in August, taken to Auschwitz in October, and died there on January 3, 1944. She was young; she was forty-three when she died.

Leonie Frankenstein left her mother's home immediately, knowing only that Walter was somewhere in Berlin. "When I returned to Berlin without knowing how to find my husband in this big city I panicked a bit about being all alone there; all I had was Edith Hirschfeldt's telephone number."

Edith Hirschfeldt was called Edith Berlow at the time (she had been married to the film director Georg Zoch between 1929 and 1934 and after the divorce had assumed her maiden name again) and had been friends with the Jewish orthopedist Kurt Hirschfeldt since 1936. At the time, in summer 1943, Kurt Hirschfeldt was already underground, hiding in Edith Berlow's apartment at Menzelstrasse 9 in the Grunewald district. Kurt Hirschfeldt and Walter Frankenstein were cousins, and so it was clear to Leonie and Walter Frankenstein that it would be safe for them to go to Edith Berlow. Leonie Frankenstein recalled:

> I rang her and said who I was and that I was looking for Walter. She didn't want to tell me where he was, of course. I understood that. But I pleaded so much. I told her that I was all alone, that they had taken my mother away and what was I to do? So she gave me the Königsallee address. But I didn't have the courage to go there. I walked up and down the street with the baby for hours and by chance my husband came out at some stage. What were we to do now? Of course we called Edith again and told her that we were standing there and did not know where to go. And then she said, 'Of course, come in. It will be all right for a few nights with the child.' And so she took us in. And then she arranged it with Mr. Ketzer that we could also sleep at Königsallee.

Edith Berlow devoted the years 1941–45 to supporting the persecuted people that she met through Kurt Hirschfeldt. Kurt's half-brother, Fritz Hirschfeldt, was deported to the Lódz ghetto with the first deportation transport on October 18, 1941, and, having received no news from him, Edith wanted to visit him there. She undertook the difficult journey there and even managed to speak with the German camp director, but achieved nothing.

She and Kurt Hirschfeldt were also close friends of Werner Scharff, an electrical technician for the Jewish Community who did many good works in the assembly camps by smuggling in news, food, and so forth. He prepared himself and others to go underground by arranging the printing of fake work cards. He

*They asked me right away if I was from Berlin, since I was brunette at the time. "Yes, why?" "Because you're so dark." I answered, "Why, are all people from Berlin blonde, then?"*

was soon seized and deported to Theresienstadt but was able to escape with his friend Fancia Grün in early September 1943. From the fall of 1943 he formed a resistance group together with Hans Winkler, who worked as a non-Jewish judicial employee in Luckenwalde (ca. 70 km south of Berlin). The group assumed the task of hiding Jews but also informing the population about the criminal character of the Nazi regime and urging passive resistance to the war. In the first half of 1944, the group formed by Scharff and Winkler under the name Society for Peace and Reconstruction (Gemeinschaft für Frieden und Aufbau) produced and distributed three flyers.[10]

Edith had also helped house Kurt Hirschfeldt's former receptionist and her husband.[11] Mrs. and Mr. Michalowicz stayed with her and apparently were not careful enough about being quiet in the apartment, opening the door to strangers, and similar matters. When they later fell into the hands of the Gestapo, their capture was a great blow to Edith and increased her sense of the risks involved. Her willingness to help, however, never weakened, and she gave a great deal in terms of practical living arrangements and providing psychological support. She never saw herself as a special or courageous person—she acted out of love for her husband and out of humanity.[12]

When the three members of the Frankenstein family called on Edith Berlow's help in August 1943, she was in a very difficult situation herself. Werner Scharff had just been deported to Theresienstadt at the beginning of August, and no one could be certain that the same fate would not also befall Kurt Hirschfeldt. Werner Scharff's wife Gertrud, who was also living under a false identity, was not arrested but worked for Mr. Ketzer, who managed a pharmaceutical company on Königsallee.[13] Edith Berlow set up the contact between the Frankensteins and Mr. Ketzer. He offered them a small room in the basement of his house. The tablet presses were next door.

It is not certain how long the family lived on Königsallee. The house was destroyed by an air mine, probably in the fall of 1943, and Mr. Ketzer suggested that it would be a practical solution for Leonie to register with the baby at an assembly point for people who had been bombed out of their homes. After thoroughly weighing the risks, Leonie Frankenstein went there. She was told that, as a mother, she had to leave Berlin immediately with the child and was sent to Briesenhorst near Landsberg/Warthe, where she was met by a woman representative of National Socialist Welfare (the Nationalsozialistische Volkswohlfahrt [NSV]). Leonie Frankenstein thinks the woman may have suspected something. "I had no ration cards, and this women sent me back to Berlin where there had just been a daylight bombing raid, everything was in chaos, and the woman at the ration card center got really worked up: 'How could she send you back to

Berlin with the little one? That's crazy. Here are your ration cards—and make sure that you get out of Berlin again.' Thus I was able to give her [the NSV woman] the ration cards. I didn't have any identity papers, but that satisfied her for a while. She never came to see if I was looking after the baby properly—thank goodness—and that everything was clean, and so on. No, she never did that."

USING A FALSE IDENTITY, Leonie Frankenstein and her child stayed "with a farmer's wife, who lived there with her daughter and an old Polish prisoner of war. Her husband and son were in Russia." Briesenhorst appeared very quiet and harmless, but every day Leonie had to be ready to face awkward questions. At the beginning of 1944 she became pregnant again.

Walter Frankenstein remained in Berlin and struggled through. He was only responsible for himself and tried to earn the money that he needed for himself and for his wife in Briesenhorst. As when Leonie was still in Leipzig, Walter found shelter in bombed-out ruins.

During the day, Walter Frankenstein had to work odd jobs or look like he was occupied. Edith Berlow had obtained a bicycle for him. "You look busy with a bicycle. It was much too dangerous to wander around! For a while, I worked as a projectionist in a daytime cinema in the arcades beneath the Friedrichstrasse tracks. The first reel ran. It was a Wehrmacht newsreel. Suddenly I heard peals of laughter from the auditorium. I looked down through the control window and saw on the screen that, instead of jumping out of the trenches and taking Russian positions as part of an assault, the German soldiers were running backward! I had forgotten to rewind the film! That was sabotage. Had a single Nazi been in the auditorium and reacted, he would have attacked me. I left everything running and ran away—I didn't even collect my pay for the last week."

Walter Frankenstein found such jobs through advertisements in the daily press. Casual work was less risky than official posts obtained through the employment office. Walter Frankenstein told various stories to explain why he had not been called up for army service. He said that he had tuberculosis or that his conscription had been deferred or that he was studying. Because of the acute labor shortage, employers were mostly satisfied with his excuses and did not ask to see his papers. During this period, Walter Frankenstein attended a cultural event every evening.

*There in a garage stood an old jacked-up car, the wheels had been taken off. It had been used by the military. I slept in it for weeks until the situation in that area became a bit dicey and then I disappeared again.*

The theater and concert halls were the safest places. There were no military checks, but the worst thing was that the advance ticket sales for the whole week took place on Sunday mornings. Opera, concert, and theater tickets were very much in demand, and the queues for the advance sales began on Friday evening.

Lists were drawn up. You put your name down and had to turn up every two hours, they put a cross by your name or you would lose your place in the queue. [This was the procedure] at the Schauspielhaus on Gendarmenmarkt, the Staatsoper, the Deutsches Theater, and the Admiralspalast. From Friday evening to Sunday morning one went round in circles. And then you would come across one of the illegals, then a second, then a third—the word had gotten around that one could sit there in peace, even sleep. I once slept through the whole of *Tristan* on a Sunday afternoon. After all, I had not slept from Friday evening to Sunday morning, and on Sunday I had been hanging around. Then *Tristan* started very early since it is so long, and I sat down on the third row of the upper tier—those were the cheapest seats—went to sleep, and woke up when the performance was over. Thus I was able to sleep for three and a half hours in peace without having to keep my eyes and ears open!

Walter Frankenstein, who kept precise records of his visits to concerts and to the theater, attended the Staatsoper for the last time on October 5, 1944. Herbert von Karajan was conducting Bruckner's Eighth Symphony.

Leonie and Walter kept in touch with each other via letters, which they picked up at the post office. Between September and October 1944 Leonie Frankenstein heard nothing from her husband, a situation she remembers as torturous and indescribable. He had just witnessed an arrest at "his" Berlin post office and did not dare to go and pick up his mail for several weeks.

**Figure 16.4**
Leonie and Peter (Uri) Frankenstein in Briesenhorst, 1944

Her second son Michael was born on September 26, 1944. She went to a clinic in Landsberg/Warthe to give birth, leaving her older son in the care of the farmer's wife in Briesenhorst, where she was living. The only problem was her false identity. "Then they wanted to know my name and date of birth and I had taken the name of a Christian acquaintance from Leipzig, and I thought I could remember when her birthday was and used that date. Then the registry office wrote to say that they could find no 'Martha Gerhard' born on such and such a date in Leipzig. Then I wrote something back—I can't remember what—and they replied that they could not find anything and asked whether my mother had given birth in a private hospital or at home, that could be the reason why they could not find me. Then I realized I had to get away and I went straight back to Berlin." She made this decision at the start of November 1944, when little Michael was five weeks old.

IN THE MEANTIME Walter Frankenstein was getting by alone in Berlin and secured contacts with the black market as well as with other people living underground. His connection to Arthur Katz turned out to be extremely important. The Frankenstein and Katz families had been neighbors in Flatow. "We knew nothing of each other. I met him—I can still picture it today—at the Savignyplatz S-Bahn station. I could see him from a distance. He saw me. We turned around and walked away from one another. No one knew [if the other was a spy]. I knew the names of some of the spies, but not all of them. Another day we again met by chance at Savignyplatz—he must have been living near there, yes, and then we went up to each other and resumed contact."

Walter Frankenstein avoided the traps that constantly lay in wait for those living underground—often only narrowly. Edith Berlow warned the Frankensteins about two *Greifer* (Jewish "snatchers," or spies), Günther Abrahamson and Stella Kübler (see chap. 15).[14] Both Frankensteins knew Günther Abrahamson personally from the Auerbachsche orphanage, where he had previously worked. Walter Frankenstein once saw Abrahamson on the tram, and was relieved when the latter did not recognize him. Luckily, Stella Kübler never crossed the couple's path.

For young men of conscription age, checks and checkpoints were highly dangerous. Walter Frankenstein recalls his only narrow escape.

After a night in a bombed-out ruin, I traveled the next morning by S-Bahn toward Friedrichstrasse. I was dog tired. Normally I would stand at the door of the subway and S-Bahn, since I get out quickly in case a conductor came by. [But] I sat down and nodded off. Suddenly there was a sergeant major standing in front of me, one of these "*Kettenhunde*" [military policemen, who wore badges decorated with chains (*Ketten*)]. He tapped me on the shoulder and said, "Your papers!" That was back in 1944, and I was already well versed in how to respond. I rummaged in my pockets and said in broken German, "Foreigner, work in Borsigwerke, come from night-shift, forget papers in work clothes." "Okay," he said, "we'll get out at Friedrichstrasse and go to the next police station. They'll ring up the company and then the whole thing will be sorted." It was the lowest S-Bahn platform, and on the escalator I stopped him: "Now I'll tell you something. I'm a Jew. I'm living illegally. If you take me to the next police station I'll be gassed in Auschwitz tomorrow." "Have you got proof?" "The only thing I have is my birth certificate."

**Figure 16.5** The Frankenstein boys, Peter (Uri) and Michael, in Hadera, Israel, 1949

I showed it to him and explained that Frankenstein was a Jewish name. "Is that true?" he wanted to know. "Yes." He gave me my birth certificate back and said, "Be off with you. I'm not looking for Jews. I'm looking for deserters."

Walter Frankenstein knew how lucky he had been, for there were certainly members of the military police who would have gladly turned in any illegal Jew to the responsible authorities.

Arthur Katz found accommodation for Walter Frankenstein with Mrs. Döhring at Emser Strasse 16. The building was adjacent building to the RSHA offices where Walter Frankenstein had worked before becoming "illegal." Since the apartment had been damaged by a bombing raid, Mrs. Döhring herself lived with a friend on Pariser Strasse.

This Arthur Katz knew her. I don't know how. And he arranged for me to live in this bombed-out apartment. I had to give her my word that I would not leave the apartment. She knew that I had done forced labor next door and that the Gestapo knew me. I was in the apartment and then she said one day: "Could you perhaps help me to fix the apartment? Arthur Katz told me that you were a handyman." "Yes, of course" I said. "Then I'll put you in touch with a man from Organisation Todt [OT, a state contractor for large-scale, often military, construction]. He'll come over, look at the apartment, and provide you with the materials that you need." A senior official from the OT came over who was able to get hold of some materials, and we went through the apartment. I said, "I thought we'd do it like so," and "I need such and such," and he delivered it. And then I did up the apartment.

Mrs. Döhring's husband was a Wehrmacht officer stationed in the Generalgouvernement in Poland, and as far as Walter Frankenstein could tell, he must have been a staunch National Socialist. He knew nothing about the assistance his wife provided, but she shared the food rations he sent her with "her two illegals," Walter Frankenstein and Arthur Katz.

As a strong young man, Walter Frankenstein needed additional food, and to get it, he connected with other *U-Boote* (submarines)—that is, Jews living underground. The black market played a role as well. "I was living with Mrs. Döhring and tried to get hold of food, and somehow I came across a deaf-mute. He wrote on a piece of paper, 'I've got meat.' I wrote back, 'Yes, I'd like to buy a piece.' Mrs. Döhring took it and cooked it. The meat remained tough. I ate it then and a few weeks later I met the deaf mute again and he asked me: 'Did you eat the meat?' 'Yes.' 'Sorry, it was dog, I did not know either.' It didn't kill me."

The fate of Arthur Katz and those close to Katz touched Frankenstein.

His situation was really tragic. He was engaged to a girl whose parents were also living illegally. The girl, too. They were living in the Friedrichshain district. I was up where they were living and had arranged to meet another illegal. There was a square down on the street—I can't remember what it was called. I looked down from the window—they were on the third or fourth floor—and then this illegal acquaintance approached. And at the same moment, two people dressed in plain clothes went up and arrested him. Two minutes later I would have been there, too. I was just waiting for him. He was supposed to come over and then we wanted to go somewhere together. The girl's parents had false papers. And they wanted to buy new ones. They were supposed to get Spanish passports. They sent their daughter to a place where she was supposed to pick up the passports. And that place was raided and she was taken away. I don't know whether her parents survived.[15]

Then, in November 1944, Leonie arrived in Berlin in a desperate state with her two small children. It was impossible to house the whole family on Emser Strasse. Arthur Katz helped once again, putting the family in contact with a woman called Mary. Walter recalls that "Mary was a madam of a brothel who lived on Blumenstrasse near Jannowitz bridge. She had a room down there in the basement apartment and she rented it out to us. She did it for money. We

*And then this man in the uniform of the SS Sturmbannführer came up to us and asked, "What's your name?" "Kranz." "Do you know where to go with your family?" "No." "Come to my office tomorrow"—he mentioned some SS office—"and I'll get you and your family an apartment and I'll propose that you get the Kriegsverdienstkreuz [decoration for civilian service in wartime]. Your actions must be rewarded!" "Okay," I said. But of course we never went.*

paid three hundred marks a month for that room. That was a lot of money. Mary had a black poodle, which slept in a little four-poster bed. And our Michael—he was dark, had dark eyes and dark hair. Out of the four-poster bed went the poodle and in went Michael. We lived there until around January or February 1945." Then, during a daylight bombing raid, the house burned down. "I tried to save the house with a man in uniform. We were extinguishing the fire but were overcome by smoke poisoning. The building burned, and we were left standing in the street with no idea of where to go."

In this situation of homelessness and extreme danger, a woman—Fräulein Dora—appeared like a good angel. Walter Frankenstein recalls that "she had met us now and again in the apartment but didn't know who we were. She heard the little children, whom she found so adorable: 'Oh God, the poor children. Where will you go now? What are you going to do?' Then Leonie told her the truth that we were Jews, living illegally, and we did not know where to go."[16]

*Then she took a key out of her bag and said, "Here you are, this is the key to my apartment. I won't come back, but you can live there."*

The Frankenstein family was able to live in Fräulein Dora's apartment until shortly before liberation. They spent the long last days of the street battles at the end of April 1945 in the Kottbusser Tor subway station, which had been converted into a bunker. Walter Frankenstein recalls, "I lay on a plank bed with a straw mattress on it, put the children on it, and there we stayed until liberation." "We had no water, no food, nothing." Recalls Leonie Frankenstein, "We could not go out either to cook something, [because] the Russians flew so close to the ground. Many people who were standing at the hydrants to get water were shot down by the planes."

FOR LEONIE, WALTER, PETER, and Michael Frankenstein, the end of the war was a true liberation. They were part of a tiny group of about 1,500 Jews who managed to survive underground in and near Berlin.[17]

It took some time for the Frankensteins to get used to the fact that the situation of complete fear for their children and each other had come to an end. Leonie Frankenstein can still remember the psychological trauma the bombings caused. On the one hand, each Allied attack brought them a step closer toward the end of the Nazi regime. On the other hand, the bombs could kill her and her family. The memory of this mortal fear still accompanies the Frankenstein couple today.

Arthur Katz also survived. When he registered with the Jewish Community in the summer of 1945 he gave Mrs. Döhring's address: Emser Strasse 16 in Wilmersdorf.[18]

The Frankensteins moved into an apartment at Emser Strasse 6 in the neighboring district of Neukölln, where Nazis had lived. They registered with the

 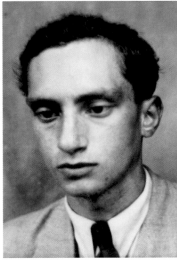

**Figures 16.6 and 16.7**
Leonie and Walter Frankenstein after liberation, 1945

Jewish Community, and a Jewish-American organization advised them to leave Berlin because of the food shortage. Leonie Frankenstein traveled with her two sons to Palestine via Paris and Marseilles, while Walter Frankenstein was detained in Cyprus. They were not reunited until 1947 in Palestine. In the 1950s, they left Israel and moved to Sweden.

AFTER GIVING THE FRANKENSTEIN family history in chronological stages, it is helpful to return to the beginning and see the picture that emerges. The people who helped them in Leipzig were Beate Kranz, Leonie's mother; Leonie's stepfather, Theodor Kranz, a low-level Communist; members of the Jehovah's Witnesses; and Mr. Koch, the old "leftist" carpenter. In Berlin, they were: Edith Berlow (later Hirschfeldt); the manager Mr. Ketzer; Arthur Katz, who lived underground; Mrs. Döhring and a female friend; the brothel keeper "Mary"; and the prostitute "Fräulein Dora."

Other people who came into contact with members of the Frankenstein family while they were living underground were either ignorant of their Jewish identities or played the role of helper by chance or out of humanity. The NSV woman and the farmer's wife in Briesenhorst are examples of the former. So, too, is the woman at the ration card point in Berlin. The military police sergeant who did not denounce Walter Frankenstein is an example of the latter. These instances were of course a matter of immense and unforeseeable luck for the Frankensteins.

There are many cases of people who survived underground with the help of even more people.[19] In the case of the Frankenstein family, the number and

**Figure 16.8** The Frankenstein family in Tel Aviv, 1949

social as well as political background of the conscious helpers delivers a clear message. The first helpers belonged to the family circle; everyone assumed that it would be safe to go to Leonie Frankenstein's mother, Beate Kranz, even though she was Jewish. Beate's non-Jewish husband was a devoted communist and diametrically opposed to the Nazi regime. In the 1930s it was suggested to him on several occasions that he divorce his Jewish wife, but each time he firmly opposed this. In Berlin, Edith Berlow was also part of this family context. As the non-Jewish partner of Walter Frankenstein's Jewish cousin, she had known Walter for a long time and had also offered assistance to Walter's mother (although these efforts came to nothing; in the course of the *Fabrik-Aktion* Mrs. Frankenstein was suddenly arrested and deported).

The pharmaceuticals manager Mr. Ketzer fits the profile of the "classic helper"—somebody who assisted people who were previously completely unknown to him. One can only speculate about his motives. Mrs. Döhring and her female friend also belonged to this category. Even if, for whatever reasons, they may have felt indebted to Arthur Katz, they were in no way obliged to help his acquaintance Walter Frankenstein.

A typical scenario, clearly recognizable in the case of the Frankenstein family, was the frequency of helpers who stood outside of the political system: the "leftist" stepfather Theodor Kranz, the leftist carpenter Mr. Koch, the Jehovah's Witnesses, the two women of the red-light district. These people lived more or less on the margins of National Socialist society and were very aware that they could at any stage come into fatal conflict with the police, the Gestapo, or the law. Mr. Koch, the Jehovah's Witnesses, and the prostitutes did not help because of political or religious "duty" but because they had kept their "human orientation." The fact that "Mary" took money for the room was an economic necessity for her. But the Frankensteins were also quite happy with this arrangement; it was a contract between equal partners, a completely normal "deal" based on paying something for a service. The advantage of payment was that people living underground did not have to feel morally dependent.

Of great interest, although little known or researched until now, are the helpers who lived underground themselves. For example, Arthur Katz, the Frankenstein's pre-1933 neighbor, later played a decisive role. Such individuals have not been acknowledged as helpers up to now due to the official guidelines of the postwar institutions set up to honor those who gave assistance to persecuted Jews.[20] According to this official framework, "helpers" were only defined as those who did not themselves face National Socialist repression. Jews who lived underground were thus excluded. So were the non-Jewish spouses of Jews and those who took—or had to take—money, goods, or services in return for their aid. And so a fixed image of the helpers has emerged, one that often does not coincide with the reality of the day.

Because it has been assumed—inaccurately—that fellow sufferers aided one another as a matter of course, helpers who themselves lived underground have not been acknowledged. Walter Frankenstein emphasizes the caution with which he established contact with Arthur Katz. Each person living underground was a potential enemy to each of his fellows. It was by no means a foregone conclusion that they would assist each other with tips and advice, contacts, or by sharing their own accommodations and networks. Katz knew Frankenstein well enough to take a risk with him. Nonetheless, he was under no obligation to share his own contacts and opportunities. Indeed, he might have improved his own chances of survival had he kept to himself his connection to Mrs. Döhring, Mary, and the black-market traders.

Arthur Katz acted out of an old and deep-rooted impulse for solidarity—anachronistic, considering the dog-eat-dog conditions of living underground. In 1944 Walter Frankenstein was twenty, and Arthur Katz thirty-four. Somehow, both young men were able to show each other a trace of humanity in the midst of this stressful and dangerous life that was below human dignity. As the Frankenstein and Katz stories attest, the "success" or "failure" of an attempt to survive underground often depended on coincidences and circumstances over which individuals had no control. The risks were crystal clear to anyone who took the decision to go underground. Despite the grave danger, an unknown but rather high number braved the step.[21] Courage and conviction in one's own strength were required to be able to decide at all to follow an incalculable, dangerous path that could in some cases lead to death but that left more scope for action and room for maneuver than the path that led to the ominous camps.

At this late stage, however, few Jews had this strength. After all they had gone through during ten years of Nazi terror, many were worn down. The initiative taken by those who went underground has something of the spirit of resistance.

**Figure 16.9** Leonie and Walter Franken- stein in Berlin, 1991

Even when the goal was to save one's own life, the broad concept of resistance applies. The murder of the Jews was a clearly defined state goal of the Nazi regime, though the practical implementation was kept secret from the public. The independent actions of Jews who went underground were marked by an oppositional stance toward National Socialist policy. They devised workable plans, methods, and opportunities; they made new contacts and called on old friends and acquaintances. In short, the Jews who went and lived underground were active. Although dependent on many people, in critical situations they had to take active decisions themselves.[22] They took their lives into their own hands.

My description of the active role played by underground Jews in saving their own lives is not intended to lessen the contribution of those who helped them.

All helpers, both acknowledged and unknown, deserve public acknowledgment and praise.

My article merely seeks to shift the emphasis somewhat. The Frankenstein family account shows that there was never a distinction between active non-Jewish helpers and passive Jewish victims at the mercy of others. Jews who had gone underground and the Gentiles who offered them help in many areas of existence had to work together in the "business of saving lives." The better the action of the two sides dovetailed, the more the various possibilities could be mutually devised and implemented, the smoother the whole project could run. The fact that most incidences of rescue—even the successful ones—did not function according to a set pattern of course lies in the nature of different people, their temperaments and characters. Of course, external influences, both known and unknown, also played a role.

In the summer of 1991, I had the honor of witnessing a reunion between the Frankensteins and Edith Hirschfeldt, née Berlow, whom they had not seen since the 1950s. All of us were moved by the obvious delight these three people showed at coming together again. By joining forces many years ago, they had successfully undertaken a life-threatening project. I can still hear Edith Hirschfeldt's heartfelt words upon seeing the Frankensteins again. "Wie schön, dass ihr lebt!" (How wonderful that you are alive!)[23]

**1** Publications include Gad Beck, *Und Gad ging zu David*, ed. Frank Heibert (Berlin, 1997); Else Behrend-Rosenfeld, *Ich stand nicht allein. Leben einer Jüdin in Deutschland, 1933–1944* (Munich, 1988); Inge Deutschkron, *Ich trug den gelben Stern* (Cologne, 1978); Eugen Herman-Friede, *Für Freudensprünge keine Zeit. Erinnerungen an Illegalität und Aufbegehren, 1942–1948*, with an afterword by Barbara Schieb (Berlin, 1991); Joel König, *Den Netzen entronnen* (Göttingen, 1967); Max Krakauer, *Lichter im Dunkel. Flucht und Rettung eines jüdischen Ehepaares im Dritten Reich* (Stuttgart, 1975); Larry Orbach and Vivien Orbach-Smith, *Soaring Underground. Autobiographie eines jüdischen Jugendlichen im Berliner Untergrund, 1938–1945* (Berlin, 1998); Ilse Rewald, *Berliner, die uns halfen, die NS-Diktatur zu überleben* (Berlin, 1975); Hans Rosenthal, *Zwei Leben in Deutschland* (Bergisch-Gladbach, 1980); Marga Spiegel, *Retter in der Nacht* (Frankfurt am Main, 1969); and Lotte Strauss, *Über den grünen Hügel. Erinnerungen an Deutschland* (Berlin, 1997).

**2** There are many grounds for the emphasis on saviors. One wanted to find out what distinguished those who helped from those who did not; they were in ideological hindsight interesting—proof that there were not just Nazis in Germany; and they were and are favored topics of study with regard to the question as to what motivates people to help complete strangers.

**3** Paul Eppstein (1901–44) first worked as a sociology professor in Mannheim and then, from 1933 on, in various Jewish institutions in Berlin. He was a member of the board of the Reichsvereinigung until 1943, and in 1943–44 he was chairman of the Council of Elders in Theresienstadt (see chaps. 18 and 19). *Enzyklopädie des Holocaust. Die Verfolgung und Ermordung der europäischen Juden*, ed. Israel Gutman et al. (Berlin, 1993) vol. 1, pp. 417–18.

**4** Jizchak Schwersenz, *Die versteckte Gruppe. Ein jüdischer Lehrer erinnert sich an Deutschland* (Berlin, 1988), p. 91.

**5** Michael Kreutzer, *Die Suche nach einem Ausweg, der es ermöglicht, in Deutschland als Mensch zu leben. Zur Geschichte der Widerstandsgruppen um Herbert Baum*, in: *Juden im Widerstand*, ed. W. Löhken and W. Vathke (Berlin, 1993), p. 95 ff.

**6** Schwersenz, *Die versteckte Gruppe*, p. 94.

**7** Leonie und Walter Frankenstein, interviewed by Barbara Schieb and Martina Voigt, Berlin 14 July, 1991. All of their quotes in this article are drawn from the (unpublished) sixteen-page transcript of the audio interview.

**8** This would have been the house at number 14, which is still standing. A memorial plaque recalls its former function.

**9** She called him Peter, but for the official birth certificate she chose the name Uri from the list of authorized Jewish first names (see chap. 1).

**10** On the Gemeinschaft für Frieden und Aufbau, see Herman-Friede, *Für Freudensprünge*; and Barbara Schieb, "Die Gemeinschaft für Frieden und Aufbau," in *Juden im Widerstand*, ed. Löhken and Vathke, pp. 37–82.

**11** According to an indictment against members of the "Europäische Union" (European Union), a resistance group led by Robert Havemann, the group supported a couple named Michailowitsch, later arrested. Despite the spelling difference, it is likely that this was the same couple. See Heinrich-W. Wörmann, *Widerstand in Charlottenburg*, vol. 5 of *Gedenkstätte Deutscher Widerstand* (Berlin, 1991), p. 112.

**12** Edith and Kurt Hirschfeldt married in 1945 and emigrated to the United States in 1948. Following Kurt's death in 1971 Edith returned to Berlin, where she died in 1995. Between 1991 and 1995, I had many conversations with her.

**13** Using a false identity, Gertrud Scharff had responded to a job notice from the Bauer Company at Königsallee 23 and worked there as a secretary. Over time, Mr. Ketzer found out his secretary's true identity. Walter Frankenstein later learned that Mr. Ketzer was the head of the Reichsstelle Chemie (Reich Department for Chemistry). Gertrud Scharff and the Frankenstein family concealed their Jewish identities from one another, although they lived in the same building and received assistance from the same helper.

**14** See chapter 15 above and Peter Wyden, *Stella: One Woman's True Tale of Evil, Betrayal, and Survival in Hitler's Germany* (New York, 1992).

**15** Another survivor, Heinrich Liebrecht describes his own arrest in connection with the discovery of an operation for forging passports. See Heinrich Liebrecht, *"Nicht mitzuhassen, mitzulieben bin ich da." Mein Weg durch die Hölle des Dritten Reiches* (Freiburg, 1990), pp. 45–76.

**16** Prostitutes often figure in the accounts of people who lived underground, mostly in a positive and helpful way. Inge Deutschkron has written about some of these in *Sie blieben im Schatten. Ein Denkmal für "stille Helden"* (Berlin, 1996), pp. 119–25.

**17** There is still no exact figure of how many people survived by living illegally. According to the research carried out by Martina Voigt and myself, there were more than 1,500.

**18** List I, List of Jews registered in Berlin following Allied liberation, August 1945, p. 38; CJA 5 A 1. Arthur Katz was born in 1910 in Flatow. According to the Jewish Community list of 1947, he was still living at Emser Straße 16. The Frankensteins state that he worked for the RIAS (Radio in the American Sector) and later emigrated to England.

**19** An extreme example is that of a married couple named Krakauer, who cite some sixty helpers. See footnote 1 (Krakauer).

**20** More than seven hundred Berlin residents were honored by the Berlin Senate between 1958 and 1966 in the course of the *Unbesungene Helden* (Unsung Heroes) campaign. Up to the present, all other German helpers have been awarded the *Bundesverdienstkreuz* (the Federal Republic's Cross of the Order of Merit). Since 1953, the Israeli memorial site at Yad Vashem in Jerusalem has honored all proven helpers throughout Europe as "The Righteous among the Nations." It is the highest honor that non-Jews can receive from the State of Israel. The criteria for the group of people to receive the honors are similarly high for all the different types of honor awarded.

**21** It will never be possible to establish the number of people who actually went underground. The estimates for the greater Berlin area lie between five and ten thousand Jews.

**22** See Barbara Schieb and Martina Voigt, "Der Widerstand der Ohnmächtigen. Untergetauchte Juden und ihre Helfer in der NS-Zeit," in *Die Neue Gesellschaft, Frankfurter Hefte* (February 1998), pp. 163 ff. As in this joint paper, the current chapter is based on detailed discussions with Martina Voigt, to whom I would like to extend my thanks. The change of perspective can be found in some articles included in a recent publication edited by Wolfgang Benz, *Überleben im 3. Reich, Juden im Untergrund und ihre Helfer* (Munich, 2003).

**23** Nominated by the Frankensteins, Edith Hirschfeldt was honored by Yad Vashem as one of the "Righteous among the Nations" in 1994 in Berlin.

# Chapter Seventeen

## Banished from the Fatherland: How Hans Rosenthal Survived the Nazi Regime

MICHAEL SCHÄBITZ

"Looking back on my life," wrote Hans Rosenthal in his 1982 autobiography, "the help I received from the three women from the Trinity Garden Allotments—Mrs. Jauch, Mrs. Schönebeck, and Mrs. Harndt—has made it possible for me to live uninhibited in Germany up until today, after a time that was so terrible for us Jews. It has allowed me to feel German and to be a citizen of this country without hatred. For these women risked their lives for me." Protected by these three "completely normal" women, the young Hans Rosenthal lived underground in Berlin from March 1943 to April 1945. They shielded him from deportation, and from near-certain death in an extermination camp. "I was not related to them. They knew me only in passing, if at all. They could have been indifferent to me. But they were good and righteous people, they were Germans, just as I once was—and just as I have once again become, now that the nightmare of National Socialism has passed from our fatherland."[1]

Hans Rosenthal, who was born in Berlin in 1925, survived to become a celebrated and beloved television host in Germany in the postwar years. He had just turned twenty at the time of Berlin's liberation. His family originally lived with his mother's parents at Winsstrasse 63 in the Prenzlauer Berg district. Hans's father, Kurt Rosenthal, had been a bank clerk for Deutsche Bank. His mother, Else Rosenthal, née Isaac, looked after Hans and his younger brother Gert, born in 1932. Along with childhood's pleasant experiences, grief and suffering soon became part of young Hans's everyday life. At the age of two, Gert fell ill with polio. Despite successful treatment he remained sickly and weak.

Hans's father, who had for many years suffered a kidney ailment, died in September 1937. Hans Rosenthal suspects that the anti-Jewish measures of the period contributed to his father's early death. "The bank where my father worked initially allowed him to keep his job. But in 1935 he was transferred to the headquarters and given only menial tasks. He was dismissed in 1937. . . . Although Deutsche Bank acted nobly, considering the circumstances at the

**Figure 17.1** Kurt Rosenthal (1900–37)

**Figure 17.2** Else Isaac Rosenthal (1899–1941)

time, and showed courage in keeping its Jewish employees on as late as 1937 (my father was one of the last to be dismissed), the discrimination completely undermined his already weak constitution and made his kidneys worse. He suffered indescribably from the ostracism. It made him sicker than he already was."[2]

At the time of his father's death, Hans was a pupil at the Jewish middle school on Grosse Hamburger Strasse, and his performance at school began to decline considerably.[3] No doubt, other circumstances contributed as well. German Jews as a whole were suffering an extraordinary level of discrimination and defamation, and Hans, too, would have witnessed a dramatic shrinking of career opportunities available to him.[4] After finishing middle school and completing a one-year apprenticeship in the basics of carpentry and metalwork, from the spring of 1940 Hans Rosenthal moved on to a Zionist-run vocational *Hachshara* (preparatory) center in the countryside. Here in Jessen (Niederlausitz) the fifteen-year-old received agricultural training. He hoped—in vain—to be able to emigrate to Palestine with the Youth Aliyah organization (see chap. 7).

After the Jessen center was closed, Hans Rosenthal was brought to the former *Hachshara* farm in Neuendorf, which had been converted by the Nazis into an agricultural labor camp. He worked as a forced laborer in the municipal graveyard in nearby Fürstenwalde. During this time, his mother became seriously ill. She died on November 8, 1941. Hans now did all he could to return to his younger brother Gert, who was housed in the Jewish orphanage at Schönhauser

**Figure 17.3**
Hans Rosenthal at
his father's grave
in the Jewish cemetery
in Weissensee

Allee 162. A memo dated December 20, 1941, from the Reichsvereinigung to the
Berlin Jewish Community describes the bond between the two boys.

> Re.: Hans Israel Rosenthal, born April 2, 1925.
> This youth, who is currently deployed as a laborer at the Neuendorf agricultural
> camp, would like to return to Berlin, as he has recently lost his mother and still
> has a younger brother, nine years of age, who is in the Auerbachsche orphanage
> there. He wants to be with his brother whatever the circumstances, and, above
> all, does not want to be separated from him in the case of emigration. Is there the
> possibility of him being housed together with his brother at the Auerbachsche
> orphanage? He would have to participate in labor deployment here.
>     We would be most grateful for a prompt reply, as the boy is really suffering
> from the separation from his brother following the death of the mother."[5]

In January 1942 Hans received permission to move to the orphanage. While Gert
went to school and had to remain with his group at all times, Hans was a forced
laborer in Alfred Hanne's metal packaging factory. The brothers only had time

**Figure 17.4**
The brothers Gert and Hans Rosenthal, around 1940

together on weekends, which they usually spent with their grandparents, Max and Agnes Rosenthal.[6]

The older boy apparently found it very difficult to get used to life in the orphanage. A report from the orphanage directors indicates that he received many disciplinary warnings. Finally, in summer 1942, when he broke the rules by traveling to Fürstenberg to visit friends from the Neuendorf camp, the orphanage directors transferred him that August to the Jewish Youth Home at Rosenthaler Strasse 26.[7]

Expulsion from the Jewish orphanage saved Hans Rosenthal's life. The orphanage was closed down on October 19, 1942, and its inmates, including the ten-year-old Gert Rosenthal, were deported to Riga. Gert perished. His precise date of death is unknown.[8]

IN NOVEMBER 1942 the metal packaging firm sent Hans Rosenthal out of Berlin to work in the branch located in Torgelow. Once again, the move spared him deportation; his Jewish co-workers at the main branch in the capital's Weissensee district were arrested in the course of the late-February *Fabrik-Aktion* and deported at the beginning of March 1943.[9] After such close calls, Hans was all too aware of danger on the horizon. "Although at the time I still did not know what was in store for us, I was slowly gripped by a mortal fear. There was nothing to suggest that Torgelow would remain a little oasis of survival. I thought of running away and of going into hiding."[10]

At the end of March 1943, Hans Rosenthal did run away. He returned briefly to his grandparents in Berlin, but could not of course stay with them. On his grandmother's advice, he asked a family acquaintance of extremely modest means, Mrs. Jauch, if she would take him in. She lived in a garden cottage at the Trinity (Dreieinigkeit) Garden Allotments in the Lichtenberg district of Berlin and eked out a living by selling clothes. Despite having little money and space, and despite the risk it posed to her own life, Mrs. Jauch took Hans into her home and shared her small house and her meals with him. The cottage had a tiny lean-to, which was reached through a concealed door and was otherwise unnoticeable. Here Hans Rosenthal lived for almost a year and a half.

Rosenthal, a talented athlete with an unbounded desire for freedom, naturally found it extremely difficult to keep quiet for days, weeks, and months in a tiny hiding place with nothing to do. His best hours were during the nightly bombing raids. "Only then, when the others who were higher up in the pecking order sat trembling in the bunkers . . . , did I feel safe. My heart beat faster when the

85.

Mein Lebenslauf.

Ich, Hans Rosenthal bin am 2.4.25. geb. Meine Kindheit verlief bis zum 6. Lebensjahre normal. Ich besuchte dann die 58. Volksschule. Nachdem ich die Schule m 4 Jahre besucht hatte, wurde ich auf die jüd. Mittelschule umgeschult. In dieser Zeit trat ich in einen Sportklub ein. Mit 13 Jahren verlor ich meinen Vater. Er war mir in jeder Beziehung insbesondere in Schulangelegenheiten, einer Mensch, der mich auf meine Pflicht hinwies. Nach seinem Tode vernachlässigte ich sehr die Schule. Mein Wunsch in die Vorlehre zu gehen wurde dann auch bald erfüllt. 1 Jahr blieb ich in der Vorlehre wo ich die Anfänge der Schlosserei - und Tischlerei erlernte. Allerdings war sonst mein ganzes Denken nur auf fußball eingestellt und ging ich nicht so mit Interesse an die Arbeit. Nach diesem Jahr kam ich in die Umschichtung Niederschönhausen. In dieser Zeit ging ich abends immer noch in die Alijah-Schule. Meine Ideen waren folgende. Schlosser wurde damals jeder zweite Jude, besonderes Interesse hatte ich an diesem Beruf auch nicht. Allerdings hatte ich viel Interesse an Landarbeit. Und so ging ich auf Hachschara. Den Zionismus als ernst-zunehmende Bewegung lernte ich erst dort kennen. Langsam verband ich mich auch mit dieser Idee. Als dann Jessen aufgelöst worden war, kam ein Teil von uns nach Neuendorf. Wir kamen dort mit anderen (Gewrot) Gruppen zusammen. Und da unsere Erziehung eine andere war als die der anderen Gruppen konnte ich keine Fühlung mit Ihnen bekommen. Zu dieser Zeit starb meine Mutter und war mein Bruder, der sehr an mir hängt, in Berlin allein. Ich gab dadurch ungerne mein Landarbeit auf und zog nach Berlin zu meinem Bruder ins Waisenhaus. Da ich aber noch nie solch ein Heimleben kannte, fiel mir das Einleben erst schwer. Nach dem ich mich dort längere Zeit dann war beging ich eine kleine Dummheit. Die Folge davon war, ich sollte ins Lehrlingsheim. Da ich aber mit meinem Bruder zusammen sein wollte, ging ich ungerne ins Heim. Nun bin ich hier und mein Lebenslauf ist beendet.

Hans Rosenthal

**Figure 17.5** A handwritten *Lebenslauf* (curriculum vitae), which dates to the time of Hans Rosenthal's move to the Jewish Youth Home in August 1942, shortly after he was expelled from the orphanage. In it, the seventeen-year-old describes that his "childhood was normal up until my sixth year." He mentions that, after transferring to the Jewish middle school in fifth grade, he entered a sports club. "I lost my father when I was thirteen. . . . After his death I fell very behind in school." He admits that, after leaving to learn carpentry and metalwork, "all of my thoughts were devoted to soccer and I had little interest for work. His first encounter with Zionism came through the Aliyah school, which he attended in the evenings. "I thought the following: every other Jew was a mechanic [*Schlosser*] at the time, and I had no particular interest in that profession. But I was very interested in farming. And so I went on the *Hachshara* [farm, in Jessen]. There for the first time I got to know Zionism as a movement worth taking seriously. Slowly I, too, attached myself to its ideas. Because Jessen was closed, a few of us went on to [the farm at] Neuendorf and we were joined with other . . . groups. Since our education had been different from that of the other groups, it didn't agree with me at all." He then mentions his mother's death and his move back to Berlin to join his little brother "who is very attached to me" at the Jewish orphanage. The biography concludes: "Because I hadn't yet known life in such a home, it was very hard to get used to it at first. After I had been there for a while, I did something dumb. I left the house against my will, since I wanted to be with my brother. Now I am here and that is the end of my *Lebenslauf*."

303

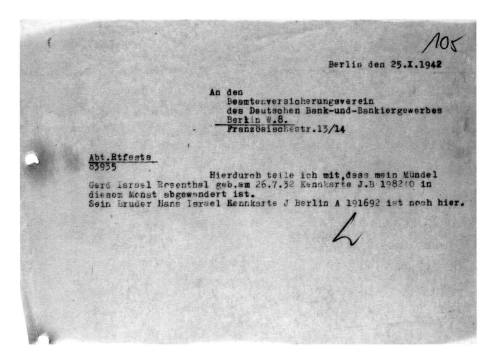

**Figure 17.6** Carbon copy of the letter in which Rosenthal's official guardian informs the pension insurance authorities of young Gert Rosenthal's "emigration"—that is, the deportation. "His brother, Hans Rosenthal, . . . is still here."

sirens announced an air raid with their rising and falling wailing tone. As soon as the others had disappeared into the bunker I went, I ran, I raced out. . . . In the summer I would lie in the grass, put my arms behind my head, and look out into the Berlin night sky. Then life was almost beautiful. . . . They [the bombers] signified life to me. Their vapor trails were beacons from a better world where I, too, could live in freedom."[11]

Hans did not want to be deported under any circumstances; he would rather have died. When an Allied bomb attack in fact damaged the Allottments, two Nazi officials came to the cottage. Hans hid under his bed. As both men sat on the bed and talked to Mrs. Jauch, "I was stiff with fear. Dust that I had breathed in from the floor was tickling my throat and I wanted to cough. I held my breath. I had brought a knife with me under the bed just in case. I had made up my mind: if they discovered me, I would take one of them with me into the next world!"[12] Yet it did not come to this.

With a small crystal radio set that Mrs. Jauch had obtained for him, Hans Rosenthal was able to listen to Goebbel's incendiary speeches, Wehrmacht reports, and sometimes, BBC German-language broadcasts. On a map of Europe, he marked the Allied fronts approaching the Reich borders with little red and blue flags.[13]

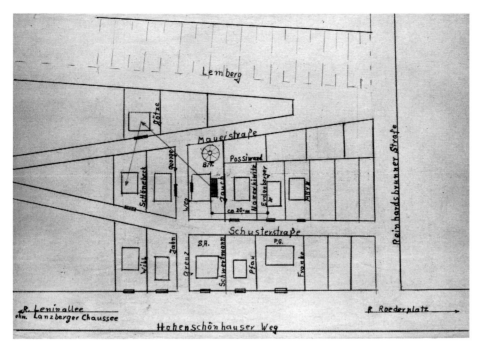

**Figure 17.7** Hans Rosenthal's drawing of the site plan of the garden allotment area. "H.R." marks the lean-to attached to Frau Jauch's cottage in which Hans Rosenthal lived for almost a year and a half.

IN THE MEANTIME, the wheels of bureaucracy turned slowly. As orphans, Gert and Hans had been assigned a guardian by the Jewish Community. Their first guardian was Fritz Lamm, who was later replaced by an Oskar Guttmann. However, the city's Family Welfare Department (Prenzlauer Berg district) remained officially responsible for the boys. At the end of May 1943 it inquired of the Jewish Community as to the whereabouts of Hans Rosenthal. Nobody knew. Fritz Lamm had been murdered,[14] Oskar Guttmann deported,[15] and a third guardian had not been appointed. The question was then put to the Hanne Company in Torgelow, where Rosenthal had last worked.

"Hans Israel Rosenthal was transferred back to our Berlin branch on March 26, 1943," replied the company in a letter dated June 15, 1943, "and as far as we know after a few days at work he did not turn up again. It is presumed that R.[osenthal] as well as the other Jewish laborers employed there were seized by the Stapo in the course of the emigration process. As with other employers, we have not received any news from there. R.'s *Arbeitsbuch* [work book—a compulsory record of work and training] was confiscated by the employment office on Fontane-Promenade in Berlin, so it is presumed that he has emigrated."[16]

The Jewish Community accepted this supposition without checking up on it and informed the Family Welfare Department, the chief finance office, and other institutions that Hans Rosenthal had "emigrated"—that is, that he had been deported. Whereupon the inheritance of Hans and Gert Rosenthal—amounting to a little more than RM 1,000—was duly transferred to the head of finance, and the guardianship file was closed.

One suspicious employee at the chief finance office carried out some research of his own, however, and on November 5, 1943, reported to the Gestapo's Berlin regional office that, "According to my inquiries, the aforementioned Jew [Hans Rosenthal] had moved away to an unknown address and is probably on the run."[17] It is not known whether the Gestapo then made concerted efforts to look for Hans Rosenthal. He does not mention anything about his grandparents being interrogated.

THE SUDDEN DEATH OF Mrs. Jauch in the summer of 1944 brought another great blow: "I lost a mother for the second time."[18] It meant, moreover, that Hans needed a new hiding place. Mrs. Harndt, the only neighbor aware of his circumstances up to then, could not take him into her home because of her husband's Communist past, which meant that he himself was under observation from the Gestapo. Desperate, Hans asked for the help of another neighbor, Mrs. Schönebeck. She was indeed prepared to take him in, even though, as Rosenthal relates, staying with her almost starved him to death. Mrs. Schönebeck was even poorer than Mrs. Jauch, and Hans was obliged to inform more of the neighbors of his presence, despite the great risk in doing so. Indeed, he was lucky that nobody betrayed him and that he was able to experience liberation by the Red Army in April 1945.[19]

Even then, Rosenthal's difficulties did not end. A misunderstanding shortly after liberation almost cost him his life.

I then returned to the Trinity Allotments with my "yellow star" and was suddenly surrounded by some Russians at the waterworks. They pointed their machine guns at me. I pointed to my star and smiled, although my heart was in my mouth. What was wrong with them? Their threatening stance left no doubt that they intended to put me up against the wall and shoot me. I was violently shoved against a wall. I stood there with my hands up and did not know what was going on. . . . Just then an officer came cycling up. He stopped, got off his bicycle and went past the soldiers toward me. . . . The officer was a Jew. A weight was lifted from my heart. He asked me in Yiddish if I was also a Jew. "Yes," I said, "I'm a Jew. Not an SS man. I was in hiding . . ." I was stammering from pure fear, since one of the men surrounding me had uttered a word that sounded like "SS." The officer remained suspicious. He demanded that I say the profession of faith, in Hebrew. As I recited it, I felt like I understood the meaning for the first time: *Shema Yisrael Adonai Elohenu Adonai Echad,* "Hear O Israel, the Lord Our God, the Lord Is One."

The officer seemed to be moved. He shook my hand and looked down at the ground in silence. "You are a Jew," he said after a long pause. "You can go." "Take that star off," he continued. "Why?" I asked. "You were lucky," said my savior. "This division liberated the concentration camp at Majdanek. Some of the SS guards there had taken the "yellow star" from the clothes of the prisoners and attached them to their own clothes. When we discovered that, the order was to immediately shoot anyone we encountered wearing such a star."[20]

On other occasions, too, Hans's experience of Soviet soldiers was less than positive, but in dealing with them, he was able to pay back some of the debt he owed to the women who had saved his life. "When the Russians came, I was able to say thank-you to the women. I shielded them when they were threatened with rape. Once I was beaten up badly for this, but it was a price I was glad to pay."[21]

THE MANY HOURS he had spent listening to the radio in hiding had kindled Hans Rosenthal's desire to work in broadcasting: "I wanted to go to a radio station when it was all over. To make radio programs! The 'right ones.' The free. The respectable. They were to be political broadcasts."[22]

With this attitude and as a convinced democrat he soon encountered difficulties at the Berliner Rundfunk (Berlin Radio), which was controlled by the Soviets, and in 1948 he moved to the RIAS (Radio in the American Sector) broadcasting company. Here he began a career as a quizmaster. Later, with shows such as *Dalli, Dalli* (On the double!) and *Rate mal mit Rosenthal* (Guess it with Rosenthal), Hans Rosenthal became one of Germany's most popular emcees. He was also active in the Jewish Community. In 1971 he became chairman of the Berlin Jewish Community's Assembly of Representatives and, in 1973, a member of the directorate of the Central Council of Jews in Germany (Zentralrat der Juden in Deutschland). As president of the football club Tennis-Borussia Berlin, he remained true to his passion for football.

Hans Rosenthal died on February 10, 1987, in Berlin and was buried in the Berlin Jewish Community cemetery on Scholzplatz.

The question of how the orphan Hans Rosenthal managed to escape the deadly persecution of the National Socialist regime cannot really be answered. A great many coincidences made it possible for him to survive. His unconditional will for freedom, his youthful rebelliousness, and his realistic view of the circumstances also contributed to his survival, along with his cheerfulness and optimism, which allowed him to keep living despite the many blows of destiny.

**1** Hans Rosenthal, *Zwei Leben in Deutschland* (Bergisch-Gladbach, 1982), pp. 79–80.

**2** Ibid., pp. 34–35.

**3** Ibid., p. 24; CJA 1, 75 Be 2, no. 412, no. 14144, sheet 85.

**4** Joseph Walk, *Jüdische Schule und Erziehung im Dritten Reich* (Frankfurt am Main, 1991), pp. 63–66, 154–55; Clemens Vollnhals, "Jüdische Selbsthilfe bis 1938," in *Die Juden in Deutschland, 1933–1945. Leben unter nationalsozialistischer Herrschaft,* ed. Wolfgang Benz (Munich, 1988), pp. 314–411, here p. 389.

**5** CJA 1, 75 Be 2, Nr. 412, no. 14144, sheet 16.

**6** The grandparents were Max (1866–1946) and Agnes Rosenthal, née Fischer (1873–1945). Agnes Rosenthal converted to Judaism before marrying but left the faith again during the Nazi period. She thus was considered non-Jewish. Her husband was exempt from deportation because of the mixed marriage. The grandparents on the mother's side, Isaac Wilhelm (b. 1867) and Clara, née Benschner (b. 1874), had died in 1939 and 1941, respectively.

**7** CJA 1, 75 Be 2, no. 412, no. 14144, sheets 83–84 ff., 92. Shortly afterward the youth home appears to have moved to Rosenstrasse 2–4, sheets 86, 98, 129–30.

**8** Recent research has revealed that all of the people on this transport from Berlin, with the exception of 81 men, were murdered on arrival in Riga on October 22, 1942. See

Wolfgang Scheffler and Diana Schulle, editors, *Buch der Erinnerung. Die ins Baltikum deportierten deutschen, österreichischen und tschechoslowakischen Juden* (Munich, 2003).

**9** At least nine Jewish forced laborers working at the Hanne firm were deported between February 19 and March 17, 1943.

**10** Rosenthal, *Zwei Leben,* p. 57.

**11** Ibid., p. 64.

**12** Ibid., p. 75.

**13** Ibid., p. 67.

**14** Together with six or seven other employees of the Jewish Community, Dr. Fritz Lamm (1876–1942) was a victim of the hostage shootings carried out by the Gestapo on November 20, 1942, in connection with the *Gemeinde-Aktion* (see chap. 18).

**15** Oskar Guttmann (1885–194?) was deported with the eighty-ninth old-age transport to Theresienstadt on May 19, 1943, and later to Auschwitz, where he was murdered.

**16** CJA 1, 75 Be 2, no. 412, no. 14144, sheet 184 b.

**17** Rosenthal, Hans file, A Rep. 092, No. 31966, n.p, LAB.

**18** Rosenthal, *Zwei Leben,* p. 79.

**19** Ibid., pp. 79–88.

**20** Ibid., pp. 88–90.

**21** Ibid., pp. 82–83.

**22** Ibid., p. 96.

# 10

# Jewish
# Organizations

# Chapter Eighteen

The Fine Line between Responsible
Action and Collaboration:
The Reichsvereinigung der Juden
in Deutschland and the Jewish
Community in Berlin, 1938–45

BEATE MEYER

## Part 1: The Establishment and Role of the Reichsvereinigung and Jewish Community

The Reich Representation of German Jews—Reichsvertretung der deutschen Juden—was founded on September 17, 1933, to respond to the newly elected Nazi regime's repressive policies. Led by Leo Baeck, the Reichsvertretung aimed to serve as a coordination point and give voice to German Jews both within the National Socialist state and with regard to foreign Jewish organizations.[1] Its concern was to promote the internal life of the Jewish Community (instruction, education, training, welfare, economic aid, and emigration), to maintain its institutions, and to at least alleviate, if not avert, the state's anti-Jewish measures through joint intervention.

When, however, on March 28, 1938, the Jewish Communities lost their status as public corporations and had to reestablish themselves as registered associations with formal membership, the Reichsvertretung sought a solution to counter the feared decrease in members.[2] The idea was that all members of the religious organizations could belong to an umbrella association, which would provide a kind of financial compensation in return.[3] Nazi leaders initially opposed this but at the end of 1938 decided that it would be sensible to commission a Jewish central organization with the task of arranging Jewish emigration as well as finance.[4]

Meanwhile, a shift in responsibility for the "Jewish question" was underway within the regime. Before the Reich Security Main Office (Reichssicherheitshauptamt [RSHA]) was established in September 1939, the SD (Sicherheitsdienst, Security Service of the SS) had already collected a broad range of information on Jewish organizations and had presented its concept of "forced emigration" as a "solution to the Jewish question." However, it was not until after the pogrom of November 9, 1938, that the SS and SD took overall control of the administration of "Jewish policy" (*Judenpolitik*) according to this concept.[5] With a constant focus on inducing emigration, the SD favored Zionist organizations, opposed "assimilationist" ones (particularly the Centralverein—the Central Organization of German Citizens of Jewish Faith),[6] and tried to cause a split among the Jewish groups.[7]

From the Nazi point of view, Adolf Eichmann had been successful in Vienna with his Zentralstelle für jüdische Auswanderung—Central Office for Jewish Emigration—to which Jewish organizations had been assigned during the Anschluss.[8] Within a few months the Zentralstelle had driven over 40 percent of Austrian and stateless Jews from Austrian territory.[9] It became a model organization for the Altreich. A similar office was to be established in Berlin to set in motion a process of mass emigration within the shortest possible time—without bureaucratic obstacles. Here, too, emigration would be financed by the victims themselves. In January 1939 Hermann Göring, then in charge of the "Jewish Question," announced the establishment of a *Zentralstelle* for the Altreich. That July he stated that a similar office would be set up in Prague for the protectorates of Bohemia and Moravia.[10]

The Reichsvertretung's proposal to form a "Reich Organization" (*Reichsverband*) did not come to fruition at first on account of the events of the pogrom of November 1938.[11] The organization eventually came into being in July 1939 with the formal establishment of the Reich Association of Jews in Germany—Reichsvereinigung der Juden in Deutschland—implemented by the Reich Citizenship Law. The Jewish proposal had thus been accepted. But its main elements were modified. The Jewish Communities had no rights of codetermination or control; representatives were not elected but appointed; and the RSHA and the Gestapo were to act as its "supervisory authority." To this extent, the Reichsvereinigung did not represent a mere continuation of the Reichsvertretung but rather a clear break: the former, a democratic organization, was now under Nazi control. In the words of Saul Friedländer, the Reichsvereinigung "for all practical purposes" became "the first of the Jewish Councils, the Nazi-controlled organizations that, in most parts of occupied Europe, were to carry out the orders of their German masters regarding life and death in their respective communities."[12]

The Reichsvereinigung's responsibilities were initially similar to those of the Reichsvertretung. These included social and professional support measures such as "emigration assistance," welfare, schooling, vocational training, and retraining.[13] The Jewish Community and the finance department also remained intact. In 1941, its tasks were almost entirely restricted to welfare and participation in the deportation process. These included producing statistical lists of Jews, physically concentrating them in certain areas, and implementing their widespread financial impoverishment by the regime.

About 16,000 Berlin Jews emigrated from Germany in the years 1938 and 1939, almost all with the help of the offices and advice centers of the Jewish organizations.[14] The organizations provided information about the requirements of the host countries and provided language and training courses in new professions, among other things.[15]

After the November pogrom, Jewish pupils were no longer allowed to attend state schools and had to transfer to Jewish schools. The Reichsvereinigung supported the education system within the city of Berlin and the entire Altreich. In 1940, at a time when emigration had brought about a steep decrease in the number of schoolchildren, some 2,200 pupils were still attending Jewish educational establishments in the Reich capital.[16] Between 1938 and 1942 the Reichsvereinigung continually had to move, merge, and close schools. It was, moreover, under constant pressure to make financial cuts and to sell the real estate transferred to it under property law when Jewish organizations were dissolved.

On June 20, 1942, the date of the Nazi decree that completely abolished the Jewish educational system, there were six elementary, middle and high schools open in Berlin.[17] Some Jewish pupils had also attended a few schools maintained by foreign organizations. There was also the Family School for Non-Aryan Christians (Familienschule für nichtarische Christen) run with the Reichsvereinigung's approval by the aid office of a Lutheran pastor named Grüber for the children of dissidents and baptized children who were nonetheless classed as Jews according to Nazi racial definitions. The Jewish schools were not only hindered by the lack of resources but also by the emigration of many teachers, to say nothing of everyday persecution such as the ban on using public transportation.

The Reichsvereinigung also sought to provide training opportunities for young people so that they could obtain professional qualifications and thereby increase their chances of emigration.[18] It offered courses such as manual apprenticeships and kindergarten teacher training until March 1942.[19] Up until July 1941 the Reichsvereinigung had maintained thirty-one agricultural and eighteen technical training companies, including three vocational colleges and a music institute.[20] The Zionist *Hachshara* agricultural centers were of particular significance. These prepared people for emigration to Palestine (see chap. 7 by Chana Schütz). The Nazis, too, showed an interest in this vocational retraining. The Reichsvereinigung was thus able to use estates on Lake Wannsee, for example,

*In the course of time many of my classmates emigrated. In the final years, when it was no longer possible to emigrate, fewer pupils came to school almost each day. They had been collected the night before. I heard terrible stories—that the people in the train starved, that they were hit, that they were gassed in trucks—but we believed none of these things.*

EUGEN HERMAN-FRIEDE, 1999

to provide training in gardening, forestry, and agriculture.[21] After the remaining centers had been dissolved, the RSHA retained part of the Wannsee center as a forced labor camp for Zionist youth.

Among so many centers that focused on manual training, the College for Jewish Studies had a special role because of its focus on Judaism and philosophy. The students were primarily young men who had been excluded from state universities and colleges. Likewise, the lecturers had lost their jobs. The subjects taught at the institute gave many students the feeling of living on an "island" untouched by the times. But the reality of persecution often broke through, for example, when students were called in to serve as curates (*Hilfsprediger*) by the Community or were drafted into forced labor by the employment office.[22] Other Jews also attended the lectures—particularly Leo Baeck's lectures—as auditors. The institute, which had been compulsorily renamed the "Teaching Institution" (*Lehranstalt*), was abolished in June 1942 with the general termination of the Jewish educational system.

The Jewish Community continued to be responsible for religious guidance after 1938. In 1937 there were still seventeen synagogues and seventeen prayer halls in Berlin, with a total congregation of some 37,000.[23] "Religion had an incredible status at the time. The synagogues were packed when particular rabbis spoke. Religion was the only thing the Jews had left. . . . People streamed into the synagogues to find comfort and encouragement. Religion was a rock in a time of need."[24]

The extremely active religious life that had emerged as a result of the ever-increasing Nazi persecution was, however, destroyed by the November pogrom. From then on the Gestapo intervened massively as a "supervisory authority" in Jewish religious life. The Communities traditionally sold seats in the synagogue. When at the end of August 1941 the Jewish Community wished to sell seats for the upcoming High Holidays, the Reichsvereinigung had to ask permission from the RSHA. Permission entailed the condition that, after covering costs, it would also raise at least 50 percent in additional revenue.[25]

In the summer of 1941 only three of Berlin's synagogues could still be used for worship: those on Münchner Strasse, Heidereutergasse, and Levetzowstrasse. There were, in addition, a few prayer halls, plus the hall of representatives at the New Synagogue on Oranienburger Strasse.[26] To enable Jewish laborers who had been forced to work on the Sabbath to attend services, the Community coordinated services to fit their working hours.[27] It was risky to attend services, however, since the Gestapo often took advantage of such gatherings as an opportunity to abuse and arrest worshippers. The synagogue, once a place of comfort, had become a place of danger, and Community members increasingly avoided it. Soon it was only possible to worship in private. After December 15, 1942, public announcements of religious services were forbidden.[28]

## The Relationship between the Reichsvereinigung and the Jewish Community

The headquarters of the Reichsvereinigung remained in Berlin, but its organizational structure changed at the lower levels.[29] Newly established "district offices" were now assigned to the Jewish Communities. The district offices did not operate autonomously but had to have all their plans and personnel matters approved by the main office, which was in turn directly under RSHA control. Until it was closed down in summer 1943, the headquarters was in charge of the *Jüdisches Nachrichtenblatt*, a strictly censored newspaper that circulated new instructions from its "supervisory authority" as well as details of religious events. The paper also had an extensive classifieds section and provided tips on day-to-day life (see chap. 6 by Clemens Maier).

Operating under joint management, the Berlin Reichsvereinigung served simultaneously as national headquarters and regional office. The Jewish Community of Berlin existed alongside it, remaining formally independent until January 29, 1943. On April 2, 1941, the Community was forced to change its name to the Jüdisches Kultusvereinigung (Jewish Religious Association, JKV).[30] The institutions were housed in separate premises. The Reichsvereinigung operated from Kantstrasse, while the Jewish Community offices were near the New Synagogue on Oranienburger Strasse.

Up to 1939–40 the Reichsvereinigung and Jewish Community of Berlin had a tense relationship. This was particularly evident in the relations between the chairman of the Berlin Community, Heinrich Stahl, and the board of the more secular Reichsvereinigung, especially Leo Baeck.[31] Stahl, fearing that Community's fate could be determined by "Jews far removed from any religious beliefs,"[32] tried to retain the Community's independence and its control of previous areas of responsibility. His proposal was supported neither by the Reichsvereinigung's board nor by the RSHA; the Communities were intended to be subordinate within the Reichsvereinigung's structure, acting merely as a kind of department.[33]

Stahl ultimately resigned from both boards, but the RSHA prevented his emigration. Hermann Simon has suggested that Heinrich Stahl "did not want to take on anything morally dubious, anything that may have associations, however

*It was freezing in the room. . . . Then we got a coat, sat down, and sang songs, and we said afterward that it would be nice to celebrate Chanukah the next time, when it was all over. . . . And we could then later celebrate freely again in our country.*

EVA FRANK-KUNSTMANN, 1999

distant, with collaboration."[34] Simon mentions Siegmund Weltlinger—another member of the board of the Jewish Community in the late 1930s—who attributed Stahl's deportation on June 11, 1942, to the fact that he "valiantly refused to cover certain measures."[35] Unfortunately, Weltlinger gave no further details about these "measures," and there is no explanation from Stahl either. Nor could Stahl fully escape the Gestapo's excessive demands. This is clear from a memo by Paul Eppstein on the funding of the first Berlin deportation transport. Eppstein states that "the former chairman of the Berlin JKV (Heinrich Israel Stahl)," asked "a range of wealthy Jews in Berlin" for contributions "on behalf of the Gestapo regional headquarters in Berlin."[36]

"For eight years I was the primary chairman of the largest Community, in Germany and I campaigned honestly and reliably for the interests of the Jews without letting the Nazis dictate their wishes to me," wrote Stahl in a letter before his deportation. Stahl harshly rebuked not only the Nazi power holders but also the Reichsvereinigung representatives as well. "I often opposed their measures. . . . In the process, I provoked the hatred of a cruel man, who in his own circles is described as the *Judengeissel* [Jewish scourge] of Europe [presumably Eichmann]. He ordered my evacuation and with this fulfilled the Reichsvereinigung's wish."[37] Stahl died of a lung disease five months after being deported to Theresienstadt.

The work of the remaining representatives of the Reichsvereinigung and the Community was both thankless and dangerous.[38] They sought to form a "buffer zone" between the Nazi state and the Jews[39] and to maintain the last remaining Jewish institutions—such as the Jewish hospitals in Berlin and Hamburg. As Nazi policy against Jews became more drastic, so the tasks of the Reichsvereinigung became more difficult—and morally questionable.

The remainder of this article examines the fine line between acting responsibly on behalf of the Jewish Community and contributing to its downfall. If a shift is to be identified, the starting point was certainly the organization's decision to participate in the first deportation, work that ranged from "preparations for emigration" to running the assembly camps. Those who worked for the Reichsvereinigung and their next of kin were temporarily spared deportation—unless they provoked the anger of a Gestapo official and were taken into "protective custody." The grace period ran out, however, in October 1942 with the *Gemeinde-Aktion*—the Nazi operation against the Community—which I will describe in detail below. By the time the Reichsvereinigung was dissolved in June 1943, all but a few of the remaining employees and the Community board had been deported.

## Part 2: Jewish Community Involvement in the Deportations

*Accommodation Advice, Questionnaires, and Index Files*

Jews were stripped of tenant protection on April 30, 1939. Thereafter the Berlin authorities, led by Albert Speer (then general building inspector), pushed for their eviction. Jewish tenants were to be housed with Jewish homeowners, and their apartments were, in turn, to accommodate non-Jews who had been obliged to move in the course of Speer's ambitious redevelopment plans to turn Berlin into "Germania."[40] The Jewish Community was burdened with the task of finding new housing for the evicted Jews. It set up an accommodation advice center headed by the lawyer Martha Mosse. The center was on Oranienburger Strasse from the summer of 1939 to November 1942; from November 1942 to January 1943, the staff had to carry out their duties from the assembly camp on Grosse Hamburger Strasse. Although the first mass wave of rehousing represented for Martha Mosse a major intervention in the private lives of those concerned, the department had at first a relatively broad scope for action. The situation was to change by October 1941 at the latest, when the advice center had to prepare the first deportation of Berlin Jews.

> It was on October 1 or 2, 1941, . . . that two board members and myself—as head of the accommodation advice center—received a phone call summoning us to the Gestapo on Burgstrasse. There Detective Secretary Prüfer put it on record that we would be immediately taken to a concentration camp if we discussed what he was about to say with third parties. . . . Mr. Prüfer then told us that the "resettlement" of the Berlin Jews was starting and that the Jewish Community had to participate in it or it would be carried out by the SA and SS—and "you know what that would be like." Several thousand Jews were to be summoned using the Jewish Community *Kataster* [tax register], and Community officials would go over Gestapo-provided questionnaires with them. The completed questionnaires then had to be submitted to the Gestapo. . . . The Jewish population was to be led to believe that this was an eviction operation. The Gestapo would then . . . put together a transport of around one thousand people, which would go to Lódz. The Jewish Community was to make sure that people on the transport were suitably clothed, and it had to provide food and ensure that the train carriages provided by the Gestapo were suitably equipped. As we were leaving, he said, "Well, it's not so easy for me to have to tell you this on Yom Kippur."[41]

The boards of the Reichsvereinigung and the Jewish Community discussed the matter the same evening and, "despite grave misgivings," decided to participate in the so-called resettlement, "because one hoped in this way to be able to do as much good as possible for those concerned."[42]

In her 1963 essay *Eichmann in Jerusalem*, Hannah Arendt criticized the "role of the Jewish leaders in the destruction of their own people," which she described as "undoubtedly the darkest chapter of the whole dark story."[43] Despite individual differences, Arendt saw the Jewish representatives as caught up in the actions, as "voluntary 'bearers of secrets,' either in order to assure quiet and prevent panic . . . or out of 'humane' considerations." Arendt wrote that "if the Jewish people had really been unorganized and leaderless, there would have been chaos and plenty of misery but the total number of victims would hardly have been between four and a half and six million people."[44] Arendt reached this view with knowledge of the subsequent murder of the deportees. She assessed all cooperation entirely in terms of the later consequences. When the boards met in October 1941, however, they presumed that resettlement—not extermination—would take place. They believed their efforts could alleviate the severity of the campaign, which they assumed would only affect a portion of the Jews. Those who were in positions of responsibility and hoped to be able to prevent anything bad from happening to their members justified their actions, as Moritz Henschel did in 1946. "One can ask: how can you let yourselves be drawn into cooperating? We cannot decide whether we did the right thing or not. But the thought that guided us was: if we do these things then they will be carried out better and less harshly than if the others do it."[45]

*Naturally one didn't know then . . . that war would break out and that I wouldn't know what would happen to my parents, where they were, or if they were alive.*

MARIANNE GIVOL, THE DAUGHTER OF MORITZ AND HILDE-GARD HENSCHEL, 1999

The Reichsvereinigung and the Jewish Community decided to cooperate "to prevent anything worse from happening." Martha Mosse received three thousand questionnaires from the Gestapo, which disguised the deportation as an "eviction operation."[46] Her department had to use the Jewish tax register to summon an appropriate number of Jews and then fill out the forms with them. A new department headed by Berta Mendelsohn was set up for this purpose. It was to make sure that there was a complete listing of people. It also had to process the documents so that "the authority . . . can take measures."[47] Subsequently the Gestapo selected a third of the three thousand forms, each one receiving a four-figure number—which turned out to be a transport number.[48] The Community got the forms back, drew up transport lists, and then returned everything to the Gestapo. The leftover forms were kept with the Gestapo for the next transports.

During these first deportations, the accommodation advice center selected names and addresses at random. Those chosen received the sixteen-page Declaration of Assets (*Vermögenserklärung*) form—which had to be completed for the authorities of the chief of finance. They also received orders to report to the synagogue on Levetzowstrasse. Also enclosed was a notice in which the JKV mentioned the possibility of depositing personal documents with the JKV and informed those concerned of the necessity to wear suitable "travel clothing." It reminded deportees to attach the "Jewish stars" to clothing per regulations but to remove the stars from all clothing they did not take with them. Above all it emphasized that it was forbidden to take along assets, and that breaches of this order would be punished. The contents of hand luggage and suitcases were also stipulated down to the last detail.[49]

From then on the Jewish Community was obliged to convert its tax register into a continuously updated system of card files. Duplicates of these files—which in the meantime filled more than one room—then had to be handed in to the Gestapo's department for Jewish matters, which, after the first deportations, drew up the transport lists on its own. The Community was in the dark as to the criteria used to assemble the later deportation lists.

Word soon spread that "resettlement," "emigration," "sending away," "evacuation," and "labor deployment abroad" were euphemisms for a completely unknown fate "in the east." As the reports of deaths piled up, more and more people on the "lists" interpreted the letters they received as a final warning and vanished underground. After a few months, the procedure was changed. Now those to be deported were picked up directly by Gestapo officials, criminal police (Kripo), and police officers (Shutzpolizei), and brought to the assembly camps.[50]

## The Assembly Camp on Levetzowstrasse

The synagogue at Levetzowstrasse 7–8, opened in 1914, had been one of three synagogues in which the Jewish Community was still permitted to hold services after 1941.[51] After the Yom Kippur services of October 1941, the Gestapo ordered the synagogue board to hand over the keys.[52] The Jewish Community was obliged to convert the premises into an assembly camp for one thousand deportees. It had to provide food and clothing for them as well as to organize auxiliary staff. Mattresses would only be available for the elderly and the frail. Younger people had to make due with the seating in the women's gallery. A room for children was also set up.

On October 16 and 17, the first arrivals to the camp stood in the pouring rain in the yard waiting to be checked in the lobby. They had to hand over all money, jewelry, and food. Community-appointed marshals (Ordner) carried the luggage to another checkpoint, where Gestapo officials weighed and searched it, confiscating items that were not permitted—or anything else that they fancied. The suitcases were assigned a transport number; deportees were given a sign with the same number. Their identity cards were withheld and only returned after deportation, marked clearly with the word "evacuated." Those assigned to the balcony had to undergo a body search in front of everyone else.

Once in the camp, inmates had to formally declare their assets, which would later be confiscated for Reich use by the head of finance. Siegmund Weltlinger described the assignment: "I sat there all night with a team of colleagues, taking down the registers of assets and drawing up lists. . . . There were heart-breaking scenes. There were constant suicides and attempted suicides. Some of the women threw themselves from the balcony and landed on the marble floor below; one could not imagine a more horrific desecration of a place of worship."[53]

The first transport of approximately a thousand Jewish Berliners left for Łódz on October 18, 1941 (see my chap. 10 and the tables included there). After arranging the first transport, the Jewish Community was forced to staff the camp with marshals, doctors, and nursing staff. It prepared food in Community kitchens. It looked after the children. Edith Dietz, who had trained as a kindergarten teacher and worked in an after-school club for Jewish schoolchildren, held this unhappy job from October 1941 until late summer 1942.

> The official sent me to the "children's room" in the synagogue's former marriage hall. Now it contained camp beds piled with straw mattresses, with a few tables and benches in the middle. To reach the children I had to go through a large room in which people were packed together, sitting or lying on the floor. The fetid air in the children's room was hard to bear. The little room could have held twenty children at the most, but there were more than seventy. The Gestapo had, moreover, crammed in all of the elderly and frail people. . . . We tried to keep the children busy. A dreadful future awaited them, and some of them already guessed this. . . . The older ones wanted to be left alone . . . . The smaller ones cried for their mothers, from whom they were cruelly separated in the same building.[54]

Two days after arriving, the detainees were given back their suitcases—a sign that their deportation was imminent.[55] During these two days, as well as during subsequent deportation processes, the marshals and nursing staff took on a particularly significant role. Marked with their white armbands, they were the only people allowed to circulate in the assembly camp or leave it. Theoretically they could help the inmates, passing messages, picking up medications, and alerting the inmates' relatives. But under threat of severe punishment the staff was bound to secrecy with regard to all events taking place in the camp (see chap. 13 by Christian Dirks). "In some cases," said Dietz in a 1999 interview, "they could be of some small help to the people they knew personally . . . But they could not help somebody they did not know—even if he wore the Jewish star! . . . They could not trust him!"[56]

The marshals thus had to wrestle with their own consciences. Neither the Reichsvereinigung nor the Jewish Community could make the decision for them. Eyewitness reports confirm that marshals often served as important intermediaries when they had social connections with the detainees.[57] Dietz, for example, often found out and passed on information about the destination of the deportation trains.[58]

Further transports followed. As Hildegard Henschel, wife of Moritz Henschel and an employee of the Jewish Community, described it in the early 1970s, "the work of the Community in the assembly camp had started to go smoothly and, as far as was possible, the terrible circumstances were alleviated."[59] Exemption from deportation was only possible in exceptional cases.

If, for example, there was concern that a candidate's health problems might impair his or her ability to go on the transport, authorities at the Jewish hospital were consulted. Dr. Walter Lustig, later a notorious figure, headed the Jewish hospital's Department to Investigate Claims for Exemption from Transport (Untersuchungsabteilung für Transportreklamationen). He managed several doctors (Jews who had, by Nazi law, been stripped of their titles and forced to call themselves "caregiver"—Behandler—instead). The staff then diagnosed candidates either "fit" or "unfit" for transport, and in the case of the latter, Lustig would check the results himself before passing them on to the Gestapo. At best, the person concerned was exempted from that particular deportation. Generally the entire procedure meant little more than postponement.[60]

Gestapo officials often arrested those who formally belonged to "protected groups"—that is, people living in mixed marriages (Mischehe) or the children of mixed-marriage partners (Mischlinge). Martha Mosse, was able to postpone such cases. In addition, over two hundred Jews were granted special protection from deportation. These were mostly artists, whose names appeared on list personally drawn up by Göring. The Gestapo was supposed to consult this list before each transport.[61]

## Part 3: 1942, Escalation of Violence, and Breakdown of Cooperation

*The Attack on the "Soviet Paradise" Exhibition and Its Consequences*

On May 18, 1942, members of a resistance group led by Herbert Baum carried out an arson attack on the Nazi propaganda exhibition Sowjetparadies in

*During the night . . . I went through the whole synagogue with a flashlight to see if anyone needed medication or something else. . . . Standing on the third floor, I looked down to the large hall below where people lay jumbled together on the floor and it resembled a huge tomb. Men, women, children, old men and women, boys and girls, it was no longer possible to distinguish them from one another.*

EDITH DIETZ, 1999, DESCRIBING THE LEVETZOWSTRASSE SYNAGOGUE, WHICH HAD BEEN CONVERTED INTO AN ASSEMBLY CAMP

Berlin.[62] Eleven people were slightly injured in the attack, which caused only a small amount of damage. The Gestapo soon found and arrested those involved, members of a group with decidedly Communist leanings that had targeted the exhibition for its anti-Soviet content. With two exceptions, the group consisted of Jews and Jewish *Mischlinge,* most of whom were sentenced to death.[63] Although only one of the participants had had any previous connection to the Reichsvereinigung or the Jewish Community, Propaganda Minister Goebbels used the attack as the pretext for a crackdown on Berlin's Jews. Goebbels won Hitler's support for a campaign of revenge. "The Führer has also given me permission to take around five hundred Jewish hostages and to respond ruthlessly with shots to any new attacks. . . . I instructed the Berlin police to draw up a list of hostages. During the course of the next week I will then order the arrests."[64]

On May 27 the Berlin Gestapo arrested Jews with "previous convictions" and took them to the Levetzowstrasse camp. Some were later released, but 154 were taken the next day to Sachsenhausen, and shot dead upon arrival. A further 96 Jews already detained in the concentration camp and mostly of Polish origin were singled out and shot that evening. Shortly afterward the relatives of the dead were summoned for deportation. On May 29 and 30 the Gestapo arrested another 250 Berlin Jews and sent them to Sachsenhausen. Those who were still alive in October 1942 were taken to Auschwitz, where they were murdered.[65]

As the reprisals were taking place, the boards of the Berlin Jewish Community, the Reichsvereinigung, the Israelite Religious Association in Vienna, and the Prague Jewish Religious Association had been ordered to gather at the RSHA, where they waited for hours with their faces to the wall. A curt explanation was eventually provided, along with the threat that further hostages would be shot if something similar to Baum's attack ever happened again.[66]

After 1945, Moritz Henschel reported that "five Germans" were killed during the attack on the exhibition.[67] Leonard Baker, a biographer of Leo Baeck, refers to the death of "five Nazis."[68] Paul Eppstein's file notes, however, make it clear that the Gestapo told the board of the Reichsvereinigung that five *Jews* had been involved in the arson attack, and that fifty Jews had been shot for each participant. If such an attack happened again, "under certain circumstances, a multiplied number of Jews will be shot."[69]

The representatives of Jewish organizations were told to pass on the warning to their members. For this purpose, the representatives drafted a short text entitled "Responsibility for the Community," which culminated in the sentence: "It should not be overlooked for an instant that each of us is responsible for all of us and that the consequences of the behavior of each individual affect the Community."[70] Although the article was written according to Gestapo instructions, the Gestapo banned its publication. The Reichsvereinigung was left with the unhappy task of sending death notices out to the relatives of those murdered.[71]

Faced with this situation, Reichsvereinigung representatives tried as best they could to prevent an escalation of the murder. Baeck instructed Norbert Wollheim, who had casual contact with Communist circles, to inform the latter of the threat posed to the Community if events were repeated. Wollheim's message met with little sympathy.[72]

The escalation of terror and the fruitless attempts to intervene underlined the powerlessness of the Reichsvereinigung and Jewish Community, neither of which had any room to maneuver. The period in which the Gestapo would inform or involve them in advance was over. They could no longer alleviate matters or argue for change. During and after the reprisal shootings, the representatives, too, were in the position of hostages. This was indeed the intention of Gauleiter Goebbels. Referring to reprisals in Bohemia and Moravia after the deadly attack on RSHA director Reinhard Heydrich, Goebbels wrote in his diary that he would act "as brutally as possible" and "conduct my campaign against the Jews in Berlin in a similar way. . . . I don't fancy the prospect of being shot in the stomach by a twenty-two-year-old Eastern Jew—such types were among those who carried out the attack on the Anti-Soviet exhibition."[73]

## The Gemeinde-Aktion

Five months later, in October, 1942, the violence escalated with the RSHA's so-called *Gemeinde-Aktion* ([Jewish] Community Operation). The Jewish staff that had been forced to organize the deportations had heretofore been spared deportation (even though some individuals had been put into "protective custody" for alleged misdemeanors). Now it, too, was drawn into the terror.

Since the start of the deportations in October 1941 both the Reichsvereinigung and the Jewish Community had intentionally sought to employ as many people as possible. Paid work in its offices and advice centers, in clothing stores, as caretakers in buildings, among other places, spared such individuals and their families from deportation. Personnel had thus not dwindled; as before, there were more than 1,500 people officially employed, not counting the wives of male workers (who carried out work without pay) and "youth helpers" (who were, however, not protected from deportation). If a department was shut down, the heads of the Community and Reichsvereinigung—who were often the same people—tried to find positions for the staff in another department. When, for example, the last Jewish schools were closed in the summer of 1942, making the department of schools superfluous, some of the teachers and principals continued to work for the Community as marshals and heads of assembly camps.

On one hand, the Community and Reichsvereinigung needed competent staff who could carry out instructions efficiently. On the other hand, they tried to protect the elderly or frail—or people unused to physical work—by giving them work them in a Jewish institution. As Martha Mosse described the situation in her memoirs, "We knew that everyone who was dismissed (unless he or she belonged to the temporarily protected groups such as people in mixed marriages) would be assigned to the next transport. This situation was particularly difficult for the [Jewish Community] board, since among the large number of employees there were of course some whose work could not, in principle, be considered of any real value."[74]

In the face of constant pressure from the Gestapo and RSHA to cut their staffs, the Community and Reichsvereinigung cited the increasing burden of work caused by new regulations from the "supervisory authority"—such as the order to hand in all typewriters, the new guidelines restricting possessions (*Verfügungsbeschränkungen*), and the implementation of "emigration transports." Such bureaucratic matters were, they claimed, very labor-intensive.[75] The guidelines meant, for example, that Jews had to obtain authorization from the Gestapo for every change in their moveable or nonmoveable properties. The applications were checked by a Reichsvereinigung official, passed on to the Gestapo, and the decision then had to be communicated to the applicant.

Despite the mountain of bureaucratic work that it had created, the Gestapo continued to demand a reduction in Community personnel.[76] Already in 1940–41, it had demanded the release of Jewish staff for forced "labor deployment" in the armaments industry. In the summer of 1942 additional "staff cuts" affected Reichsvereinigung employees, who were deported.[77] The *Gemeinde-Aktion* followed on October 20, 1942, and in November half of the welfare department's employees were "made redundant." In January, March, and May 1943, additional employees of the Community, the Reichsvereinigung, and the Jewish hospital were dismissed. Their jobs were taken over by *Mischlinge* and Jews living in mixed marriages.[78] Then, in June, a "punishment operation" first reduced the number of employees, then dissolved the Reichsvereinigung entirely. Most of those remaining were deported.

Although staff cuts were an unhappy part of the Jewish organizations' everyday life, the *Gemeinde-Aktion* of October 1942 was a particular blow. The operation's scale, the dramatic course of events, the frightening hostage-taking and brutal shootings all combined to ingrain the event in the memories of its few survivors.[79]

On October 19, 1942, Moritz Henschel, the chairman of the Berlin Jewish Community board, was summoned by telephone to the Gestapo headquarters. This happened often enough, but the chief detective secretary Franz Prüfer's aggressive tone of voice led Henschel to leave his watch, wedding ring, and other valuables on his desk—his secret danger signal to employees and his wife.[80] In fact, he returned to the Oranienburger Strasse offices with precise instructions: a major roll call of all Community staff—more than a thousand souls—was to take place the next morning. There were feverish attempts to find enough space for everyone in the building. The Community instructed all departments to summon their staff to Oranienburger Strasse 31 at 7 A.M. the next day. Indispensable emergency services such as those offered in the Jewish hospital would be on hand, though limited to the bare minimum.[81] Those who already worked on Oranienburger Strasse had to assemble in the offices and corridors in front of the offices. Staff from the other buildings were to gather in the larger rooms, especially the hall of representatives, in rows of five.[82] The commercial staff gathered in a side corridor in the basement.[83]

The next day, a terrified staff followed the order punctually. After several hours, Sturmbannführer Rolf Günther, Hauptsturmführer Fritz Wöhrn, and several Gestapo officials, among them Franz Prüfer, appeared. Günther announced that five hundred of those assembled would lose their jobs. The department heads were instructed to name those "whose continued work was superfluous."[84] Some, such as Dora Silbermann, head of youth welfare, refused to comply.[85] Others, as Siegbert Kleemann (head of the Winter Relief and the Welfare Department) himself reports, avoided the task without anyone noticing.[86] In such cases, the Gestapo officials took over the selection process. Hilde Kahan, who had waited in the hall of representatives for four hours with other employees of the Jewish hospital, reported that first the physically handicapped were dragged out and then others were called out by name.[87] (Later, a few were taken back as indispensable employees following the objections of either Henschel or Lustig. Selmar Neumann, head of Community payroll, was one of them.)[88]

Ultimately, 533 employees and 328 of their relatives—a total of 861 people—were selected to "move away."[89] Günther ordered those selected to go to the assembly camp on Grosse Hamburger Strasse on October 22 together with their families. The dismissed employees were then taken to the accommodation advice center to fill out the usual questionnaires.[90]

Paul Scheurenberg, who was a Community employee but had on the day of the summons by coincidence been "borrowed" along with some colleagues to unload potatoes, wrote: "Oh God in heaven, you have protected me again. The twenty-five of us were unloading potatoes and escaped this tragedy. All of the caretakers were selected for evacuation. When I lost my caretaker's job, I moaned . . . If I had been at the roll call I would surely have met the same fate."[91] A few days later, Scheurenberg and his colleagues had to "help dispatch the transport of Community staff. Oh, it was hard. So hard. Staff who had worked for the Jewish Community for decades were loaded onto a drafty animal truck along with all of the others. . . . I don't want to suggest that these had more rights than the other Jews. But the situation is more beastly, barbaric, and tyrannical than it has ever been before and hopefully than it will ever be again. . . . At the station, these people facing an unknown future were given some food, and each received a packet of sandwiches. We were not allowed to speak to each other, but we did. . . . This transport cost me much money, tobacco, and food."[92]

Those selected to be deported "to the east" and to Theresienstadt[93] more or less knew the significance of the order to report to the assembly camp. Sturm-bannführer Günther had threatened to shoot one leading member of the Reichs-vereinigung or the JKV for every person who failed to appear.[94] Nonetheless, twenty people, including sixteen women, did not appear. According to notes on the missing persons list, eight of them threatened that they would commit suicide if they were deported.[95] On Gestapo orders, the Community hastily carried out detailed investigations into the family situations of these people and their possible whereabouts. It was an attempt to avert a major wave of arrests.[96] Some of those who had fled were caught. Others turned themselves in after a few days, like one woman who had taken her lame child to acquaintances.[97] All the same, the Gestapo arrested twenty hostages. Four, possibly five of them were released, including Adolf Wolffsky, who headed the Community's application office.[98] On November 20, 1942, however, at least seven leading employees were shot dead in Sachsenhausen and Lichterfelde, and their relatives were deported. The notices of death are dated December 1, 1942.[99] Postwar investigations by the prosecuting attorney's office in the 1960s revealed the victims to be Dr. Fritz Lamm (welfare department), Dr. Bruno Mendelsohn (head of central administration), Alfred Selbiger (formerly head of the Palestine Office, later employed in the personnel department of the Reichsvereinigung), Dr. Julius Blumenthal (legal department), Dr. Goldstein (arbitration and consultation board), Arnold Looser (Community employee), and Dr. Adler (audit section).[100]

Next to the murder of hostages in May 1942, the *Gemeinde-Aktion* of October 1942 marked another peak in RSHA and Gestapo brutality. The campaign clearly showed the futility of the strategy of cooperating with the Nazis in order to protect people and alleviate suffering.

Between fall 1941 and fall 1942 more than 16,000 Berlin Jews were deported according to Gestapo instructions.[101] The Gestapo assumed the task of picking up the people to be deported, "sifting through" the luggage (*Schleusung*), and arranging deportation from the assembly camp. For this purpose it used several haulage firms. The Community, meanwhile, appointed marshals to carry luggage, was responsible for the internal organization of the assembly camp (marshals, food, medical care), and had to provide the premise for the subsequent complete expropriation of the deportees.[102] They could postpone deportation or alleviate circumstances in certain cases. The hope, however, of satisfying the RSHA's demands with the "resettlement" of several thousand Jews and thereby protecting the majority of Berlin's remaining Jews had long since vanished.

If those responsible in the Community still thought that they had some room for maneuver they discovered their powerlessness in May 1942 at the latest, when the Gestapo shot 250 Jewish hostages and arrested a further 250. In this case there was no prior warning, no decision-making process, no possibility of intervention, and no plan for moderation. Five months later, the *Gemeinde-Aktion* again gave more than ample proof that the hope of "preventing worse things" was an illusion. The employees of the Community were now the target of the selections.

### The End of the First Wave of Deportations, Fall 1942

Decisive changes took place during the deportation of the Community employees. Between October 1942 and January 1943, Viennese Gestapo officials temporarily ran the Gestapo's "Jewish office" in the Berlin regional headquarters, following a corruption affair in the Berlin Gestapo. Alois Brunner was put in charge of the operation. Harry Schnapp, a former marshal, recalled the change in personnel: "Between November 7 and 10, 1942, members of the Viennese Gestapo came to Grosse Hamburger Strasse and halted the work of the Berlin Gestapo. We heard violent disputes between the two Gestapo groups. Even [Walter] Dobberke [who headed the Gestapo and ran the assembly camp] was no longer allowed to go to the camp."[103] (For a portrait of Dobberke, see chap. 15 above.)

Theft and embezzlement were signatures of the Berlin Gestapo's behavior. The Berlin officials had been preying on the inmates of the Levetzowstrasse assembly camp as well as taking advantage of abandoned "Jewish apartments." Detective commissioner Gerhard Stübs, head of the Office for Jewish Affairs, had "a whole store of Jewish possessions"; senior detective secretary Franz Prüfer had a chest full of gold, most likely from bribes.[104] Stübs had quite clearly conducted a brisk trade with his colleagues in objects belonging to Jews.[105]

Ten Gestapo officials were arrested, but that was just the tip of the iceberg. In the summer of 1944, the internal SS and police court in Berlin apparently sentenced around eighty more Gestapo and Kripo staff in connection with the deportations.[106] Even Otto Bovensiepen, the head of the Berlin Gestapo headquarters, was transferred for disciplinary reasons as a result of the affair. It was deemed that he "should have been more careful selecting the men in charge of the operation."[107] All the same, allowances were made for the fact that "incidences of corruption" had already been part of the Gestapo's professional culture before Bovensiepen arrived on the job. Stübs avoided arrest by committing suicide. Other officials—Walter Dobberke among them—returned to their posts.[108] Still others were transferred for disciplinary reasons to "workers' educational camps" (*Arbeitserziehungslager*).[109]

Of course this disciplinary action in no way put an end to the impoverishment, intimidation, and robbery of Berlin's remaining Jews. Jewish witnesses report that the Gestapo officials regularly accepted bribes right through to the end of the war. They deployed Jewish prisoners for private work, commissioned Jewish "odd-jobbers" to obtain scarce goods on the black market, and trafficked in clothing produced by Jewish forced laborers at the assembly camp on Schulstrasse (see below).[110]

Before the Viennese officials launched their reign of terror in Berlin, the Berlin Gestapo's corruptibility may in some cases have helped the Jewish Community alleviate circumstances. The actions of their officials had been to some degree a predictable factor of their greed. Now, however, Brunner cracked down, reorganizing the deportations and the assembly camp system according to his efficient Viennese model.[111] On November 14, 1942, he ordered the Community board to convert the Levetzowstrasse and Grosse Hamburger Strasse assembly camps to accommodate up to 1,200–1,500 people. The former home for the elderly at Grosse Hamburger Strasse 26 had served since June 1942 as an assembly camp for smaller deportation groups, generally fifty to one hundred people bound for Theresienstadt.[112] It was now supposed to accommodate more than ten times this number.[113] Within a few days the building was radically expanded. The furniture was removed. It was refitted into a virtual prison.

Meanwhile, the former home for the elderly at Gerlachstrasse 19–21 was equipped to take on a variety of people in "protective custody" (*Schutzhäftlinge*). These had the "right" to go to Theresienstadt for reasons of their advanced age or because they were veterans or lived in mixed marriages. Another assembly camp at Auguststrasse 17 was modernized. For a time there were also camps at Gormannstrasse 3, Johannisstrasse 16, and on Kleine Hamburger Strasse.[114] From the fall of 1942 until the spring of 1944, the assembly camp on Grosse Hamburger Strasse replaced Levetzowstrasse as the camp for deportations "to the east."[115]

## The Assembly Camp on Grosse Hamburger Strasse

The former home for the elderly on Grosse Hamburger Strasse was transformed into a prison, complete with bars on its windows, a surrounding fence, and nighttime illumination. A guard of twenty-five to thirty armed policemen was posted there with instructions to shoot any prisoner who tried to escape.

The Gestapo had several rooms of its own on the premises. The Jewish Community index files were transferred here—the "small file system" (*kleine Kartei*)—and managed by two Jewish women who also registered new arrivals at the camp. "There were cards in different colors," recalled Martha Ehrlich (later Martha Raphael). "I still remember that those who counted as Jews by religion and race received white cards if they had no Aryan genealogical background, and that children of mixed marriages brought up as Jews received blue cards. Furthermore, I think that the Jewish wife in a mixed marriage received a yellow card if her children were raised as Jews. There were cards in different colors, but I can no longer remember their details."[116] Duplicates of the files—the "large file system" (*grosse Kartei*)—were kept at the Gestapo department on Burgstrasse, a two-minute walk from Grosse Hamburger Strasse. The Gestapo moved the relevant card files there and drew up lists for the "collectors" (*Abholer*) assigned to bring in deportees. When the files were destroyed in a bombing raid at the end of November 1943, Brunner's subordinates replaced the destroyed files with an incomplete file system they had produced on their own.[117] To keep the files up to date, any Jews still in Berlin were expected to inform the assembly camp records office—the Jewish Registration Point (*Jüdische Meldestelle*)—of such matters as change of address.[118]

The camp inmates slept on straw mattresses in overcrowded, locked rooms. The doors to the toilets had been removed for monitoring purposes.[119] Likely escapees were held in the basement along with those who had been mistreated and were segregated from the other prisoners until their wounds had begun to heal.

The role of the Jewish marshals at the camp changed fundamentally in the fall of 1942. Heretofore they had only provided secondary services: carrying luggage, distributing food, and supervising. Now, for the camp on Grosse Hamburger Strasse the Community had to provide forty "capable" men who, though paid by the Community, took their orders from the Gestapo.[120] They were placed in groups under two "guards" (*Wachthabenden*), senior marshals of a sort,[121] who were to report to Walter Dobberke.

After Alois Brunner took over the "Jewish office," marshals had to accompany the SS commando on its raids. If those they sought were not found at home, the

*My parents were arrested [on Christmas] in December 1942. This is of course a major holiday. But the death machine did not stop on that day, either.*

ERNEST FONTHEIM, 1999

*Men, women, children, all together. Completely packed. . . . Indescribable sanitary conditions. Lockable doors were then installed on the individual floors. Not proper doors but they could be locked. For when a transport was being assembled, the floors were always sealed off. It was initially very quiet in the building until all of the names were known. And then of course the sound of crying started.*

HORST GESSNER, 1999

**Figure 18.1**
Entrance to the Grosse Hamburger Strasse assembly camp

Jewish marshals were ordered on threat of deportation to locate and turn them over.[122] Later on, the marshals sometimes had to cooperate with such "snatchers" (*Greifer*) as Stella Kübler and Rolf Isaaksohn, too (see chap. 15).

Other Jews worked within the camp as well. Brunner's people had used Curt Naumann as a personal slave. He survived on account of his role as a general drudge in the assembly camps on Grosse Hamburger Strasse and Schulstrasse. The former Jewish camp leader Werner Simon had been deported during the *Gemeinde-Aktion* and now Max Reschke, former rector of the Jewish elementary school on Kaiserstrasse, was appointed in his place. Reschke ruled with an iron rod, insisted on discipline, and responded particularly harshly to escape attempts.

According to one inmate, the camp was divided into three sections. The "east rooms" (*Ostzimmer*) housed people who were designated for deportation to Auschwitz, the "Theresienstadt rooms" (*Theresienstadtzimmer*) housed those who were to be taken to this camp, and the "accommodation rooms" (*Unterkunftszimmer*) housed the remaining inmates whose destination and deportation dates had yet to be determined. Shortly before deportations, the "east rooms" and stairwells were locked so that the prisoners could not pass on any information.[123] Most survivors describe abuse that took place during interrogations, after attempted escapes, in the bunkers, and above all during transport to the station. The Jewish Community negotiated with Alois Brunner to post at least one medical team and set up some sick rooms in the camp.[124]

Brunner moved around three hundred Jewish forced laborers to the assembly camp on Auguststrasse. From here they often had a long and difficult route to their workplaces and were only temporarily exempted from deportation because they worked at firms that were essential to the war effort.[125] In rapid succession Brunner now assigned orphans, doctors and dentists, the blind and deaf-mute, the infirm, recipients of welfare, and over one thousand people not deployed as laborers to the deportation lists.[126] The former practice of collecting individuals was abandoned in favor of targeting entire buildings, particularly those known to house many Jewish tenants. Those Jewish marshals forced to take part in the "collection service" had to fill a given "head count," a "daily quota" that they were forbidden to fall short of.[127]

The *Fabrik-Aktion* on February 27 and 28, 1943, represented the brutal conclusion of the second wave of deportations that decisively marked Alois Brunner's regime (see chap. 9 by Diana Schulle). During Brunner's three months in Berlin, the Jewish Community continued to bear the costs of the camps, transport, and staff, but it had lost all possibility of intervention.

## Dilemma: Knowledge and Silence

To what degree were the leading representatives of the Reichsvereinigung aware of what was happening to the "resettled" Jews in the east? Did they know that Jews were being shot, gassed, and driven to death through labor, hunger, and disease? Postwar witness statements give a very diverse picture. Some had learned of the massacres from soldiers who had come from the eastern front. Some regarded the rumors as credible, while others dismissed them as "gruesome propaganda" (see chap. 16 by Barbara Schieb). News of deaths, in particular, had spread. Some Community employees drew on their own experiences to piece together an idea of what their fellow Jews could expect on the transports. Such was the case for one marshal who had been forced to clean a train in which the Jewish passengers had clearly been shot through the wooden partitions.

**Figure 18.2**
A "bunker" in the cellar of the assembly camp

The Jewish Community leader Moritz Henschel, however, claimed ignorance of the events. "Neither in Berlin nor in Theresienstadt did we hear anything about the gassings in Auschwitz. In Berlin I knew next to nothing about Theresienstadt and life there. Later in Theresienstadt one was not aware that the transports led to the gas chambers, since in Theresienstadt the main issue was the luggage to be taken along."[128]

What did Leo Baeck know? Max Plaut, chairman of the Hamburg Reichsvereinigung, states that at the end of 1939 the *Judenreferent* of the Hamburg Gestapo informed him that special labor and concentration camps were planned for Jews. Plaut immediately informed the central office in Berlin of this.[129] At the time, the term "special camp" (*besondere Lager*) could not—and indeed still cannot—be equivalent to the term "extermination camp" (*Vernichtungslager*). After the war, Baeck stated that a non-Jewish woman who had accompanied her husband to Poland came to him in the summer of 1941 and apparently told him about gas wagons in which hundreds of Polish Jews were murdered.[130] This information preceded the Berlin deportations, but it must be presumed that other people came to Baeck and passed on information as well. In Theresienstadt

**Figure 18.3** Leo Baeck in Theresienstadt

Baeck was informed about the gassings in Auschwitz. "So it was not just a rumor, as I had hoped, the illusion of a diseased imagination." Still he decided to keep silence with the inmates and the Council of Elders: "Living in the expectation of death by gassing would have been harder. And this death was not certain for all: there was selection for slave labor; perhaps not all transports went to Auschwitz. So I came to the grave decision to tell no one."[131] Herbert Strauss reported that Leo Baeck had agreed only against his will to the Gestapo's demands to participate in the "resettlement." Surely Baeck's colleagues had reservations and concerns as well.[132]

As the deportations began, Baeck faced a dilemma. On the one hand he supported the policy of cooperating with the Gestapo.[133] On the other, he advised younger acquaintances to go underground and flee. In the wake of Nazi reprisals for the "Soviet Paradise" attack, the Gestapo's threat to shoot not just fifty but 250 hostages for every Jew involved in any subsequent act of resistance was serious enough for Baeck to try to persuade Communist-oriented groups to abandon further campaigns.[134] The historians Avraham Barkai, Konrad Kwiet, and Helmut Eschwege have interpreted this behavior as meaning that in 1942 Baeck and the Reichsvereinigung still held to the principle of legality and tried to prevent *all* resistance activities.[135] Baum and his group had planned their attack not in response to the persecution of the Jews but in defense of the Soviet Union. The action had harmed rather than helped the Jewish Community because of the reprisals it brought down on the Community as a whole. The thesis that Baeck held fast to the principle of legality can only be validated in light of the decisions he made, however. And he made no decisions regarding other acts of resistance—resistance to assignment to the assembly camps, to the deportations, or to the Gestapo's *Judenreferat*—because such acts were not carried out.

Baeck kept whatever he knew hidden from his fellow Community members. Even when he was asked for advice—for example, from a woman who wanted to accompany her husband to a concentration camp—he did not pass on his knowledge. Would openness have helped the situation? The majority of Jews remaining in Berlin were old and impoverished. Would they have had the option of going underground? Did they have a realistic chance of lasting for two or three years in hiding? Even in Theresienstadt, Baeck kept trying to maintain the hope of desperate Community members and to give them comfort. Should he have stated what he knew and, with this, robbed the victims of all hope? This objective lack of alternatives and prospects reveals the tragic dilemma that the Reichsvereinigung and its representatives were in.[136]

### The Reichsvereinigung's Termination and Its Successor Organization

The Jüdisches Kultusvereinigung (JKV) was dissolved on January 29, 1943, a few days after Leo Baeck, Philipp Kozower, and Paul Eppstein were deported to Theresienstadt. The dissolution was itself brief and brutal. According to a Community secretary, "various Gestapo members stood around with riding whips, forcing us to make haste."[137] Already two days later, the Reichsvereinigung had presented a "Reorganization Plan for the Headquarters and the Berlin Jewish Religious Association" outlining the new responsibilities. At the time the finance and administration departments still existed, as did the Berlin district office of the JKV and the welfare department.[138] The Berlin JKV in turn had its own administration and welfare department and the task of organizing "special work commissioned by the authorities" (*Sonderarbeiten im behördlichen Auftrag*), namely, the construction teams for the RSHA. It was responsible for the few remaining Jewish homes, the department for "accommodation advice and emigration," the clothing store, the cemetery, and the Jewish hospital on Iranische Strasse. Dr. Walter Lustig was in charge of health care and the hospital.[139]

Robbed of their leading members, the remaining employees—in the fourth and fifth years of the war and facing an acute lack of resources and ever more persecution—tried as best they could to feed and house the remaining (forced) members as well to prepare for deportations. Major Nazi crackdowns such as the *Gemeinde-Aktion, Fabrik-Aktion,* and later, the *Krankenhaus-Aktion,* reduced the number of Jews in Berlin by thousands. The Reichsvereinigung had become powerless, a mere organ of the Gestapo, even before it was officially dissolved on June 10, 1943. The organization was taken over by Dr. Walter Lustig, Ph.D., who ran the "Rest-Reichsvereinigung"—the Residual Reich Association, sometimes called the Neue Reichsvereinigung—with a small team of devoted colleagues based at the Jewish hospital. An executive body of the Gestapo, its purview consisted of people living in mixed marriages, *Geltungsjuden,* and the dwindling group of Jews who had not yet been deported from Berlin.

## Part 4: The Jewish Hospital and the Schulstrasse Assembly Camp

The significance that the Jewish hospital already had for Berlin's Jewish population increased under the Nazis.[140] Here the wounds of concentration camp victims were treated after the pogrom of November 9, 1938. Here necessary operations were carried out—later, operations that would postpone deportation. Children were born and attempts were made to save people who had tried to commit suicide. (According to estimates a total of seven thousand Berlin Jews took their own lives during the period.)[141] The doctors and medical staff who remained fought to heal the sick and maintain the hospital despite scarce resources and the hopeless situation. Not just Jewish patients but the staff as well were at risk.

In the summer of 1942 Jewish psychiatric patients from the whole German Reich were brought to the hospital. These were largely foreign citizens or people protected by non-Jewish relatives who would otherwise already have been murdered in the Nazi euthanasia program. Before the mentally ill patients were deported, the psychiatric ward was one of the hospital's largest. Hilde Kahan, a secretary there at the time, stated after the war that, after the deportation of these patients, the staff had by chance read a secret order from Berlin Gestapo headquarters on the back of a list of names. It stated that "the mentally ill Jews are to be shot on the spot in Sachsenhausen forest near Oranienburg."[142]

The Jewish hospital was under the direct control of the RSHA. Adolf Eichmann had already assigned Fritz Wöhrn (cited previously in connection with the *Gemeinde-Aktion*) the task of supervising the hospital. After the war, his judges ruled that "he was one of the most ruthless and well-known functionaries from the [Gestapo's] *Judenreferat,* who spread fear and terror, particularly during his inspections of the Jewish hospital. During his visits to the hospital, which he generally carried out unannounced at all possible times of day, the Jewish employees had to stand at attention and state their respective jobs. The defendant went around shouting at the top of his voice and threatened to send people to a concentration camp if all was not done per his instructions."[143]

During his inspections, Wöhrn was in the habit of checking whether the yellow star was sewn on according to Nazi regulations. On June 28, Ruth Ellen Wagner, a twenty-two-year-old shorthand typist, was not even wearing a star

When the mass deportations began, the number of suicides mounted. There are around two thousand such graves in the cemetery [in Weissensee]. Special "security measures" had to be taken in the case of the death of an "illegal" person: a frightened landlady or neighbor gave an address by phone, usually anonymously, and the driver then went there with the former delivery van that had been converted into a hearse . . . in order to collect the unfortunate load as inconspicuously as possible.

LIESELOTTE
CLEMENS, 1999

**Figure 18.4** The main building of the Jewish hospital in the 1930s

when Wöhrn summoned her. All of her colleagues' attempts to rescue her failed, and Wöhrn had the young woman put into preventative detention. Her parents were not informed initially but then received several letters from a concentration camp near Braunschweig and finally the notice of death from Auschwitz dated December 8, 1943.[144] After the war, Wöhrn was sentenced to twelve years in a penitentiary for this case. For his leading role in the *Gemeinde-Aktion* and *Krankenhaus-Aktion* he was charged as an accessory to murder.[145]

On March 10, 1943, the Gestapo had attempted to deport all patients and staff from the hospital. The *Krankenhaus-Aktion* was the next ordeal in the history of Berlin's Jews. Trucks were already waiting in front of the hospital when Dr. Lustig—who incidentally had not intervened on Ruth Ellen Wagner's behalf—prevented the mass deportation at the last minute. He pointed out to the Gestapo that the hospital was under the direct control of the RSHA. The next day Wöhrn appeared and himself drew up a list, which Hilde Kahan had to take down: "A colleague and I were given the task of writing up the list ordered by the Gestapo the previous night; the names were dictated to us to type. Around three hundred people . . . were affected. . . . A week later the employees were arrested in their homes along with their families, and we never heard anything from them again."[146]

Officially, the Jewish hospital did not even have its own grounds, and the buildings at Iranische Strasse 2 and 4 had to be transferred to the Akademie für Jugendmedizin e.V. (Academy for Youth Medicine) and rented by the hospital for RM 8,400 per month.[147] Confiscations and bombing damage also decreased capacity. In 1943 came the instruction to clear the psychiatric and gynecology wards as well as the nurses' home in order to make room for a reserve military

**Figure 18.5** The pathology department of the Jewish hospital on Schulstrasse, 1934

**Figure 18.6** Frau Dr. Wundsch with a colleague, probably Dr. Maier

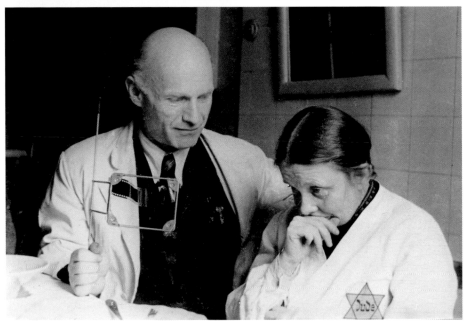

hospital.[148] For a short time the Bund Deutscher Maedel, the girls' organization in the Hitler Youth, also had an office here. Fifty to sixty Jews from the western part of Germany who were living in mixed marriages or classed as *Geltungsjuden* were also detained in the hospital.[149] They were later joined by over three hundred mixed-marriage spouses from the Rhineland and Westphalia who had been deemed no longer fit to work.[150] In addition, the Rest-Reichsvereinigung had been instructed by the Gestapo to detain all Jews coming into Berlin and to house them in the hospital.[151] The hospital thus increasingly resembled an improvised

**Figure 18.7**
Hauptsturmführer
Fritz Wöhrn, who
supervised the Jewish
hospital for the RSHA

**Figure 18.8**
Ruth Ellen Wagner,
a typist in the Jewish
hospital, early 1940s

emergency accommodation camp. There were "protected Jews" (*Schutzjuden*) and people who were claimed by the RSHA or other departments.

Meanwhile, many of the Jews who figured on Göring's list of "protected prominent figures" (*Schützlinge von hohen Persönlichkeiten*) were now detained as well, albeit not openly in the assembly camps. They, too, were brought to the hospital section.[152] Many employees, including Walter Lustig and the head of administration, Selmar Neumann, also lived on the premises.[153] There was also accommodation for children (*Kinderunterkunft*) with over sixty orphans whose racial origins were unclear and needed to be checked.[154]

The prisoners' hospital was separate from these emergency accommodations, and there was also a police station (with bars on the windows and without door handles) to which prisoners from the Alexanderplatz police prison and the Wuhl-heide workers' educational camp were assigned.[155] According to Bruno Blau, who survived his time in the hospital, forced labor was also reintroduced during the final months of the war: "In the final months of the Thousand-Year Reich the Gestapo had also converted a large hall in the hospital into a workroom, where children's clothing were produced. . . . Inmates of the assembly camp were also deployed to this factory, and those who performed especially well were spared for as long as possible from deportation; some escaped deportation alto-gether. . . . The firm was extremely profitable, since it had no costs apart from raw materials. . . . There were two shifts—one of them at night. When the Nazi regime collapsed, there was a whole stack of finished children's clothes, which were distributed among the Jews in the hospital."[156]

At the war's end there were up to a thousand inhabitants in the hospital, 370 of whom were patients.[157] According to another source, fifty "fully Jewish" employees (including their family members) survived, along with 93 orphans and 76 prisoners in the police station.[158]

From March 1, 1944, the deportation camp on Grosse Hamburger Strasse was designated for use by the Gestapo as an auxiliary prison. At that time the porter's lodge of the Jewish hospital on Schulstrasse (one of the streets bordering the complex in Wedding) and the pathology (anatomy) sections were taken over for use as another assembly camp, and both buildings were marked off from the rest of the hospital with barbed wire. "Jews who had been living illegally and had been arrested ended up in the assembly camp," testified an eyewitness in 1966.[159] A former prisoner described the layout:

> There was a three-story building, not particularly big. The grounds were divided from the buildings on Iranische Strasse by a wall topped with barbed wire. This wall also restricted the inner courtyard in which prisoners had to, for example, clean the tiles. The windows of the lower stories were . . . barred. [As on Grosse Hamburger Strasse,] Dobberke was again camp leader. . . . Reschke was again appointed Jewish camp leader. . . . The Jewish woman [Martha] Raphael was still responsible for the Jewish files. . . . There were an average of one hundred to one hundred fifty Jews detained in the camp. They were divided between the individual rooms, where they slept on mattresses. Prisoners who were marked out for the next transport were housed on the first floor. The prisoners on the upper floors were those for whom it had not yet been determined whether they should be deported and, if so, where. These people were usually deployed in various forms of labor including tailoring, cleaning, or special work outside the camp. Labor commandos were also put together and put to work, for example, in . . . clearing up [bomb] damaged authority buildings.[160]

As the war came to an end the inmates of the assembly camp were at the greatest risk yet. On April 19, 1945, "a day before the general collapse"—that is, before the RSHA staff abandoned the sinking ship—there were heated debates on the fate of the Jews housed in the official buildings. A secretary participating via telephone heard the following: "'The Jews will all be bumped off.' There was a loud dispute. Someone said: 'You can't do that.'"[161] Curt Naumann, who had worked as an odd-job man at the hospital, had also listened in on the dispute. In agreement with the non-Jewish secretary he subsequently telephoned from inside the camp to announce

Dr. Wundsch was also in a mixed marriage and for this reason she was able to survive. After her husband's death she went to England. . . . She worked with my father from 1939 to 1945. They were responsible for the bacteriological department of the Jewish hospital.

CLEMENS MARCUSE, SON OF THE PHYSICIAN DR. KURT MARCUSE, 1999

an alleged RSHA order for the immediate release of the prisoners. The secretary confirmed Naumann's words to the camp leader.[162] If this version of events is correct—and up to now there has been nothing to suggest otherwise—Naumann's courage and presence of mind saved the lives of the prisoners literally at the last minute.

Historian Rifka Elkin has called the Jewish hospital and Jewish cemetery in Weissensee the final relics of the once flourishing Jewish life in Berlin, "all that remained of Jewish life in Germany." She writes that, through the changes the hospital underwent, "it lost its character as a medical establishment over the years, even if attempts were made to present this image to the outside world so as not to give a premise for its liquidation."[163] Ultimately, both aspects—the survival of the hospital as well as its transformation into a camp—are the doing of Walter Lustig. Though he saved the hospital from closure, he is also known to have obediently filled deportation orders—sometimes before they were even given.

### Dr. Walter Lustig: The "One-Man Jewish Council"

Even today, the name Walter Lustig provokes violent aversion among Jewish survivors. His persona has been shrouded in a negative myth, particular since 1945. The medical doctor was and is still seen by many of his contemporaries as a beneficiary of the Nazi regime, immune to repression and terror—a powerful individual who, between 1943 and 1945, could deal with the Berlin Jews as he pleased. In their opinion he was not just the henchman of the Gestapo but also their drinking companion, someone who sexually abused women and drew up deportation lists on his own initiative. The former Oberregierungsrat (senior civil servant) was called "Oberlustrat Gierig" (Captain Lust-Greed) by many.

Only a few statements contradict this view, referring tentatively to his merits with regard to the Jewish hospital, its staff, and individual patients. Who was this man who lives on in the memories of his contemporaries but of whom so few traces remain? Rather than personal memoirs, he left behind a long bibliography of medical books and essays. And it was not until the year 2000 that a photo of him was discovered.

Walter Lustig was born August 19, 1891, in Ratibor in Upper Silesia, the son of the Jewish trader Bernhard Simon Lustig and his wife Regina, née Besser.[164] He attended grammar school and took his university entrance exams on March 7, 1910. In October of the same year he started as a medical student at the University of Breslau, finishing his studies there in winter 1914–15 with a specialization in surgery. He was awarded his license to practice and became a doctor

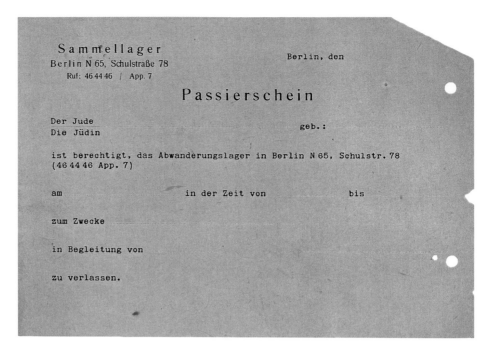

**Figure 18.9**

At the end of the war there were blank passes in the Jewish hospital, which the Jewish Community used as writing paper on account of the paper shortage.

in March/April 1915. Just a year and a half later, he completed a philosophical dissertation, which indicates his exceptionally hard-working nature, especially since he won his academic laurels while completing his military service in Breslau. He was very proud of his two titles and always insisted that his employees use both when addressing him.

After World War I, Lustig started work as a medical officer. During this period it is said that he and his colleagues were involved in the campaign against the socialist Spartacus League. In the 1920s, while running his own practice, he also gathered information on national health and communicated it to the Prussian Ministry for National Welfare. In 1927 he moved to Berlin and married Annemarie Preuss, a non-Jewish doctor with whom he had been friends for years. He started work at police headquarters in Berlin, advancing to become head of the medical department. He authored several publications, which became standard literature for students, interns, and instructors.[165] His tasks included monitoring health standards in schools, homes, and mass housing as well as the vocational training of medical staff. Politically, Lustig leaned toward the Social Democrats.

Due to the Nazi Law for the Restoration of the Professional Civil Service, Lustig was dismissed from his job in October 1933. He was not recognized as a frontline veteran and so had only his pension to live on. (This nonetheless

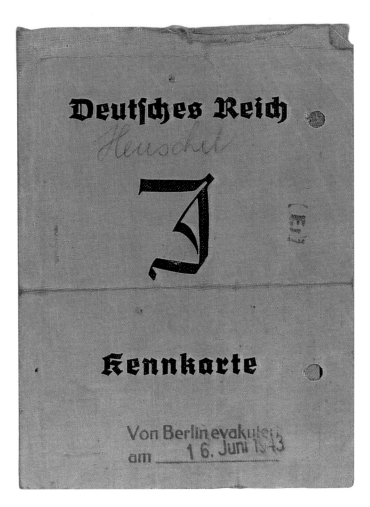

**Figure 18.10**
Hildegard Henschel's identity card with the deportation date "16. Juni 1943" stamped on it

amounted to some RM 500 per month).[166] Up to that point Lustig had felt no sense of affiliation with the Jewish faith. It was not until the age of forty-three that he became more closely associated with the Jewish Community. Starting in 1935, he probably worked several years for the health administration of the Community, and during this time he made initial contacts with the Jewish hospital. At the end of September 1938, along with all other Jewish doctors, he lost his license to practice. He also had to give up the private practice that he had managed up to then.

In July 1939 the *Jüdisches Nachrichtenblatt* described Lustig as the person responsible for health services,[167] and in 1940–41 he joined the Reichsvereinigung board, replacing the head of the health department, who had emigrated. Shortly after the start of the deportations he ran the aforementioned Department to

Investigate Claims for Exemption from Deportation at the Jewish hospital. He apparently managed to postpone deportations in several cases for medical reasons, but by 1942 the guidelines had become stricter, and it was very rare for exemptions to be made.[168] The department was closed down shortly afterward.

Eyewitnesses emphasize Lustig's good connections with the Gestapo, his administrative talent, and his negotiating skills.[169] Despite this he, too, was subject to the regime's anti-Jewish measures, for example, the ban on owning or using vehicles. On one occasion he received a warning from the Gestapo when he was caught driving his wife's car.[170] He also had to pay the Jewish Property Levy (*Judenvermögensabgabe*), which was fixed at RM 21,400. His assets were frozen in blocked accounts and he, too, had to hand over his valuables: a "mink fur with otter collar," gold jewelry, skis, and a Stassfurt Imperial brand radio.[171]

In 1942 the "supervisory authority" appointed Lustig head of the Jewish hospital, which fell under the jurisdiction of Department IV B 4 of the RSHA.[172] A range of reports from patients and colleagues bear witness to the fact that Lustig, on the one hand, adhered strictly to Gestapo orders but, on the other hand, in March 1943 prevented the whole hospital from being closed down and all staff and patients deported. Though he was not able to prevent staff cuts, which meant deportation for those concerned, there is proof that he successfully intervened for the release of workers he considered indispensable.[173] When the remaining Reichsvereinigung staff was arrested in 1943, Lustig was the only one left. He was not even able to save his father, who was deported to Theresienstadt.[174] His wife had in the meantime been drafted for forced labor as an assistant doctor in the municipal hospital in Traunstein.[175]

It is not possible to ascertain whether Lustig was aware of the precariousness of his situation. Perhaps he believed he was in a special position. For when the other representatives and leading staff of the Jewish Community and Reichsvereinigung were deported, he took over the chair of the New Reich Association—a "one-man Jewish Council" with an office in the Jewish hospital. He was now responsible for all of Berlin's Jews who had thus far been spared from deportation. Under him, during this last chapter of Nazi rule, the Jewish hospital also became the "final refuge and trap" for Jews from all over Germany.[176] As a "one-man Jewish Council," Lustig no longer had any room to maneuver. He mainly had to administer and carry out instructions. His "scope for action was above all about the *how.*"[177] His superior, Hauptsturmführer Wöhrn, was a former colleague from police headquarters. Lustig now carried Wöhrn's orders out to the letter, sometimes with obviously eager obedience. Thus, under his management patients and staff were deported, but he also succeeded in rescuing around fifty "full Jews" and *Geltungsjuden.*[178] He apparently intervened especially on behalf of the children in the orphanage. Despite all this, his activities are more than contentious,[179] since he for instance proposed people for deportation who had tried to escape. He had a reputation of saving friends and acquaintances above others. And, moreover, he hid shattering information from the inmates.[180] This almost cost the prisoners in the military hospital section their lives when the war had just come to an end.

After liberation in 1945 Lustig provided his services to the Wedding district of Berlin as a medical officer and head of the health department. With other functionaries from the Reichsvereinigung he tried to get the Soviet occupying powers to recognize the organization—despite its problematic wartime role—as a legitimate representation of the interests of the Jewish survivors.

On June 6, 1945, he sent the Berlin mayor a memo in which he described the Reichsvereinigung as a "justified and authorized body" and called for immediate measures to be taken. When all National Socialist organizations were to be closed down it was Lustig who applied for the organization to change its name to "Jüdische Gemeinde Berlin" (Jewish Community of Berlin). He did so not because he thought that the Reichsvereinigung had become discredited but because its activities were now centered "mainly in the Greater Berlin area." He himself wanted to be appointed the highest "functionary," with his colleagues of the past two years assuming ranks two through twelve in the appended list.[181] Lustig called for better food, for surviving Jews to be exempted from rubble-clearing operations, and for Jews to enjoy preferential treatment when it came to allocating clothing and shoes.[182] A dedication to Stalin from one of Lustig's colleagues concluded this letter: "The few surviving Jews of Berlin thank you, *Herr Marshal,* from the bottom of their hearts that the glorious Red Army liberated them from the dreadful National Socialist regime."[183] This is particularly ironic, since Lustig had saved only his own skin during the Red Army's occupation of the hospital, abandoning the inmates of the prisoners' hospital (and probably also the other wards of the hospital) to their own fates. The Soviet soldiers rearrested these prisoners and took them to Weissensee, where they were supposed to be shot dead. It was only with difficulty that they could explain that they were Jewish inmates. They narrowly escaped with their lives.

Needless to say, Lustig was not appointed head of the Jewish Community, which had already been reestablished in May by other Jews, most of whom had survived underground. Regarding other attempts at postwar Jewish reorganization, Lustig continued to claim that his was the sole legitimate representation.[184] At the end of 1945 he was arrested by the Soviet occupying force on charges brought by the inmates of the hospital assembly camp; he died, probably killed by Soviet soldiers. There are no further details.[185] His date of death was later given as December 31, 1945.

His wife subsequently applied for a surviving dependent's pension for victims of Nazi persecution. She attempted to make the authorities believe that her husband had been arrested in 1943, taken to a concentration camp (by which she meant the assembly camp on Schulstrasse at the hospital) from which he never returned.[186] The audacity of her request led a former inmate of the prisoners' hospital to object vehemently to the restitution payment. The investigations he launched could have provoked a debate on the classification and assessment of Lustig's activities.[187] However, the responsible authorities were not interested in an explanation and only made lackluster inquiries in Berlin about how to assess Lustig's activities. They rejected the Berlin Jewish Community's proposal to solicit witnesses in a published appeal in the Jewish press.

In the end Lustig's old colleagues—those he had included on his list of proposed Community functionaries—put down on record that he had "done all in his power in the interests of the Jews."[188] The only person to raise an objection was Alexander Rotholz, a Berliner who had been active underground and in the resistance and had worked for the Community after the war (see chap. 15). According to Rotholz, Lustig "did not put himself out for the latter in any way but rather carried out his tasks, which were in Gestapo interests, with extreme conscientiousness."[189] Rotholz shattered Lustig's status as a murdered victim of a concentration camp, but the Jewish Community missed the opportunity as a whole to deal with this part of its past.

During the Reichsvereinigung's lifespan, the Gestapo showed no scruples in filling senior posts with people it trusted.[190] It preferred men (it rarely chose women) who through their professional occupation already had experience with official hierarchies, organization, and administration processes—men who were not used to questioning orders but carried them out as quickly and efficiently as possible.

What drove a man like Walter Lustig to carry out his so-called "obligations" right up to the end without even indicating the slightest doubt, antipathy, or despondency to his closest colleagues? For one thing, Lustig brought a fundamental criterion with him to the job: his experience. He had acquired the necessary "virtues" for fitting into and being subordinate to an authoritarian system not only at police headquarters but also during his time in the military and via his strictly hierarchical medical training. His publications show him to be an experienced practitioner who was less interested in theoretical and conceptual questions than practical solutions. In political terms Lustig was someone who could adapt. Very much drawn by achievement and promotion, his dismissal in 1933 under Nazi Law hit him particularly hard. So it is not surprising that he sought new work, aided by the personnel shortage in the Jewish Community following the wave of emigration in 1938–39. Nor is it surprising that he proved to be a capable administrator.

A similar career path can be applied to others—Martha Mosse, for example. But further aspects of Lustig's personality undoubtedly contributed to the controversy surrounding him. He had a very specific disposition, which the retiring Professor Seligmann described as "so torn up on the inside and so inhibited on the outside."[191] This psychological profile probably contributed to his unconditional acceptance of RSHA orders. His inhibitions in dealing with colleagues and subordinates, particularly women, suggest a difficulty communicating with people. In an extreme power structure that constantly focused on matters of life and death, it was, however, neither necessary nor desirable to open up on a personal level and establish relationships. Instructions or (implied) threats replaced communication, just as orders replaced relationships.

Lustig's relations with Wöhrn, for example, were marked by exclusivity; no other person was allowed to participate in their discussions. All eyewitnesses stress that on every inspection Wöhrn went straight to Lustig and talked with him in his office or on site. Although Wöhrn refused to address Lustig by his title—which Dr. Lustig insisted that his all subordinates use—Lustig received exclusive information, which he passed on at his own discretion to other Reichsvereinigung or hospital staff or, as was often the case, kept to himself. Successful intervention against the deportation of a Jew, for example, would have confirmed his sense of power. That Lustig clearly enjoyed the high position he had acquired is clear from his activities after liberation and his effort to maintain the Reichsvereinigung in the service of the next regime.

## Part 5: Conclusion and Perspectives

The activities of the Reichsvereinigung (and the Jewish Communities that were subordinate to it) underline the two-faced nature of this institution. These stemmed on the one hand from the Reichsvereinigung's role as a forced tool of the Gestapo, but on the other hand from its status as the only representation of Jewish interests in the National Socialist state. Several phases should be distinguished with regard to its impact.

Between 1939, the year of the Reichsvereinigung's establishment, and 1941, its representatives assumed that the organization's work could "prevent worse things from happening" and improve the living circumstances of Jews in Germany. Indeed, that assumption most accurately describes the situation. During this period, the Reichsvereinigung engaged in a variety of activities with regard to emigration. It sought to provide religious and social support to the Community (which had a disproportionate number of elderly people) and to alleviate hardship caused by the homelessness, disorientation, and impoverishment of its members.

The fall of 1941 saw a decisive change in the Reichsvereinigung's working conditions, as the ban on emigration and the start of deportations from Berlin coincided in October 1941. By taking up the Gestapo's "proposal" to participate in "resettlement," the Reichsvereinigung was unavoidably drawn to an ever greater extent into Nazi "Jewish policy" and the dynamic of extermination. Its scope for action diminished. At the end of 1941 it must have been clear to every representative of the Reichsvereinigung and each leader in the Jewish Community that "resettlement" did not just affect one sector of Berlin's Jews and that the majority of Jews still living in the capital would not be rescued through cooperation with the Nazis. It was only possible to pull someone from a deportation transport in isolated cases—and in any case, this only resulted in a brief reprieve, a postponement. The Nazi shootings of Jewish hostages in May 1942 and the deportation of Community employees that October, above all, underlined the intensity of the violence. The strategy of cooperation was a failure. From the fall of 1942 there was no more room for maneuver. The Reichsvereinigung, namely Walter Lustig, had become a tool of the Gestapo.

Despite all these considerations, there should be no irrefutable judgments on the behavior of the Reichsvereinigung representatives. What in retrospect seems like a one-way street, a route without any alternatives, was in the view of those who, for example, assumed responsibilities at the Reichsvereinigung between 1939 and 1940, a process with an uncertain conclusion. For these individuals, the "breakdown in civilization" (*Zivilisationsbruch*)[192] into systematic mass murder was not only outside the breadth of their experience but also the bounds of their imagination.

Even in retrospect there seems to be no alternative strategy that would definitely have been more successful. To claim that demonstrative refusal, open resistance, and a mass movement underground would have enabled a greater number of people to survive is mere speculation—and assumes that the majority of German Jews would have been prepared for this. Ultimately, Germany's Jews lived in a society that was predominantly loyal to the Nazi regime, a society in which the majority was not prepared to support the victims of persecution. Above all, the tragedy of the Reichsvereinigung and its representatives is marked by the objective hopelessness of all attempts. The representatives became entangled in the Nazi policy of extermination, for which they were at the same time not responsible.

The troubled history of the Reichsvereinigung effected the postwar period, when a small number of concentration camp survivors and those who had re-emerged from hiding decided—despite all their harrowing experiences—to remain in Germany and to reestablish the Jewish Community. In view of the wartime Community's implication in the deportation process—and the involvement of individual employees in particular—it was laborious to build up a new Jewish Community. The unexplained circumstances of Walter Lustig's violent death, the trials against the "snatcher" Stella Kübler, and the execution of the marshal Heinrich Koplowitz (who was sentenced during the Waldheim trials) were some of the specific cases marked by these difficulties.

Mistrust and accusations continued on a lower level as well, and the newly founded Jewish Community tried to respond to these with internal "tribunal proceedings" (Ehrengerichtsverfahren). These were initiated by accusers, and even the accused themselves, seeking to rid themselves of suspicion and rumors. Following questioning of witnesses and examinations of evidence, a committee consisting of a chairman, a legal assessor, and a lay assessor decided whether the accused had "acted against the interests of the Jewish Community."

Subordinate wartime employees, who were themselves constantly threatened with deportation, often saw themselves as plunged into major conflicts of conscience brought on by the board's decision "to prevent worse things from happening." This became clear during the trial of Martha Raphael, née Ehrlich, the woman who had been in charge of the Reichsvereinigung files: "The tribunal did not underestimate the major danger faced by the Jewish Community . . . when it chose to conform to the Gestapo's suggestion that it work for them. The Jewish employees who had to follow this command were presented with a difficult conflict between their Jewish consciences and the tasks given to them. They needed great strength of character to fulfill this unpleasant dual requirement."[193] The tribunal certified that Raphael had shown "great enthusiasm for her work," which ultimately had a detrimental impact on her fellow Jews. It was also attested, however, that she had successfully and helpfully intervened in particular cases. The judgment would certainly have applied to many Reichsvereinigung employees, both in leading and in subordinate positions.

The Community's attempt to clarify the historical responsibility of individuals in internal trials without external pressure was without parallel in postwar

German history. However, within the small group of survivors who dealt with these issues beyond the borders of responsibility, it was also necessary to cover complicity in order to move forward and reestablish the Community. The tribunal proceedings channeled anger, mistrust, and perhaps even a desire for revenge against actual or presumed collaborators who would otherwise, as in the first months after the war, have been brought to trial at Soviet institutions.

It is impossible here to judge the ultimate success of the internal process of reconciliation within the Jewish Community of Berlin, a process that continued until the 1950s. Yet it was probably the only way for Jews to be able to live with one another again and to preserve themselves in a society in which the basic attitude of anti-Semitism was far from overcome.

## Representatives and Employees of the Jewish Community and the Reichsvereinigung

**Dr. Leo Baeck**, born May 23, 1873, rabbi of the Jewish Community, member of the board of the Jewish Community and the Reichsvereinigung, and teacher at the College for Jewish Studies. He was deported to Theresienstadt on January 26, 1943, where he worked for the Council of Elders. After liberation he emigrated to Great Britain and, after 1948, taught at the Hebrew College in Cincinnati. Baeck died on November 2, 1956, in London.

**Dr. Cora Berliner**, born January 23, 1890, professor of economics, worked in the Reichsvereinigung's emigration department and dealt, in particular, with the emigration of women and girls. After a control visit by the Gestapo on June 19, 1942, she was selected for deportation and deported to Minsk between June 24 and 26, where she was murdered at the age of fifty-two.

**Dr. Conrad Cohn**, born November 25, 1901, member of the board of the Berlin Jewish Community, head of the welfare department. He was arrested in the spring of 1942, ostensibly for bureaucratic errors regarding the delivery of some soap to a children's home. Died August 15, 1942, in the Mauthausen concentration camp at the age of forty-one.

**Elieser Ehrenreich**, born November 5, 1883, religious official of the Jewish Community. He was arrested on January 21, 1941, probably for his involvement in a fast that protested the deportation of Jews from the Baden region. He was first assigned to the "Workers' Educational Camp" (*Arbeitserziehungslager*) in Wuhlheide, then transferred to Sachsenhausen. He died at Ravensbrück on November 21, 1941, at the age of fifty-eight.

**Dr. Paul Eppstein**, born March 4, 1902, was an adjunct lecturer in national economics and, like Baeck, a member of the board of the Jewish Community and the Reichsvereinigung. He was one of the most important negotiators with the authorities, above all the Gestapo as "supervisory body." He was arrested and rereleased on several occasions before being deported to Theresienstadt with his wife Dr. Hedwig Eppstein, a social worker, on January 26, 1943. There he was appointed Jewish Elder. It is likely that he was shot there—after detention—on September 27, 1944, at the age of forty-two. Hedwig Eppstein carried out unpaid work for the youth welfare department of the Community. She was murdered either at Theresienstadt or Auschwitz at the age of forty.

**Dr. Erich Fabian**, born September 22, 1902, headed the organization department of the Reichsvereinigung. He was deported to Theresienstadt in June 1943. Fabian survived in Berlin's Theresienstadt. He emigrated to the United States in 1949 and died there in 1974 at the age of seventy-two.

**Recha Freier**, born November 29, 1892, founded the Jugend-Alijah (Youth Aliyah), which helped young people emigrate to Palestine. Dismissed from the Palestine Office in 1940 because of her efforts to rescue Polish Jews illegally, she fled to Palestine via Yugoslavia in 1941. She subsequently founded a training center for underprivileged children on a kibbutz in Palestine. She died in Jerusalem in 1984.

**Paula Fürst**, born August 6, 1894, headmistress and head of the Reichsvereinigung's department of schools. In 1939 she accompanied a Kindertransport to England but returned to Germany despite the possibility of escape. She was deported to Minsk between June 24 and 26, 1942, where she was murdered at the age of forty-eight.

**Hildegard Henschel**, born April 29, 1897, employee of the Jewish Community's health administration. She and her husband Moritz Henschel were deported to Theresienstadt on June 16, 1943. Both survived and subsequently emigrated to Palestine, where she was obliged to work as a cleaning lady. She served as a witness during the Eichmann trial. She died in Israel in 1983 at the age of eighty-six.

**Dr. Moritz Henschel**, born February 17, 1879, lawyer and Heinrich Stahl's successor to the chair of the Jewish Community (1940–43). After deportation to Theresienstadt in June 1943, he first headed the department of leisure activities and, later, the post office. Weakened by his detention in the camp, he died in 1947 in Palestine at the age of sixty-eight.

**Dr. Otto Hirsch**, born January 9, 1885, served in the Würtemberg government cabinet and was president of the senior council of the Israelite religious association in Würtemberg. He moved to Berlin in 1933 to lead the Reichsvertretung, later serving on the board of the Reichsvereinigung. One of his main concerns was creating possibilities for emigration. Despite numerous trips abroad, he did not make use of the opportunities to emigrate. He was taken to the police prison located on the Alexanderplatz. He was then moved to the Mauthausen concentration camp on May 23, 1941, where he was murdered on June 19, 1941, at the age of fifty-six.

**Hanna Karminski**, born July 24, 1897, kindergarten teacher and social worker, very active in the Association of Jewish Women, and head of the Reichsvereinigung's department of social work. She was deported to Auschwitz where she was murdered on June 4, 1943, at the age of forty-five.

**Philipp Kozower**, born January 29, 1894, lawyer and notary. He served on the board of the Reichsvereinigung and was responsible for housing and benefits. He was moved to Theresienstadt and then deported to Auschwitz on October 12, 1944, where he was murdered at the age of fifty.

**Leo Kreindler**, born September 23, 1886, the most senior member of Jewish Community staff, head of the department for welfare and later editor-in-chief of the *Jüdisches Nachrichtenblatt*. He suffered a heart attack in November 1942, when the Gestapo had his department summoned for a roll call. He was fifty-six at the time of his death.

**Dr. Fritz Lamm**, born December 21, 1876, head of the office for social work and youth welfare, guardian of many Jewish children. He was held as a hostage after the *Gemeinde-Aktion* for other employees who had escaped underground. He was taken and then shot on December 3, 1942, in the Sachsenhausen concentration camp. He was sixty-six years old.

**Arthur Lilienthal**, born March 13, 1899, member of the Reichsvereinigung's board. He was selected for deportation in June 1942 during a Gestapo check and was reported "missing, presumed dead in the east," at the age of forty-three.

**Dr. Martha Mosse**, born May 29, 1884, studied music and law and worked as an administrative lawyer in the Berlin police headquarters until her dismissal in 1933. She headed the Reichsvereinigung's accommodation advice center. Deported to Theresienstadt on June 16, 1943, she survived and after the war returned to Berlin, where she reentered the city's judicial service. She later worked at the police headquarters. She died in 1977 at the age of ninety-three.

**Martin Riesenburger**, born in 1896, worked from 1933 as a spiritual guide in the Berlin Jewish Community's home for the elderly, located on Grosse Hamburger Strasse, and regularly delivered sermons during religious services. From June 1943 to May 1945 he headed the Reichsvereinigung's funerary department. After the war he organized services for the Berlin Jewish Community from 1945 to 1953 and was ordained as a rabbi there after 1953; in 1961 he was appointed regional rabbi for the Jewish Community in East Germany. He died in 1965.

**Alfred Selbiger**, born May 16, 1911, Zionist leader.
He headed the Zionist youth movement and worked in
the Palestine Office until 1941, thereafter in the Reichsvereinigung's finance department. He worked undercover
for the Hechalutz (Pioneers). After the *Gemeinde-Aktion*
he, too, was taken hostage. He was shot on December 1,
1942, in the Sachsenhausen concentration camp at the
age of thirty-one.

**Julius Seligsohn**, born May 7, 1890, lawyer, worked for
the Reichsvereinigung board, particularly in the emigration
department. He allegedly was behind the Reichsvereinigung's call for a day of fasting to protest the deportation of
the Baden Jews and was consequently arrested in November 1940. At Sachsenhausen, he was tortured and died on
February 28, 1942 at the age of fifty-one.

**Heinrich Stahl**, born April 13, 1868, director of the Victo-
ria insurance company, chairman of the Jewish Community
in Berlin until his removal from office in 1940. The Gestapo
refused to allow him to emigrate, and he was deported
to Theresienstadt with his wife on June 11, 1942. He died
there on November 4, 1942, at the age of seventy-four.

**Fritz Wisten**, born March 25, 1890, actor, director, and head of the Jüdische Kulturbund. He was able to survive the Nazi years in Berlin in a "privileged mixed marriage," and from 1945 on, he worked again as a director in various Berlin theaters. He died on December 12, 1962, in Berlin.

**Edith Wolff**, born April 13, 1904, worked with Recha Freier at the Palestine Office and, like Freier, lost her job because of her illegal efforts on behalf of Polish Jews. A "first-degree Mischling" she used her extensive freedom of movement to support Jews living underground. She was captured by the Gestapo in 1944, tortured, and sentenced. She survived seventeen prisons as well as Ravensbrück. She emigrated to Israel in 1954 and died there.

**1** On the Reichsvertretung (Reich Representation), see especially Otto Dov Kulka, editor, *Deutsches Judentum unter dem Nationalsozialismus*, vol. 1, *Dokumente zur Geschichte der Reichsvertretung der deutschen Juden, 1933–1939* (Tübingen, 1997).

**2** It is above all Otto D. Kulka who, using sources from East German archives, has brought about a change in the formerly prevailing view that the compulsory association was a Gestapo idea. His focus is on the considerations and proposals from representatives of the Reichsvertretung. See Otto D. Kulka, "The Reichsvereinigung and the Fate of the German Jews, 1938/1939–1943. Continuity or Discontinuity in German-Jewish History in the Third Reich," in *Die Juden im nationalsozialistischen Deutschland*, ed. Arnold Paucker (Tübingen, 1986), pp. 353–63, here pp. 357 ff.

**3** Günther Plum, "Deutsche Juden oder Juden in Deutschland?" in *Die Juden in Deutschland, 1933–1945*, ed. Wolfgang Benz (Munich, 1988), pp. 35–74, here pp. 69 ff.

**4** Saul Friedländer, *Nazi Germany and the Jews*, vol. 1, *The Years of Persecution, 1933–1939* (New York, 1997).

**5** Michael Wildt, *Die Judenpolitik des SD 1935 bis 1938. Eine Dokumentation* (Munich, 1995); Ulrich Herbert, "Von der 'Reichskristallnacht' zum 'Holocaust.' Der 9. November und das Ende des 'Radauantisemitismus,'" in *Arbeit, Volkstum, Weltanschauung* (Frankfurt am Main, 1995), pp. 59–77.

**6** Ibid., p. 46.

**7** Ibid., p. 15.

**8** Ibid., pp. 53–54.

**9** Ibid., doc. 32, pp. 202 ff.

**10** Ibid., p. 60.

**11** Ibid., doc. 32, p. 197

**12** Friedländer, *Nazi Germany and the Jews*, 318. See also Beate Meyer, "Das unausweichliche Dilemma: Die Reichsvereinigung der Juden in Deutschland, die Deportationen und die untergetauchten Juden" in *Solidarität und Hilfe für Juden während der NS-Zeit*, Beate Kosmala and Claudia Schoppmann, eds. (Berlin, 2002), pp 273–96.

**13** The responsibilities were laid down, for example, in the tenth supplementary decree to the Reich Citizenship Law, July 4, 1939, RGBl. I, p. 1146.

**14** Wolf Gruner, *Judenverfolgung in Berlin, 1933–1945. Eine Chronologie der Behördenmassnahmen* (Berlin, 1996), p. 95.

**15** See also chapters in this volume by Michael Schäbitz and Chana C. Schütz on emigration and Zionism, respectively; Scholem Adler-Rudel gives an impressive ac-

count of the major efforts of the Jewish organizations with regard to emigration between 1938 and 1941 in *Jüdische Selbsthilfe unter dem Nazi-Regime, 1933–1939* (Tübingen, 1974), particularly pp. 109–20.

**16** Rita Meyhöfer, *Gäste in Berlin? Jüdisches Schülerleben in der Weimarer Republik und im Nationalsozialismus* (Hamburg, 1996), p. 212.

**17** On the Jewish education system see Jörg H. Fehrs, *Von der Heidereutergasse zum Roseneck. Jüdische Schulen in Berlin, 1712–1942* (Berlin, 1993); and Willi Holzer, *Jüdische Schulen in Berlin* (Berlin, 1992).

**18** See Adler-Rudel, *Jüdische Selbsthilfe*, pp. 47 ff., although the period after 1938 is largely excluded.

**19** Joseph Walk, *Jüdische Schule und Erziehung im Dritten Reich* (Frankfurt am Main, 1991), pp. 154–60.

**20** Esriel Hildesheimer, *Jüdische Selbstverwaltung unter dem NS-Regime* (Tübingen, 1994), p. 166.

**21** Ibid., p. 165.

**22** Memoirs of former student Herbert Strauss, *Über dem Abgrund. Eine jüdische Jugend in Deutschland, 1918–1943* (Frankfurt am Main, 1997), pp. 99 ff.

**23** The 1937 administrative report of the board of the Jewish Community in Berlin (Berlin, 1938), pp. 5–6.

**24** Interview with Lutz Ehrlich conducted by Beate Meyer on November 24, 1999, transcript, p. 2.

**25** CJA, 2 B1/2, file note no. 141, August 23, 1941, p. 4.

**26** Ibid., 2 B1/2, file note no. 109, July 16, 1941.

**27** Elisa Klapheck, editor, *Fräulein Rabbiner Jonas. Kann die Frau das rabbinische Amt bekleiden?* (Teetz, 1999), p. 74.

**28** Report by Bruno Blau, doc. 37, in *Jüdisches Leben in Deutschland*, ed. Monika Richarz (Stuttgart, 1982), p. 471. Also see CJA, 2 B1/5, file note from December 15, 1942.

**29** Comparing the Reichsvereinigung to its predecessor the Reichsvertretung, Historian Avraham Barkai calls it a "fundamentally different organization" even though "the same people continued to work in the same offices." Avraham Barkai, "Von Berlin nach Theresienstadt. Zur politischen Biographie von Leo Baeck, 1933–1945," in Barkai, ed., *Hoffnung und Untergang. Studien zur deutsch-jüdischen Geschichte des 19. und 20. Jahrhunderts* (Hamburg, 1998), p. 152.

**30** Charlottenburg district court, entry of the change of name, entry no. 5, April 30, 1941. (Both the Jüdische Gemeinde and the Jüdisches Kultusvereinigung (JKV) are generally referred to as "Jewish Community" throughout this English edition. The Berlin Jewish Community was a kind of independent department of the Reichsvereinigung. Other Jewish Communities could exist as long as they had more than 3,000 members. If not, they were dissolved and incorporated in the local departments of the Reichsvereinigung. See Glossary.)

**31** On Heinrich Stahl see Hermann Simon, "Heinrich Stahl, 13. April 1868—4. November 1942," (Berlin, 1993). On the differences between Stahl and Baeck see also Barkai, "Von Berlin," pp. 152–53.

**32** Heinrich and Jenny Stahl to their children and grandchildren, letter, quoted in Simon, "Heinrich Stahl," p. 35.

**33** CJA, 2 B1/1, file note of June 26, 1939, pp. 2 ff., and July 1, 1939, p.1.

**34** Simon, "Heinrich Stahl," pp. 21 ff.

**35** Ibid., p. 24.

**36** CJA, 2 B1/4, file note K 22, November 12, 1941, p. 2.

**37** See note 32.

**38** Hans Erich Fabian, "Die letzte Etappe," in *Festschrift zum 80. Geburtstag von Leo Baeck am 23. Mai 1953*, Council for the Protection of the Rights and Interests of Jews from Germany ed. (London, 1953), pp. 85–97.

**39** Ibid.

**40** On the policy on living space see Susanne Willems, *Der entsiedelte Jude. Albert Speers Wohnungsmarktpolitik für den Berliner Hauptstadtbau* (Berlin, 2000). On Jewish persecution in Berlin see also Wolf Gruner, "Die Reichshauptstadt und die Verfolgung der Berliner Juden, 1933–1945," in *Jüdische Geschichte in Berlin. Essays und Studien*, ed. Reinhard Rürup (Berlin, 1995), pp. 229–66.

**41** Martha Mosse, memoirs, appendix: *Die Jüdische Gemeinde zu Berlin, 1934–1943*, report of July 23–24, 1958, pp. 1–2, B Rep. 235–07, MF 4170–4171, Landesarchiv Berlin (LAB).

**42** Ibid.

**43** Hannah Arendt, *Eichmann in Jerusalem: A Report on the Banality of Evil*, excerpted in *The Portable Hannah Arendt*, ed. Peter Baehr (New York, 2000), p. 348.

**44** Ibid., pp. 354.

**45** Yad Vashem 01/51, Moritz Henschel, lecture "Die letzten Jahre der Jüdischen Gemeinde Berlin (The final years of the Jewish Community in Berlin)," held in Tel Aviv on September 13, 1946, p. 3.

**46** Questioning of Martha Mosse, July 11, 1967, p. 2, B Rep. 057–01, 1 Ks 1/69 no. 17, LAB.

**47** Ibid., R 34/1, trial against Schotte et. al., questioning of Martha Mosse, August 19, 1942, sheets 100–1.

**48** Ibid., 1 Ks 1/69, no. 17, questioning of Martha Mosse, July 11, 1967, p. 4.

**49** Notice for the participants in deportation transports, quoted in Inge Hartwig-Scharnberg and Jan Maruhn, "Das kann doch nicht mehr lange dauern," (manuscript, 1995).

**50** Mosse, *Erinnerungen*, p. 10; and questioning of the Gestapo official "Karl B.," December 2, 1965, p. 3, B Rep. 057–01, 1 Js 1/67, R 34/17, LAB.

**51** CJA, 2 B1/2, file note 109/B19. See also "Die Synagoge Levetzowstrasse als Sammellager," in *Erbe und Auftrag*, Hermann Simon, New Synagogue Foundation, and Museum Educational Service eds. (Berlin, 1996), pp. 44–47; Klaus Dettmer, "Die Deportationen aus Berlin," in Wolfgang Scheffler and Diana Schulle, editors, *Buch der Erinnerung. Die ins Baltikum deportierten deutschen, österreichischen und tschechoslowakischen Juden* (Munich, 2003), pp. 191–197.

**52** Report by Jacob Jacobson, Doc. 32, in *Jüdisches Leben in Deutschland*, ed. Richarz (see note 28), pp. 401–428, here p. 402.

**53** Siegmund Weltlinger, *Hast Du es schon vergessen? Erlebnisbericht aus der Zeit der Verfolgung*, ed. Berlin Society for Jewish-Christian Cooperation (Berlin, 1954), p. 27.

**54** Edith Dietz, *Den Nazis entronnen* (Frankfurt am Main, 1990), pp. 36–37.

**55** Interview with Max Reschke on May 11, 1959, StA LG Berlin, 1 Js 5/65, Gestapo regional headquarters Berlin/documents, accompanying file 30, collection Dr. Wolfgang Scheffler, pp. 2–3; pp. 166–67.

**56** Interview with Edith Dietz conducted by Beate Meyer on July 7, 1999, CJA, Ausstellungsunterlagen, no transcript, cassette 2, side B.

**57** For example, the former math teacher Ernst Günter Fontheims, who had to work as a marshal, communicated a hidden warning to his mother. See interview with Ernest Fontheim conducted by Beate Meyer on May 26, 1999, CJA, *Ausstellungsunterlagen*, transcript, pp. 7–8.

**58** See note 56.

**59** Hildegard Henschel, "Aus der Arbeit der Jüdischen Gemeinde Berlin während der Jahre 1941–1943. Gemeindearbeit und Evakuierung von Berlin 16. Oktober 1941—16. Juni 1943," in *Zeitschrift für die Geschichte der Juden* 9 (1972), pp. 34–52, here p. 37.

**60** Questioning of Hilde Kahan, October 30, 1968, B Rep. 057–01, 1 Ks 1/69, R 11/20, p. 3, LAB.

**61** Questioning of Johanna Heym, June 14, 1967, B Rep. 057–01, no. 385, p. 3; see also ibid., 1 Js 1/67, R 34/3, p. 1,326, LAB.

**62** For a detailed account see Wolfgang Scheffler, "Der Brandanschlag im Berliner Lustgarten im Mai 1942 und seine Folgen. Eine quellenkritische Betrachtung," in *Berlin in Geschichte und Gegenwart. Jahrbuch des Landesarchivs Berlin 1984,* ed. Hans J. Reichardt (Berlin 1984), pp. 91–118; see also Eric Brothers and Michael Kreutzer, "Die Widerstandsgruppen um Herbert Baum," in *Im Kampf gegen Besatzung und "Endlösung." Widerstand der Juden in Europa, 1939–45,* ed. Georg Heuberger (Frankfurt am Main, 1995), pp. 23–42.

**63** On the individuals involved see Scheffler, "Der Brandanschlag," pp. 93–96.

**64** Goebbels diary entry for May 24, 1942, in *Die Tagebücher von Joseph Goebbels,* ed. Elke Fröhlich, part 2, 1941–1945, vol. 4 (Munich, 1987), pp. 351ff.

**65** Scheffler, "Der Brandanschlag," pp. 106, 109–10.

**66** That the boards of the Vienna and Prague Reichsvereinigung were present at this summons suggests that Nazi retaliation for the arson attack and revenge for the attack on Heydrich were linked.

**67** Henschel, "Die letzten Jahre," p. 4.

**68** Leonhard Baker, *Hirt der Verfolgten. Leo Baeck im Dritten Reich* (Stuttgart, 1982), p. 366.

**69** "Summons to the Reich Security Main Office, May 29, 1942," Bundesarchiv (BArch), 75 C Re 1, no. 1.1.1/8/2, file note, p. 116. Also see Goebbels, *Die Tagebücher,* p. 432.

**70** "Summons," p. 107.

**71** Ibid., R 8.1.5.0, 1.1.1./8/1, p. 35, 47–61.

**72** Baker, *Hirt der Verfolgten,* p. 367; Barkai, "Von Berlin," p. 161.

**73** Goebbels diary entry for May 28, 1942, in *Die Tagebücher,* p. 386.

**74** Report by Dr. Martha Mosse on "resettlement" of the Berlin Jews taken down by Dr. Wolfgang Scheffler on July 23–24, 1958, Yad Vashem 02/769, p. 5.

**75** File note F 53, p. 69 ff., here p. 3, p. 70, 75 C Re 1, no. 112/46/3, BArch.

**76** Ibid.

**77** Questioning of Hans-Erich Fabian by the state prosecutor on October 28, 1968, B Rep. 057–01, 1 Ks 1/69, R 11/16, pp. 4–5, LAB.

**78** File note no. 243, March 9, 1943, 75 C Re 1, no. 1.3/50/6, BArch.

**79** The significance of this operation for the survivors emerges from the fact that memoirs on this operation blend together many things that are related to other events. These include Leo Kreindler's fatal heart attack—he died during a roll call on November 19, 1942—and the appearance of Adolf Eichmann (who was not present during the *Gemeinde-Aktion*).

**80** See Henschel, "Aus der Arbeit" and Henschel's testimony in the Eichmann trial, trial proceedings in the CJA library, Strafakt 40/61, minutes of the meeting 37, p. O01. <sic>

**81** Only four "careers" remained in the Jewish hospital to care for the sick. Questioning of Dr. Helmut Cohen, October 31, 1968, B Rep. 057–01, 1 Ks 1/69, R 11/16, LAB. The emergency services are listed in CJA, complete archive 00239, p. 289.

**82** Questioning of Siegbert Kleemann, February 14, 1969, B Rep. 057–01, 1 Ks 1/69, R 11/16p. 31, LAB; and affirmation by Liselotte Pereles, January 14, 1961, AG–RSHA F II b–796 (Israeli Eichmann-Document), quoted here according to the copy in StA LG Berlin 1 Js 5/65, Gestapo regional headquarters Berlin/documents, accompanying file no. 30.

**83** CJA, 1, 75 A Be 2, no. 14 (no. 239), room allocation, p. 280.

**84** Sentence against Fritz Wöhrn, October 13, 1969, B Rep. 057–01, no. 406, p. 40, LAB.

**85** See note 82 (Liselotte Pereles).

**86** Questioning of Siegbert Kleemann, February 14, 1969, B Rep. 057–01, 1 Ks 1/69, R 11/16, p. 32, LAB.

**87** Ibid., questioning of Hilde Kahan, October 30, 1968.

**88** Ibid., R 11/20, questioning of Selmar Neumann, August 11, 1968, p. 2; Henschel, "Aus der Arbeit," p. 42.

**89** Report by the JKV to RMdI/RSHA, Kozower, October 22, 1942, 75 C Re 1, no. 1.3/50/2, p. 130, BArch.

**90** Henschel to Lustig, letter dated January 7, 1943, CJA, 1, 75 A Be 2, no. 14 (no. 239), p. 15.

**91** Paul Scheurenberg, memoirs written in Theresienstadt 1943–44, pp. 59–60, copy in the CJA archive, pp. 14–15.

**92** Ibid.

**93** CJA, 1, 75 A Be 2, no. 14 (no. 239), Listen, pp. 18–37 and 56.

**94** See note 84 (Wöhrn), p. 42.

**95** CJA, 1, 75 A Be 2, no. 14 (no. 239), list VIII: Still missing after investigation, p. 16.

**96** Ibid., file note Henschel, October 29, 1942, p. 44; Report by the JKV (see note 89), p. 131; the enclosure contains a list of people to be deported, see pp. 132–148, for details on individuals who had fled see pp. 145 ff. and JKV to Reichsvereinigung, November 2, 1942, Henschel, p. 149.

**97** Ibid. and CJA, 1, 75 A Be 2, no. 14 (no. 239), note by Kleemann, February 9, 1943, p. 17.

**98** The reasons for these releases are unknown. Questioning of Adolf Wolffsky, December 1, 1965, B Rep. 057–01, 1 Ks 1/69, R 34/4, pp. 5 ff, LAB.

**99** Henschel, "Aus der Arbeit," p. 43. The notices of death are dated December 1, 1942.

**100** B Rep. 057–01, 1 Ks 1/69, R 11/18 note of March 27, 1968, p. 79, LAB. Also see Yad Vashem 01/197 Georg Glückstein, Report "In Berlin 1933–1945," p. 5.

**101** A list of deportation transports is found in Gruner, *Judenverfolgung*, p. 98.

**102** Henschel, "Aus der Arbeit," p. 35; Certificate from the JKV, accommodation advice center, November 24, 1942, signed by Martha Mosse, Rep. 200 Acc. 2334 no. 37 sheet 56, LAB.

**103** Questioning of Harry Schnapp, April 27, 1965, B Rep. 057–01, 1 Js 1/67, R 34/8, p. 3, LAB.

**104** Wilfried Meyer, *Unternehmen Sieben. Eine Rettungs-aktion für vom Holocaust Bedrohte aus dem Amt Ausland/ Abwehr im Oberkommando der Wehrmacht* (Frankfurt am Main, 1993), pp. 377–78.

**105** Questioning of H. G. Werner, n.d., B Rep. 057–01, 1 Ks 1/69, R 34/4, pp. 2 ff., pp. 562 ff, LAB.

**106** Meyer, *Unternehmen Sieben*, p. 378.

**107** RSHA to the RFSS, personal staff, Wolff, letter dated March 10, 1943, BDC, 640000/4484, BArch.

**108** Questioning of Ursula Prietzel, October 9, 1967, B Rep. 057–01, 1 Ks 1/69, R 34/4, p. 6, LAB.

**109** Questioning of H. G. Werner, n.d., B Rep. 057–01, 1 Ks 1/69, R 34/4, pp. 9, 570, LAB.

**110** Questioning of Ursula Prietzel, October 9, 1967, B Rep. 057–01, 1 Ks 1/69, R 34/4, p. 8, LAB; in the same file, questioning of Rehfeld, January 27, 1965, p. 1.

**111** Mosse, *Erinnerungen*, p. 4; Henschel, "Aus der Arbeit," p. 43.

**112** Questioning of Harry Schnapp, December 10, 1965,

**113** File note Moritz Henschel November 14, 1942, CJA, 2 B1/5. For further details, in the same file see note by Rockmann, November 14, 1942.

**114** Little information about the assembly camps on Kleine Hamburger Strasse and Johannisstrasse is available. Questioning of Margarete Sch., June 8, 1967, B Rep. 057–01, 1 Js 1/67, no. 34/3, pp. 2–3, LAB.

**115** The site on Gerlachstrasse was sold in March 1943, the assembly camp closed down, and the inmates moved to Auguststrasse. CJA, 1 75A Be 2, no. 112/1 (no. 14218), sheets 43–45. This site was sold to the Nationalsozialistische Volks-swohlfahrt (NSV). Ibid., sheets 104 ff.

**116** Questioning of Martha Ehrlich, July 4, 1967, B Rep. 057–01, no. 383, p. 2, LAB.

**117** Questioning of Curt Naumann, July 14, 1965, B Rep. 057–01, 1 Js 1/67, R 34/33, 7, LAB; in the same fine, questioning of Staats, p. 7a.

**118** Questioning of Johanna Heym, June 14, 1967, B Rep. 057–01, no. 385, LAB.

**119** Ibid., 1 Js 1/67, R 34/8, questioning of Harry Schnapp, December 10, 1965, pp. 15 ff., here p. 17.

**120** File note by Kozower following a discussion with Brunner, November 17, 1942, CJA, 2 B1/5; and summons of Werner Simon to Henschel, November 18, 1942.

**121** Questioning of Bruno Goldstein, November 30, 1965, B Rep. 057–01, 1 Ks 1/69, no. 13, LAB.

**122** Ibid., copy of the sentence passed by Lichterfelde district court (Pks 9/48, StA Berlin), July 2, 1947, p. 3.

**123** Questioning of Heinz Muskatblatt, B Rep. 057–01, 1 Js 1/67, R 34/7, p. 2, LAB.

**124** Henschel, "Aus der Arbeit," pp. 43–44.

**125** CJA, 2 B1/5, file notes, December 14, 1942.

**126** CJA, 2 B1/5, file notes November 20, 1942, November 21, 1942, November 24, 1942, November 26, 1942, December 7, 1942, December 10, 1942, and January 27, 1943; Henschel, "Aus der Arbeit," p. 41.

**127** CJA, 2 B1/5, file notes from December 11, 1942, December 15, 1942, and January 4, 1943.

**128** See note 45 (Moritz Henschel, "Die letzten Jahre"), p. 4.

**129** Max Plaut, account of life after 1933, Archive Institute for the History of German Jews, 14.–001.1, p. 1.

**130** "Leo Baeck, "A People Stands before Its God," in *We Survived*, ed. Erich Böhm (Yale, 1949), pp. 284–298.

**131** Eric H. Boehm, editor, *We Survived: The Stories of Fourteen of the Hidden and Hunted of Nazi Germany* (New Haven, 1949), p. 293.

**132** Strauss, *Abgrund*, p. 158.

**133** Baker, *Hirt*, p. 365.

**134** Ibid., pp. 367 ff.

**135** See note 29 (Barkai, "Von Berlin,"), p. 161.

**136** Barkai points out that the Czech-Jewish leaders also decided in this way. Barkai, "Von Berlin," pp. 163–64.

**137** Questioning of Stella Borchers, July 14, 1966, Rep. 057–01, 1 Js 1/67, R 34/21, p. 2, LAB.

**138** The finance expert Erich Fabian was even brought back from Theresienstadt to continue the complex transfer of remaining Reichsvereinigung assets to the German Reich. See notes 38 and 77 (Fabian, *Die letzte Etappe*; questioning of Fabian, October 28, 1968).

**139** All information from JKV reorganization plan, January 31, 1943, CJA, 2 B 1.

**140** A good overview of the history of the hospital is provided in Dagmar Hartung von Doetinchem and Rolf Winau, editors, *Zerstörte Fortschritte. Das Jüdische Krankenhaus in Berlin* (Berlin, 1989); Rifka Elkin, *Das Jüdische Krankenhaus in Berlin zwischen 1938 und 1945* (Berlin, 1993).

**141** Hartung von Doetinchem and Winau, *Zerstörte Fortschritte*, p. 179.

**142** Questioning of Hilde Kahan, October 30, 1968, B Rep. 057–01, 1 KS 1/69, R 11/20, p. 9, LAB; for a divergent account see Hilde Kahan, *Chronik deutscher Juden, 1939–1945*, Leo Baeck Institute Jerusalem, 207, manuscript 1980, p. 32.

**143** Sentence against Fritz Wöhrn, October 13, 1969, B Rep. 057–01, no. 406, p. 59, LAB.

**144** Indictment of Fritz Wöhrn, Rep. 057–01, no. 405, 1 Js /65 (RSHA), pp. 638–39.

**145** Of Wöhrn's twelve-year sentence, five years were suspended. Ibid., pp. 2–3.

**146** Questioning of Hilde Kahan, October 30, 1968, B Rep. 057–01, R 11/20, p. 10, LAB.

**147** This emerges from the file note of May 24–28, 1944 (Kleemann), 75 C Re1, no. 111/9/1, BArch.

**148** Questioning of Heinz Pagel, April 11, 1968, B Rep. 057–01, 1 KS 1/69, R 11/20, p. 45, LAB.

**149** Questioning of Stella Borchers, July 14, 1966, B Rep. 057–01, 1 KS 1/69, R 43/21, p. 4; and in the same file, questioning of Selmar Neumann, April 11, 1968, p. 12.

**150** See Blau, in *Jüdisches Leben in Deutschland*, p. 469.

**151** Ibid.

**152** Kahan, *Chronik deutscher Juden*, p. 32.

**153** 75 C Re1, no. 1.1.1./9/7, p. 587; and 1.1.3/61/2, p. 97, BArch.

**154** Kahan, *Chronik deutscher Juden*, pp. 32–33.

**155** See note 137 (questioning of Stella Borchers), p. 4.

**156** See Blau, in *Jüdisches Leben in Deutschland*, p. 464.

**157** Hartung-von Doetinchem and Winau, *Zerstörte Fortschritte*, p. 214. Blau refers to about eight hundred people. See *Jüdisches Leben in Deutschland*, note 28, p. 470.

**158** Entry by Kleemann, added to the testimony of February 22, 1957, Düsseldorf Restitution Office, Restitution files ZK 14012.

**159** See note 137 (questioning of Stella Borchers), p. 2.

**160** Questioning of Heinz Paul Meissl, July 12, 1967, Sta LG Berlin, 3 PKs 1/7 (Bovensiepen et al.), vol. 31, pp. 12–14.

**161** Questioning of Margarete Schindler, June 8, 1967, B Rep. 057–01, 1 Js 1/67, R 34/3, pp. 4–5, LAB.

**162** Curt Naumann makes a similar statement in his questioning of July 14, 1965, B Rep. 057–01, 1 Js 1/67, R 34/33, p. 6, LAB.

**163** Elkin, *Das Jüdische Krankenhaus*, p. 70.

**164** Daniel S. Nadav and Manfred Stürzbecher, "Walter Lustig," in Hartung von Doetinchem and Winau, *Zerstörte Fortschritte*, pp. 221–26. Unless indicated, all further details are from this essay.

**165** Lustig's publications, most of which appeared before 1933, included *Der kleine Lustig,Leitfaden der gerichtlichen Medizin einschliesslich der gerichtlichen Psychiatrie"* (1926), *"Die theoretischen Grundlagen der praktischen Krankenpflege"* (1933/1936); *"Recht und Gesetz im Krankenhaus"* (1930) and *"Laboratorium und Röntgeninstitut in Gesetz und Recht"* (1931).

**166** Evidence of instructions on benefit amounts, January 11, 1934, Pr Br Rep. 042, Kap. 60 Ti 21b/L7, LAB.

**167** *Jüdisches Nachrichtenblatt*, 21 July, 1939, p. 1.

**168** Elkin, *Das Jüdische Krankenhaus*, p. 46.

**169** Ibid., p. 55.

**170** CJA, 2 B1/3, file note K 30, December 19, 1941.

**171** Decision on the Jewish Property Levy, January 3, 1939, Chief Finance Department, 8 WGA 2176.50.

**172** Ibid.

**173** Elkin, *Jüdische Krankenhaus,* pp. 49 ff.

**174** CJA, 2 B1/5, file note, December 10, 1942.

**175** The Lustigs' childless marriage was considered a "nonprivileged mixed marriage," that is, it provided no protection from deportation. CJA, display documents Lustig, Traunstein district hospital, index sheet and salary declaration from the mayor of Traunstein, July 1, 1943.

**176** Ulrike Eckhardt and Andreas Nachama, *Jüdische Orte in Berlin* (Berlin, 1996), p. 137.

**177** Dagmar Hartung von Doetinchem, "Das Krankenhaus im Nationalsozialismus," in Hartung von Doetinchem and Winau, *Zerstörte Fortschritte,* pp. 146–215.

**178** Entry by Kleemann (n.d. [June 1945]), Düsseldorf Restitution Office, ZK 14012, pp. M 71 and 72.

**179** Eckhardt and Nachama, *Jüdische Orte,* p. 137.

**180** Elkin, *Jüdische Krankenhaus,* pp. 58–59. The employees in turn kept matters such as religious services secret from him, p. 64.

**181** Walter Lustig, letter dated June 15, 1945, Rep. 20, no. 4616–4617, LAB.

**182** Ibid., letter appendix, pp. 1–3, Rep. 20, no. 4616–4617.

**183** Ibid., Dr. Hirschfeld to Marshal Joseph Stalin, telegram.

**184** See note 182, pp. 17–18.

**185** It remains to be established whether there was a tribunal proceeding or a court case.

**186** Düsseldorf Restitution Office, ZK 14 012, decision of the district special assistance committee, October 1, 1948.

**187** Sworn witness statement by F. H., March 31, 1953, Düsseldorf Restitution Office, ZK 14 012.

**188** Entry by Kleemann, p. M 71 and 72, enclosed the statement of February 22, 1957, Düsseldorf Restitution Office, ZK 14 012.

**189** letter from Alexander Rotholz, April 17, 1957, p. M 83, Düsseldorf Restitution Office, ZK 14 012.

**190** See Wildt, *Die Judenpolitik des SD 1935 bis 1938,* p. 46.

**191** Hartung von Doetinchem and Winau, *Zerstörte Fortschritte,* p. 172.

**192** Dan Diner, "Jenseits des Vorstellbaren. Der "Judenrat" als Situation," in *"Unser einziger Weg ist Arbeit." Das Getto in Lódz, 1940–1944,* ed. Jewish Museum and Frankfurt am Main (Frankfurt am Main, 1990), pp. 32–40.

**193** Ruling in the tribunal proceedings against Martha Raphael, May 7, 1947, Rep. 20, no. 4860–4861, p. 2, LAB.

# Chapter Nineteen
## Oranienburger Strasse 28–31

DIANA SCHULLE

Citizens of the Third Reich were required to have an *Ariernachweis,* proof that their "German-blood," or "Aryan," identity extended back to their grandparents' generation. Regardless of their religious affiliation, all Jews—as defined by the *Arierparagraph* ("Aryan Clause") of the 1935 Nuremberg racial laws—were excluded. Failure to possess an *Ahnenpass* (proof of "Aryan" ancestry) meant, among other things, that it was not possible to marry or to change professions.[1] Anyone wishing to join the National Socialist German Workers' Party (NSDAP) or one of its suborganizations had to furnish proof of pure "Aryan" ancestry as far back as 1800, and in some cases, earlier. What was to be done if the relevant documents were no longer in the family's possession? Who made the decision on whether an individual was of "German" or "foreign" blood if, despite all efforts, it was no longer possible to obtain the birth certificate in question? How could the problem be solved in the case of adoptive children and foundlings?

Beginning in April 1933, the Reich Ministry of the Interior employed a Racial Research Expert (*Sachverständiger für Rasseforschung*) to address such questions. The department was renamed the Reich Office for Genealogical Research (Reichsstelle für Sippenforschung [RfS]) in 1935 and was affiliated with the NSDAP Department for Genealogical Research (Amt für Sippenforschung [AfS]). In the event of a doubtful racial pedigree, this office alone was to make the final decision on the "racial" classification of the person in question. Initially it checked up only on employees of the ministry—civil servants and officials. Soon, however, the group of people to be examined expanded, as more and more ministries and other public bodies approached the RfS for quick checks on their employees.

To help supply the missing information, the two institutions of the RfS and AfS needed access to a variety of sources. These included, among other things, archives from courts and municipal administrations, church records, personal files from major institutions, registry office records, autobiographical publications, dissertations containing the author's curriculum vita, published and unpublished family biographies, reference works, family notices in daily newspapers, and genealogical newspapers.

Heading both the RfS and the AfS was Kurt Mayer, a historian and SS member who also held an emeritus position in the Office for Race and Resettlement. Mayer was constantly in search of materials that would make it less costly and time-consuming to prove Jewish origins. It was not until the pogrom of November 9–10, 1938, that the Gestapo accomplished in one night what he had been trying to do for years.

For the Gestapo, the pogrom yielded—in addition to vandalized synagogues; plundered shops and apartments; destroyed children's homes, schools, and other institutions—the "extensive Jewish archive and special documents of all kinds from synagogues, Jewish religious communities, and other Jewish departments." Reinhard Heydrich, head of the SD (SS security service) and chief of the security police, subsequently announced that "a large amount of the materials are located in Gestapo departments, some of them . . . however, with other authorities and departments." Since it was essential first to bring these materials together in order to allow standardized examination and assessment, Heydrich ordered that the "archive and written materials gathered during the Jewish campaigns"—his euphemism for the pogrom—"be immediately handed over in their entirety and without amendment to the responsible Gestapo office."[2]

Mayer greeted the Gestapo cache of confiscated materials with enthusiasm. He hoped that the personal details on family background and origin that they contained would fill the gaps that remained, even after five years of work, and that they would make his archive virtually unassailable. He used his still-intact personal connections to Heinrich Himmler to get his hands on the material. Soon thereafter, Mayer had, at least theoretically, in his possession a huge and diverse quantity of material related to individuals. It came from all manner of sources, and it was thus difficult to get an overview. Mayer was now faced with a purely practical problem: the impossibility of housing it all in the RfS offices at Schiffbauerdamm 26, which were already short of space.

The problem was solved with the help of the Reich Security Main Office (Reichssicherheitshauptamt [RSHA]). With the Gestapo's blessing, an official from both the RfS and the AfS would move to the business premises of the Gesamtarchiv der deutschen Juden (General Archive of German Jews).[3] The move was "effective immediately" (at the end of March 1939). The Gesamtarchiv had been housed next door to the New Synagogue on Oranienburger Strasse 28. Now, in order to draw up documents based on Jewish registers of births, deaths, and (if they were required for a proof of origin) marriages, the RfS and

**Figure 19.1**

The New Synagogue (built 1866) on Oranienburger Strasse

AfS researchers would be able to consult all of the Gesamtarchiv's confiscated files along with those of the Jewish Community. Most useful of all was the register detailing the not insubstantial number of Jews who had over generations voluntarily withdrawn from the Berlin Jewish Community, many of them having converted to Christianity. The records extended back to about 1873.[4]

Meanwhile, the remaining staff of the Gesamtarchiv continued to work for "solely Jewish purposes"—that is, using the archive to confirm identity cards, organize emigration, issue certificates of nationality and membership in the Jewish Community, and so forth. Mayer granted them use of the two rooms formerly belonging to the archive's library. "The Jewish Community has not raised any objections," he reported to the minister of the interior, Wilhelm Frick.[5]

Mayer anticipated that the newly accessible materials would attract more researchers and so thought it sensible to give the institution a special name. The Central Office for Jewish Registers of Births, Deaths, and Marriages (*Zentralstelle für jüdische Personenstandsregister*) opened on April 6, 1939.[6] The "Central Office" was to have a completely separate entrance to that used by the Jewish Community, and the Community was, moreover, to "provide a porter at its own expense" to guard it.[7]

The head of the Gesamtarchiv, Dr. Jacob Jacobson, urged by the Berlin Jewish Community's chairman, Heinrich Stahl, eventually negotiated to have the decision to confiscate the archive and Jewish Community's library overturned. The decision in fact only meant that the RfS would transfer its Register of People of Foreign Origin (*Fremdstämmigenkartei*) to the premises as well—since it, too, related to Jews. As time went by, the RfS laid claim to more and more space for itself.[8]

In 1940, the Central Office had in its possession about half of the Jewish registers of personal details and similar sources for all of the Altreich. It now seemed "extremely important" to the authorities to merge the Register of People of Foreign Origin and the Gesamtarchiv into one archive. Those in favor of the move argued that the facilities at Oranienburger Strasse 28 were "particularly suited to this."[9] And so, on June 24, 1940, the RfS's two major collections of files—its Register of Ancestry of the German People (*Ahnenstammkartei des deutschen Volkes*) and the Register of People of Foreign Origin—were moved to Oranienburger Strasse.

The first of these, the Register of Ancestry, had been made available by the Leipzig-based Central Office for German Personal and Family Biographies in September 1933.[10] The register—which still exists—extends from the first recorded genealogical sources to the present. It is not structured as a register of names but rather of genealogy. Each card listed the youngest member of a family line, the respective living descendant, with his or her direct predecessors, and the women related by marriage. The lines of descent entered on record cards were sorted phonetically, classed according to family names, and within these classifications, listed according to places of origin. The sources of the data were also listed precisely.[11]

The importance of the Register of People of Foreign Origin, which comprised over a million card files, was that it only contained facts that could be proven with documentary evidence. It listed all racial Jews currently or previously living in in the territory of the German Reich—regardless of whether they belonged to the "Jewish Religious Community," had no religious denomination, or had in fact been baptized as Christians. It registered *Mischlinge* as well. Lastly, it included data gathered during background checks on dubious Gentiles. The details were duly entered on record cards and integrated with the rest of the information.[12]

Jacob Jacobson, who knew his well-ordered archive intimately, held a post that was of great interest to the RfS.[13] Consequently, only his wife and son were granted permission by the Gestapo to emigrate to England; Jacobson was too important to let go. He was charged with providing appropriate assistance to the RfS as well as to people obliged to furnish proof of origin. In return, the office intervened in the fall of 1941 to exempt him from wearing the yellow star. Jacobson refused the privilege.[14]

Jacobson was in a dangerous position, especially, as he later wrote, "when people [who] came to me to prove their [Gentile] origin . . . urged me to suppress incriminating entries or to tear out the relevant pages. I could never be sure if those proposing such risky undertakings were agent provocateurs. I had, moreover, to consider the fact that official departments had copies of the registers that my information must have been based on."[15]

For all the "incriminating" evidence it contained, the Gesamtarchiv could also be a source of help. Those Jews still in Berlin consulted the files to prove, for example, that they had relatives living in the United States. Such evidence could greatly aid them in obtaining the coveted immigration visas.[16]

**Figure 19.2**
Jacob Jacobson

THE JEWISH ARCHIVES THAT had been appropriated during the November pogrom were housed in three different locations. The most recent material was stored in police departments for use by the police themselves; material relevant to general historical research was set aside for archives; and material that could be used to prove origin was to be collated by the RfS. In the process, however, the RSHA and the security police expressly reserved the right to the entire stock of materials, particularly with regard to deciding the extent to which and at what time the materials should be made available.[17]

The guidelines were fuzzy, even to those in the know. Gerhard Kayser, the head of the department for the Register of People of Foreign Origin and the *Schriftdenkmalschutz* (protection of historical documents), classified the entire contents of the Gesamtarchiv according to these guidelines. Jacobson, who was most familiar with the materials, assisted him. In other words, Kayser removed all the materials that he considered unnecessary for the work of the newly renamed Reichssippenamt (Reich Office for Genealogy [RfS]). The contents "were apparently . . . greatly reduced in the process. Two departments were formed . . . from the remaining materials: A) the sources of personal details (Jewish register, tax lists, lists of pupils, and so on), and B) historical materials."[18]

The historical materials occupied an area of about 120 square meters in the national archive. The Reichssippenamt was prepared to hand the material over to the archive administration right away, but it required the SD's permission.[19]

Only in 1942 did the supervisory authority—Department VII of the RSHA, which was responsible for "Weltanschauung research and assessment" and led by Franz Six—decide to give the files of the "historical department" stored on Oranienburger Strasse to the Secret State Archive (Geheime Staatsarchiv) in Dahlem for archival assessment. The sole right of disposal, however, remained with Department VII. The secret state archive could not obtain fuel for transporting the "Jewish files" to Dahlem. Between November 30 and December 8, 1942, the materials were moved to storage far away from Berlin, along with other archive materials.

In the meantime "messengers from the Secret State Archive" picked up collections of files, which Jacobson saw as a clear sign of the impending demise of his Gesamtarchiv.[20] When he was deported to Theresienstadt in May 1943 "the Gesamtarchiv was completely finished."[21] Even at Theresienstadt, however, Jacobson continued his research into Jewish history on Gestapo orders. He translated marriage and circumcision books from the eighteenth and nineteenth centuries, which the Reichssippenamt had given to him from their collections.[22]

Oranienburger Strasse 28 now housed under one roof the Central Office for Jewish Registers (of Births, Deaths, and Marriages) and the Register of People of Foreign Origin as well as the Gesamtarchiv. In addition, on August 5, 1942, the Reich Office for Statistics handed over the supplementary forms (*Ergänzungskarten*) from the census of May 17, 1939. These contained personal details on people with one or several "fully Jewish" grandparents as well as information about their origin and background.[23] Added to this were the Jewish identity card register, the register of the Reich Ministry of Labor on people of "foreign origin" employed in the Reich, and around 20,000 personal files released by various authorities.[24] Director Kurt Mayer vehemently opposed a move of the whole Reichssippenamt to Oranienburger Strasse after some renovation measures there were rejected. He remained at the Schiffbauerdamm offices, along with the central department with the records office, the information section, and the picture department. Meanwhile, his deputy director, Friedrich A. Knost—who was both editor and one of the publishers of the Newspaper for Registry Offices (*Zeitschrift für Standesamtswesen*)[25]—established his office on Oranienburger Strasse.

On July 5, 1943, Knost announced that "the supervisory authority of the Reichsvereinigung der Juden in Deutschland [Reich Association of Jews in Germany], the Gestapo . . . [has] dissolved all Jewish Communities and local offices of the Reich Association of Jews in the Altreich, effective June 10, 1943. . . . All available files on Jews who have emigrated and moved away—likewise on mixed marriages and privileged [mixed] marriages—which were located housed by the

Jewish Community in Berlin and the Reich Association of Jews in Germany at Kantstrasse 158, Berlin, have been taken over by Department III."[26] To make the Reichsvereinigung's documents at all usable, the Reichssippenamt first took on fifteen Jewish employees. Five days before it was closed, the Reichsvereinigung had to sell the building at Oranienburger Strasse 28 to the German government; on June 10 it was confiscated.

In the night from November 22 to 23, 1943, the New Synagogue was severely damaged by bombardment. The top two floors of the adjacent building became unusable. Administration of the complex was transferred to the head of finance on April 1, 1944. In November 1944 the latter fixed with the Reichssippenamt "the appropriate rent at 5 percent of the assessed value plus all running costs." The building's assessed value was RM 407,000; hence the Reichssippenamt would have had to pay annual rent of RM 20,350 and monthly rent of around RM 1,700 for a six-story building—an almost laughably high amount. Mayer objected to this and got the price reduced to between RM 700–800, as his institution could only claim the basement and the first two floors. The archive rooms important for his office had become unusable "because of the impact of air raids."[27] In the end, the rent was RM 505 per month.

From August 9, 1943—a few weeks after the materials from the Reichsvereinigung had been taken over—the approximately 10,000 Jewish registers from the eastern territories housed in the archive building on Oranienburger Strasse were loaded onto police trucks and deposited in a tunnel at the Stassfurt salt mine. This would protect them from further bomb attacks. The Reichssippenamt's film archive was already located here at .85 meters below ground level. Experts meanwhile declared the basement of the archive building on Oranienburger Strasse to be secure against bomb attacks, even after the upper floors had collapsed.[28] For this reason, current files on ancestry as well as the library of the Berlin heraldic association Der Herold were moved to the vaults of the synagogue complex.[29]

The "Jewish register," which was constantly consulted and included 7,000 volumes with details on "German Reich" Jews, the Register of People of Foreign Origin, the register of identity cards, and around 160,000 separate files on descent,[30] as well as selected materials taken over from the Reichsvereinigung, was to be taken to a confiscated Moravian castle for safekeeping.[31] This plan presumably changed, since the Reichssippenamt had a location in Thuringia from mid-October 1943 at the latest. The director fundamentally refused a complete evacuation of the Reichssippenamt with the reason that around sixty people still came to Schiffbauerdamm every day during consultation hours. These were mainly soldiers on leave from the front seeking, by means of a quick marriage, to bind their wives to them. The Reichssippenamt continued to issue "declarations of origin" (*Abstammungsunterlagen*). Some 750 to 850 new applications were made each month, mainly by members of the Wehrmacht.[32]

There were sometimes up to eleven Jews from "mixed marriages" working to enter the Notices of Amendment (*Veränderungsmeldungen*) sent in by intermediaries of the Reichsvereinigung into the Reichsvereinigung files. Although these people worked on Oranienburger Strasse, the "Neue Reichsvereinigung" was now based at the Jewish hospital at Iranische Strasse 2, in the Wedding district.

For example, queries coming from the Office for the Utilization of Assets of the head of finance for Berlin-Brandenburg or from other finance offices were directed to the so-called *Kataster* (tax register), which was housed on Oranienburger Strasse. The *Kataster* staff provided information from Reichsvereinigung materials on the final address or the whereabouts of Jews. Finance authorities could thus seize the possessions left behind by Jews who had emigrated or been deported. The Notices of Amendment from the intermediaries, which did not come in regularly but were certainly not absent, ensured that the Jewish *Kataster* was kept more or less up to date, with the result that it became indispensable, for example, for the head of finance, who apparently lost an overview of the confiscation of assets at the beginning of 1945.[33]

There was frequent talk of splitting the property at Oranienburger Strasse 28–30 into three parts until a land surveyor confirmed that this would be unwise, "especially as the synagogue at Oranienburger Strasse 30 will probably go over to the state (*Land*) of Berlin to be put up for sale."[34]

After British air raids on the complex during the night of November 22–23, 1943, mention was made of an Army Uniform Department (*Heeresbekleidungsamt*) at Oranienburger Strasse 30—the synagogue building. At present there are no further details as to whether this office moved into the synagogue, and if so, when.[35]

THE GESTAPO ESTABLISHED THE "most notorious and horrific torture chamber in Berlin" in the basement of the building at Oranienburger Strasse 31, on the New Synagogue's western flank.[36] Before the November pogrom, the building had housed another Jewish institution and important cultural site: the Jewish Museum.[37] Among the Gestapo prisoners held in the building was Werner Scharff, a founder member of the resistance group Society for Peace and Reconstruction (Gemeinschaft für Frieden und Aufbau). Eyewitnesses report that the building served, at least temporarily, as the Oranienburger Strasse office of the Gestapo regional headquarters. In 1990, the wife of Henri Higuet, a

former forced laborer, related the following in a letter to the Centrum Judaicum: "My husband was brought to the synagogue every day. They all had to spend the whole day in the yard. . . . Upstairs in the offices . . . they were then interrogated and beaten." [38]

The ground floor contained cells that faced the synagogue. The prisoners were sorted according to sex and nationality. Jennie Lebel, who was imprisoned here as a "Serb" rather than a "Jewess," recalls that "the doors were made of heavy wood, hard big locks, and small hatches, on which the number of prisoners was written in chalk. . . . In my cell, which was two-by-three meters in size, there were a minimum of nine and sometimes as many as twenty-three prisoners. . . . When it came to an interrogation, the name of the prisoner concerned was called out from the entrance to the corridor and [he] had to report through the control hatch. The interrogations took place on the upper floors, in the rooms facing the street. . . . When there were bomb attacks the guards locked us in and brought themselves to safety." [39]

Distressing evidence from the Nazi period was discovered during renovation work on the building in the spring of 1961. Beneath wallpaper that had been put up at the end of the war, the names and addresses of prisoners had been scratched into the walls. [40]

**Figure 19.4**
Prisoners' inscriptions,
August and October
1944

**1** The *Ahnenpass* was introduced in 1934 by the registrars "to overcome the . . . many difficulties" that arose when a person had to present his *Abstammungsunterlagen* (documents of origin) at various institutions. Multiple inquiries to registry offices and church authorities could thereby be avoided. Anhalt State Ministry, Department for Interior Affairs, September 24, 1934, in *Zeitschrift für Standesamtswesen* 19 (1934): 359.

**2** HA I, Rep. 178/VII, 2 E 8, vol. 2, sheet 82, RdErl. d. RMI, April 15, 1939; Pol. S-V no. 852 II/38–151 (on behalf of Heydrich), unpublished, Geheimes Staatsarchiv Preußischer Kulturbesitz (GStPK).

**3** Kurt Mayer to Wilhelm Frick, copy of letter dated March 31, 1939, HA I, Rep. 178/VII, 2 E 8, vol. 2, sheets 22–24, GStPK.

**4** Barbara Welker and Hermann Simon, "Die Stiftung 'Neue Synagoge Berlin—Centrum Judaicum,'" in *Der Archivar* 3 (1992): column 369. The remaining portion of the register of members leaving the Community begins around 1890. I would like to thank Barbara Welker, archivist at the CJA, for her supplementary and expert clarifications.

**5** GStPK, HA I, Rep. 178/VII, 2 E 8, vol. 2, sheets 22–24; copy of the letter from Mayer to Frick of March 31, 1939.

**6** Letter to the RmdI, March 31, 1939, R 39/39, Bundesarchiv (BArch).

**7** Ibid.

**8** Jacob Jacobson, *Bruchstücke 1939–1945, Memoiren*, p. 2, M.E. 560, Leo Beck Institute, New York (LBI N.Y.).

**9** Letter from Jahnke to Frick regarding a statistical monthly report of June 27, 1940, R 39/9, BArch.

**10** Deutsche Zentralstelle für Genealogie Leipzig (DZfG), DA, vol. 2 (1928–37); circular "An unsere Mitglieder!" (To our members!) and copy of the agreement between both institutions on taking over the Register of Ancestry of the German People.

**11** On the register, see Martina Wermes, *Die Ahnenstammkartei des deutschen Volkes. Einführung in den Bestand*, manuscript, 1994. The registry was preceded by the Circular of Lists of Ancestry (*Ahnenlistenumläufen*) of the Association of Researchers (Forscherbund), founded by Karl Förster in 1921 in Dresden. In 1930 this became the Registered German Society for Ancestry (Deutsche Ahnengemeinschaft e.V.) The Central Office for German

Personal and Family Biographies in Leipzig thereby was paid to compile the second copy of the lists of ancestry into an archive of lists of ancestry and provide information.

**12** This also listed people who, during an examination by nonspecialist departments, were suspected to be of "non-Aryan" origin on account of their name.

**13** Stefi Jersch-Wenzel, "Zum Tode von Jacob Jacobson," in *Jahrbuch für die Geschichte Mittel- und Ostdeutschlands* 18 (1969): 700.

**14** Jacobson, *Bruchstücke.*

**15** Ibid.

**16** Jersch-Wenzel, "Zum Tode," p. 701.

**17** HA I, Rep. 178/VII, 2 E 8, Bd. 2. sheets 92–93, GStPK.

**18** Ibid., Bl. 117; file note.

**19** Ibid., HA I, Rep. 178/VII, 2 E 8, Bd. 2, sheets 128 and 132, GStPK.

**20** Jacobson, *Bruchstücke*, p. 23.

**21** Letter from Jacobson to Max Kreutzberger, April 7, 1966, M.E. 560, LBI NY. The "Jewish register," which remained on Oranienburger Strasse and was not taken to Thuringia, was put in the vault, which was apparently very large. Mayer told the district courts that they could put their Jewish materials from the period 1847 to 1874 there. HA I, Rep. 178, 2 E 8, vol. 2, sheet 150, GStPK.

**22** J. Jacobson to M. Kreutzberger, letter dated April 7, 1966, M.E. 560, LBI NY.

**23** Note by Jahnke, August 5, 1942, n.p., R 39/803, BArch.

**24** R 39/802, BArch. The Charité hospital in Berlin was among the institutions from which the personal files came.

**25** Friedrich August Knost founded the International Association of Civil Officials (Vereinigung der Beamten des Zivilstandes) in 1934. After 1945 he was a legal advisor at the Registry Office Organization (Organisation der Standesbeamten), from 1957 to 1980 its president, and until 1982 the honorary president of the Federal Association of Registrars (Bundesverband der Standesbeamten). See Heinrich Stülten, "Dr. Friedrich August Knost," in *Die deutschen Standesbeamten und ihr Verband. Rückblick auf 75 Jahre Verbandsgeschichte* (Frankfurt/Main and Berlin, 1995), pp. 147–50.

**26** Kaebernick (individual file of information), 15.09/42, BArch. Many of the files of the Reichsvereinigung and the Jewish Community were apparently destroyed on Gestapo orders after the office was closed. Others were said to have been destroyed by fire during a bombing on January 15, 1944. The head of finance took the more valuable items such as typewriters and property. See Ball-Kaduri, *Berlin wird judenfrei*, p. 227.

**27** R 39/39, 1, BArch.

**28** Security measures for the Reichssippenamt and the Reich Office for Genealogical Research, August 17, 1943, R 39/21, BArch.

**29** Der Herold's library comprised around 25,000 books and writings, including extensive materials on family trees and heraldry as well as valuable collections of letter seals. Kurt Mayer, an enthusiastic collector of coats-of-arms and heraldic seals, used the Herold's dire financial straits for his own interests. Using the AfS's budget, he bought its valuable collection for a fraction of its actual worth. When the association had to clear out of its quarters in the Marstall (a building on the river Spree) for financial reasons, Mayer offered rooms on the premises of the Berlin Jewish Community. The library's move to Oranienburger Strasse took place on November 18–23, 1940. See HA I, Rep. 309/810, GStPK. See also the negotiations on the transfer and takeover of November 25, 1940. It was affiliated in administrative terms with the AfS.

**30** BArch, R 39/21; security measures for the Reichssippenamt and the Reich Office for Genealogical Research, August 17, 1943.

**31** Air-raid protection measures of the Reichssippenamt, August 5, 1943, R 39/46, BArch.

**32** See note 30.

**33** Rep. 92, Ac 3924, No. 10217/43, LAB.

**34** Hermann Simon, "Die Neue Synagoge einst und jetzt," in *"Tuet auf die Pforten." Die Neue Synagoge, 1866–1995* (Berlin, 1995), pp. 10–42, quotation on p. 31.

**35** Ibid. A list headed "Public Buildings" from the Berlin State Archive states that the Army Uniform Store III (Heeresbekleidungsamt III) at Oranienburger Strasse 30 had been "totally destroyed."

**36** Letter from Edith Hirschfeldt about Werner Scharff to Ricarda Huch, in Hermann Maas and Gustav Radbruch, editors, *Den Unvergessenen. Opfer des Wahns* (Heidelberg, 1952), pp. 17–18.

**37** See Hermann Simon, *Das Berliner Jüdische Museum*, 3rd ed. (Berlin, 2000).

**38** Letter from Henri and Lieselotte Higuet (née Mewes) to the Centrum Judaicum (March 1990).

**39** Letter from Jennie Lebel to Hermann Simon, September 16, 1995.

**40** *Der Morgen*, 14 June, 1961.

# Acknowledgments

We would like to thank all who made the exhibition Juden in Berlin 1938–1945 possible. Special thanks to the Stiftung Deutsche Klassenlotterie, which financed the 2000 exhibition and the publication. The German Foreign Ministry generously supported this English edition.

Judith Angress, Maayan Zwi, Israel
Frank Bajohr, Hamburg
Marina Bartsch-Rüdiger, Berlin
Bayer-Archiv, Leverkusen
Gad Beck, Berlin
Vera Bendt, Jewish Museum Berlin
Jürgen Bogdahn, Entschädigungsamt
Cornelia Böhnstätt, Stiftung Stadtmuseum
    Berlin
Barbara Borowy, Museumspädagogischer
    Dienst
Jael Botsch-Fitterling, Berlin
Edna Brocke, Alte Synagoge Essen
Gabriel Bron, Jerusalem
Allison Brown, Berlin
Claus Bründel, Deutsches Technikmuseum
    Berlin
Werner Buchwald, Edition Hentrich Berlin
Liselotte Clemens, Berlin
Marlies Coburger, Stiftung Stadtmuseum
    Berlin
Zwi Cohen, Maabarot, Israel
Klaus Dettmer, Landesarchiv Berlin

Deutsches Apotheken-Museum, Heidelberg
Deutschlandradio, Berlin
Edith Dietz, Karlsruhe
Ernst Ludwig Ehrlich, Riehen
Renate Evers, Leo Baeck Institute New York
Herbert Fiedler, Luckenwalde
Ernest Fontheim, Ann Arbour, MI
Eva Frank, Holon
J. Fränkel, Berlin
Leonie and Walter Frankenstein, Bandhagen,
    Sweden
Arkady Fried, Bibliothek der Jüdischen
    Gemeinde zu Berlin
Edith Gamson, Berlin
Thomas J. Garbáty, Ann Arbour, MI
Sandra Gebbeken, Leo Baeck Institute New
    York
Martha Gerson, Berlin
Horst Gessner, Berlin
Marianne Givol, Holon
Pit Goldschmidt, Hamburg
Ruth Gross, Berlin
Wolf Gruner, Berlin

Renate Grunert, Schwarzenbek
Kai Gruzdz, Ausstellung Blindes Vertrauen
  Berlin
David Hamilton, London
Elieser Günter Hammerstein, Berlin
Wolfgang Haney, Berlin
Michael Haring, Kindermann Photo Service
  Berlin
Heimatmuseum Hohenschönhausen, Berlin
Horst Helas, Berlin
Eugen Herman-Friede, Kronberg
Erika Herzfeld, Berlin
Rudolf Hirsch, Berlin
Hans Israelowicz, Berlin
Helga Isvoranu, Berlin
Gisela Jacobius, Berlin
Thomas Jersch, Berlin
Anne Jobst, Jewish Museum Berlin
Rolf Joseph, Berlin
Irmgard Jourdain, Karlsruhe
Jüdisches Museum, Berlin
Renate Kirchner, Bibliothek der Jüdischen
  Gemeinde zu Berlin
Gerd Koch, Berlin
Günter Kopplin, Archiv Landgericht Berlin
Margit Korge, Berlin
Reiner Korsen, Hamburg
Ferdinand Kroh, Berlin
Ariane Kwasigroch, Ausstellung Blindes
  Vertrauen Berlin
Simone Ladwig-Winters, Berlin
Landesarchiv Berlin
Kurt Landsberger, New Milford, CT
Frank Leimkugel, Mülheim
Anette Leo, Berlin
Evi und Walter Levin, Basel
Judith Levin, Yad Vashem Jerusalem
Christa Liebscher, Sportmuseum Berlin
Jutta Liesen, alias Film, Berlin
Peter Loewy, Berlin
Ina Lorenz, Hamburg
Jürgen Lottenburger, Satz-Rechen-Zentrum
  Berlin
Wendy Luterman, Steven Spielberg Jewish
  Film Archive Jerusalem
Gudrun Maierhof, Frankfurt

Clemens Marcuse, Raisting
Monika Marschel, Centrum Judaicum Berlin
Peter Matuschek, Stiftung Stadtmuseum
  Berlin
Auguste Meder, Berlin
Kersti Mellberg, Schwedische Victoriage-
  meinde Berlin
Miriam Merzbacher, Stamford, CT
Albert Meyer, Berlin
Winfried Meyer, Berlin
Rita Meyhöfer, Berlin
Gisela Mießner, Berlin
Ragnhild Münch, Berlin
Hans Nisblé, Berlin
Markus Oppermann, Satz-Rechen-Zentrum
  Berlin
Bodmar Ottow, Berlin
Evelyn Pearl, New York
Maja Peers, Deutsches Historisches Museum
  Berlin
Stefan Peetz, Berlin
Frank Pfeiffer, Pandora Neue Medien GmbH
  Berlin
Walter Philipp, West Hills, CA
Lutz Prieß, Berlin
Marion Proft, Stiftung Stadtmuseum Berlin
Ruth Recknagel, Wiedergutmachungsämter
  von Berlin
Monika Richarz, Hamburg
Heiner Ross, Metropolis Kommunales Kino
  Kinemathek Hamburg e.V.
Michael Rüdiger, Berlin
Christiaan Frederik Rüter, Amsterdam
Irene Ruschin, Berlin
Rosa Sacharin, Glasgow
Carola Sachse, Berlin
Mali Scharf-Berger, New York
Wolfgang Scharnberg, Hamburg
Ellen Scheurenberg, Wunstorf
Barbara Schieb, Berlin
Kurt Schilde, Siegen
Alisah Schiller, Beit Theresienstadt Givat
  Haim Ihud, Israel
Lothar Schirmer, Stiftung Stadtmuseum
  Berlin
Sabine Schleiermacher, Berlin

Peter Schmalfuß, Technikmuseum Berlin

Manfred Schnapp, Berlin

Bärbel Schönefeld, Polizeihistorische Sammlung Berlin

Winfried Schultze, Archiv der Humboldt-Universität zu Berlin

Detlef Schwarz, Entschädigungsbehörde von Berlin

Jizchak Schwersenz, Berlin

Anna Shannon, Los Angeles

Helga Simon, Berlin

Uwe Splett, Berlin

Stadtteilarchiv Ottensen, Hamburg

Hellmut Stern, Berlin

Herbert Strauß, New York

Manfred Stürzbecher, Berlin

Martin Tessmer, In And Around Media Workshop, Berlin

Johannes Tuchel, Gedenkstätte deutscher Widerstand Berlin

Daniel Uziel, Yad Vashem, Jerusalem

Günther Wagenlehner, Bonn

Herman Wagner, Beit Iizchak, Israel

Henry Walton, Cheshire, Great Britain

Bianca Welzing, Landesarchiv Berlin

Jürgen Wetzel, Landesarchiv Berlin

Karin Wieckhorst, Berlin

Thomas Willerscheck, Sportmuseum Berlin

Ruth Wing, London

Kurt Winkler, Stiftung Stadtmuseum Berlin

Angelika Winkler-Wulkau, Wiedergutmachungsämter von Berlin

Anna Winn, Entschädigungsamt Berlin

Eva-Maria Wittke, ARD-Studio London

Hans-Udo Wittkowski, Berlin

Christine Zahn, Berlin

Special thanks to the entire staff of the Centrum Judaicum Berlin

# Abbreviations

**AfS** Amt für Sippenforschung der NSDAP / Nazi Party Department for Genealogical Research

**BArch** Bundesarchiv / National Archive

**BDC** Berlin Document Center

**BLHA** Brandenburgisches Landeshauptarchiv

**BstU** Der Bundesbeauftragte für die Unterlagen des Staatssicherheitsdienstes / former GDR

**CJ** Centrum Judaicum

**CJA** Centrum Judaicum Archive

**CV** Centralverein deutscher Staatsbürger jüdischen Glaubens / Central Association of German Citizens of Jewish Faith

**DA** Deutsche Ahnengemeinschaft Dresden / Registered German Society for Ancestry

**DAF** Deutsche Arbeitsfront / German Labor Front

**DZfG** Deutsche Zentralstelle für Genealogie Leipzig / Central Office for German Personal and Family Biographies, Leipzig

**EZA** Evangelisches Zentralarchiv in Berlin

**FWA** Friedrich-Wolf-Archiv

**GDW** Gedenkstätte Deutscher Widerstand / German Resistance Memorial Center

**Gestapa** Geheimes Staatspolizeiamt / Office for State Secret Police

**Gestapo** Geheime Staatspolizei / State Secret Police

**GFA** Gemeinschaft für Frieden und Aufbau / Society for Peace and Reconstruction (resistance group)

**GStPK** Geheimes Staatsarchiv Preußischer Kulturbesitz

**IMG** Internationaler Militärgerichtshof / International Military Tribunal

**JGMOD** *Jahrbuch für die Geschichte Ost- und Mitteldeutschlands*

**JKV** Jüdische Kultusvereinigung / Jewish Religious Association, as the Jewish Community was called after April 1941

**JuPo** Judenpolizei / Jewish Police (Vienna)

**Kripo** Kriminalpolizei / Criminal Police

**LAB** Landesarchiv Berlin / Berlin State Archive

**LBI NY** Leo Baeck Institute, New York

**LBI YB** Leo Baeck Institute Yearbook (Jerusalem)

**LG** Landgericht / District Court

**LG** Ministerium für Staatssicherheit (der ehemaligen DDR / Ministry for National Security (in the former GDR)

**MBliV** *Ministerialblatt für die innere Verwaltung*

**NSDAP** Nationalsozialistische Deutsche Arbeiterpartei / German National Socialist Workers' Party

**OdF** Opfer des Faschismus / Victim of Fascism

**OFD** Oberfinanzdirektion / (Nazi) Office of Finance

**OFP** Oberfinanzpräsident / (Nazi) President of Finance

**OPG** Oberstes Parteigericht / Highest Party Court

**ORB** Ostdeutscher Rundfunk Brandenburg / West German Radio, Brandenburg

**OstF** Obersturmführer / First Lieutenant

**Ostubaf** Obersturmbannführer / Lieutenant Colonel

**RarbMin** Reichsarbeitsministerium / Reich Ministry of Labor

**RBG** Reichsbürgergesetz / Reich German Citizenship Law

**RdErl** Runderlaß / General Decree

**RfS** Reichsstelle für Sippenforschung / Reich Office for Genealogical Research

**RFSS** Reichsführer SS / Reich Leader of the SS

**RGBl** *Reichsgesetzblatt*

**RJM** Reichsjustizminister(-ium) / Reich Ministry of Justice

**RM** Reichsmark

**RMdI** Reichsministerium des Innern / Reich Ministry of the Interior

**RMfVuP** Reichsministerium für Volksaufklärung und Propaganda / Reich Ministry of Propaganda

**RMI** Reichsminister des Innern / Reich Minister of the Interior

**RPA** Rassenpolitisches Amt der NSDAP / NSDAP Office for Race

**RSA** Reichssippenamt / Reich Office for Genealogy

**RSHA** Reichssicherheitshauptamt / Reich Security Main Office

**RuSHA** Rasse- und Siedlungshauptamt / Main Office for Race and Colonization

**Reichsvereinigung** Reichsvereinigung der Juden in Deutschland / Reich Association of Jews in Germany

**RVerwBl** *Reichsverwaltungsblatt*

**RWiMi** Reichswirtschaftsminister(ium) / Reich Ministry of Business

**SA** Sturmabteilungen / Storm Troopers

**SAdK** Stiftung Archiv der Akademie der Künste

**SBZ** Sowjetische Besatzungszone / Soviet Zone of Occupation

**Schf** Scharführer / Corporal

**SD** Sicherheitsdienst / Security Service of the SS

**SFB** Sender Freies Berlin / Radio Station

**SfR** Sachverständiger für Rasseforschung / Experts for Race Research

**Sopade** Sozialdemokratische Partei Deutschlands (im Exil) / Social Democrat Party of Germany (in Exile)

**SS** Schutzstaffel / Protection squadron

**Sta LG** Staatsanwaltschaft beim Landgericht Berlin / Office of the Berlin State Prosecutor

**StAZ** *Zeitschrift für Standesamtswesen*

**StM** Staatsministerium(ien) / State Ministry

**SWR** Südwestdeutscher Rundfunk / South-west German Radio

**VB** *Völkischer Beobachter* / Nazi newspaper

**VfZ** *Vierteljahreshefte für Zeitgeschichte*

**VO** Verordnung / Decree

**VVSt** Vermögensverwertungsstelle / Center for Evaluation of Assets

**WL**

**YV** Yad Vashem Archive, Jerusalem

**YVS** *Yad Vashem Studies*

**ZfG** *Zeitschrift für Geschichtswissenschaft*

**ZH** Zeugenheft / Witness book

**ZVfD** Zionistische Vereinigung für Deutschland / German Zionist Organization

# Glossary

**Altreich**  Germany according to its 1937 borders, excluding Austria and other regions that subsequently became part of the Third Reich.

**Aryan**  Terms such as "Aryan" (*arisch*), "Aryan person" (*Arier*), "Aryanhood" (*Ariertum*), and "Aryan descent" (*arische Abkunft*) entered the Nazi vocabulary with the enactment of the Law for the Restoration of the Professional Civil Service and the first supplementary decree on its implementation of April 11, 1933. The pseudo-racial term had become popular in the nineteenth century during a time of revived enthusiasm for the Teutonic world. It commonly denoted the opposite of "Jew" or "Semite." The linguistic origins of the term—which technically describes the Indo-Iranian or Indo-European linguistic groups—could not be negated, however, and this caused jurisdictional difficulties. The Nuremberg Laws of September 1935 replaced the terminology with abstract but no less problematic terms such as "German-blooded" (*deutschblütig*) or "of German or related blood" (*deutsches oder artverwandtes Blut*).

**Fabrik-Aktion** (Factory Operation)  See chapter 9. The large-scale campaign launched on February 27, 1943, against the German Reich's remaining Jews. It was coordinated by the Gestapo with the factory security service (Werkschutz) to arrest Jews in the factories where they worked as forced laborers—some 15,000 of whom were in the armaments industry in Berlin. Jews who were not captured at work were taken from their homes and elsewhere. At the time there were only around 51,000 Jews still living in the Reich, more than half of whom were in Berlin. Those

arrested were for the most part detained in several large buildings in Berlin. Most "*Mischlinge,*" Jewish partners in "mixed marriages," and employees of the Reichsvereinigung and the Berlin Jewish Community (the JKV) were eventually released. All of the others were deported to Auschwitz on five transports from March 1 to 6, 1943.

**Forced Labor**  Any kind of labor or service demanded from an individual on a nonvoluntary basis under threat of punishment.

**The Jewish Community of Berlin (*Jüdische Gemeinde Berlin*)**  See chapter 18. Berlin's religious community (*Gemeinde*) of Jews was founded in September 1671. Stripped of its legal status as a public corporation on March 29, 1938, it was forced to call itself a "registered association"—the "Jüdische Gemeinde zu Berlin e.V."—after August 1939. On April 2, 1941 it was again forced to change its name to the Jüdische Kultusvereinigung zu Berlin (Jewish Religious Association of Berlin [JKV]). Based on a January 28, 1941, order from the Reich Ministry of the Interior, the Community was struck from the register of associations that February. The Jewish Community of Berlin remained formally independent of the Reichsvereinigung until January 29, 1943.

**Jew (Nazi legal definition)**  "A Jew is anyone descended from at least three grandparents who are racially full Jews [*Volljuden*]" (first supplementary decree to the Reich Citizenship Law, November 14, 1935, § 5, section 1). A grandparent was automatically classed as a "full Jew" if he or she had belonged to the Jewish religious Community. A

Jew could not be a "Reich citizen," had no right to vote on political matters, and was banned from public office. It was forbidden for Jews to marry or have sexual relations outside marriage with non-Jews or "second-degree *Mischlinge.*"

**Geltungsjude ("Jew by definition")** Again according to the first supplementary decree to the Reich Citizenship Law, § 5, "a Jew is also a Jewish national of mixed blood who is descended from two full Jewish [*Volljüdische*] grandparents." If he belonged to the Jewish religious Community when the law was enacted [September 15, 1935] or joined it later, If he was married to a Jew when the law was issued or subsequently married a Jew, If he is the offspring of a marriage with a Jew, in the sense of § 1, which was contracted after the enactment of the "Law on the Protection of German Blood and Honor" of September 15, 1935 . . . , If he is the offspring of an extramarital relationship with a Jew . . . and was born out of wedlock after July 31, 1936."

**First-degree *Mischlinge*** Although people with two "full Jewish" grandparents were considered "provisional Reich citizens" (*vorläufige Reichsbürger*), they were not racially "Aryan" and therefore required permission to marry non-Jews as well as "second-degree *Mischlinge*" (according to § 3 of first supplementary decree on the implementation of the Law on the Protection of German Blood.)

**Second-degree *Mischlinge*** People with one "full Jewish" grandparent, also considered "provisional Reich citizens" but not "Aryan." According to §§ 2 and 4 of the above-cited decree, they were forbidden to marry other "second-degree *Mischlinge*," and could only marry "first-degree Mischlinge" with permission.

**Mixed Marriage (*Mischehe*)** A marriage involving a Jew and a Gentile.

**"Privileged" and "Nonprivileged" Mixed Marriages** The term "privileged mixed marriage" never officially appeared in the *Reichsgesetzblatt* (Reich Law Gazette) yet it entered the vocabulary in December 1938. It referred to a mixed marriage in which the children had not had a Jewish upbringing (that is, did not fall into the category of *Geltungsjuden*), or to a childless mixed marriage in which the husband was "German-blooded." The marriage was considered "nonprivileged" if the children "counted" as Jews or if the husband was a Jew. Although Jews in mixed marriages were subject to all the regulations that applied to Jews, Jews in "privileged mixed marriages" were exempt from some provisions, from wearing the yellow star in particular.

**Reichsvereinigung der Juden in Deutschland (Reich Association of Jews in Germany)** See chapter 18. The Reichsvertretung der deutschen Juden (Reich Representation of German Jews) was founded on September 17, 1933, as an umbrella organization for Jewish institutions. It was initially able to function autonomously. In 1935, it was forced to change its name to the Reichsvereinigung der Juden in Deutschland (Reich Association of Jews in Germany), which emphasized that its members were Jews in Germany rather than German Jews. On July 4, 1939, it became a compulsory organization to which all racial Jews (as defined by the Nuremberg Laws) had to belong. The Jewish Communities lost their de facto independence. By the time the Gestapo dissolved all the Jewish Communities and Reichsvereinigung regional offices on June 10, 1943, the Reichsvereinigung had already been largely depleted through deportation and arrest.

# Contributors

**Christian Dirks** is currently writing his doctoral dissertation with the aid of a 2003 grant from the Friedrich Ebert Foundation. His topic is "The Crimes of Others: Nazi Trials in the German Democratic Republic; The Proceedings against Concentration Camp Doctor Horst Fischer." He studied history, political science, and sociology in Munster and Berlin and was an assistant at the Berlin branch of the Institute for Contemporary History in 1996–97. Between 1998 and 2000 he was an assistant at the New Synagogue Berlin—Centrum Judaicum Foundation, where he served as project coordinator for the exhibition Juden in Berlin, 1938–1945.

**Clemens Maier** is at work on a doctoral dissertation entitled "Resistance and Treason: Scandinavian Postwar Collective Memory" with a grant from the European University Institute in Florence, Italy. He studied history, political science, and sociology at the Free University in Berlin.

**Albert Meirer** fulfilled his community civil service for the Republic of Austria as an intern (*Gedenkdiener*) at the New Synagogue Berlin—Centrum Judaicum Foundation in 1999. He studied philosophy and German philology at the University of Vienna.

**Dr. Beate Meyer** has been a research associate at the Institute for the History of German Jews in Hamburg since 2001 and is currently preparing a study on deportation and the Reich Association of Jews in Germany (the Reichsvereinigung). She studied history and political science at the University of Hamburg and then was a research associate at the Research Institute for Contemporary History there. She held a research fellowship at the International Institute for Holocaust Research, Yad Vashem in Jerusalem in 2000–1. She has published on women and race politics in the Nazi era as well as regional studies and oral histories for the period. Her books include *"Jüdische Mischlinge," Rassenpolitik und Verfolgungserfahrung, 1933–1945* (1999).

**Dr. Rita Meyhöfer** holds a degree in political science and is currently engaged in freelance scholarly and educational activities for the memorial site Yad Vashem in Jerusalem and the Topography of Terror Foundation in Berlin, among others. She is the author of a book on Jewish schoolchildren in Weimar and Nazi Germany, *Gäste in Berlin? Jüdisches Schülerleben in der Weimarer Republik und im Nationalsozialismus* (1996).

**Alexandra von Pfuhlstein** holds a degree in social pedagogy. She studied social pedagogy at the Fachhochschule Münster and political science at the University of Munster. After a year of social work in Costa Rica, she studied political science at the Free University in Berlin and was an assistant at the Bürgerstiftung Berlin (Berlin Community Foundation).

**Barbara Schieb** has been an independent historian since 1986 and has worked for the German Resistance Memorial Center and the House of the Wannsee Conference, among others. She studied history and literature in Freiburg im Breisgau and Berlin. Her research topics include underground Jews and their helpers, Jewish resistance, and the attitude of the Church toward the "Jewish question" in the Nazi era. Among her publications are a chapter on the Society for Peace and Reconstruction (Gemeinschaft für Frieden and Aufbau) in *Juden im Widerstand*, Löhken and Vathke, editors (1993); a biography of the artist Walter Herzberg (1998); and *Nachricht von Chotzen—"Wer immer hofft, stirbt singend"* (2000), a book about a mixed-marriage family in Nazi Berlin.

**Michael Schäbitz** is writing a doctoral dissertation entitled "Emancipation and Acculturation of Jews in the Kingdom of Saxony in the Nineteenth Century." He studied history, psychology, and philosophy at the Free University in Berlin and the Hebrew University in Jerusalem.

**Dr. Diana Schulle** works independently as a freelance researcher for national, business, and private employers. She studied history, philosophy, and religion at the Free University in Berlin, earning her doctorate in 2000 with a dissertation on the Nazi-era Office for Genealogy. Her publications include *Das Reichssippenamt. Eine Institution nationalsozialistischer Rassenpolitik* (based on her dissertation) and, with Wolfgang Scheffler, *Buch der Erinnerung. Die ins Baltikum deportierten deutschen, österreichischen and tschechoslowakischen Juden* (Book of Remembrance. The German, Austrian and Czechoslovakian Jews Deported to the Baltic States).

**Dr. Chana C. Schütz** is research associate and vice-director of the New Synagogue Berlin—Centrum Judaicum Foundation. She studied art history and history in Berlin, Jerusalem, and Bonn, earning her doctorate in Bonn in 1988. Curator and project organizer of numerous exhibitions, her publications include *Preußen und Jerusalem (1800–1861)* and numerous articles on German-Jewish art history and the history of Jews in Berlin.

**Dr. Hermann Simon** has been the director of the New Synagogue Berlin—Centrum Judaicum Foundation since its inception in 1988. From 1988 to 1995 he supervised the restoration of the New Synagogue. He studied history and oriental studies at the Humboldt University in Berlin and undertook graduate work on oriental numismatics in Prague, receiving his doctorate in 1976 with a thesis on oriental coins of the medieval period. From 1977 to 1988 he was active in this field on behalf of the National Museums in Berlin. He has directed various exhibitions at the New Synagogue Berlin—Centrum Judaicum Foundation and elsewhere, including "Juden in Berlin, 1938–1945" (with Beate Meyer), upon which this book is based. He has authored numerous articles the history of Jews in Germany and numismatics as well as the book *Das Berliner Jüdische Museum in der Oranienburger Straße*, the third edition of which appeared in 2000. He is editor of the book series Jewish Memoirs as well as Jewish Miniatures.

**Karin Wieckhorst** has since October 1997 been a research associate of the German-Israeli joint research project "Reconstructing German-Jewish Childhood and Literature for German-Jewish Children under National Socialism." She is business manager of the Zurückgeben Foundation, a Berlin-based organization that supports Jewish women in the arts and scholarship. She studied German language and literature and political science at the Free University in Berlin and graduated with a thesis on German-Jewish children and children's literature in the Nazi era.

# Illustration Credits

Figures preface 1–5, 1.1, 2.1–2.4, 11.1–11.4, 15.2, 15.9, 16.3, 18.9: CJA

Figure 1.2: J. Moriyah private collection

Figure 1.3: Stadtteilarchiv Ottensen

Figures 1.4, 1.6: Wiener Library, London

Figure 1.5: Staatsbibliothek Preußischer Kulturbesitz (PKB)

Figures 1.7, 6.1, 8.2, 9.1, 19.1–19.2: Abraham Pisarek photo archive

Figures 1.8, 3.1, 3.4–3.5, 18.1–18.2: Preußischer Kulturbesitz photo archive

Figure 1.10: David Hamilton private collection

Figures 2.5, 4.3, 15.8, 15.11: Gedenkstätte Deutscher Widerstand

Figures 3.2–3.3: By kind permission of Ruth Wing (née Spanier)

Figures 3.6–3.7: Irene Lehmann private collection

Figure 3.8: American Jewish Joint Distribution Committee, New York

Figure 3.9: Walter Philipp private collection

Figures 3.10, 5.4, 19.3–19.4: Photo by Margit Billeb

Figures 3.11–3.12: Irmgard Jourdain private collection

Figures 4.1–4.2, 4.4–4.9: Printed with the kind permission of Thomas Garbáty

Figure 5.1: PK photo archive

Figure 5.2: Heimatmuseum Hohenschönhausen, Berlin

Figures 5.3, 6.2–6.7: Bibliothek der Jüdischen Gemeinde, Zweigstelle Oranienburger Str.

Figure 6.8: Stiftung Akademie der Künste

Figures 7.8–7.12: Jizchak Schwersenz private collection

Figures 7.1, 7.5–7.6: Walter Levin private collection

Figure 7.2: Archiv für Kunst und Gerschichte Berlin

Figures 7.3–7.4, 7.7, 7.13: Herbert Fiedler private collection

Figures 7.14–7.15: Kibbutz Maayan Tzwi

Figure 8.1: Auguste Meder private collection

Figures 8.3–8.4: YIVO Institute for Jewish Research, New York

Figures 9.2, 18.7–18.8: Landesarchiv Berlin

Figures 12.1–12.2: Stiftung Stadtmuseum Berlin, Theatre Collection

Figure 12.3: Geheimes Staatsarchiv Preußischer Kulturbesitz

Figures 13.1–13.9: Ellen Scheurenberg private collection

Figures 14.1–14.13: Karin Wieckhorst private collection

Figures 15.1, 15.3–15.4, 15.10, 15.13, 15.15, 15.18: Bundesarchiv Berlin

Figures 15.5–15.7: Gabriel Bron, Journalist, private collection

Figure 15.12: Helga Isvoranu private collection

Figure 15.14: Archiv der Staatsanwaltschaft beim Landgericht Berlin

Figure 15.16: Pressebilderdienst Kindermann

Figure 15.17: Ullstein Bilderdienst

Figures 16.1–16.2, 16.4–16.9: Barbara Schieb private collection

Figures 17.1–17.7: Traudl Rosenthal private collection

Figure 18.3: LBI New York

Figures 18.4–18.5: Jüdisches Krankenhaus

Figure 18.6: Clemens Marcuse private collection

Figure 18.10: Entschädigungsbehörde von Berlin

Representatives and Employees of the Jewish Community and the Reichsvereinigung (pp. 349–356)

P. 349 (*top and center*), 352 (*center*): LBI New York

P. 349 (*bottom*), 350 (*top*), 351 (*center*), 354 (*top*), 355 (*top and center*): © 1965 Deutsche Verlags-Anstalt Stuttgart

P. 350 (*center and bottom*), 352 (*bottom*), 353 (*center and bottom*), 354 (*bottom*): Jizchak Schwersenz private collection

P. 351 (*top*): Encyclopedia Judaica

P. 351 (*bottom*): Marianne Givol private collection

P. 352 (*top*), 354 (*center*): CJA

p. 353 (*top*): used without permission

p. 355 (*bottom*): Abraham Pisarek photo archive

p. 356 (*bottom*): Jizchak Schwersenz private collection

Section Openers

Section 1: CJA

Section 2: American Jewish Joint Distribution Committee, New York

Section 3: Printed with the kind permission of Thomas Garbáty

Section 4: Süddeutscher Verlag picture service

Section 5: Jizchak Schwersenz private collection

Section 6: YIVO Institute for Jewish Research, New York

Section 7: Landesbildstelle Berlin

Section 8: Bundesarchiv Berlin

Section 9: Barbara Schieb private collection

Section 10: Jizchak Scwersenz private collection

# Name Index